OXFORD MANAGEMENT READER

RESOURCES, FIRMS, AND STRATEGIES

The OXFORD MANAGEMENT READERS series reflects the inter-disciplinary nature of much teaching of management. The aim of the series is to bring together carefully selected contributions on particular issues. The volumes will be based around either key themes or topics on the management curriculum.

Also published in the series

Firms, Organizations, and Contracts
Edited by Peter J. Buckley and Jonathan Michie

Leadership
Edited by Keith Grint

RESOURCES, FIRMS, AND STRATEGIES

A Reader in the Resource-Based Perspective

Edited by

Nicolai J. Foss

OXFORD
UNIVERSITY PRESS

Great Clarendon Street, Oxford OX2 6DP

Oxford University Press is a department of the University of Oxford.
It furthers the University's objective of excellence in research, scholarship,
and education by publishing worldwide in

Oxford New York

Auckland Cape Town Dar es Salaam Hong Kong Karachi Kuala Lumpur
Madrid Melbourne Mexico City Nairobi New Delhi Shanghai Taipei Toronto

With offices in

Argentina Austria Brazil Chile Czech Republic France Greece
Guatemala Hungary Italy Japan South Korea Poland Portugal
Singapore Switzerland Thailand Turkey Ukraine Vietnam

Oxford is a registered trade mark of Oxford University Press
in the UK and in certain other countries

Published in the United States
by Oxford University Press Inc., New York

Introduction and compilation
© Nicolai J. Foss 1997

First published 1997

British Library Cataloguing in Publication Data

Data available

Library of Congress Cataloging in Publication Data

Resources, firms, and strategies: a reader in the resource-based perspective/edited by Nicolai J. Foss.
p. cm.–(Oxford management readers)
Includes bibliographical references.
1. Industrial organization (Economic theory). 2. Strategic planning. 3. Natural resources..
I. Foss, Nicolai, J., 1964- . II. Series.
HD2326.R474 1997 338.7–dc21 97-19447

ISBN 978-0-19-878180-6 (hbk)
ISBN 978-0-19-878179-0 (pbk)

Printed in Great Britain
on acid-free paper by
Biddles Ltd., King's Lynn, Norfolk

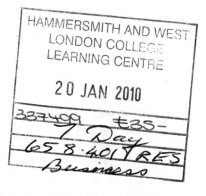

Acknowledgements

Extracts from the conclusion of Philip Selznick, *Leadership in Administration* (Harper & Row, 1957). Copyright © 1957 Philip Selznick. This book was republished in 1984 by the University of California Press and is reprinted here by permission.

Extracts from Edith Penrose, *The Theory of the Growth of the Firm* (OUP 3rd edn., 1995). Reprinted by permission of Oxford University Press.

Extracts from 'Introduction, Strategy and Structure', in Alfred D. Chandler, Jr., *Strategy and Structure* (MIT Press, 1962). Copyright © 1962 Massachusetts Institute of Technology. Reprinted by permission.

Extracts from Kenneth R. Andrews, *The Concept of Corporate Strategy* (Richard D. Irwin, Inc., 1980). Reprinted by permission.

G. B. Richardson, 'The Organisation of Industry', *Economic Journal*, 82 (1972), 883–92 and 895–96. Reprinted by permission of Blackwell Publishers.

Harold Demsetz, 'Industrial Structure, Market Rivalry, and Public Policy', *The Journal of Law and Economics*, 16 (1973), 1–3. © 1973 The University of Chicago Law School. Reprinted by permission.

Extracts reprinted by permission of the publisher from *An Evolutionary Theory of Economic Change* by Richard R. Nelson and Sidney G. Winter, Cambridge, MA: Harvard University Press. Copyright © 1982 by the President and Fellows of Harvard College.

Extracts reprinted from David J. Teece, 'Economies of Scope and the Scope of the Enterprise', *Journal of Economic Behavior and Organization* 1 (1980), 223–33, by permission of Elsevier Science.

Birger Wernerfelt, 'A Resource-Based View of the Firm', *Strategic Management Journal* 5 (1984), 171–80. Copyright © 1984 by John Wiley & Sons, Ltd. Reprinted by permission of John Wiley & Sons, Ltd.

Richard P. Rumelt, 'Towards a Strategic Theory of the Firm', in R. B. Lamb (ed.) *Competitive Strategic Management*, © 1984. Reprinted by permission of Prentice Hall, Upper Saddle River, New Jersey.

Acknowledgements

Jay B. Barney, 'Strategic Factor Markets: Expectations, Luck, and Business Strategy', *Management Science* 32/10 (1986), 1231–41. Copyright © 1986, The Institute of Management Sciences, 290 Westminster Street, Providence, RI 02903, USA. Reprinted by permission.

Ingemar Dierickx and Karel Cool, 'Asset Stock Accumulation and the Sustainability of Competitive Advantage', *Management Science*, 35/12 (1989), 1504–11. Copyright © 1989, The Institute of Management Sciences, 290 Westminster Street, Providence, RI 02903, USA. Reprinted by permission.

Cynthia A. Montgomery and Birger Wernerfelt, 'Diversification, Ricardian rents, and Tobin's *q*', *RAND Journal of Economics*, 19/4 (1988), 623–32. Copyright © 1988. Reprinted by permission of RAND.

Margaret A. Peteraf, 'The Cornerstones of Competitive Advantage: A Resource-Based View', *Strategic Management Journal*, 14 (1993), 179–88. © 1993 by John Wiley & Sons, Ltd. Reprinted by permission of John Wiley & Sons, Ltd.

Joseph T. Mahoney and J. Rajendran Pandian, 'The Resource-Based View Within the Conversation of Strategic Management', *Strategic Management Journal*, 13 (1992), 363–80. © 1992 by John Wiley & Sons, Ltd. Reprinted by permission of John Wiley & Sons, Ltd.

Reprinted by permission of *Harvard Business Review*. 'The Core Competence of the Corporation' by C. K. Prahalad and Gary Hamel, *Harvard Business Review*, 66 (May/June 1990). Copyright © 1990 by the President and Fellows of Harvard College; all rights reserved.

Extracts from Richard R. Nelson, 'Why Do Firms Differ, and How Does It Matter?', in Richard P. Rumelt, Dan E. Schendel, and David J. Teece (eds.), *Fundamental Issues in Strategy: A Research Agenda* (Harvard Business School Press, 1994). This article first appeared in *Strategic Management Journal*, 14 (1991), 61–74 and is reprinted by permission of John Wiley and Sons, Ltd.

Extracts from David J. Teece, Gary Pisano, and Amy Shuen, 'Dynamic Capabilities and Strategic Management', *Strategic Management Journal*, 18:7 (1997), 509–33. © by John Wiley & Sons, Ltd. Reprinted by permission of John Wiley & Sons, Ltd.

Extracts from Richard N. Langlois, 'Transaction-Cost Economics in Real Time', *Industrial and Corporate Change* 1/1 (1991), 99–127. Reprinted by permission of Oxford University Press.

Bruce Kogut and Udo Zander, 'Knowledge of the Firm, Combinative Capabilities, and the Replication of Technology', *Organization Science*, 3 (1992), 383–97.

Copyright © 1992, The Institute of Management Sciences, 290 Westminster Street, Providence, RI 02903, USA. Reprinted by permission.

Constantinos C. Markides and Peter J. Williamson, 'Related Diversification, Core Competences and Corporate Performance', *Strategic Management Journal*, 15 (1994), 149–57. © 1994 by John Wiley & Sons, Ltd. Reprinted by permission of John Wiley & Sons, Ltd.

Contents

I. INTRODUCTION

II. THE HISTORICAL ORIGINS

Contents

Contents

List of Contributors

Kenneth R. Andrews	Donald K. David Professor of Business Administration, Emeritus, Graduate School of Business Administration, Harvard University
Jay B. Barney	Professor, Bank One Chair For Excellence in Corporate Strategy, Max M. Fischer College of Business, the Ohio State University
Alfred D. Chandler	Strauss Professor of Business History, Emeritus, Graduate School of Business Administration, Harvard University
Karel Cool	Professor of Strategic Management, INSEAD
Harold Demsetz	Professor of Economics, University of California, Los Angeles.
Ingemar Dierickx	Professor of Strategy, INSEAD
Bruce Kogut	Professor, the Wharton School, University of Pennsylvania
Richard N. Langlois	Professor of Economics, University of Connecticut
Joseph T. Mahoney	Associate Professor of Business Administration, University of Illinois, Urbana-Champaign
Constantinos Markides	Associate Professor, Strategic and International Management, London Business School
Cynthia A. Montgomery	Professor, Graduate School of Business Administration, Harvard University
Richard R. Nelson	Professor of International and Public Affairs, Columbia University
J. Rajendran Pandian	Lecturer, Department of Management, University of Wollongong
Edith T. Penrose	The late Edith Penrose was Professor, School of Oriental and African Studies, the University of London, and Professor, the Institut Europeén d'Administration, Fontainebleau

Contributors

Margaret Peteraf	Associate Professor of Managerial Strategy, University of Minnesota
Gary Pisano	Associate Professor, Production and Operations Management, Graduate School of Business Administration, Harvard University
C. K. Prahalad	Harvey C. Fruehauf Professor of Business Administration, Graduate School of Business Administration, University of Michigan, Ann Arbor
George B. Richardson	Former Warden of Keble College, former Secretary to the Delegates, Oxford University Press
Richard P. Rumelt	Professor, INSEAD; Professor and Kunin Chair in Business and Society, Graduate School of Management, University of California, Los Angeles
Philip Selznick	Professor, University of California at Berkeley
Amy Shuen	Assistant Professor, University of California at Berkeley
David J. Teece	Mitsubishi Bank Professor in International Business and Finance, Haas School of Business, University of California
Birger Wernerfelt	Deloitte and Touche Professor of Management, Sloan School of Management, MIT
Peter J. Williamson	Professor, Strategic and International Management, London Business School
Sidney G. Winter	Professor, The Wharton School, University of Pennsylvania
Udo Zander	Associate Professor, Institute of International Business, Stockholm School of Economics

Illustrations

Foreword

Birger Wernerfelt

Today, it is very difficult to imagine teaching business strategy without more or less explicitly relying on some insights from the resource-based view of the firm; at least to the degree that one espouses the maxim that resources are a major determinant of strategy. However, this is a quite recent development.

Like other streams of research, the resource-based view is a puzzle under construction. When the first pieces were put down, there was no clear relationship between them. In my original article, 'A Resource-Based View of the Firm', I *assumed* that resources were leveraged inside the firm and *took as given* that firms had heterogeneous resource endowments. Several years passed before we realized that David Teece and Richard Rumelt had supplied those pieces of the puzzle. Only then, in the late 1980s, did the resource-based view pick up steam. We now have substantial convergence and something which looks like a research stream. While the words differ, the last five papers in Part III of this Reader are clearly all about the same theory. In particular, most researchers associated with the resource-based view by now agree at least with the general statement that (1) resources are fixed inputs and (2) sustainable competitive advantages are conferred by resources which are hard to imitate and scarce relative to their economic value.

As illustrated in Part IV, different groups of researchers are currently investigating the firm and market level effects of different classes of resources. The more prominent examples include knowledge assets ('competencies'?), resources for which change is largely stochastic ('the evolutionary perspective'), first-mover advantages ('commitments'), and second-order resources ('dynamic capabilities'?). As we explore these angles it is important that we maintain the links to the larger set of resources, such that we, as a group, can develop a more cumulative body of knowledge. By bringing several of these efforts together, this Reader has the potential to help in this integrative process.

As someone who has been away from the area for a while, I am impressed by the way different parts of the perspective are converging. My sense is, however, that many resources remain mystical. We have made progress discussing them in terms of their effects, but we do not really know what they are. I feel that we need to move towards a more specific understanding of the *nature* of different resources, rather than of their effects. We have some understanding of reputational resources, including brand names, as well as irreversible investments in physical assets. However, many resources are only known indirectly. A good example of this is 'group resources'. What exactly is it that makes one group of people better at doing something than another? I suspect that this class of resources contains most of the critical ones. However, at the moment its contents are in a black box, and unless we open it, we will not be able to say much about it.

I. INTRODUCTION

1 Resources and Strategy: A Brief Overview of Themes and Contributions

Nicolai J. Foss

1. Introduction

During the last five years, strategy—both as an aspect of business practice and as a field of inquiry—seems to have been regaining some of the reputation and influence that was lost by the end of the 1970s and the beginning of the 1980s. There are many reasons for this situation. One is that the strategy field has become academically more respectable: there is a growing feeling that practical strategic advice can be based on sound deduction and systematic observation. At the same time, research in, and the teaching of, strategy has become increasingly professionalized. Taken as a whole, the field has become, if not coherent and homogeneous, then certainly less fragmented than it was, for example, fifteen years ago.

A key factor in this development has been the emergence of a new and rigorous perspective on strategy with a huge potential for integrating diverse perspectives in strategy and organization, and of clear appeal to managers. It has already left a clear imprint on practical management thinking. Arguably, firms are now increasingly prone to begin the strategy process by asking questions such as, 'Which are our central resources?', 'How can we augment and leverage our critical capabilities?', 'Is it desirable to try and build a new competence within this technical area?' etc. This is different, both in substance and focus, from such broad(er) question as, 'What is our corporate mission?' or 'What businesses are we in?'

Much of this reorientation in the way that the practical strategy-making process is carried out is undoubtedly due to the breakthrough in academic as well as practical strategy thinking of what is often referred to as *'the resource-based perspective'* (henceforth, 'the RBP'). The perspective begins from two basic empirical generalizations:

- There are systematic differences across firms in the extent to which they control resources that are necessary for implementing strategies.
- These differences are relatively stable.

The basic structure of the RBP emerges when these two generalizations are combined with fundamental assumptions that are to a large extent derived from economics. Among these assumptions are:

- Differences in firms' resource endowments cause performance differences.
- Firms seek to increase (if not necessarily maximize) their economic performance.

The overall managerial implication is that firms may secure a strong performance by building or otherwise acquiring certain endowments of resources. More generally, the overall objective that informs the RBP is *to account for the creation, maintenance and renewal of competitive advantage in terms of the resource side of firms*. More specifically, we are interested in linking the explanation of competitive advantage, and the dynamics of competitive advantages, to the characteristics of resources, and how these characteristics change over time.

One may safely infer from this that the RBP is prone to asking fundamental questions—indeed, *the* fundamental questions.[1] Arguably, this is another important reason for the recent success of the RBP: it is only by clarifying foundations and asking the truly fundamental questions that a sound theory of strategy can be built. Economics has played a key role here, since basic economic tools have allowed strategy researchers to pose and answer such fundamental questions in a more satisfactory way.[2]

This Reader incorporates the key contributions to the RBP, and documents the gradual emergence of a resource-based approach to strategy. In order to understand the context of the emergence of the RBP, and in order to understand some of the reasons for why it is increasingly possible to be optimistic on behalf of the strategy enterprise, it is instructive to look back at why strategy, for some time, suffered a loss of reputation.

Undoubtedly, the downswing in popularity and respect that strategy suffered at the end of the 1970s was both a matter of strategic planning tools not being able to deliver what was expected from them and a result of critique of some of the important premises of the strategy enterprise. Thus, during the turmoil of the 1970s, firms had to learn the hard way that what was then called 'long-range planning' and somewhat less ambitiously, 'strategic planning', did not lead to the necessary adaptiveness or even survival. Fundamental critique of the epistemic presuppositions—in fact, pretenses—of the planning school, and also of its unrealistically optimistic view of strategy implementation, raised by the likes of Henry Mintzberg and James Brian Quinn, similarly did much to undermine the heavily rationalistic planning ideal.[3] All this meant that earlier hubris had to give way to a new pessimism. As David J. Collis and Cynthia A. Montgomery (1995: 118) noted in a recent article in *Harvard Business Review*:

As recently as ten years ago, we thought we knew most of what was needed to know about strategy. . . . Leading companies, such as General Electric, built large staffs that reflected growing confidence in the value of strategic planning. Strategy consulting boutiques expanded rapidly and achieved widespread recognition. How different the landscape looks today. The armies of planners have all but disappeared, swept away by the turbulence of the last decade. On multiple fronts, strategy has come under fire.

In the place of ambitious long-range planning, scenarios, attempts to grab market share at virtually any price, ride the experience curve, etc., came a much more introverted—and also more timid—tendency, where (roughly) the focus shifted from the corporate and even business strategy level to the functional level.

The success of such practices as Total Quality Management, Business Process Reengineering, the learning organization, etc. are relatively recent manifestations of the more introverted stance. In its own way, Thomas Peters and Robert Waterman's *In Search of Excellence* (1982) also belongs to this current, as does the general interest in corporate culture which this book, among others, inspired. The net effect of the more introverted stance was arguably an increasing emphasis on identifying, and wherever possible, extending, the strengths of individual firms.

What is important in the present connection, the more introverted stance probably also helped foster and sustain the basic resource-based idea that firms are *essentially different* and that the analysis of strategy and competitive advantage has to begin from this fact, rather than from the analysis of more aggregate competitive forces (e.g. in the industry). The importance of this basic assumption is discussed in the present collection by Richard Nelson in his 1991 *Strategic Management Journal* article on 'Why Do Firms Differ, and How Does It Matter?'[4]

Nelson is an economist, and ideas that are closely related to the RBP are becoming ever more important in economics. The stylized, black-box view of the firm, characteristic of neoclassical price theory, in which firms in an industry are seen as essentially alike, is increasingly giving way to a much richer understanding of the firm in which incentives, contracts, and firm-specific resources are seen as crucial (Williamson, 1985).

Nelson and Sidney Winter's 1982 book, **An Evolutionary Theory of Economic Change**, constituted a strong impetus to this development in economics. The book has also been influential in strategy thinking, because Nelson and Winter make an extremely convincing case that firms should be seen as essentially heterogeneous entities, characterized by their unique resource-bases (rather than simply by scale). On the whole there is now—both within economics and within strategic management—a growing realization that essential firm heterogeneity is surely the most important basic assumption that is needed for building strategically relevant models of the firm.

At the face of it, this may seem obvious, even trivial: *of course*, firms have to be different in some way in order to obtain a competitive advantage! However, the increasing emphasis on firm heterogeneity should be seen against the intellectual background of almost complete concentration on *industries* in economics, rather than on firms—a tendency that has also raised its head in strategy thinking (Porter, 1980). To the extent that firms in an industry-level approach are seen as different, it is because they bear the stamp of the industry they operate in, not because they have themselves created differences relative to other firms in the industry. Therefore, what is crucial in an industry approach is structural differences between industries, not differences among individual firms.[5] The pendulum would now seem to have swung in almost the opposite direction.

It is probably no exaggeration to say that the dominant overall framework in strategic management is one that is normally seen as conceived of by Kenneth Andrews in his **The Concept of Corporate Strategy** (Foss *et al.*, 1995). According to Andrews, the role of the strategist is to match the opportunities of the environment with what the firm is capable of doing at an acceptable level of risk, while safeguarding the weaknesses of the firm from the threats of the same environment. It is readily seen that this involves an assessment of internal phenomena and an external analysis of the environment, most directly, the industry.[6]

Clearly, this is a version of what is also often called 'fit' or 'alignment', as captured by the SWOT (Strengths–Weaknesses–Opportunities–Threats) framework. Although it has often been criticized as being inherently static and as making unrealistic claims as to the possibilities of identification of supposedly objective opportunities, strengths, etc. (see Spender, 1992), the basic Andrews framework remains immune to these criticisms. It is consistent with such dimensions as change, complexity, uncertainty, etc.[7] Moreover, it is not a model that claims to deliver objective knowledge about the environment or the inside of the organization; it is a framing device that is useful in the strategy process. As such, it is clearly related to the notion of 'productive opportunity'—the productive possibilities that the management team of the firm can see and take advantage of—put forward by Edith Penrose in 1959 in her seminal contribution, **The Theory of the Growth of the Firm**.

In a way, the basic Andrews framework also allows us to put some of the changes and perspectives in the strategy field into perspective. For many of the changes that have taken place in the strategy field have been a matter of shifting attention between external and internal analysis, and it has been a characteristic of most approaches to strategy that they have primarily emphasized either an externally oriented perspective or an internally oriented perspective.

For example, the extremely successful five forces framework proposed by Michael Porter in 1980 was wholly oriented towards industry analysis, and had really next to nothing to say about firms' strengths and weaknesses. On the other hand, the tendency around the mid-1980s was to go in the opposite direction and put relatively little emphasis on external analysis. Although most strategy scholars would stand prepared to acknowledge the essential soundness of Andrews' analysis, we have not yet witnessed the emergence of a unified, rigorous approach to strategy that can satisfactorily accommodate his main idea: that both internal and external aspects should be featured on an equal footing.

At any rate, there can be little doubt that the increased interest in the strengths of individual firms that began in the aftermath of the collapse of strategic planning models helped pave the ground for the RBP. In its modern manifestation, the resource-based approach may conveniently—if admittedly somewhat arbitrarily—be dated to 1984 when two seminal articles were published.[8] One of these is 'A Resource-Based View of the Firm' by Birger Wernerfelt, published in the *Strategic Management Journal*, and the other is a paper by Richard P. Rumelt, 'Towards a Strategic Theory of the Firm', which was published in a conference volume. These papers were quickly followed by a spate of important work, much of which is reprinted in the present collection. Like the contributions of Wernerfelt and Rumelt, this work was also explicitly drawing on the older work of Philip Selznick, Edith Penrose, and Alfred Chandler. Thus, although the RBP has often been seen as an almost revolutionary development, it is in reality firmly rooted in older, classical work on firms and firm strategies.

In little more than a decade, the RBP has emerged as perhaps the dominant contemporary approach to strategy. All the major academic strategy journals and also the more popular business periodicals regularly feature articles written from a resource-based perspective. A few resource-based strategy textbooks have appeared (Grant, 1991; Kay, 1993). In the business press, concepts such as 'resources', 'capabilities' and 'competences' are everywhere. In fact, what may be the perhaps ultimate litmus test of the general acceptance of the overall ideas of the resource-based perspective, the weekly publication, *The*

Economist—known for its acerbic comments on strategy thinking—is now routinely employing resource-based concepts such as 'core competences'.

The rest of this Introduction will be primarily concerned with presenting the strengths of the resource-based approach. The concluding chapter, on the other hand, is concerned with discussing whether the strengths of the resource-based approach can be successfully matched with the opportunities presented by the space of discourse in strategic management on the one hand and the space of application on the other hand. It also highlights some weaknesses of the RBP in its present form.

2. Main Themes of the Resource-Based Perspective

Clearly the RBP is an emerging perspective. For example, the reader of this collection of articles cannot help but notice that the perspective is characterized by a certain amount of terminological confusion. This is perhaps most conspicuously seen with respect to the terminology that is used for characterizing the key strengths of firms. According to many authors, these strengths are 'resources'. In his 1984 article, Birger Wernerfelt defines resources as 'anything which could be thought of as a strength or weakness of a given firm'. Jay Barney (1991), on the other hand, reserves the term 'resources' for virtually anything 'that enables the firm to conceive of and implement strategies that improve its efficiency and effectiveness' (p. 101).

C. K. Prahalad and Gary Hamel, in their enormously successful 1990 *Harvard Business Review* article, '**The Core Competence of the Corporation**', prefer instead to talk about what in Wernerfelt and Barney's terminology is a specific type of resource, namely 'core competence', They take this to be 'the collective learning of the organization, especially how to coordinate diverse production skills and integrate multiple streams of technology'. Additional complexity is introduced by other reprints in the present collection. For example, Richard Langlois in his 1992 contribution on '**Transaction Costs in Real Time**', and Bruce Kogut and Udo Zander in their '**Knowledge of the Firm, Combinative Capabilities, and the Replication of Technology**' (1992) prefer instead to talk about 'capabilities', while David Teece, Gary Pisano, and Amy Shuen in '**Dynamic Capabilities and Strategic Management**' talk about 'dynamic capabilities' as the key assets of the firm.

There may be different rationales behind the introduction of concepts such as 'capabilities' or 'competencies', particularly when they are seen as different from 'resources'. One such rationale may be that it captures the distinction between stocks, for example, resources, and flows, that is, the services that may be obtained from resources—a distinction that is crucial to Penrose's **The Theory of the Growth of the Firm**.

Another—though not unrelated—reason is that some resource-based theorists apparently feel that it is desirable to make distinctions between assets based on their ability to contribute to competitive advantage. Clearly, not all assets are significant in these terms. The fountain pen with which the firm's strategic plan is drafted is presumably not a strategically important asset. BMW's competence in high-precision engineering, on the other hand, is a crucial strategic asset to BMW. Those who use concepts such as competencies or capabilities normally feel that it is knowledge assets that are the most likely candidates for bringing firms sustained competitive advantage. However, while entirely plausible, this may at most be a matter of empirical generalization, not of strict logic. For although intuition would support the view that knowledge assets are on the whole the most important ones, there are in fact numerous examples of physical assets bringing firms sustained competitive advantage. For example, telephone and cable companies are certainly advantageously positioned in the emerging multimedia industry because of their possession of nets of transmission, that is, of certain physical resources (Collis and Montgomery, 1995: 119).

This suggests that it is more sensible to begin by developing insight into which criteria *any* asset should meet in order to yield sustained competitive advantage, rather than determine and settle on a given asset category on the basis of casual empiricism or arbitrary choice. In fact, this is exactly what resource-based strategy scholars have done, and this is also where economics enters the scene.

If strategic management is ultimately about achieving sustained competitive advantage, then surely an inquiry into the determinants of this must be considered a fundamental issue. However, it is probably no exaggeration to say that it is only really with the advent of the RBP in the mid-1980s that clarity was obtained here. Arguably, this clarity is to a large extent based on an increasing reliance on economics.

Basic economics tells us that *valuable* resources that are in short supply relative to demand, and are therefore *rare*, may yield a distinct return that is related to the resource being both valuable and rare. This return is called a *rent*. When for some reason it is impossible or prohibitively costly to *imitate* the resource, or *substitute* it with another resource that can perform the same tasks, the rent from the resource may be long-lived. Basically, the resource-based conception of competitive advantage is based on this analysis.

The perhaps most systematic exposition of a resource-based perspective on the conditions for sustained competitive advantage is that contained in Margaret Peteraf's 1993 *Strategic Management Journal* article, 'The Cornerstones of

Competitive Advantage'. The 'cornerstones' in question refer to the insights that for resources to yield a sustained competitive advantage, they should meet four basic criteria:

Heterogeneity—i.e. in lieu of efficiency differences across resources, there cannot be any differences in the rents firms earn (in fact, there cannot be any rents at all). This indicates that resource heterogeneity, leading to efficiency differences and therefore rents, is a basic necessary condition for competitive advantage. An alternative formulation—put forward by Jay Barney (1991)—is that with homogeneous resources, all firms can implement the same strategies; hence, no firm can differentiate itself from other firms, and nobody will have a competitive advantage.[9]

Ex ante limits to competition—i.e. resources have to be acquired at a price below their discounted net present value in order to yield rents. Otherwise future rents will be fully absorbed in the price paid for the resource. This important point is further clarified in Barney's 1986 article, **'Strategic Factor Markets: Expectations, Luck, and Business Strategy'**.

Ex post limits to competition—i.e. it should be difficult or impossible for competitors to imitate or substitute rent-yielding resources. As Ingemar Dierickx and Karel Cool clarify in their 1989 article, **'Asset Stock Accumulation and the Sustainability of Competitive Advantage'**, there are a number of mechanisms at work that often make it hard for competitors to copy the sources of competitive advantage of a successful firm. For example, there may be 'causal ambiguity', which means that competitors confront difficulties ascertaining precisely how a bundle of resources contributes to success.

Imperfect mobility— i.e. the resource should be relatively specific to the firm. Otherwise, the superior bargaining position that is obtained from not being tied to a firm can be utilized by the resource (or the resource's owner) to appropriate the rent (or, at least a large portion of the rent) that the resource helps create. In other words, the key question to ask here is, who captures value from the resource, and how may the firm capture more value from the resource?[10]

Now, these are formal conditions, and seemingly quite hard to make operational. Indeed, this is the usual first reaction from students and practitioners alike. However, it is surely possible to bring these concepts into practical action (see Collis and Montgomery (1995) for numerous examples). Think, for example, of the waves of acquisitions of companies that have swept Western business in the last decade. The motive force has usually been the wish to obtain synergy from complementary resources possessed by the acquired firm. In this connection, the condition for sustained competitive advantage summarized under the heading 'ex ante limits to competition' directs our attention to the price that firms pay for their acquisition. In reasonably well-functioning markets for corporate control, prices paid for acquisition targets will offset the rents from acquiring these targets.[11] Many firms have had to learn this basic lesson the hard way, as waves of divestments followed acquisitions.

Inspection of the above conditions also reveals an interesting feature: the competitive environment is a crucial part of all four conditions. This should perhaps be noted to counter Michael Porter's (1994: 445) recent claim that the RBP is overly 'introspective'. For, trivially, it only makes sense to talk about heterogeneity in the context of an environment of other firms. More interestingly, the concepts of ex post and ex ante competition and imperfect mobility bring into play rather specific players, such as suppliers (whose pricing decisions influence how much rent can be captured), competing would-be imitators, and employees (who are engaged in a bargaining game with the firm over the rents that their human capital yield).

Thus, although the RBP may be said to be an 'introverted' perspective in the sense that the strategy process is ideally seen as starting from an analysis of the firm's resource-portfolio, the environment is certainly not forgotten. In fact, as in Porter's five forces framework (Porter, 1980), it is a key idea that value is rather continuously subject to a complex bargaining game that is being played between employees, suppliers, distributors, customers, and owners.

If the inquiry into the conditions for sustained competitive advantage defines the one major research theme of the RBP, diversification studies surely constitute the other main theme. Clearly, the two themes are related on an overall level (as Wernerfelt emphasized in his 1984 paper). For example, as David Teece's 1980 article on '**Economies of Scope and the Scope of the Firm**' and Cynthia Montgomery and Birger Wernerfelt's '**Diversification, Ricardian Rents, and Tobin's *q***' from 1988 clarify, diversification may be an important means to better exploit rent-yielding resources that are for some reason in excess.

Although the basic story is much refined now, this is in itself no novel point, as it was the key idea of Penrose's **The Theory of the Growth of the Firm**. What is new, however, is the point that diversification may in turn help building *new* resources, as Constantinos Markides and Peter Williamson argue in their 1994 paper, '**Related Diversification, Core Competences, and Corporate Performance**'.

Diversification studies may arguably be where the resource-based approach has had the greatest impact. The commonly accepted theory of diversification is roughly the resource-based theory. The basic story is the following one: firms gradually accumulate excess resources as a (non-intended) consequence of their normal operations. Tasks become routinized and this releases human resources, such as managerial resources; some physical resources are indivisible, which means that they may not be fully exploited in their present use; etc. In principle, these resources could be traded over markets; however, the presence of transaction costs—that is, the costs of actually making the exchanges—

will often hinder trading excess resources. As David Teece clarifies in 'Economics of Scope and the Scope of the Enterprise', this is particularly likely to be the case if the resources in question are knowledge resources. An important implication of the theory that is developed and tested in Cynthia Montgomery and Birger Wernerfelt's 'Diversification, Ricardian Rents, and Tobin's q' is that firms earn decreasing average rents as they diversify more widely.

In a broader context, the resource-based theory of diversification suggests a link to the modern economic theory of organization exemplified by the work of Oliver Williamson (1985). This type of work is concerned with the general issue of how transactions are best (most efficiently) organized, whether it be in-house, in various types of cooperative relations, or in more traditional arms-length market relations. The link between the resource-based view and the theory of economic organization is discussed on a methodological level by Joseph Mahoney and J. Rajendran Pandian in their 1992 *Strategic Management Journal* paper, 'The Resource-Based View Within the Conversation of Strategic Management', as part of an overall argument that because of its strong integrative capabilities, the RBP is eminently suited to further conversation within the strategy field.

On a more substantial level, the connection between economic organization and resources is discussed in the classic 1972 contribution by George B. Richardson on 'The Organisation of Industry'. In this paper, Richardson coins the concept of capabilities and builds a theory of inter-firm cooperation from this concept. His main idea is that firms enter into cooperative relations when they need access to the services of the 'dissimilar, but complementary' capabilities of other firms. The economic organization/resource-based approach link is also explored by Richard Langlois in 'Transaction Costs in Real Time' and by Bruce Kogut and Udo Zander in 'Knowledge of the Firm, Combinative Capabilities, and the Replication of Technology'.

3. The Organizing Principles of the Reader

Strategic management is a field of inquiry with no more than at most four decades of existence. True, the first business policy course was taught by Arch Shaw at Harvard Business School as early in 1911, integrating the overall points of the functional courses and adopting the perspective of the top-level manager. However, to the extent that professionalization is an integral part of the establishment of a field of inquiry, strategic management dates back to the beginning of the 1960s. But arguably the main idea of the RBP, that firms are essentially different in terms of their endowments of productive resource and that the resulting efficiency differences yield differential rents, is just as old!

This idea is anticipated, most notably, by Edith Penrose. As she argues in **The Theory of the Growth of the Firm** (1959: 149), the firm 'is essentially a pool of resources the utilization of which is organized in an administrative framework'. Now firms utilize resources differently and (the same type of) resources yield different services when organized in different firms. For example, as Philip Selznick points out in **Leadership in Administration** (1957), different firms develop different 'distinctive competence'. While Selznick is primarily concerned with the role of leadership for the development of distinctive competence, Alfred Chandler in his 1962 study of **Strategy and Structure** adds to leadership the importance of organizational structure, and thus details how the administrative framework influences the utilization of resources. Together these three seminal contributions anticipate much of the essence of the modern resource-based approach.

The approach taken in this Reader is to present the resource-based approach in what is arguably the most natural way—namely in terms of chronology and in terms of themes. Thus, we begin in 1957 with an extract from Selznick, and one of the last selections is David J. Teece, Gary Pisano, and Amy Shuen's 1997 *Strategic Management Journal* article on '**Dynamic Capabilities and Strategic Management**'. In addition to the chronological organizing principle, there is also a thematic organization to the Reader. Thus, we begin with the historical origins, continue with the main resource-based contributions, and end with what may be seen as a development or branching of the resource-based ideas in a more dynamic direction, namely the dynamic capabilities/core competence approach(es).

Undeniably, the chronological approach taken here introduces an element of what historians of thought call 'rational reconstruction'. That is to say, we look back at the contributions that bear a resemblance to modern resource-based thought and see these as precursors to present-day contributions. Moreover, we look at the work of Selznick, Penrose, and Chandler with the lens provided by the modern resource-based approach. Undeniably, this procedure obtains much legitimacy simply from the fact that the works that we 'rationally reconstruct' were written only three decades ago, and are constantly being cited and quoted by modern resource-based strategy theorists. However, one may still question whether there really was a genuine flow of influence in this case, or whether quoting and citing the works of older scholars is simply an ex post ritual, designed to lend added credibility to modern resource-based contributions.

In fact, Jay Barney—one of the prime movers behind the emergence of the resource-based approach in the 1980s—recently argued that the chronological approach, according to which the development of the resource-based approach can be dated back to Selznick and Penrose and seen to progress rather smoothly from there, simply is a 'myth' (Barney, 1995). Instead, Barney argued that the modern RBP owes its origin largely to the interaction, at UCLA and elsewhere, between such economists and strategy scholars as William Ouchi, Michael Porter, Richard Rumelt, Oliver Williamson, Sidney Winter, and Barney himself. Out of this interaction came two seminal contributions that played a founding role for the resource-based approach, namely Lippman and Rumelt's 1982 essay, 'Uncertain Imitability: An Analysis of Interfirm Differences Under Competition' and Barney's 1986 *Management Science* article on '**Strategic Factor Markets**'. And only subsequently came the realization that much of the early work of Selznick, Penrose, Chandler, and Andrews anticipated modern resource-based thought.

Professor Barney's critique is a welcome warning towards too eagerly ascribing to older writers views that, only by twisting the facts, can they be seen to be anticipating. His argument may also be strengthened by observing how much is happening in strategy research around the year of 1980 that is really quite close to the modern RBP. For example, there is Caves (1980) in which strategy is explicitly seen as the quest for efficiency rents; Quinn (1980) where strategy is defined as a means of allocating resources to a *unique* posture: Hofer and Schendel (1979) where the importance of competences is stressed, etc. Thus, much can be said for the view that the RBP not only takes off, but actually begins around 1980 and grows out of the American mainstream in strategy research. This would seem to be consistent with Barney's account of what happened.

However, this account of the emergence of the RBP leaves out a number of important considerations. It neglects David Teece and Birger Wernerfelt's role and the fact that both Wernerfelt and Teece in their early papers explicitly draw on Penrose's work. It also neglects the role of UCLA economist Harold Demsetz. Demsetz was probably the first economist to develop an understanding of barriers to entry as essentially informational in nature. This is clearly related to the overall resource-based idea that the primary barriers that hinder the equalization of rents across firms are informational in nature (e.g. causal ambiguity). Moreover, Demsetz also pioneered and refined an efficiency approach to industrial concentration, according to which the simultaneous occurrence of high returns and high concentration could be explained as a result of the past success of efficient firms. These firms would grow and earn substantial rents on their scarce, efficient assets, and both concentration and aggregate returns would rise as a consequence. The extract from Demsetz's 1973 *Journal of Law and Economics* article, '**Industry Structure, Market Rivalry, and Public Policy**', demonstrates how much of resource-based reasoning Demsetz really anticipated. For example, a rudimentary outline of Barney's 1986 strategic factor market reasoning can be founded in the Demsetz extract.

Thus, the resource-based approach can claim honorable ancestors and equally honorable related contemporaries: it has a background in the mainstream of American management thinking, for example, via the Selznick, Chandler, and Andrews link. But it also connects to Chicago industrial organization theory and to transaction cost economics. And notions such as 'capabilities' and 'competences'—anticipated by Penrose's notion of 'services'—clearly imply links to organizational behaviour and organizational learning studies.

This may be regarded as a major asset of the RBP: it implies that the perspective has integrative capabilities in the sense that it may align different, but complementary, perspectives on firms and strategy. However, the many connections that the RBP establishes to other approaches is not an unqualified virtue. For the other side of the coin is that because the RBP is open to a number of influences, there is a real danger that it may become increasingly fragmented. For example, one may conjecture a situation with one branch of the RBP being primarily inspired by economics, and another branch being primarily inspired by organizational behaviour and learning studies, and therefore following different, and divergent, paths of development.

In fact, it may be argued that such a branching has already begun, and that it now makes sense to talk of two different ways of framing the RBP (Mahoney, 1995). At any rate, this is to some extent reflected in the organization of the present Reader: while Part II is devoted to 'The Historical Origins', featuring extracts from the works of Penrose, Selznick, Chandler, and others, Part III is devoted to what may be called 'the traditional resource-based approach', while Part IV includes extracts from 'The Dynamic Capabilities/Core Competences Approach'.

The distinction is primarily one of whether dynamic factors are included in theorizing. While dynamics (innovation, organizational learning, resource-accumulation, competence-building, the development of the mental models of the management team, etc.) comes first in recent work on core competences and dynamic capabilities, statics comes first in the traditional resource-based approach. That is, in the traditional resource-based approach one begins by clarifying and examining the conditions that must obtain in order for resources to yield rents in equilibrium. This is the procedure followed in, for example, Barney's **'Strategic Factor Markets'** or Peteraf's **'The Cornerstones of Competitive Advantage'**. The more dynamic issues relating to processes of accumulation of resources enter subsequently, or are simply suppressed.

One may interpret this branching in different ways. In one (plausible) reading, the two branches of the RBP are not in conflict. They are different, but complementary (Mahoney, 1995), the one being preoccupied with strategy content research, the other one with strategy process research. The task ahead is to integrate more fully these two ways of framing the RBP. Indeed, one may argue, with Spender (1992), that what he calls 'resource-learning'—human resources learning about the services of other resources—is the RBP's key to advancement (cf. Mahoney, 1995: 96). That would bring us back to Penrose once more, for her story of firm growth is very much such a theory of resource-learning.

These issues are treated further in the concluding chapter in this Reader, which provides an assessment of the future development potential of the RBP, including both 'the traditional resource-based approach' and 'the dynamic capabilities/core competence approach'.

Notes

1. This aspect is highlighted and discussed by several contributors in Rumelt *et al.* (1994).
2. This also holds for the Porter industry analysis approach to strategy (Porter, 1980) which is solidly built on industrial organization economics.
3. Much of this critique is presented in a detailed and elaborate way in Mintzberg (1994).
4. In this Introduction, when articles or extracts from books that are reprinted in this Reader are mentioned, they are set in **bold**.
5. Arguably, this is not completely true of the new game-theoretic industrial organization economics (Tirole, 1988), which is less given to aggregative, industry-level thinking than the older type of industrial organization economics associated with economists such as Joe Bain (1959).
6. Actually, Andrews' formulation would seem to be most directly relevant to *business* strategy—in spite of the title of his book. It should perhaps be noted that the 'alignment model' proposed by Andrews was anticipated long before he wrote. Spender (1992: 6) argues that the model in its SWOT manifestation goes back to the 1920s.
7. Itami (1987) contains interesting extensions of the basic framework, for example, the concept of 'dynamic fit'.
8. One reason why the year 1984 is a somewhat arbitrary benchmark for dating the beginning of the resource-based perspective is, for example, that another seminal article that may have been almost as influential as Wernerfelt's article, namely Richard P. Rumelt and Stephen Lippman's article on 'Uncertain Imitability: An Interfirm Differences in Efficiency Under Competition', was published in 1982. Lippman and Rumelt demonstrated that, if one assumed that firms had difficulties imitating the firm-specific sources of superior performance, an equilibrium with a firm of diverging efficiencies could be sustained. This is a basic idea underlying the resource-based approach. The Lippman and Rumelt article is not reproduced here because of its highly formal nature.

9. It is no escape to say that otherwise homogeneous resource-bundles may be organized differently, for in the RBP, organization is normally treated as part of the resource-bundle.
10. The difference between the first-best and second-best use value of the resource—often called Paretian rent (after Italian economist, Vilfredo Pareto)—is what the firm may appropriate to achieve above-normal returns.
11. In point of fact, these prices will often more than offset rents, because of the 'winner's curse' phenomenon: those who bid the most, and therefore win the price, are those that have the most optimistic (and possibly unrealistic) expectations.

References

Bain, Joe (1959), *Industrial Organization*, Wiley, New York.

Barney, Jay B. (1991) 'Firm Resources and Sustained Competitive Advantage', *Journal of Management*, 17, 99–120.

Barney, Jay B. (1995), 'The Resource Based View: Evolution, Current Status, and Future', handout for a presentation, Third International Workshop on Competence-Based Competition, Ghent, Belgium, November.

Caves, Richard E. (1980), 'Industrial Organization, Corporate Structure, and Strategy', *Journal of Economic Literature*, 18, 64–92.

Collis, David J. and Cynthia A. Montgomery (1995), 'Competing on Resources: Strategy in the 1990s', *Harvard Business Review* (July–August), 118–28.

Foss, Nicolai J., Christian Knudsen, and Cynthia A. Montgomery (1995), 'An Exploration of Common Ground: Integrating Evolutionary and Strategic Theories of the Firm', in Cynthia A. Montgomery, ed. (1995), *Resource-Based and Evolutionary Theories of the Firm*, Kluwer Academic Publishers, Boston.

Grant, Robert M. (1991), *Contemporary Strategy Analysis*, Blackwell, Cambridge, MA.

Hofer, Charles and Dan Schendel (1979), *Strategy Formulation: Analytical Concepts*, West, St. Paul, MN.

Itami, Hiroyuki (1987), *Mobilizing Invisible Assets*, Harvard University Press, Cambridge, MA.

Kay, John (1993), *The Foundations of Corporate Success*, Oxford University Press, Oxford.

Lippman, Stephen A. and Richard P. Rumelt (1982), 'Uncertain Imitability: An Analysis of Interfirm Differences Under Competition', *Bell Journal of Economics*, 13, 418–38.

Mahoney, Joseph T. (1995), 'The Management of Resources and the Resource of Management', *Journal of Business Research*, 33, 91–101.

Mintzberg, Henry (1990), 'Strategy Formation: Schools of Thought', in J. W. Fredrickson, ed. (1990), *Perspectives on Strategic Management*, Harper, New York.

Mintzberg, Henry (1994), *The Decline and Fall of Strategic Planning*, Prentice-Hall, New York.

Montgomery, Cynthia A. (1995), 'Of Diamonds and Rust: A New Look at Resources', in Cynthia A. Montgomery, ed. (1995), *Resource-Based and Evolutionary Theories of the Firm*, Kluwer Academic Publishers, Boston, MA.

Peters, Thomas J. and Robert H. Waterman (1982), *In Search of Excellence*, Harper & Row, Cambridge, MA.

Rorter, Michael E. (1980), *Competitive Strategy*, Free Press, New York.

Porter, Michael E. (1994), 'Toward a Dynamic Theory of Strategy', in Richard P. Rumelt, Dan E. Schendel, and David J. Teece, eds., *Fundamental Issues in Strategy*, Harvard Business School Press, Boston, MA.

Quinn, James Brian (1980), *Strategies for Change: Logical Incrementalism*, Irwin, Homewood, IL.

Rumelt, Richard P., Dan E. Schendel, and David J, Teece, eds. (1994), *Fundamental Issues in Strategy: A Research Agenda*, Harvard Business School Press, Boston, MA.

Spender, J.-C. (1992), 'Strategy Theorizing: Expanding the Agenda', *Advances*

Tirole, Jean (1988), *The Theory of Industrial Organization*, MIT Press, Cambridge, MA.

Williamson, Oliver E. (1985), *The Economic Institutions of Capitalism*, Free Press, New York.

II. THE HISTORICAL ORIGINS

Leadership in Administration: A Sociological Interpretation

Philip Selznick

It is easy to agree to the abstract proposition that the function of the executive is to find a happy joinder of means and ends. It is harder to take that idea seriously. There is a strong tendency not only in administrative life but in all social action to divorce means and ends by overemphasizing one or the other. The cult of efficiency in administrative theory and practice is a modern way of over-stressing means and neglecting ends. This it does in two ways. First, by fixing attention on maintaining a smooth-running machine, it slights the more basic and more difficult problem of defining and safeguarding the ends of an enterprise. Second, the cult of efficiency tends to stress techniques of organization that are essentially neutral, and therefore available for any goals, rather than methods peculiarly adapted to a distinctive type of organization or stage of development.

Efficiency as an operating ideal presumes that goals are settled and that the main resources and methods for achieving them are available. The problem is then one of joining available means to known ends. This order of decision-making we have called *routine*, distinguishing it from the realm of *critical* decision. The latter, because it involves choices that affect the basic character of the enterprise, is the true province of leadership as distinct from administrative management. Such choices are of course often made unconsciously, without awareness of their larger significance, but then the enterprise evolves more or less blindly. Leadership provides guidance to minimize this blindness.

In many situations, including those most important to the ultimate well-being of the enterprise, goals may not have been defined. Moreover, even when they are defined, the necessary means may have still to be created.

Creating the means is, furthermore, not a narrow technical matter; it involves molding the social character of the organization. Leadership goes beyond efficiency (1) when it sets the basic mission of the organization and (2) when it creates a social organism capable of fulfilling that mission. A company's decision to add a new product may be routine if the new is but an extension of the old. It is a critical decision, however, when it calls for a re-examination of the firm's mission and role, e.g., whether to remain primarily a producer of a raw commodity or to become a manufacturer of consumer goods. The latter choice will inevitably affect the outlook of management, the structure and control of the company, and the balance of forces in the industry.

The design and maintenance of organizations is often a straightforward engineering proposition. When the goals of the organization are clear-cut, and when most choices can be made on the basis of known and objective technical criteria, the engineer rather than the leader is called for. His work may include human engineering in order to smooth personal relations, improve morale, or reduce absenteeism. But his problem remains one of adapting known quantities through known techniques to predetermined ends.

From the engineering perspective, the organization is made up of standardized building blocks. These elements, and the ways of putting them together, are the stock-in-trade of the organization engineer. His ultimate ideal is complete rationality, and this assumes that each member of the organization, and each constituent unit, can be made to adhere faithfully to an assigned, engineered role. Furthermore, the role assigned does not stem so much from the peculiar nature of *this* enterprise; rather, the roles are increasingly generalized and similar to parallel roles in other organizations. Only thus can the organization engineer take advantage of the growth of general knowledge concerning the conditions of efficient administrative management.

The limits of organization engineering become apparent when we must create a structure *uniquely adapted to the mission and role of the enterprise*. This adaptation goes beyond a tailored combination of uniform elements; it is an adaptation in depth, affecting the nature of the parts themselves. This is really a very familiar process, brought home to us most clearly when we recognize that certain firms or agencies are stamped by distinctive ways of making decisions or by peculiar commitments to aims, methods, or clienteles. In this way the organization as a technical instrument takes on values. As a vehicle of group integrity it becomes in some degree an end in itself. This process of becoming infused with value is part of what we mean by institutionalization. As this occurs, *organization management* becomes *institutional leadership*. The latter's main responsibility is not so much technical administrative management as the maintenance of institutional integrity.

The integrity of an enterprise goes beyond efficiency, beyond organization forms and procedures, even beyond group cohesion. Integrity combines organization and policy. It is the unity that emerges when a particular orientation becomes so firmly a part of group life that it colors and directs a wide variety of attitudes, decisions, and forms of organization, and does so at many levels of experience. The building of integrity is part of what we have called the 'institutional embodiment of purpose' and its protection is a major function of leadership.

The protection of integrity is more than an aesthetic or expressive exercise, more than an attempt to preserve a comforting, familiar environment. It is a practical concern of the first importance because the defense of integrity is also a defense of the organization's *distinctive competence*. As institutionalization progresses the enterprise takes on a special character, and this means that it becomes peculiarly competent (or incompetent) to do a particular kind of work. This is especially important when much depends on the creation of an appropriate atmosphere, as in the case of efforts to hold tight transportation schedules or maintain high standards of quality. A considerable part of high-level salesmanship is an effort to show the firm's distinctive capability to produce a certain product or perform a special service. This is important in government too, where competing agencies having similar formal assignments work hard to develop and display their distinctive competencies.

The terms 'institution,' 'organization character,' and 'distinctive competence' all refer to the same basic process—the transformation of an engineered, technical arrangement of building blocks into a social organism. This transition goes on unconsciously and inevitably wherever leeway for evolution and adaptation is allowed by the system of technical controls; and at least some such leeway exists in all but the most narrowly circumscribed organizations. Leadership has the job of guiding the transition from organization to institution so that the ultimate result effectively embodies desired aims and standards.

The study of institutions is in some ways comparable to the clinical study of personality. It requires a genetic and developmental approach, an emphasis on historical origins and growth stages. There is a need to see the enterprise as a whole and to see how it is transformed as new ways of dealing with a changing environment evolve. As in the case of personality, effective diagnosis depends upon locating the special problems that go along with a particular character-structure; and we can understand character better when we see it as the product of self-preserving efforts to deal with inner impulses and external demands. In both personality and institutions 'self-preservation' means more than bare organic or material survival. Self-preservation has to do with the maintenance of basic identity, with the integrity of a personal or institutional 'self.'

As the organization becomes an institution new problems are set for the men who run it. Among these is the need for institutional responsibility, which accounts for much of what we mean by statesmanship.

From a personal standpoint, responsible leadership is a blend of commitment, understanding, and determination. These elements bring together the selfhood of the leader and the identity of the institution. This is partly a matter of self-*conception*, for whatever his special background, and however important it may have been in the decision that gave him his office, the responsible leader in a mature institution must transcend his specialism. Self-*knowledge* becomes an understanding not only of the leader's own weaknesses and potentialities but of those qualities in the enterprise itself. And the assumption of command is a self-*summoning* process, yielding the will to know and the will to act in accordance with the requirements of institutional survival and fulfillment.

From a policy standpoint, and that is our primary concern, most of the characteristics of the responsible leader can be summarized under two headings: the avoidance of opportunism and the avoidance of utopianism.

Opportunism is the pursuit of immediate, short-run advantages in a way inadequately controlled by considerations of principle and ultimate consequence. To take advantage of opportunities is to show that one is alive, but institutions no less than persons must look to the long-run effects of present advantage.

Opportunism also displays itself in a narrow self-centeredness, in an effort to exploit other groups for immediate, short-run advantages. If a firm offers a product or service to other firms, expectations of dependability are created, especially in the matter of continuing supply. If supplies are abruptly discontinued, activities that depended upon them will suffer. Hence a firm's reputation for dependability and concern for others becomes a matter of great importance wherever continuing relationships are envisioned. To act as if only a set of impersonal transactions were involved, with no responsibility beyond the strict terms of a contract, creates anxiety in the buyer, threatens to damage *his* reputation for dependability, and in the end weakens both parties.

Utopian wishful-thinking enters when men who purport to be institutional leaders attempt to rely on overgeneralized purposes to guide their decisions. But when guides are unrealistic, yet decisions must be made, more realistic *but uncontrolled* criteria will somehow fill the gap. Immediate exigencies will dominate the actual choices that are made. In this way, the polarities of utopianism and opportunism involve each other.

Responsible leadership steers a course between utopianism and opportunism. Its responsibility consists in accepting the obligation of giving direction instead of merely ministering to organizational equilibrium; in adapting aspiration to the character of the organization, bearing in mind that what the organization has been will affect what it can be and do; and in transcending bare organizational survival by seeing that specialized decisions do not weaken or confuse the distinctive identity of the enterprise.

To the essentially conservative posture of the responsible leader we must add a concern for change and reconstruction. This creative role has two aspects. First, there is what we have called the 'institutional embodiment of purpose.' Second, creativity is exercised by strategic and tactical planning, that is, analyzing the environment to determine how best to use the existing resources and capabilities of the organization.

The art of the creative leader is the art of institution-building, the reworking of human and technological materials to fashion an organism that embodies new and enduring values. The opportunity to do this depends on a considerable sensitivity to the politics of internal change. This is more than a struggle for power among contending groups and leaders. It is equally a matter of avoiding recalcitrance and releasing energies. Thus winning consent to new directions depends on how secure the participants feel. When many routine problems of technical and human organization remain to be solved, when the minimum conditions for holding the organization together are only precariously met, it is difficult to expend energy on long-range planning and even harder to risk experimental programs. When the organization is in good shape from an engineering standpoint it is easier to put ideals into practice. Old activities can be abandoned without excessive strain if, for example, the costs of relatively inefficient but morale-saving transfer and termination can be absorbed. Security is bartered for consent. Since this bargain is seldom sensed as truly urgent, a default of leadership is the more common experience.

On the same theme, security can be granted, thereby releasing energies for creative change, by examining established procedures to distinguish those important to a sense of security from those essential to the aims of the enterprise. Change should focus on the latter; stability can be assured to practices that do not really matter so far as objectives are concerned but which do satisfy the need to be free from threatening change. Many useless industrial conflicts have been fought to protect prerogative and deny security, with but little effect on the ultimate competence of the firm.

If one of the great functions of administration is the exertion of cohesive force in the direction of institutional security, another great function is the creation of conditions that will make possible in the future what is excluded in the present. This requires a strategy of change that looks to the attainment of new capabilities more nearly fulfilling the truly felt needs and aspirations of the institution. The executive becomes a statesman as he makes the transition from administrative management to institutional leadership.

3 The Theory of the Growth of the Firm

Edith Penrose

So far as I know, no economist has as yet attempted a general theory of the growth of firms. This seems to me so very strange that I am sure anyone attempting it should indeed watch his (or her) step, for naturally there is always a good reason for what economists do or do not do. Perhaps such a theory is impossible to construct, unnecessary, trivial, or outside the pale of economics proper. I do not know, but I offer this study in the hope that all four possibilities will be rejected.

We shall be concerned with the growth of firms, and only incidentally with their size. The term 'growth' is used in ordinary discourse with two different connotations. It sometimes denotes merely increase in amount; for example, when one speaks of 'growth' in output, exports, sales. At other times, however, it is used in its primary meaning implying an increase in size or an improvement in quality as a result of a *process* of development, akin to natural biological processes in which an interacting series of internal changes leads to increases in size accompanied by changes in the characteristics of the growing object. Thus the terms 'economic growth' and 'economic development' are often used interchangeably where 'growth' implies not only an increase in the national product but also a progressive changing of the economy. 'Growth' in this second sense often also has the connotation of 'natural' or 'normal'—a process that will occur whenever conditions are favourable because of the nature of the 'organism'; size becomes a more or less incidental result of a continuous on-going or 'unfolding' process.

But this is not the way the size of firms is looked at in traditional economic analysis, which examines the advantages and disadvantages of *being* a particular size and explains movement from one size to another in terms of the net advantages of different sizes. Growth becomes merely an adjustment to the size appropriate to given conditions; there is no notion of an *internal* process of *development* leading to cumulative movements in any one direction. Still less is there any suggestion that there may be advantages in *moving* from one position to another quite apart from the advantages of *being* in a different position. It is often presumed that there is a 'most profitable' size of firm and that no further explanation than the search for profit is needed of how and why firms reach that size. Such an approach to the explanation of the size of firms will be rejected in this study; it will be argued that size is but a by-product of the process of growth, that there is no 'optimum', or even most profitable, size of firm.

1. The Nature of the Argument

A comprehensive theory of the growth of the firm must explain several qualitatively different kinds of growth and must take account not only of the sequence of changes created by a firm's own activities but also of the effect of changes that are external to the firm and lie beyond its control. Not all of these things can be discussed at the same time, however, without creating such a serious confusion between very different types of causal relationships that the discussion degenerates into a generalized description of a sequence of events that appears largely fortuitous and to have been introduced for the convenience of a pre-determined conclusion, like the coincidences of a poorly constructed detective story. Hence the development of the theory must proceed in stages.

After a discussion of the characteristics of the business firm, its functions, and the factors influencing its behaviour, we shall turn to an examination of the forces inherent in the nature of firms which at the same time create the possibilities for, provide the inducements to, and limit the amount of the expansion they can undertake or even plan to undertake in any given period of time. It will then be shown that this limit is by its nature temporary, that in the very process of expansion the limit recedes, and that after the completion of an optimum plan for expansion a new 'disequilibrium' has been created in which a firm has new inducements to expand further even if all external conditions (including the conditions of demand and supply) have remained unchanged.

In all of the discussion the emphasis is on the internal resources of a firm—on the productive services available to a firm from its own resources, particularly the productive services available from management with experience within the firm. It is shown not only that the resources with which a particular firm is accustomed to working will shape the productive services its management is capable of rendering (where management is defined in the broadest sense), but also that the experience of management will affect the productive services that all its other resources are capable of rendering. As management tries to make the best use of the resources available, a truly 'dynamic' interacting process occurs which encourages continuous growth but limits the rate of growth. In order to focus attention on the crucial role of a firm's 'inherited' resources, the environment is treated, in the first instance, as an 'image' in the entrepreneur's mind of the possibilities and restrictions with which he is confronted, for it is, after all, such an 'image' which in fact determines a man's behaviour; whether experience confirms expectations is another story.[1] Even 'demand' as seen by a firm is largely conditioned by the productive services available to it, and hence the 'direction of expansion'—the products a firm becomes interested in producing—can be analyzed with reference to the relationship between its resources and its own view of its competitive position. This will be discussed in an extensive analysis of the economics of diversification.

The theory of growth is developed first as a theory of internal growth, that is, of growth without merger and acquisition. The significance of merger can best be appraised in the light of its effect on the process of and limits to internal growth. Some attention to merger is given in the discussion of diversification, but not until Chapter VIII does the full analysis of growth through merger appear, and with this the development of the theory of growth is completed. The emphasis of the analysis is then shifted from the internal resources of the firm to the impact of particular types of external conditions as firms grow larger and to the particular situation of small as compared with large firms in the economy. This permits the development of an analysis of changes in the rate of growth of firms as they grow, and finally leads to a discussion of the process of industrial concentration, which is, after all, primarily a question of the relative rates of growth of large and small firms in a changing economy.

The 'theory of the firm'—as it is called in the literature—was constructed for the purpose of assisting in the theoretical investigation of one of the central problems of economic analysis—the way in which prices and the allocation of resources among different uses are determined. It is but part of the wider theory of value, indeed one of its supporting pillars, and its vitality is derived almost exclusively from its connection with this highly developed, and still basically unchallenged general system for the economic analysis of the problem of price determination and resource allocation.[2] In this context only those aspects of the behaviour of firms are considered that are relevant to the problems that the wider theory is designed to solve.

When the 'theory of the firm' is kept in its proper habitat there is not much difficulty with any of the explanations of the 'size' of firms. Difficulties arise when an attempt is made to acclimatize the theory to an alien environment and, in particular, to adapt it to the analysis of the expansion of the innovating, multiproduct, 'flesh-and-blood' organizations that businessmen call firms. It makes little difference in the theory of the firm whether changes in the characteristics of the individual firm, for example its managerial ability, or changes in the expectations of the entrepreneur about the future course of events, are treated as causing changes in the size of a single firm or as causing the creation of a series of 'new firms'.[3] The theorist is free to adopt the technique most suited to his problem. But how such changes are treated makes a great deal of difference to the theorist concerned with the growth of the firm defined, say, as an administrative organization in the real world.

2. The Function and Nature of the Industrial Firm

Probably it would be generally agreed that the primary economic function of an industrial firm is to make use of productive resources for the purpose of supplying goods and services to the economy in accordance with plans developed and put into effect within the firm. The essential difference between economic activity inside the firm and economic activity in the 'market' is that the former is carried on within an administrative organization, while the latter is not.

The cohesive character that an administrative organization imparts to the activities of the people operating within it provides the justification for separating for analytical purposes such a group from all other groups. The activities of the group which we call an industrial firm are further distinguished by their relation to the use of productive resources for the purpose of producing and selling goods and services. Thus, a firm is more than an administrative unit; it is also a collection of productive resources the disposal of which between different uses and over time is determined by administrative decision. When we regard the function of the private business firm from this point of view, the size of the firm is best gauged by some measure of the productive resources it employs.

The physical resources of a firm consist of tangible things—plant, equipment, land and natural resources, raw materials, semi-finished goods, waste products and by-products, and even unsold stocks of finished goods. Some of these are quickly and completely used up in the process of production, some are durable in use and continue to yield substantially the same services for a considerable period of time, some are transformed in production into one or more intermediate products which themselves can be considered as resources of the firm once they are produced, some are acquired directly in the market, and some that are produced within the firm can neither be purchased nor sold outside the firm. All of them are things that the firm buys, leases, or produces, part and parcel of a firm's operations and with the uses and properties of which the firm is more or less familiar.

There are also human resources available in a firm—unskilled and skilled labour, clerical, administrative, financial, legal, technical, and managerial staff. Some employees are hired on long-term contracts and may represent a substantial investment on the part of the firm. For some purposes these can be treated as more or less fixed or durable resources, like plant or equipment; even though they are not 'owned' by the firm, the firm suffers a loss akin to a capital loss when such employees leave the firm at the height of their abilities. Such human resources may well be on the payroll for considerable periods of time even though their services cannot be adequately used at the time. This may sometimes be true also of daily or weekly workers. They, too, may often be considered as a permanent 'part' of the firm, as resources the loss of whose services would involve a cost—or lost opportunity—to the firm.

Strictly speaking, it is never *resources* themselves that are the 'inputs' in the production process, but only the *services* that the resources can render.[4] The services yielded by resources are a function of the way in which they are used— exactly the same resource when used for different purposes or in different ways and in combination with different types or amounts of other resources provides a different service or set of services. The important distinction between resources and services is not their relative durability; rather it lies in the fact that resources consist of a bundle of potential services and can, for the most part, be defined independently of their use, while services cannot be so defined, the very word 'service' implying a function, an activity. As we shall see, it is largely in this distinction that we find the source of the uniqueness of each individual firm.

The productive activities of such a firm are governed by what we shall call its 'productive opportunity', which comprises all of the productive possibilities that its 'entrepreneurs' see and can take advantage of.[5] A theory of the growth of firms is essentially an examination of the changing productive opportunity of firms; in order to find a limit to growth, or a restriction on the rate of growth, the productive opportunity of a firm must be shown to be limited in any period.

Of the three classes of explanation why there may be a limit to the growth of firms—managerial ability, product or factor markets, and uncertainty and risk—the first refers to conditions within the firm, the second to conditions outside the firm, and the third is a combination of internal attitudes and external conditions.

3. The Nature of the Managerial Limit

Expansion does not take place automatically; on the contrary, the composition and extent of an expansion programme, as well as its execution, must be planned. Planning implies on the one hand a purpose, and on the other, the organization of resources to accomplish this purpose in some desired manner. Specifically, the creation of an 'optimum' plan for expansion requires that the resources available to a firm, whether already acquired by the firm or obtainable in the market, be used to 'best' advantage.[6] It is obvious that if all necessary productive services, including managerial and entrepreneurial services, were available in unlimited amounts at constant prices, and if demand for products were infinitely elastic, no 'best' plan could be constructed: a larger plan would always be better than a smaller one. It follows that there must be some limiting consideration to which the plan is anchored.

The assumption that a firm can obtain in the market any type of resource or quality of management implies that the specialized resources or managerial abilities it may need to take advantage of market opportunities are available to it. We assume that there are numerous opportunities for profitable production open to the individual firm. Nevertheless, the firm cannot, and in general will not attempt to, extend its expansion plans, and with them its 'management team', in an effort to take advantage of *all* such opportunities. It *cannot* do so because the very nature of a firm as an administrative and planning organization requires that the *existing* responsible officials of the firm at least know and approve, even if they do not in detail control all aspects of, the plans and operations of the firm; it *will not* even try to do so if the officials of the firm are themselves concerned to maintain its character as an organized unit.

4. The Management 'Team'

Since there is plainly a *physical* maximum to the number of things any individual or group of individuals can do, there is clearly some sort of limit to the rate at which even the financial transactions of individuals or groups can be expanded. It the present discussion, however, we are dealing with the rate of expansion of the firm as an administrative and planning organization. It follows that the existing officials of such an organization must have something to do with any operations that are to be treated as an expansion of that organization's operations; for to call a group of activities which are unconnected with a given organization an expansion of that organization is a contradiction in terms. This being so, the capacities of the *existing* managerial personnel of the firm necessarily set a limit to the expansion of that firm in any given period of time, for it is self-evident that such management cannot be hired in the market-place.

Businessmen commonly refer to the managerial group as a 'team', and the use of this word implies that management in some sense works as a unit. An administrative group is something more than a collection of individuals; it is a collection of individuals who have had experience in working together, for only in this way can 'teamwork' be developed. Existing managerial personnel provide services that cannot be provided by personnel newly hired from outside the firm, not only because they make up the administrative organization which cannot be expanded except by their own actions, but also because the experience they gain from working within the firm and with each other enables them to provide services that are uniquely valuable for the operations of the particular group with which they are associated.

These are services which make possible a working relationship between particular individuals making decisions and taking action in a particular environment, and they determine the efficiency and confidence with which action can be taken by the group as a whole. Unless such services are provided by its members, the group cannot function as a unit. It is for this reason that it is impossible for a firm to expand efficiently beyond a certain point merely by drawing up a management 'blueprint' for an extensive organization and then proceeding to hire people to fill the various positions and carry out the functions laid down in detailed 'job descriptions'.[7]

If a group is to gain experience in working together, it must have work to do. The total amount of work to be done at any time in a firm depends on the size of the firm's operations, which is in turn limited by the plans and actions of the past and thus by the managerial resources existing at the time the plans were made. Hence not only does existing management limit the amount of new management that can be hired (after all the services of existing management are required even to greet, let alone to install and instruct, the new personnel) but the plans put into effect by past management limit the rate at which newly hired personnel can gain the requisite experience.[8] Extensive planning requires the co-operation of many individuals who have confidence in each other, and this, in general, requires knowledge of each other. Individuals with experience within a given group cannot be hired from outside the group, and it takes time for them to achieve the requisite experience.[9] It follows, therefore, that if a firm deliberately or inadvertently expands its organization more rapidly than the individuals in the expanding organization can obtain the experience with each other and with the firm that is necessary for the effective operation of the group, the efficiency of the firm will suffer, even if optimum adjustments are made in the administrative structure; in extreme cases this may lead to such disorganization that the firm will be unable to compete efficiently in the market with other firms, and a period of 'stagnation' may follow.[10]

In Chapter II a distinction was made between resources and productive services. Managerial services of the type described here are as much productive services in a firm as are the services of engineers in the physical production process; and they are a necessary part of the 'inputs' of which the productive activities of a firm are composed. Of all the various kinds of productive services, managerial services are the only type which every firm, because of its very nature as an administrative organization, must make use of. Since the services from 'inherited' managerial resources control the amount of new managerial resources that can be absorbed, they create a fundamental and inescapable limit to the amount of expansion a firm can undertake at any time.[11]

5. Release of Managerial Services

If the argument is accepted that a firm will expand only in accordance with plans for expansion and that the extent of these plans will be limited by the size of the experienced managerial group, then it is evident that as plans are completed and put into operation, managerial services absorbed in the planning processes will be gradually released and become available for further planning.

6. The Growth of Managerial Services

In most circumstances one would expect new managerial services to be created in the process of expansion and to remain available to the firm. Any substantial expansion normally involves both acquisition of new personnel and promotion and redistribution of the old. Not infrequently a new subdivision of managerial organization is effected and a further decentralization of managerial functions takes place.

7. The Continuing Availability of Unused Productive Services

Resources were defined in Chapter II to include the physical things a firm buys, leases, or produces for its own use, and the people hired on terms that make them effectively part of the firm. Services, on the other hand, are the contributions these resources can make to the productive operations of the firm. A resource, then, can be viewed as a bundle of possible services.

For any given scale of operations a firm must possess resources from which it can obtain the productive services appropriate to the amounts and types of product it intends to produce. Some of the services will be obtained from resources already under the control of the firm in the form of fixed plant and equipment, more or less permanent personnel, and inventories of materials and goods in process; others will be obtained from resources the firm acquires in the market as occasion demands. Although the 'inputs' in which the firm is interested are productive services, it is *resources* that, with few exceptions, must be acquired in order to obtain services. For the most part, resources are only obtainable in discrete amounts, that is to say, a 'bundle' of services must be acquired even if only a 'single' service should be wanted.[12] The amount and kind of productive services obtainable from each *class* of resource are different, and sometimes, particularly with respect to personnel, the amount and kind of service obtainable from each *unit* within a resource-class are different. Having acquired resources for actual and contemplated operations, a firm has an incentive to use as profitably as possible the services obtainable from each unit of each type of resource acquired.

It follows, therefore, that as long as expansion can provide a way of using the services of its resources more profitably than they are being used, a firm has an incentive to expand; or alternatively, so long as any resources are not used fully in current operations, there is an incentive for a firm to find a way of using them more fully. Unused productive services available from existing resources are a 'waste', sometimes an unavoidable waste (that is to say, it may not pay to try to use them) but they are 'free' services which, if they can be used profitably, may provide a competitive advantage for the firm possessing them.

Of all of the outstanding characteristics of business firms perhaps the most inadequately treated in economic analysis is the diversification of their activities, sometimes called 'spreading of production' or 'integration', which seems to accompany their growth. It has often been pointed out that this process is likely to be 'inefficient' in the sense that productivity is likely to be smaller the greater the number of activities to which a given collection of resources is devoted.[13] 'Efficient' production of given products is the economist's criterion of satisfactory performance, and the primary justification for a large size of firm; yet the most successful and evidently highly efficient firms in the business world are heavily diversified, producing many products, extensively integrated, and apparently are always eager to take on more products.

The discussion of the role of diversification in the process of growth perhaps brings out more clearly than would anything else the significance of the statement made in an earlier chapter that a firm is essentially a pool of resources the utilization of which is organized in an administrative framework. In a sense, the final products being produced by a firm at any given time merely represent one of several ways in which the firm could be using its resources, an incident in the development of its basic potentialities. Over the years the products change, and there are numerous firms today which produce few or none of the products on which their early reputation and success were based. Their basic strength has been developed above or below the end-product level as it were—in technology of specialized kinds and in market positions. Within the limits set by the rate at which the administrative structure of the firm can be adapted and adjusted to larger and larger scales of operation, there is nothing inherent in the nature of the firm or of its economic function to prevent the indefinite expansion of its activities.

Notes

1. These lines were written in a slightly different form before Kenneth Boulding's imaginative little book appeared. 'Image' is so apt a word for my purposes that I promptly appropriated it. See Kenneth E. Boulding, *The Image* (Ann Arbor: Univ. of Michigan Press, 1956).
2. Consequently the various attacks on the theory of the firm, whether they come from theorists emphasizing the effect of uncertainty or from investigators of the actual behaviour of firms, have failed to dislodge it from its key position in economic theory. To do so, even for the competitive case, would, as Hicks has pointed out, involve the 'wreckage' of 'the greater part of general equilibrium theory', which can hardly be accepted until something better has been evolved to take its place. J. R. Hicks, *Value and Capital* (Oxford: Clarendon Press, 2nd ed., 1946), p. 84.
3. Kaldor, for example, has defined the firm as a 'productive combination possessing a given unit of co-ordinating ability', and hold that 'all the theoretically relevant characteristics of a firm change which changes in coordinating ability. It might as well be treated, therefore, as a different firm.' N. Kaldor, 'The Equilibrium of the Firm', *Economic Journal*, Vol. XLIV, No. 173 (March 1934), pp. 69–70. And Triffin

explicitly states that for (his) theoretical purposes it is 'better to say that a new firm has been created' when the producer's appraisal of cost and revenue conditions changes. Furthermore 'each innovation modifies the level of profit opportunities attached to a firm or rather creates a new firm, provided with profit opportunities of its own . . .'. Robert Triffin, *Monopolistic Competition and General Equilibrium Theory* (Cambridge: Harvard Univ. Press, 1940), pp. 169–171.

4. I am avoiding the use of the term 'factor of production' precisely because it makes no distinction between resources and services, sometimes meaning the one and sometimes the other in economic literature.

5. The term 'entrepreneur' throughout this study is used in a functional sense to refer to individuals or groups within the firm providing entrepreneurial services, whatever their position or occupational classification may be. Entrepreneurial services are those contributions to the operations of a firm which relate to the introduction and acceptance on behalf of the firm of new ideas, particularly with respect to products, location, and significant changes in technology, to the acquisition of new managerial personnel, to fundamental changes in the administrative organization of the firm, to the raising of capital, and to the making of plans for expansion, including the choice of method of expansion. Entrepreneurial services are contrasted with managerial services, which relate to the execution of entrepreneurial ideas and proposals and to the supervision of existing operations. The same individuals may, and more often than not probably do, provide both types of service to the firm. The 'management' of a firm includes individuals supplying entrepreneurial services as well as those supplying managerial services, but the 'competence of management' refers to the way in which the managerial function is carried out while the 'enterprise of management' refers to the entrepreneurial function. The nature of the organization of a firm and the relationships between the individuals within it have often as important an influence on the competence and enterprise of management and on the kinds of decisions taken as do the inherent characteristics of the individuals themselves. The influence of 'organizational structure' has been particularly stressed by the 'organization theorists'. See, for example R. M. Cyert and J. G. March, 'Organization Structure and Pricing Behavior in an Oligopolistic Market', *American Economic Review*, Vol. XLV, No. 1 (Mar. 1955), pp. 129–139.

6. The judgment regarding which of several alternative possibilities is 'best' will, of course, for any given firm be influenced by the attitude of the firm's entrepreneurs towards risk and by their ideas about the kind of action appropriate to their firm. We need not inquire into these things for the present but merely assume that they remain unchanged form one planning period to the next.

7. The emphasis I am placing on managerial experience within a firm does not imply that 'outside' experience is not also very valuable, especially for the 'chief executive' of a large corporation. It should be remembered that the 'management group' that we are discussing includes the entire managerial organization, subordinates as well as 'chiefs'. Herrymon Maurer, in his breezy and journalistic, but frequently shrewd discussion of the 'big corporation', points out that decisions in the modern corporation are 'group' decisions in which the president, or chief executive, of the

corporation may take little direct part; his role being that of providing relatively unobtrusive guidance, lubrication, and conciliation. It is incidentally for this reason that, while the management group as a whole must be experienced in working together, a new 'leader' from outside with the required personal qualifications and general experience, may very effectively preside over and 'lead' the 'team'. See Herrymon Maurer, *Great Enterprise: Growth and Behavior of the Big Corporation* (New York: Macmillan, 1955). Mabel Newcomer also stresses the contribution of outside experience to the successful functioning of the chief executives of large corporations. Her study dealt only with Presidents and Board Chairmen, but from the point of view of the problems of expanding an administrative organization these officials may be of less importance than their subordinates. See Mabel Newcomer, *The Big Business Executive* (New York: Columbia Univ. Press, 1955).

8. For example, in a report of the National Science Foundation it was noted that one chemical company in their survey 'has developed an optimum rate-of-growth factor expressed in terms of an annual percentage increase in personnel. The percentage is based upon the number of new employees the company believes can be successfully assimilated each year. This percentage is applied to the company's research staff, as well as to the other parts of the firm, but with modifications depending on the amount and kind of research considered necessary to assure overall company growth at the established rate.' National Science Foundation, *Science and Engineering in American Industry: Final Report on a 1953–1954 Survey* (Wash. D.C.: U.S. Government Printing Office, 1956), p. 48.

9. The former director of the Tennessee Valley Authority, in discussing the problem of developing atomic energy quickly during the war and of putting production on an industrial basis, mentioned the various types of skills that were needed, and added 'most important of all, these three capabilities of research, industrial techniques and operation had to be *combined* in the same team, with experience in working together as a unit. To go out and create such an organization was out of the question. There was not time.' This was why it was necessary, he says, to turn to already established organizations, such as the Bell telephone system. David Lilienthal, *Big Business: A New Era* (New York: Harper, 1953), p. 102.

10. One student of industrial organization has noted that '. . . business enterprise today (as we must not cease to observe) is a corporate manifestation and its capacity to cope with larger outputs is not fixed but expands with its structure—and depends on the relation . . . between the governing members of the corporation. . . . Some firms will fail with size because of management, if the immediate jump in size which they attempt is too great; or if the management is incapable of adapting its structure . . .'. P. Sargant Florence, *The Logic of British and American Industry* (London: Routledge and Kegan Paul, 1953), p. 64.

11. It should be noted that this analysis applies only to the scale of organization of the firm, not necessarily to the scale of its production measured in terms of capital investment. As we shall see, in Chapter IX, for a given capital expenditure, the organizational problem may be reduced by the use of large-scale equipment and technical processes.

12. Even those raw materials which are in principle finely divisible must usually be

acquired in minimum-sized bundles because to acquire less than the 'standard unit' is usually disproportionately expensive. However, this type of indivisibility is probably not of much practical importance.

13. Nicholas Kaldor, for example, concludes that ' "spreading of production" is always attended with some cost; i.e. the physical productivity of a *given* quantity of resources calculated in terms of *any* of the products will always be less, the greater the number of separate commodities they are required simultaneously to produce.' He gives the following as 'evidence' for his proposition: 'That this is the case for a large proportion of jointly produced commodities is shown by the fact that the development of an "industry" is always attended by "specialization" or "disintegration", i.e. the reduction of the number of commodities produced by single firms.' Nicholas Kaldor, 'Market Imperfection and Excess Capacity', *Economica*, Vol. II (New Series), 1935, p. 48.

And P. Sargant Florence writes: 'Integration within a plant or a firm must be suspected therefore of small-scale inefficient production till it is proved innocent.' *The Logic of British and American Industry* (London: Routledge and Kegan Paul, 1953), p. 74.

4 Strategy and Structure

Alfred D. Chandler

1. Motives and Methods

This investigation into the changing strategy and structure of the large industrial enterprise in the United States began as an experiment in the writing of comparative business history. The initial thought was that an examination of the way *different* enterprises carried out the *same* activity—whether that activity was manufacturing, marketing, procurement of supplies, finance, or administration—would have as much value as a study of how a *single* firm carried on *all* these activities. Such a comparative analysis could permit deeper probes into the nature of the function studied, and so provide more accurate interpretations and more meaningful evaluations of the performance of several different enterprises in that activity than could a whole series of histories of individual firms. It could thus indicate more clearly the ways in which American businessmen have handled that activity over the years.

Of the several activities carried on in American business, that of administration appeared to be among the most promising for such an experiment in comparative history. Business administration has a particular relevance for today's businessmen and scholars. The enormous expansion of the American economy since World War II has led to the rapid growth of a multitude of industrial companies. Their executives are faced with complex administrative problems that before the war concerned only those of the largest corporations. At the same time, the growth of units that carry on political, military, educational, medical, as well as business activities has brought their administration to the attention of sociologists, anthropologists, economists, political scientists, and other scholars. Yet the historians have provided social scientists with little empirical data on which to base generalizations or hypotheses concerning the administration of great enterprises. Nor have the historians formulated many theories or generalizations of their own.

If changing developments in business administration presented a challenging area for comparative analysis, the study of innovation seemed to furnish the proper focus for such an investigation. Historically, administrators have rarely changed their daily routine and their positions of power except under the strongest pressures. Therefore a study of the creation of new administrative forms and methods should point to urgent needs and compelling opportunities both within and without the firm. For a study of such forms, that of the organizational structure used to administer the largest and most complex of American industrial enterprises seemed to offer the widest possibilities.

What then has been the structure used to administer such great enterprises? And who were its innovators? A preliminary survey of the experience of fifty of the largest industrial companies in the United States helped to answer these questions.[1] This survey showed that in recent years what may be called the multidivisional type of organization has become generally used by industrial firms carrying on the most diverse economic activities. In this type of organization, a general office plans, coordinates, and appraises the work of a number of operating divisions and allocates to them the necessary personnel, facilities, funds, and other resources. The executives in charge of these divisions, in turn, have under their command most of the functions necessary for handling one major line of products or set of services over a wide geographical area, and each of these executives is responsible for the financial results of his division and for its success in the market place. This administrative form, often known in business parlance as the 'decentralized' structure, is depicted in Figure 1 (page 44).

The first companies to devise this 'decentralized' form, according to the preliminary study, included the E. I. du Pont de Nemours & Co., General Motors Corporation, Standard Oil Company (New Jersey), and Sears, Roebuck and Company. Du Pont and General Motors began to fashion their new structure shortly after World War I. Jersey Standard started its reorganization in 1925, and Sears started its in 1929. Five other firms among the fifty studied—United States Rubber, B. F. Goodrich, Union Carbide & Carbon, Westinghouse Electric, and The Great Atlantic & Pacific Tea Co.—initiated comparable changes between 1925 and 1932. Except for the last, the A. & P., these administrative reorganizations proved to be less creative innovations than those in the first group.[2] Therefore du Pont, General Motors, and Jersey Standard were selected for study. And of the two innovators of the new multidivisional form in the merchandising field, Sears was picked instead of A. & P. because its activities were more complex and because information about the company was more readily available.

Possibly, other large corporations not on the list of the top fifty began to set up the 'decentralized,' multidivisional structure in the 1920's and even earlier. But the four selected—du Pont, General Motors, Jersey Standard, and Sears— were among the very first to initiate major reorganizations of this kind. What is important for this study is that the executives of these four began to develop their new structure independently of each other and of any other firm. There was no imitation. Each thought its problems were unique and its solutions genuine innovations, as brand new ways of administering great industrial enterprises. In time, the innovations became models for similar changes in many American corporations.

2. Some General Propositions

If useful comparisons are to be made among four companies and then fourscore more, and if decisions and actions in these firms are to indicate something about the history of the industrial enterprise as an institution, the terms and concepts used in these comparisons and analyses must be carefully and precisely defined. Otherwise comparisons and findings can be more misleading than instructive. The following set of general or theoretical propositions attempts to provide some sort of conceptual precision. Without reference to historical reality, they try to explain in fairly clear-cut, oversimplified terms how the modern, 'decentralized' structure came into being.

Before developing these propositions, the term *industrial enterprise* needs to be defined. Used in a broad sense, it means here a large private, profit-oriented business firm involved in the handling of goods in some or all of the successive industrial processes from the procurement of the raw material to the sale to the ultimate customer. Transportation enterprises, utilities, or purely financial companies are not then included in this study, while those firms concerned with marketing and with the extraction of raw materials as well as those dealing with processing or manufacturing do fall within this definition. An industrial enterprise is thus a subspecies of what Werner Sombart has described as the capitalistic enterprise, which as 'an independent economic organism is created over and above the individuals who constitute it. This entity appears then as the agent in each of these transactions and leads, as it were, a life of its own, which often exceeds in length that of its human members.'[3]

While the enterprise may have a life of its own, its present health and future growth surely depend on the individuals who guide its activities. Just what, then, are the functions of the executives responsible for the fortunes of the enterprise? They coordinate, appraise, and plan. They may, at the same time, do the actual buying, selling, advertising, accounting, manufacturing, engineering, or research, but in the modern enterprise the execution or carrying out of these functions is usually left to such employees as salesmen, buyers, production supervisors and foremen, technicians, and designers. In many cases, the executive does not even personally supervise the working force but rather administers the duties of other executives. In planning and coordinating the work of subordinate managers or supervisors, he allocates tasks and makes available the necessary equipment, materials, and other physical resources necessary to carry out the various jobs. In appraising their activities, he must decide whether the employees or subordinate managers are handling their tasks satisfactorily. If not, he can take action by changing or bringing in new physical equipment and supplies, by transferring or shifting the personnel, or by expanding or cutting down available funds. Thus, the term, *administration*, as used here, includes executive action and orders as well as the decisions taken in coordinating, appraising, and planning the work of the enterprise and in allocating its resources.

The initial proposition is, then, that administration is an identifiable activity, that it differs from the actual buying, selling, processing, or transporting of the goods, and that in the large industrial enterprise the concern of the executives is more with administration than with the performance of functional work. In a small firm, the same man or group of men buy materials, sell finished goods, and supervise manufacturing as well as coordinate, plan, and appraise these different functions. In a large company, however, administration usually becomes a specialized, full-time job. A second proposition is that the administrator must handle two types of administrative tasks when he is coordinating, appraising, and planning the activities of the enterprise. At times he must be concerned with the long-run health of his company, at other times with its smooth and efficient day-to-day operation.[4] The first type of activity calls for concentration on long-term planning and appraisal, the second for meeting immediate problems and needs and for handling unexpected contingencies or crises. To be sure, in real life the distinction between these two types of activities or decisions is often not clear cut. Yet some decisions clearly deal very largely with defining basic goals and the course of action and procedures necessary to achieve these goals, while other decisions have more to do with the day-to-day operations carried out within the broader framework of goals, policies, and procedures.

The next few propositions deal with the content of administrative activities handled through the different types of posts or positions in the most complex administrative structures. The executives in a modern 'decentralized' company carry out their administrative activities from four different types of positions (see Fig. 1). Each of these types within the enterprise has a different range of

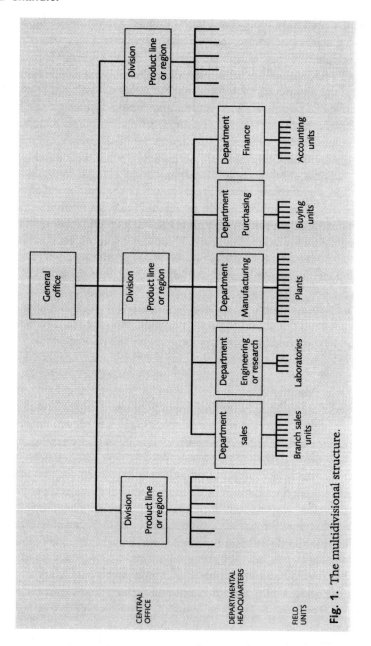

Fig. 1. The multidivisional structure.

administrative activities. Normally, each is on a different level of authority. At the top is a *general office*. There, general executives and staff specialists coordinate, appraise, and plan goals and policies and allocate resources for a number of quasi-autonomous, fairly self-contained divisions. Each division handles a major product line or carries on the firm's activities in one large geographical area. Each division's *central office*, in turn, administers a number of departments. Each of these departments is responsible for the administration of a major function—manufacturing, selling, purchasing or producing of raw materials, engineering, research, finance, and the like. The *departmental headquarters* in its turn coordinates, appraises, and plans for a number of field units. At the lowest level, each *field unit* runs a plant or works, a branch or district sales office, a purchasing office, an engineering or research laboratory, an accounting or other financial office, and the like. The four types of administrative positions in a large multidivisional enterprise are thus: the field unit, the departmental headquarters, the division's central office, and the general office. These terms are used throughout this study to designate a specific set of administrative activities. They do not, it should be stressed, refer to an enterprise's office buildings or rooms. One office building could house executives responsible for any one of the positions or conceivably those responsible for all four. Conversely, the executives in any one of the posts could be housed in different rooms or buildings.

Only in the first, the field unit, are the managers primarily involved in carrying on or personally supervising day-to-day activities. Even here, if the volume of activity is large, they spend much of their time on administrative duties. But such duties are largely operational, carried out within the framework of policies and procedures set by departmental headquarters and the higher offices. The departmental and divisional offices may make some long-term decisions, but because their executives work within a comparable framework determined by the general office, their primary administrative activities also tend to be tactical or operational. The general office makes the broad strategic or entrepreneurial decisions as to policy and procedures and can do so largely because it has the final say in the allocation of the firm's resources—men, money, and materials—necessary to carry out these administrative decisions and actions and others made with its approval at any level.[5]

It seems wise here to emphasize the distinction between the formulation of policies and procedures and their implementation. The formulation of policies and procedures can be defined as either strategic or tactical. *Strategic* decisions are concerned with the long-term health of the enterprise. *Tactical* decisions deal more with the day-to-day activities necessary for efficient and smooth operations. But decisions, either tactical or strategic, usually require *implementation* by an allocation or reallocation of resources—funds, equipment, or personnel. Strategic plans can be formulated from below, but normally the implementation of such proposals requires the resources which only the general office can provide. Within the broad policy lines laid down by that office and with the resources it allocates, the executives at the lower levels carry out tactical decisions.

The executives who actually allocate available resources are then the key men in any enterprise. Because of their critical role in the modern economy, they will be defined in this study as entrepreneurs. In contrast, those who coordinate, appraise, and plan within the means allocated to them will be termed managers. So *entrepreneurial* decisions and actions will refer to those which affect the allocation or reallocation of resources for the enterprise as a whole, and *operating* decisions and actions will refer to those which are carried out by using the resources already allocated.

Just because the entrepreneurs make some of the most significant decisions in the American economy, they are not all necessarily imbued with a long-term strategic outlook. In many enterprises the executives responsible for resource allocation may very well concentrate on day-to-day operational affairs, giving little or no attention to changing markets, technology, sources of supply, and other factors affecting the long-term health of their company. Their decisions may be made without forward planning or analysis but rather by meeting in an *ad hoc* way every new situation, problem, or crisis as it arises. They accept the goals of their enterprise as given or inherited. Clearly wherever entrepreneurs act like managers, wherever they concentrate on short-term activities to the exclusion or to the detriment of long-range planning, appraisal, and coordination, they have failed to carry out effectively their role in the economy as well as in their enterprise. This effectiveness should provide a useful criterion for evaluating the performance of an executive in American industry.

As already pointed out, executives in the large enterprise work in four types of offices, each with his own administrative duties, problems, and needs. The four types operate on different scales, and their officers have different business horizons. The managers in the field unit are concerned with one function— marketing, manufacturing, engineering, and so forth—in one local area. The executives in the departmental headquarters plan, administer, and coordinate the activities of one function on a broad regional and often national scale rather than just locally. Their professional activities and their outside sources of information concern men and institutions operating in the same specialized function. The divisional executives, on the other hand, deal with an industry rather than a function. They are concerned with all the functions involved in the overall process of handling a line of products or services. Their professional horizons and contacts are determined by industry rather than functional interests. Finally, executives in the general office have to deal with several industries or one industry in several broad and different geographical regions. They set policies and procedures and allocate resources for divisions carrying out all types of functions, either in different geographical areas or in quite different product lines. Their business horizons and interests are broadened to range over national and even international economies.

While all four types of offices exist in the most complex of industrial enterprises, each can of course exist separately. An industrial enterprise can include one, two, three, or all four of these offices. Many small firms today have only a single office managing a single plant, store, laboratory, financial operation, or sales activity. Larger companies with a number of operating units carry out a single function—such as sales (wholesale or retail), manufacturing, purchasing, or engineering. Their over-all administrative structure comprises a headquarters and field offices. So also today there are integrated industrial enterprises that handle several economic functions rather than just one. Finally, there are the great diversified industrial empires, carrying on different functions and producing a variety of goods and services in all parts of the globe.

Since each type of position handles a different range of administrative activities, each must have resulted from a different type of growth. Until the volume or technological complexity of an enterprise's economic activities had so grown as to demand an increasing division of labor within the firm, little time needed to be spent on administrative work. Then the resulting specialization required one or more of the firm's executives to concentrate on coordinating, appraising, and planning these specialized activities. When the enterprise expanded geographically by setting up or acquiring facilities and personnel distant from its original location, it had to create an organization at a central headquarters to administer the units in the field. When it grew by moving into new functions, a central office came to administer the departments carrying on the different functions. Such a central administrative unit proved necessary, for example, when in following the policy of vertical integration a manufacturing firm began to do its own wholesaling, procuring of supplies, and even producing raw materials. Finally, when an integrated enterprise became diversified through purchasing or creating new facilities and entered new lines of business, or when it expanded its several functional departments over a still larger geographical area, it fashioned a number of integrated divisional units administered by a general office.

The thesis that different organizational forms result from different types of growth can be stated more precisely if the planning and carrying out of such growth is considered a *strategy*, and the organization devised to administer these enlarged activities and resources, a *structure*. *Strategy* can be defined as the determination of the basic long-term goals and objectives of an enterprise, and the adoption of courses of action and the allocation of resources necessary for carrying out these goals. Decisions to expand the volume of activities, to set up distant plants and offices, to move into new economic functions, or become diversified along many lines of business involve the defining of new basic goals.

47

New courses of action must be devised and resources allocated and reallocated in order to achieve these goals and to maintain and expand the firm's activities in the new areas in response to shifting demands, changing sources of supply, fluctuating economic conditions, new technological developments, and the actions of competitors. As the adoption of a new strategy may add new types of personnel and facilities, and alter the business horizons of the men responsible for the enterprise, it can have a profound effect on the form of its organization.

Structure can be defined as the design of organization through which the enterprise is administered. This design, whether formally or informally defined, has two aspects. It includes, first, the lines of authority and communication between the different administrative offices and officers and, second, the information and data that flow through these lines of communication and authority. Such lines and such data are essential to assure the effective coordination, appraisal, and planning so necessary in carrying out the basic goals and policies and in knitting together the total resources of the enterprise. These resources include financial capital; physical equipment such as plants, machinery, offices, warehouses, and other marketing and purchasing facilities, sources of raw materials, research and engineering laboratories; and, most important of all, the technical, marketing, and administrative skills of its personnel.

The thesis deduced from these several propositions is then that structure follows strategy and that the most complex type of structure is the result of the concatenation of several basic strategies. *Expansion of volume* led to the creation of an administrative office to handle one function in one local area. Growth through *geographical dispersion* brought the need for a departmental structure and headquarters to administer several local field units. The decision to expand into new types of functions called for the building of a central office and a multidepartmental structure, while the developing of new lines of products or continued growth on a national or international scale brought the formation of the multidivisional structure with a general office to administer the different divisions. For the purposes of this study, the move into new functions will be referred to as a strategy of *vertical integration* and that of the development of new products as a strategy of *diversification*.

This theoretical discussion can be carried a step further by asking two questions: (1) If structure does follow strategy, why should there be delay in developing the new organization needed to meet the administrative demands of the new strategy? (2) Why did the new strategy, which called for a change in structure, come in the first place?

There are at least two plausible answers to the first query. Either the administrative needs created by the new strategy were not positive or strong enough to require structural change, or the executives involved were unaware of the new needs. There seems to be no question that a new strategy created new administrative needs, for expansion through geographical dispersion, vertical integration, and product diversification added new resources, new activities, and an increasing number of entrepreneurial and operational actions and decisions. Nevertheless, executives could still continue to administer both the old and new activities with the same personnel, using the same channels of communication and authority and the same types of information. Such administration, however, must become increasingly inefficient. This proposition should be true for a relatively small firm whose structure consists of informal arrangements between a few executives as well as for a large one whose size and numerous administrative personnel require a more formal definition of relations between offices and officers. Since expansion created the need for new administrative offices and structures, the reasons for delays in developing the new organization rested with the executives responsible for the enterprise's long-range growth and health. Either these administrators were too involved in day-to-day tactical activities to appreciate or understand the longer-range organizational needs of their enterprises, or else their training and education failed to sharpen their perception of organizational problems or failed to develop their ability to handle them. They may also have resisted administratively desirable changes because they felt structural reorganization threatened their own personal position, their power, or most important of all, their psychological security.

In answer to the second question, changes in strategy which called for changes in structure appear to have been in response to the opportunities and needs created by changing population and changing national income and by technological innovation. Population growth, the shift from the country to the city and then to the suburb, depressions and prosperity, and the increasing pace of technological change, all created new demands or curtailed existing ones for a firm's goods or services. The prospect of a new market or the threatened loss of a current one stimulated geographical expansion, vertical integration, and product diversification. Moreover, once a firm had accumulated large resources, the need to keep its men, money, and materials steadily employed provided a constant stimulus to look for new markets by moving into new areas, by taking on new functions, or by developing new product lines. Again the awareness of the needs and opportunities created by the changing environment seems to have depended on the training and personality of individual executives and on their ability to keep their eyes on the more important entrepreneurial problems even in the midst of pressing operational needs.

The answers to the two questions can be briefly summarized by restating the general thesis. Strategic growth resulted from an awareness of the opportunities and needs—created by changing population, income, and technology—to employ existing or expanding resources more profitably. A new strategy required a new or at least refashioned structure if the enlarged enterprise was to be operated efficiently. The failure to develop a new internal structure, like the failure to respond to new external opportunities and needs, was a consequence of overconcentration on operational activities by the executives responsible for the destiny of their enterprises, or from their inability, because of past training and education and present position, to develop an entrepreneurial outlook.

One important corollary to this proposition is that growth without structural adjustment can lead only to economic inefficiency. Unless new structures are developed to meet new administrative needs which result from an expansion of a firm's activities into new areas, functions, or product lines, the technological, financial, and personnel economies of growth and size cannot be realized. Nor can the enlarged resources be employed as profitably as they otherwise might be. Without administrative offices and structure, the individual units within the enterprise (the field units, the departments, and the divisions) could undoubtedly operate as efficiently or even more so (in terms of cost per unit and volume of output per worker) as independent units than if they were part of a larger enterprise. Whenever the executives responsible for the firm fail to create the offices and structure necessary to bring together effectively the several administrative offices into a unified whole, they fail to carry out one of their basic economic roles.

Notes

1. Alfred D. Chandler, Jr., 'Management Decentralization: An Historical Analysis,' *Business History Review*, 30:111–174 (June, 1956). After the article was completed, further research indicated that Westinghouse had begun its changes in 1931.
2. The United States Rubber Company's major reorganization in 1929 was completed under du Pont direction; Goodrich quickly abandoned its initial attempt at 'decentralization,' returning to it only in the 1950's; and by World War II, Union Carbide had made only tentative steps to transform the functions of its headquarters from those of a holding company into those of a modern, policy-making, appraising, and coordinating unit. The reorganization at Westinghouse between 1931 and 1936 began as an independent innovation, but the company's changes were in many ways only a repetition of those that had already been put into effect at du Pont and Jersey Standard. It seemed wise, therefore, merely to outline the Westinghouse story and to broaden the scope of the study by selecting a large merchandise firm with business activities quite different from those of the integrated manufacturing companies already chosen for study.
3. Werner Sombart, 'Capitalism,' *Encyclopedia of the Social Sciences* (New York, 1930), III, 200. This form, in turn, is one of the institutional genera that dominate our modern political, military, religious, and educational life as well as the contempo-

rary economic world that Max Weber first delineated as bureaucratic. (H. H. Gerth and C. Wright Mills, *From Max Weber* (New York, 1946), pp. 196–244). Weber stressed:

> It is the peculiarity of the modern entrepreneur that he conducts himself as the 'first official' of his enterprise, in the very same way in which the ruler of a specifically modern bureaucratic state spoke of himself as 'the first servant' of the state. The idea that the bureau activities of the state are intrinsically different in character from the management of private economic offices is a continental European notion and, by way of contrast, is totally foreign to the American way. (*Ibid.*, p. 198)

4. I am greatly indebted to Dr. Fritz Redlich for first pointing out to me this critically important distinction, see his 'Unternehmer,' *Handworterbuch der Sozialwissenschaften* (Göttingen, 1959), X, 489, and 'The Business Leader in Theory and Reality,' *American Journal of Economics and Sociology*, 8:223–237 (April, 1949).
5. The distinctions between the duties of the administrative offices at these different levels and the relation of the function of these offices to entrepreneurial activities within the enterprise are worked out in more detail in Alfred D. Chandler, Jr., and Fritz Redlich, 'Recent Developments in American Business Administration and Their Conceptualization,' *Weltwirtschaftliches Archiv*, 86:103–130 (1961).

The Concept of Corporate Strategy

Kenneth R. Andrews

1. What Strategy Is

Corporate strategy is the pattern of decisions in a company that determines and reveals its objectives, purposes, or goals, produces the principal policies and plans for achieving those goals, and defines the range of business the company is to pursue, the kind of economic and human organization it is or intends to be, and the nature of the economic and noneconomic contribution it intends to make to its shareholders, employees, customers, and communities. In an organization of any size or diversity, 'corporate strategy' usually applies to the whole enterprise, while 'business strategy,' less comprehensive, defines the choice of product or service and market of individual businesses within the firm. Business strategy, that is, is the determination of how a company will compete in a given business and position itself among its competitors. Corporate strategy defines the businesses in which a company will compete, preferably in a way that focuses resources to convert distinctive competence into competitive advantage. Both are outcomes of a continuous process of strategic management that we will later analyze in detail.

The strategic decision contributing to this pattern is one that is effective over long periods of time, affects the company in many different ways, and focuses and commits a significant portion of its resources to the expected outcomes. The pattern resulting from a series of such decisions will probably define the central character and image of a company, the individuality it has for its members and various publics, and the position it will occupy in its industry and markets. It will permit the specification of particular objectives to be attained through a timed sequence of investment and implementation decisions and will govern directly the deployment or redeployment of resources to make these decisions effective.

Some aspects of such a pattern of decision may be in an established corporation unchanging over long periods of time, like a commitment to quality, or high technology, or certain raw materials, or good labor relations. Other aspects of a strategy must change as or before the world changes, such as product line, manufacturing process, or merchandising and styling practices. The basic determinants of company character, if purposefully institutionalized, are likely to persist through and shape the nature of substantial changes in product-market choices and allocation of resources.

It would be possible to extend the definition of strategy for a given company to separate a central character and the core of its special accomplishment from the manifestations of such characteristics in changing product lines, markets, and policies designed to make activities profitable.

2. Formulation of Strategy

Corporate strategy is an organization process, in many ways inseparable from the structure, behavior, and culture of the company in which it takes place. Nevertheless, we may abstract from the process two important aspects, interrelated in real life but separable for the purposes of analysis. The first of these we may call *formulation*, the second *implementation*. Deciding what strategy should be may be approached as a rational undertaking, even if in life emotional attachments (as to metal skis or investigative reporting) may complicate choice among future alternatives (for ski manufacturers or alternative newspapers). The principal subactivities of strategy formulation as a logical activity include identifying opportunities and threats in the company's environment and attaching some estimate or risk to the discernible alternatives. Before a choice can be made, the company's strengths and weaknesses should be appraised together with the resources on hand and available. Its actual or potential capacity to take advantage of perceived market needs or to cope with attendant risks should be estimated as objectively as possible. The strategic alternative which results from matching opportunity and corporate capability at an acceptable level of risk is what we may call an economic strategy.

The process described thus far assumes that strategists are analytically objective in estimating the relative capacity of their company and the opportunity they see or anticipate in developing markets. The extent to which they wish to undertake low or high risk presumably depends on their profit objectives. The higher they set the latter, the more willing they must be to assume a correspondingly high risk that the market opportunity they see will not develop or that the corporate competence required to excel competition will not be forthcoming.

So far we have described the intellectual processes of ascertaining what a company *might do* in terms of environmental opportunity, of deciding what it *can do* in terms of ability and power, and of bringing these two considerations together in optimal equilibrium. The determination of strategy also requires consideration of what alternatives are preferred by the chief executive and are to be met if funds for reinvestment are limited. In any case, the greatest knowledge about the opportunities for a given technology and set of markets should be found at the divisional level.[1]

The strategic dilemma of a conglomerate world enterprise is the most complex in the full range of policy decisions. When the variety of what must be known cannot be reduced by a sharply focused strategy to the capacity of a single mind and when the range of a company's activities spans many industries and technologies, the problems of formulating a coherent strategy begin to get out of hand. Here strategy must become a managed process rather than the decision of the chief executive officer and his immediate associates. Bower and Prahalad have shown in important research how the context of decision can be controlled by the top management group and how power can be distributed through a hierarchy to influence the kind of strategic decision that will survive in the system.[2] The process of strategic decision can, like complex operations, be organized in such a way as to provide appropriate complementary roles for decentralization and control.

To conceive of a new development in response to market information and prediction of the future is a creative act. To commit resources to it only on the basis of projected return and the estimate of probability constituting risk of failure is foolhardy. More than economic analysis of potential return is required for decision, for economic opportunity abounds, far beyond the ability to capture it. That much money might be made in a new field or growth industry does not mean that a company with abilities developed in a different field is going to make it. We turn now to the critical factors that for an individual company make one opportunity better than another.

---

3. Identifying Corporate Competence and Resources

The first step in validating a tentative choice among several opportunities is to determine whether the organization has the capacity to prosecute it successfully. The capability of an organization is its demonstrated and potential ability to accomplish, against the opposition of circumstance or competition, whatever it sets out to do. Every organization has actual and potential strengths and weaknesses. Since it is prudent in formulating strategy to extend or maximize the one and contain or minimize the other, it is important to try to determine what they are and to distinguish one from the other.

It is just as possible, though much more difficult, for a company to know its own strengths and limitations as it is to maintain a workable surveillance of its changing environment. Subjectivity, lack of confidence, and unwillingness to face reality may make it hard for organizations as well as for individuals to know themselves. But just as it is essential, though difficult, that a maturing person achieve reasonable self-awareness, so an organization can identify approximately its central strength and critical vulnerability.

To make an effective contribution to strategic planning, the key attributes to be appraised should be identified and consistent criteria established for judging them. If attention is directed to strategies, policy commitments, and past practices in the context of discrepancy between organization goals and attainment, an outcome useful to an individual manager's strategic planning is possible. The assessment of strengths and weaknesses associated with the attainment of specific objectives becomes in Stevenson's words a 'key link in a feedback loop' which allows managers to learn from the success or failures of the policies they institute.

Although this study does not find or establish a systematic way of developing or using such knowledge, members of organizations develop judgments about what the company can do particularly well—its core of competence. If consensus can be reached about this capability, no matter how subjectively arrived at, its application to identified opportunity can be estimated.

Sources of capabilities. The powers of a company constituting a resource for growth and diversification accrue primarily from experience in making and marketing a product line or providing a service. They inhere as well in (1) the developing strengths and weaknesses of the individuals comprising the organization, (2) the degree to which individual capability is effectively applied to the common task, and (3) the quality of coordination of individual and group effort.

The experience gained through successful execution of a strategy centered upon one goal may unexpectedly develop capabilities which could be applied to different ends. Whether they should be so applied is another question. For example, a manufacturer of salt can strengthen his competitive position by offering his customers salt-dispensing equipment. If, in the course of making engineering improvements in this equipment, a new solenoid principle is perfected that has application to many industrial switching problems, should this patentable and marketable innovation be exploited? The answer would turn not only on whether economic analysis of the opportunity shows this to be a durable and profitable possibility, but also on whether the organization can muster the financial, manufacturing, and marketing strength to exploit the discovery and live with its success. The former question is likely to have a more positive answer than the latter. In this connection, it seems important to remember that individual and unsupported flashes of strength are not as dependable as the gradually accumulated product and market-related fruits of experience.

Even where competence to exploit an opportunity is nurtured by experience in related fields, the level of that competence may be too low for any great reliance to be placed upon it. Thus a chain of children's clothing stores might well acquire the administrative, merchandising, buying, and selling skills that would permit it to add departments in women's wear. Similarly, a sales force effective in distributing typewriters might gain proficiency in selling office machinery and supplies. But even here it would be well to ask what *distinctive* ability these companies could bring to the retailing of soft goods or office equipment to attract customers away from a plethora of competitors.

Identifying strengths. The distinctive competence of an organization is more than what it can do; it is what it can do particularly well. To identify the less obvious or by-product strengths of an organization that may well be transferable to some more profitable new opportunity, one might well begin by examining the organization's current product line and by defining the functions it serves in its markets. Almost any important consumer product has functions which are related to others into which a qualified company might move. The typewriter, for example, is more than the simple machine for mechanizing handwriting that it once appeared to be when looked at only from the point of view of its designer and manufacturer. Closely analyzed from the point of view of the potential user, the typewriter is found to contribute to a broad range of information processing functions. Any one of these might have suggested an area to be exploited by a typewriter manufacturer. Tacitly defining a typewriter as a replacement for a fountain pen as a writing instrument rather than as an input-output device for word processing is the explanation provided by hindsight for the failure of the old-line typewriter companies to develop before IBM did the electric typewriter and the computer-related input-output devices it made possible. The definition of product which would lead to identification of transferable skills must be expressed in terms of the market needs it may fill rather than the engineering specifications to which it conforms.

Besides looking at the uses or functions to which present products contribute, the would-be diversifier might profitably identify the skills that underlie whatever success has been achieved. The qualifications of an organization efficient at performing its long-accustomed tasks come to be taken for granted and considered humdrum, like the steady provision of first-class service. The insight required to identify the essential strength justifying new ventures does not come naturally. Its cultivation can probably be helped by recognition of the need for analysis. In any case, we should look beyond the company's capacity to invent new products. Product leadership is not possible for a majority of companies, so it is fortunate that patentable new products are not the only major highway to new opportunities. Other avenues include new marketing services, new methods of distribution, new values in quality-price combinations, and creative merchandising. The effort to find or to create a competence that is truly distinctive may hold the real key to a company's success or even to its future development. For example, the ability of a cement manufacturer to run a truck fleet more effectively than its competitors may constitute one of its principal competitive strengths in selling an undifferentiated product.

Matching opportunity and competence. The way to narrow the range of alternatives, made extensive by imaginative identification of new possibilities, is to match opportunity to competence, once each has been accurately identified and its future significance estimated. It is this combination which establishes a company's economic mission and its position in its environment. The combination is designed to minimize organizational weakness and to maximize strength. In every case, risk attends it. And when opportunity seems to outrun present distinctive competence, the willingness to gamble that the latter can be built up to the required level is almost indispensable to a strategy that challenges the organization and the people in it. Fig. 1 diagrams the matching of opportunity and resources that results in an economic strategy.

Before we leave the creative act of putting together a company's unique internal capability and opportunity evolving in the external world, we should note that—aside from distinctive competence—the principal resources found in any company are money and people—technical and managerial people. At an advanced stage of economic development, money seems less a problem than technical competence, and the latter less critical than managerial ability. Do not assume that managerial capacity can rise to any occasion. The diversification of American industry is marked by hundreds of instances in which a company strong in one endeavor lacked the ability to manage an enterprise requiring different skills. The right to make handsome profits over a long period must be earned. Opportunism without competence is a path to fairyland.

Besides equating an appraisal of market opportunity and organizational capability, the decision to make and market a particular product or service should be accompanied by an identification of the nature of the business and the kind of company its management desires. Such a guiding concept is a product of many considerations, including the managers' personal values. As such, this concept will change more slowly than other aspects of the organization, and it will give coherence to all the variety of company activities. For example, a president who is determined to make his or her firm into a

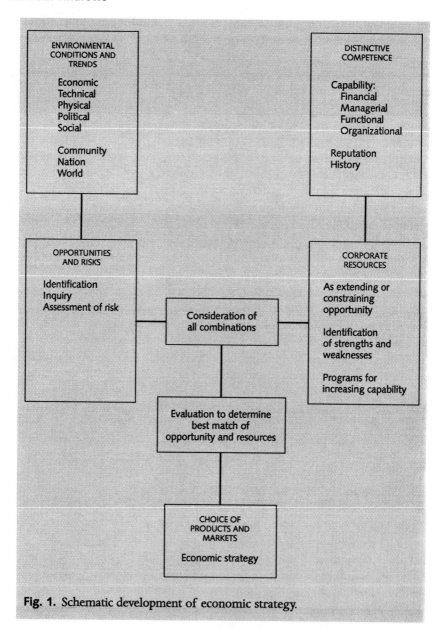

Fig. 1. Schematic development of economic strategy.

worldwide producer and fabricator of a basic metal, through policies differentiating it from the industry leader, will not be distracted by excess capacity in developed markets, by low metal prices, and by cutthroat competition in certain markets. Such a firm would not be sidetracked into acquiring, for example, the Pepsi-Cola franchise in Africa, even if this business promised to yield a good profit. (That such a firm should have an experimental division exploring off-shoot technology is, however, entirely appropriate.)

Uniqueness of strategy. In each company, the way in which distinctive competence, organizational resources, and organizational values are combined is or should be unique. Differences among companies are as numerous as differences among individuals. The combinations of opportunity to which distinctive competences, resources, and values may be applied are equally extensive. Generalizing about how to make an effective match is less rewarding than working at it. The effort is a highly stimulating and challenging exercise. The outcome will be unique for each company and each situation.

Notes

1. See Norman Berg, 'Strategic Planning in Conglomerate Companies,' *Harvard Business Review*, May–June 1965, pp. 79–92.
2. Joseph L. Bower, *Managing the Resource Allocation Process* (Boston: Division of Research, Harvard Business School, 1970); and C. K. Prahalad, 'The Strategic Process in a Multinational Corporation' (unpublished doctoral thesis, Harvard Business School, 1975), partially summarized in 'Strategic Choices in Diversified MNCs,' *Harvard Business Review*, July–August 1976, pp. 67–78.

6 | The Organisation of Industry[1]

George B. Richardson

I

I was once in the habit of telling pupils that firms might be envisaged as islands of planned co-ordination in a sea of market relations. This now seems to me a highly misleading account of the way in which industry is in fact organised. The underlying idea, of course, was of the existence of two ways in which economic activity could be co-ordinated, the one, conscious planning, holding sway within firms, the other, the price mechanism, operating spontaneously on the relations between firms and between firms and their customers. The theory of the firm, I argued, had as its central core an elaboration of the logic of this conscious planning; the theory of markets analysed the working of the price mechanism under a variety of alternative structural arrangements.

I imagine that this account of things might be acceptable, as a harmless first approximation, to a large number of economists. And yet there are two aspects of it that should trouble us. In the first place it raises a question, properly central to any theory of economic organisation, which it does not answer; and, secondly, it ignores the existence of a whole species of industrial activity which, on the face of it, is relevant to the manner in which co-ordination is achieved. Let us deal with each of these matters in turn.

Our simple picture of the capitalist economy was in terms of a division of labour between the firm and the market, between co-ordination that is planned and co-ordination that is spontaneous. But what then is the principle of this division? What kinds of co-ordination have to be secured through conscious direction within firms and what can be left to the working of the invisible hand? One might reasonably maintain that this was a key question—perhaps the key question—in the theory of industrial organisation, the most important matter that the Divine Maker of market economies on the first day of creation would have to decide. And yet, as I hope soon to show, it is a matter upon which our standard theories, which merely assume but do not explain a division between firm and market, throw little light.

Let me now turn to the species of industrial activity that our simple story, based as it is on a dichotomy between firm and market, leaves out of account. What I have in mind is the dense network of co-operation and affiliation by which firms are inter-related. Our theoretical firms are indeed islands, being characteristically well-defined autonomous units buying and selling at arms' length in markets. Such co-operation as takes place between them is normally studied as a manifestation of the desire to restrict competition and features in chapters about price agreements and market sharing. But if the student closes his textbook and takes up a business history, or the financial pages of a newspaper, or a report of the Monopolies Commission, he will be presented with a very different picture. Firm A, he may find, is a joint subsidiary of firms B and C, has technical agreements with D and E, sub-contracts work to F, is in marketing association with G—and so on. So complex and ramified are these arrangements, indeed, that the skills of a genealogist rather than an economist might often seem appropriate for their disentanglement.[2] But does all this matter? Theories necessarily abstract and it is always easy to point to things they leave out of account. I hope to show that the excluded phenomena in this case are of importance and that by looking at industrial reality in terms of a sharp dichotomy between firm and market we obtain a distorted view of how the system works. Before doing so, however, I wish to dwell a little longer on the several forms that co-operation and affiliation may take; although the arrangements to be described are no doubt well known to the reader, explicit mention may nevertheless help to draw attention to their variety and extent.

II

Perhaps the simplest form of inter-firm co-operation is that of a trading relationship between two or more parties which is stable enough to make demand expectations more reliable and thereby to facilitate production planning. The relationship may acquire its stability merely from goodwill or from more formal arrangements such as long-term contracts or shareholding. Thus, for example, the Metal Box Company used to obtain a discount from its tin plate

suppliers in return for undertaking to buy a certain proportion of its requirements from them, and the same company owned 25% of the share capital of
the firm supplying it with paints and lacquers. In the same way Imperial
Tobacco owned shares in British Sidac, which made cellophane wrapping, and
in Bunzl, which supplied filter tips. Occasionally shareholdings of this kind may
be simply investments held for their direct financial yield, but more generally
they give stability to relationships through which the activities of the parties
are co-ordinated both quantitatively and qualitatively. Not only is it made easier
to adjust the quantity of, say, lacquer to the quantity of cans which it is used
to coat but the specification and development of the lacquers can be made
appropriate to the use to be made of them. And in the synthetic fibre industry
likewise, linkages between firms at the various stages—polymer manufacture,
yarn spinning and finishing, textile weaving—help bring about the co-ordinated
development of products and processes. The habit of working with models
which assume a fixed list of goods may have the unfortunate result of causing
us to think of co-ordination merely in terms of the balancing of quantities of
inputs and outputs and thus leave the need for qualitative co-ordination out of
account.

Co-operation may frequently take place within the framework provided by
sub-contracting. An indication of the importance of this arrangement is provided by the fact that about a quarter of the output of the Swedish engineering industry is made up of sub-contracted components, while for Japan the
corresponding figure is about a third and in that country's automobile industry almost a half. Sub-contracting on an international basis, moreover, is said
to be becoming more widespread and now a dense network of arrangements
links the industries of different countries.[3] Now the fact that work has been
sub-contracted does not by itself imply the existence of much co-operation
between the parties to the arrangement. The plumbing work on a building contract may be sub-contracted on the basis of competitive tenders for the individual job. Frequently, however, the relationship between the parties acquires
a degree of stability which is important for two reasons. It is necessary, in the
first place, to induce sub-contractors to assume the risks inherent in a rather
narrow specialisation in skills and equipment; and, secondly, it permits continuing co-operation between those concerned in the development of specifications, processes and designs.

Co-operation also takes place between firms that rely on each other for
manufacture or marketing and its fullest manifestation is perhaps to be found
in the operations of companies such as Marks and Spencer and British Home
Stores. Nominally, these firms would be classified as retail chains, but in reality
they are the engineers or architects of complex and extended patterns of co-
ordinated activity. Not only do Marks and Spencer tell their suppliers how much

they wish to buy from them, and thus promote a quantitative adjustment of supply to demand, they concern themselves equally with the specification and development of both processes and products. They decide, for example, the design of a garment, specify the cloth to be used and control the processes even to laying down the types of needles to be used in knitting and sewing. In the same way they co-operate with Ranks and Spillers in order to work out the best kind of flour for their cakes and do not neglect to specify the number of cherries and walnuts to go into them. Marks and Spencer have laboratories in which, for example, there is development work on uses of nylon, polyester and acrylic fibres. Yet all this orchestration of development, manufacture and marketing takes place without any shareholding by Marks and Spencer in its suppliers and without even long-term contracts.

Mention should be made, finally, of co-operative arrangements specifically contrived to pool or to transfer technology. Surely the field of technical agreements between enterprises is one of the under-developed areas of economics. These agreements are commonly based on the licensing or pooling of patents but they provide in a quite general manner for the provision or exchange of know-how through the transfer of information, drawings, tools and personnel. At the same time they are often associated with the acceptance by the parties to them of a variety of restrictions on their commercial freedom—that is to say with price agreements, market sharing and the like.

This brief description of the varieties of inter-firm co-operation purports to do no more than exemplify the phenomenon. But how is such co-operation to be defined? And how in particular are we to distinguish between co-operation on the one hand and market transactions on the other? The essence of co-operative arrangements such as those we have reviewed would seem to be the fact that the parties to them accept some degree of obligation—and therefore give some degree of assurance—with respect to their future conduct. But there is certainly room for infinite variation in the scope of such assurances and in the degree of formality with which they are expressed. The blanket manufacturer who takes a large order from Marks and Spencer commits himself by taking the appropriate investment and organisational decisions; and he does so in the expectation that this company will continue to put business in his way. In this instance, the purchasing company gives no formal assurance but its past behaviour provides suppliers with reason to expect that they can normally rely on getting further orders on acceptable terms. The qualification 'normally' is, of course, important, and the supplier is aware that the continuation of orders is conditional on a sustained demand for blankets, satisfaction with the quality of his manufacture and so on. In a case such as this any formal specification of the terms and conditions of the assurance given by the supplier would scarcely be practicable and the function of goodwill and reputation is to render it unnecessary.

Where buyer and seller accept no obligation with respect to their future conduct, however loose and implicit the obligation might be, then co-operation does not take place and we can refer to a pure market transaction. Here there is no continuing association, no give and take, but an isolated act of purchase and sale such, for example, as takes place on an organised market for financial securities. The pure market transaction is therefore a limiting case, the ingredient of co-operation being very commonly present, in some degree, in the relationship between buyer and seller. Thus although I shall have occasion to refer to co-operation and market transactions as distinct and alternative modes of co-ordinating economic activity, we must not imagine that reality exhibits a sharp line of distinction; what confronts us is a continuum passing from transactions, such as those on organised commodity markets, where the co-operative element is minimal, through intermediate areas in which there are linkages of traditional connection and goodwill, and finally to those complex and inter-locking clusters, groups and alliances which represent co-operation fully and formally developed. And just as the presence of co-operation is a matter of degree, so also is the sovereignty that any nominally independent firm is able to exercise on a *de facto* basis, for the substance of autonomy may often have been given up to a customer or a licensor. A good alliance, Bismarck affirmed, should have a horse and a rider, and, whether or not one agrees with him, there is little doubt that in the relations between firms as well as nation states, the condition is often met.

III

It is time to revert to the main line of our argument. I had suggested that theories of the firm and of markets normally provide no explanation of the principle of the division of labour between firms and markets and of the roles within a capitalist economy of planned and spontaneous co-ordination. And I also maintained that these theories did not account for the existence of inter-firm co-operation and affiliation. It is upon the first of these two deficiencies that I now wish to concentrate.

Probably the simplest answer to the question as to the division of labour between firm and market would be to say that firms make products and market forces determine how much of each product is made. But such an answer is quite useless. If 'products' are thought of as items of final expenditure such as cars or socks, then it is clear that very many different firms are concerned with the various stages of their production, not only in the sense that firms buy in components and semi-manufactures from other firms but also in that there may be a separation of manufacture and marketing (as in the case of Marks and Spencer and its suppliers) or of development and manufacture (as in the case of licensors and licencees). If, alternatively, we simply define 'products' as what firms do, then the statement that firms make products is a tautology which, however convenient, cannot be the basis of any account of the division of labour between firm and market.

It is worth observing that we learn nothing about this division of labour from the formal theory of the firm. And this is perhaps not surprising as the theory, in its bare bones, is little more than an application of the logic of choice to a particular set of problems. It may be that the theory indeed makes it more difficult to answer our question in that, in order the better to exhibit this logic of choice, it is formulated on the assumption of 'given production functions' which represent the maximum output obtainable from different input combinations. However useful this representation of productive possibilities, it leaves one important class of ingredients out of account. It abstracts totally from the roles of organisation, knowledge, experience and skills, and thereby makes it the more difficult to bring these back into the theoretical foreground in the way needed to construct a theory of industrial organisation. Of course I realise that production functions presume a certain level of managerial and material technology. The point is not that production is thus dependent on the state of the arts but that it has to be undertaken (as Mrs. Penrose has so very well explained)[4] by human organisations embodying specifically appropriate experience and skill. It is this circumstance that formal production theory tends to put out of focus, and justifiably, no doubt, given the character of the optimisation problems that it is designed to handle; nevertheless, it seems to me that we cannot hope to construct an adequate theory of industrial organisation and in particular to answer our question about the division of labour between firm and market, unless the elements of organisation, knowledge, experience and skills are brought back to the foreground of our vision.

It is convenient to think of industry as carrying out an indefinitely large number of *activities*, activities related to the discovery and estimation of future wants, to research, development and design, to the execution and co-ordination of processes of physical transformation, the marketing of goods and so on. And we have to recognise that these activities have to be carried out by organisations with appropriate *capabilities*, or, in other words, with appropriate knowledge, experience and skills. The capability of an organisation may depend upon command of some particular material technology, such as cellulose chemistry, electronics or civil engineering, or may derive from skills in marketing or knowledge of and reputation in a particular market. Activities which require the same capability for their undertaking I shall call *similar activities*. The notion of capability is no doubt somewhat vague, but no more so perhaps than that of, say, liquidity and, I believe, no less useful. What concerns us here is the fact that organisations will tend to specialise in activities for which their capabilities offer some comparative advantage; these activities will, in other words, generally be similar in the sense in which I have defined the term although they may nevertheless lead the firm into a variety of markets and a variety of product lines. Under capitalism, this degree of specialisation will come about through competition but it seems to me likely to be adopted under any alternative system for reasons of manifest convenience. Mrs. Penrose has provided us with excellent accounts of how companies grow in directions set by their capabilities and how these capabilities themselves slowly expand and alter.[5] Dupont, for example, moved from a basis in nitro-cellulose explosives to cellulose lacquers, artificial leather, plastics, rayon and cellophane and from a basis in coal tar dyestuffs into a wide range of synthetic organic chemicals, nylon and synthetic rubber. Similarly, Marks and Spencer, having acquired marketing and organisational techniques in relation to clothing were led to apply them to foodstuffs.

There is therefore a strong tendency for the activities grouped within a firm to be similar, but this need not always be so. In the history of any business random factors will have left an influence, and the incentive to take up a particular activity will sometimes be provided, not by the prior possession of an appropriate capability, but by the opportunity of a cheap acquisition, through a family or business connection or because of management's belief that the profitability of investment in some direction was being generally under-estimated. There is no need to deny, moreover, that a variety of potential gains are provided by grouping activities irrespective of their character; risks can be spread, the general managerial capability of the firm can be kept fully employed and the allocation of finance can be planned from the centre. None of this is in contradiction with the principle that it will pay most firms for most of the time to expand into areas of activity for which their particular capabilities lend them comparative advantage. A firm's activities may also, on occasions, be more similar than they superficially appear. If a firm acquired companies irrespective of the character of their activities we should term it conglomerate; but if the motive for the purchases were the belief that the companies were being badly managed, the hope being to restore them to health before re-selling them at a profit, the management would be exercising a particular capability.

IV

I have argued that organisations tend to specialise in activities which, in our special sense of the term, are similar. But the organisation of industry has also to adapt itself to the fact that activities may be *complementary*. I shall say that activities are complementary when they represent different phases of a process of production and require in some way or another to be co-ordinated. But it is important that this notion of complementarity be understood to describe, for instance, not only the relationship between the manufacture of cars and their components, but also the relationship of each of these to the corresponding activities of research and development and of marketing. Now it is clear that similarity and complementarity, as I have defined them, are quite distinct; clutch linings are complementary to clutches and to cars but, in that they are best made by firms with a capability in asbestos fabrication, they are similar to drain-pipes and heat-proof suits. Similarly, the production of porcelain insulators is complementary to that of electrical switchgear but similar to other ceramic manufacture. And while the activity of retailing toothbrushes is complementary to their manufacture, it is similar to the activity of retailing soap. This notion of complementarity will require closer definition at a later stage, but it will be convenient first to introduce one further (and final) set of conceptual distinctions.

It is clear that complementary activities have to be co-ordinated both quantitatively and qualitatively. Polymer production has to be matched, for example, with spinning capacity, both in terms of output volume and product characteristics, and investment in heavy electrical equipment has likewise to be appropriate, in scale and type, to the planned construction of power stations. Now this co-ordination can be effected in three ways; by *direction*, by *co-operation* or through *market transactions*. Direction is employed when the activities are subject to a single control and fitted into one coherent plan. Thus where activities are to be co-ordinated by direction it is appropriate that they be *consolidated* in the sense of being undertaken jointly by one organisation. Co-ordination is achieved through co-operation when two or more independent organisations agree to match their related plans in advance. The institutional counterparts to this form of co-ordination are the complex patterns of co-operation and affiliation which theoretical formulations too often tend to ignore. And, finally, co-ordination may come about spontaneously through market transactions, without benefit of either direction or co-operation or indeed any purposeful intent, as an indirect consequence of successive interacting decisions taken in response to changing profit opportunities. Let us now make use of this somewhat crude categorisation to re-interpret the questions with which we started.

V

What is the appropriate division of labour, we should now ask, between consolidation, co-operation and market transactions?

If we were able to assume that the scale on which an activity was undertaken did not affect its efficiency, and further that no special capabilities were even required by the firm undertaking it, then there would be no limit to the extent to which co-ordination could be affected by direction within one organisation. If production could be set up according to 'given' production functions with constant returns, no firm need ever buy from, or sell to, or co-operate with any other. Each of them would merely buy inputs, such as land and labour, and sell directly to consumers—which, indeed, is what in our model-building they are very often assumed to do. But, of course, activities do exhibit scale economies and do require specialised organisational capabilities for their undertaking, the result being that self-sufficiency of this kind is unattainable. The scope for co-ordination by direction within firms is narrowly circumscribed, in other words, by the existence of scale economies and the fact that complementary activities need not be similar. The larger the organisation the greater the number of capabilities with which one may conceive it to be endowed and the greater the number of complementary activities that can, in principle, be made subject to co-ordination through direction; but even if a national economy were to be run as a single business, it would prove expedient to trade with the rest of the world. Some co-ordination, that is to say, must be left either to co-operation or to market transactions and it is to the respective roles of each of these that our attention must now turn.

Building and brick-making are dissimilar activities and each is undertaken by large numbers of enterprises. Ideally, the output of bricks ought to be matched to the volume of complementary construction that makes use of them and it is through market transactions that we expect this to come about. Brickmakers, in taking investment and output decisions, estimate future market trends; and errors in these estimates are registered in stock movements and price changes which can lead to corrective actions. As we all know, these adjustments may work imperfectly and I have myself argued elsewhere[6] that the model which we often use to represent this type of market is unsatisfactory. But this is a matter with which we cannot now concern ourselves. What is important, for our present purposes, is to note that impersonal co-ordination through market forces is relied upon where there is reason to expect aggregate demands to be more stable (and hence predictable) than their component elements. If co-ordination were to be sought through co-operation, then individual brick-makers would seek to match their investment and output plans *ex ante* with individual builders. Broadly speaking, this does not happen, although traditional links between buyers and sellers, such as are found in most markets, do introduce an element of this kind. Individual brick manufacturers rely, for the most part, on having enough customers to ensure some cancelling out of random fluctuations in their several demands. And where sales to final consumers are concerned, this reliance on the law of large numbers becomes all but universal. Thus we rely on markets when there is no attempt to match complementary activities *ex ante* by deliberately co-ordinating the corresponding plans; salvation is then sought, not through reciprocal undertakings, but on that stability with which aggregates, by the law of large numbers, are providentially endowed.

Let us now consider the need to co-ordinate the production of cans with tin plate or lacquers, of a particular car with a particular brake and a particular brake lining, of a type of glucose with the particular beer in which it is to be used, or a cigarette with the appropriate filter tip. Here we require to match not the aggregate output of a general-purpose input with the aggregate output for which it is needed, but of particular activities which, for want of a better word, we might call *closely complementary*. The co-ordination, both quantitative and qualitative, needed in these cases requires the co-operation of those concerned; and it is for this reason that the motor car companies are in intimate association with component makers, that Metal Box interests itself in its lacquer suppliers, Imperial Tobacco with Bunzl and so on. Co-ordination in these cases has to be promoted either through the consolidation of the activities within organisations with the necessary spread of capabilities, or through close co-operation, or by means of institutional arrangements which, by virtue of limited shareholdings and other forms of affiliation, come somewhere in between.

Here then we have the prime reason for the existence of the complex networks of co-operation and association the existence of which we noted earlier. They exist because of the need to co-ordinate closely complementary but dissimilar activities. This co-ordination cannot be left entirely to direction within firms because the activities are dissimilar, and cannot be left to market forces in that it requires not the balancing of the aggregate supply of something with the aggregate demand for it but rather the matching, both qualitative and quantitative, of individual enterprise plans.

VI

This article began by referring to a vision of the economy in which firms featured as islands of planned co-ordination in a sea of market relations. The deficiencies of this representation of things will by now be clear. Firms are not islands but are linked together in patterns of co-operation and affiliation. Planned co-ordination does not stop at the frontiers of the individual firm but can be effected through co-operation between firms. The dichotomy between firm and market, between directed and spontaneous co-ordination, is misleading; it ignores the institutional fact of inter-firm co-operation and assumes away the distinct method of co-ordination that this can provide.

The analysis I presented made use of the notion of activities, these being understood to denote not only manufacturing processes but to relate equally to research, development and marketing. We noted that activities had to be undertaken by organisations with appropriate capabilities. Activities that made demands on the same capabilities were said to be similar; those that had to be matched, in level or specification, were said to be complementary. Firms would find it expedient, for the most part, to concentrate on similar activities. Where activities were both similar and complementary they could be co-ordinated by direction within an individual business. Generally, however, this would not be the case and the activities to be co-ordinated, being dissimilar, would be the responsibility of different firms. Co-ordination would then have to be brought about either through co-operation, firms agreeing to match their plans *ex ante*, or through the processes of adjustment set in train by the market mechanism. And the circumstances appropriate to each of these alternatives were briefly discussed.

Let me end with two further observations. I have sought to stress the co-operative element in business relations but by no means take the view that where there is co-operation, competition is no more. Marks and Spencer can drop a supplier; a sub-contractor can seek another principal; technical agreements have a stated term and the conditions on which they may be re-negotiated will depend on how the strengths of the parties change and develop; the licensee of today may become (as the Americans have found in Japan) the competitor of tomorrow. Firms form partners for the dance but, when the music stops, they can change them. In these circumstances competition is still at work even if it has changed its mode of operation.

Theories of industrial organisation, it seems to me, should not try to do too much. Arguments designed to prove the inevitability of this or that particular form of organisation are hard to reconcile, not only with the differences between the capitalist and socialist worlds, but also with the differences that exist within each of these. We do not find the same organisation of industry in Jugoslavia and the Soviet Union, or in the United States and Japan. We ought to think in terms of the substitutability of industrial structures in the same way as Professor Gerschenkron has suggested in relation to the prerequisites for economic development. It will be clear, in some situations, that co-ordination has to be accomplished by direction, by co-operation or through market transactions, but there will be many others in which the choice will be difficult but not very important. In Great Britain, for example, the artificial textile industry is vertically integrated and the manufacturers maintain that this facilitates co-ordination of production and development. In the United States, on the other hand, anti-trust legislation has checked vertical integration, but the same co-ordination is achieved through close co-operation between individual firms at each stage. It is important, moreover, not to draw too sharp lines of distinction between the techniques of co-ordination themselves. Co-operation may come close to direction when one of the parties is clearly predominant; and some degree of *ex ante* matching of plans is to be found in all markets in which firms place orders in advance. This points, however, not to the invalidity of our triple distinction but merely to the need to apply it with discretion.[7]

Notes

1. I am grateful to Mr. J. F. Wright, Mr. L. Hannah and Mr. J. A. Kay, each of whom gave helpful comments on a draft of this article.
2. The sceptical reader might care to look up a few cases in the reports of the Monopolies Commission. The following example is found in the report on cigarette filter tips. Cigarette Components Ltd. made filter tips for Imperial Tobacco and Gallaher using machines hired from these companies. It has foreign subsidiaries, some wholly and some partially owned. It was both licensee and licensor of various patents one of which was held by the Celfil Trust, registered in Liechtenstein, with regard to the ultimate control of which Cigarette Components told the Monopolies Commission they could only surmise. Nevertheless, this patent was of key importance in that the Celfil licensees, of which Cigarette Components was only one, were bound by price and market sharing arrangement. Cigarette Components was itself owned by Bunzl Ltd., in which Imperial Tobacco had a small shareholding. The raw material for the tips is cellulose acetate tow which was made by Ectona Fibres Ltd., a company in which Bunzl had a 40% interest and a subsidiary of Eastman Kodak 60%. Agreements had been made providing that, should Bunzl lose control of Cigarette Components, then Eastman could buy out their shares in Ectona . . . ect., etc.
3. See the *Economic Bulletin for Europe*, Vol. 21, No. 1.
4. E. T. Penrose, *The Theory of the Growth of the Firm* (Oxford University Press, 1959).
5. E. T. Penrose, *ibid.*

6. In *Information and Investment* (Oxford University Press, 1961).

7. In his article, 'The Nature of the Firm,' *Economica*, 1937, pp. 386–405, R. H. Coase explains the boundary between firm and market in terms of the relative cost, at the margin, of the kinds of co-ordination they respectively provide. The explanation that I have provided is not inconsistent with his but might be taken as giving content to the notion of this relative cost by specifying the factors that affect it. My own approach differs also in that I distinguish explicitly between inter-firm co-operation and market transactions as modes of co-ordination.

7 Industry Structure, Market Rivalry, and Public Policy

Harold Demsetz

Under the pressure of competitive rivalry, and in the apparent absence of effective barriers to entry, it would seem that the concentration of an industry's output in a few firms could only derive from their superiority in producing and marketing products or in the superiority of a structure of industry in which there are only a few firms. In a world in which information and resource mobility can be secured only at a cost, an industry will become more concentrated under competitive conditions only if a differential advantage in expanding output develops in some firms. Such expansion will increase the degree of concentration at the same time that it increases the rate of return that these firms earn. The cost advantage that gives rise to increased concentration may be reflected in scale economies or in downward shifts in positively sloped marginal cost curves, or it may be reflected in better products which satisfy demand at a lower cost. New efficiencies can, of course, arise in other ways. Some firms might discover ways of lowering cost that require that firms become smaller, so that spinoffs might be in order. In such cases, smaller firms will tend to earn relatively high rates of return. Which type of new efficiency arises most frequently is a question of fact.

Such profits need not be eliminated soon by competition. It may well be that superior competitive performance is unique to the firm, viewed as a team, and unobtainable to others except by purchasing the firm itself. In this case the return to superior performance is in the nature of a gain that is completely captured by the owner of the firm itself, not by its inputs.[1] Here, although the industry structure may change because the superior firm grows, the resulting increase in profit cannot easily serve to guide competitors to similar success. The firm may have established a reputation or goodwill that is difficult to separate from the firm itself and which should be carried at higher value on its books. Or it may be that the members of the employee team derive their higher productivity from the knowledge they possess about each other in the environment of the particular firm in which they work, a source of productivity that may be difficult to transfer piecemeal. It should be remembered that we are discussing complex, large enterprises, many larger (and more productive) than entire nations. One such enterprise happens to 'click' for some time while others do not. It may be very difficult for these firms to understand the reasons for this difference in performance or to know to which inputs to attribute the performance of the successful firm. It is not easy to ascertain just why G.M. and I.B.M. perform better than their competitors. The complexity of these organizations defies easy analysis, so that the inputs responsible for success may be undervalued by the market for some time. By the same token, inputs owned by complex, unsuccessful firms may be overvalued for some time. The success of firms will be reflected in higher returns and stock prices, not higher input prices, and lack of success will be recorded in lower returns and stock prices, not lower input prices.

Moreover, inputs are acquired at historic cost, but the use made of these inputs, including the managerial inputs, yields only uncertain outcomes. Because the outcomes of managerial decisions are surrounded by uncertainty and are specific to a particular firm at a particular point in its history, the acquisition cost of inputs may fail to reflect their value to the firm at some subsequent time. By the time their value to the firm is recognized, they are beyond acquisition by other firms at the same historic cost, and, in the interim, shareholders of the successful or lucky firm will have enjoyed higher profit rates. When nature cooperates to make such decisions correct, they can give rise to high accounting returns for several years or to a once and for all capital gain if accountants could value *a priori* decisions that turn out to be correct *ex post*. During the period when such decisions determine the course of events, output will tend to be concentrated in those firms fortunate enough to have made the correct decisions.

None of this is necessarily monopolistic (although monopoly may play some role). Profit does not arise because the firm creates 'artificial scarcity' through a reduction in its output. Nor does it arise because of collusion. Superior performance can be attributed to the combination of great uncertainty plus luck or atypical insight by the management of a firm. It is not until the experiments are actually tried that we learn which succeed and which fail. By the time the results are in, it is the shareholder that has captured (some of) the value, positive or negative, of past decisions. Even though the profits that arise from a firm's activities may be eroded by competitive imitation, since information is costly to obtain and techniques are difficult to duplicate, the firm may enjoy growth and a superior rate of return for some time.

Superior ability also may be interpreted as a competitive basis for acquiring a measure of monopoly power. In a world in which information is costly and the future is uncertain, a firm that seizes an opportunity to better serve customers does so because it expects to enjoy some protection from rivals because of their ignorance of this opportunity or because of their inability to imitate quickly. One possible source of some monopoly power is superior entrepreneurship. Our patent, copyright, and trademark laws explicitly provide as a reward for uncovering new methods (and for revealing these methods), legal protection against free imitation, and it may be true in some cases that an astute rival acquires the exclusive rights to some resource that *later* becomes valuable. There is no reason to suppose that competitive behavior never yields monopoly power, although in many cases such power may be exercised not by creating entry barriers, but through the natural frictions and ignorance that characterize any real economy. If rivals seek better ways to satisfy buyers or to produce a product, and if one or a few succeed in such endeavors, then the reward for their entrepreneurial efforts is likely to be some (short term) monopoly power and this may be associated with increased industrial concentration. To destroy such power when it arises may very well remove the incentive for progress. This is to be contrasted with a situation in which a high rate of return is obtained through a successful *collusion* to restrict output; here there is less danger to progress if the collusive agreement is penalized. Evidence presented below suggests that there are definite dangers of decreasing efficiency through the use of deconcentration or anti-merger policies.

---

1. Inefficiency Through Anti-concentration Public Policy

The discussion in part II noted that concentration may be brought about because a workable system of incentives implies that firms which better serve buyers will tend to grow relative to other firms. One way in which a firm could better serve buyers is by seizing opportunities to exploit scale economies, although if scale economies are the main cause of concentration, it is difficult to understand why there is no significant trend toward one-firm industries; the lack of such a trend seems to suggest that superiority results in lower but *positively* sloped cost curves in the relevant range of large firm operations. This would set limits to the size of even the successful firms. Successful firms thus would seem to be more closely related to the 'superior land' of classical economic rent analysis than to the single firm of natural monopoly theory. Whether or not superiority is reflected in scale economies, deconcentration may have the total effect of promoting inefficiency even though it also may reduce some monopoly-caused inefficiencies.[2]

Harold Demsetz

The classic portrayal of the inefficiency produced by concentration through the exercise of monopoly power is that of a group of firms cooperating somehow to restrict entry and prevent rivalrous price behavior. Successfully pursued, this policy results in a product price and rate of return in excess of that which would have prevailed in the absence of collusion. However, if all firms are able to produce at the same cost, then the rate of return to successfully colluding firms should be independent of the particular sizes adopted by these firms to achieve low cost production. One firm may require a small scale, and hence have a smaller investment, while another may require a large scale, and corresponding large investment. At any given collusive price, the absolute amounts of monopoly profits will be proportional to output, but capital investment also will be proportionate to output, so we can expect the rate of return to be invariant with respect to size of firm.

If one size of firm earns a higher rate of return than another size, given any collusive price, then there must exist differences in the cost of production which favor the firm that earns the higher rate of return. Alternatively, if there is no single price upon which the industry agrees, but, rather a range of prices, then one firm can earn a higher rate of return if it produces a superior product and sells it at a higher price without thereby incurring proportionately higher costs; here, also, the firm that earns the higher rate of return can be judged to be more efficient because it delivers more value per dollar of cost incurred.

A deconcentration or anti-merger policy is more likely to have benign results if small firms in concentrated industries earn the same or higher rates of return than large firms, for, then, deconcentration may reduce collusion,[3] if it is present, while simultaneously allocating larger shares of industry output to smaller firms which are no less efficient than larger firms. But if increased concentration has come about because of the superior efficiency of those firms that have become large, then a deconcentration policy, while it may reduce the ease of colluding, courts the danger of reducing efficiency either by the penalties that it places on innovative success or by the shift in output to smaller, higher cost firms that it brings about. This would seem to be a distinct possibility if large firms in concentrated industries earn higher rates of return than small firms.

The problem posed is how to organize data to shed light on the probability that deconcentration will promote inefficiency. Correlating industry rate of return with concentration will not be enlightening for this problem, for even if concentrated industries exhibit higher rates of return, it is difficult to determine whether it is efficiency or monopoly power that is at work. Similarly, large firms would tend to earn high profit rates in concentrated industries either because they are efficient or because they are colluding. However, partitioning industry data by size of firm does suggest that there exists a real danger from a deconcentration or anti-merger public policy, for the rates of return earned by small firms give no support to the doctrine relating collusion to concentration. A successful collusion is very likely to benefit the smaller firms, and this suggests that there should be a positive correlation between the rate of return earned by small firms and the degree to which the industry is concentrated. By the same token, if efficiency is associated with concentration, there should be a positive correlation between concentration and the difference between the rate of return earned by large firms and that earned by small firms; that is, large firms have become large because they are more efficient than other firms and are able to earn a higher rate of return than other firms.

Tables 1 and 2 show 1963 rates of return based on internal revenue data partitioned by size of firm and industry concentration for 95 three digit industries. In these tables, C_{63} designates the four firm concentration ratio measured on industry sales; R_1, R_2, R_3, and R_4, respectively, measure accounting rates of return (profit plus interest)/total assets, for firms with asset value less than \$500,000, \$500,000 to \$5,000,000, \$5,000,000 to \$50,000,000 and over \$50,000,000. Table 1 is calculated by assigning equal weight to all industries. It is based, therefore, on the assumption that each industry, regardless of size, offers an equally good observational unit for comparing the efficiency and monopolistic aspects of industry structure. Table 2 presents the same basic data with accounting rates of return weighted by asset value. Hence, an industry with many assets owned by small firms receives a larger weight in calculating the small firm rate of return for a given interval of concentration ratios.

Table 1. Rates of return by size and concentration (unweighted)

C_{63}	Number of Industries	R_1	R_2	R_3	R_4	$\bar{R}$
10–20%	14	6.7%	9.0%	10.8%	10.3%	9.2%
20–30	22	4.5	9.1	9.7	10.4	8.4
30–40	24	5.2	8.7	9.9	11.0	8.7
40–50	21	5.8	9.0	9.5	9.0	8.3
50–60	11	6.7	9.8	10.5	13.4	10.1
over 60	3	5.3	10.1	11.5	23.1	12.5

Table 2. Rates of return by size and concentration (weighted by assets)

C_{63}	Number of Industries	R_1	R_2	R_3	R_4	$\bar{R}$
10–20%	14	7.3%	9.5%	10.6%	8.0%	8.8%
20–30	22	4.4	8.6	9.9	10.6	8.4
30–40	24	5.1	9.0	9.4	11.7	8.8
40–50	21	4.8	9.5	11.2	9.4	8.7
50–60	11	0.9	9.6	10.8	12.2	8.4
over 60	3	5.0	8.6	10.3	21.6	11.3

Harold Demsetz

Both tables fail to reveal the beneficial effects to small firms that we would expect from an association of collusion and industry concentration. The rate of return earned by firms in the smallest asset size does not increase with concentration. This seems to be true for the next two larger asset size classifications also, although in Table 1 the 11.5 per cent earned by R_3 firms in industries with concentration ratios higher than 60 per cent offers some indication of a larger rate of return than in less concentrated industries.[4] The data do not seem to support the notion that concentration and collusion are closely related, and, therefore, it is difficult to remain optimistic about the beneficial efficiency effects of a deconcentration or anti-merger public policy. On the contrary, the data suggest that such policies will reduce efficiency by impairing the survival of large firms in concentrated industries, for these firms do seem better able to produce at lower cost than their competitors.[5] Both tables indicate that R_4 size firms in industries with concentration ratios greater than 50 per cent produce at lower average cost.

Since a larger fraction of industry output is produced by larger firms in the more concentrated industries, these industries may exhibit higher rates of return than other industries. That this is so can be seen from the unweighted row averages given by column $\bar{R}$. Industries with $C_{63} > 50$ per cent seem to have earned higher rates of return than less concentrated industries. But this result, which is consistent with some earlier studies, may be attributed to the superior performance of the larger firms and not to collusive practices. Table 2 reveals this pattern even more clearly. Because the rates of return of smaller firms receive a larger weight (by total assets) in Table 2, industry rates of return are reduced even for concentrated industries in which large firms continue to perform well.

The general pattern of these data can be seen in Table 3. The results of regressing differences in profit rates on concentration ratios are shown in this table.

These regressions reveal a significant positive relationship between concentration and differences in rates of return, especially when comparing the largest

Table 3.

$R_4 - R_1 = -1.4 + .21^*C_{63}$	$r^2 = .09$
(.07)	
$R_4 - R_2 = -2.6 + .12^{**}C_{63}$	$r^2 = .04$
(.06)	
$R_4 - R_3 = -3.1 + .10^{**}C_{63}$	$r^2 = .04$
(.05)	

*, **, significant at the 1% and 5% levels respectively.
Standard errors are shown in parenthesis.

78

Table 4.

$$R_4 - R_1 = 1.5 + .21^*C_{63} + .21(C_{67} - C_{63}) \qquad r^2 = .09$$
$$(.07) \qquad (.42)$$

$$R_4 - R_2 = -2.9 + .12^{**}C_{63} + .37(C_{67} - C_{63}) \qquad r^2 = .06$$
$$(.06) \qquad (.28)$$

$$R_4 - R_3 = -3.4 + .10^{**}C_{63} + .29 (C_{67} - C_{63}) \qquad r^2 = .05$$
$$(.05) \qquad (.24)$$

*,**, respectively, 1% and 5% confidence levels.

and smallest firms in an industry.[6] The three regressions taken together indicate a nonlinear, decreasing impact of concentration on relative rates of return as the size of the smaller firms is increased from R_1 to R_3.

The competitive view of industry structure suggests that rapid changes in concentration are brought about by changed cost conditions and not by alterations in the height of entry barriers. Industries experiencing rapid increases in concentration should exhibit greater disparities between large and small rates of return because of the more significant cost differences which are the root cause of rapid alternations in industry structure. The monopoly view of concentration does not imply such a relationship, for if an industry is rapidly achieving workable collusive practices there is no reason to suppose that the difference between large and small firm profit rates should increase. At the time of writing, matching data on concentration were available for both 1963 and 1967. This time span is too short to reveal much variation in concentration ratios, and so we cannot be very confident about evidence gained by regressing differences in profit rates on changes in concentration ratios. However, the persistently positive coefficient of the variable $C_{67} - C_{63}$ in Table 4 is consistent with the competitive viewpoint, and must increase our doubts, however slightly, about the beneficial effects of an active deconcentration or anti-merger policy.

I have presented an explanation of industry structure and profitability based on competitive superiority. The problem faced by a deconcentration or anti-merger policy was posed on the basis of this explanation. Is there a danger that such a policy will produce more inefficiency than it eliminates? The data presented suggest that this danger should be taken seriously.

Notes

The author wishes to thank the Research Program in Competition and Public Policy at U.C.L.A. for assisting in the preparation of this article.

Harold Demsetz

1. A detailed discussion of the implicit notion of team production that underlies these arguments can be found in Armen A. Alchian & Harold Demsetz, Production, Information Costs, and Economic Organization, 62 Amer. Econ. Rev. 777 (1972).
2. For a discussion of the social costs that might be incurred by deconcentration, especially in the context of scale economies, see John S. McGee, In Defense of Industrial Concentration 159 (1971).
3. This statement is incorrect if a deconcentration or anti-merger policy causes firms to adopt socially less efficient methods of colluding than would be adopted in the absence of such a policy.
4. Since firms are segregated by absolute size, for some industries the R_3 firms will be relatively large. A better test could be secured by contrasting the rates of return for the 1-% largest and 10% smallest firms in each industry. But the data do not allow such a comparison. However, see footnote 6 for the result of a similar type of adjustment.
5. On the margin of output, however, these large firms need not have an advantage over small firms, just as fertile land has no advantage over poor land for producing marginal units. The failure of the large firms to become more dominant in these industries suggests the absence of such advantage.
6. Three adjustments in procedure and in variables were undertaken to analyze certain problems in the data and the theory.

    (1) It is believed by some that the profits of firms, and especially of small firms, are hidden in administrative wages. To check on the possibility that this phenomenon might have accounted for the data relationships shown above, the data were recalculated after adding back to profits all administrative salaries of firms in the R_1 asset size class. Although this increased very slightly the rates of return for this asset size class, as, of course, must be the case, no correlation between concentration and rate of return was produced. In fact, rates of return so calculated were virtually perfectly correlated with the rates of return shown above for this asset size.

    (2) The asset size categories used to calculate the above data are uniform over all industries. Some industries, however, had no firms in the largest asset size category, and these were dropped from the sample. An alternative method was used to check on the impact of this procedure. For each industry, the largest asset size class was redefined so as to include some firms in every industry. The mechanics of the procedure was to categorize asset sizes more finely and choose the largest three size categories containing some observations for each industry. These were then counted as the larger firms in each industry, and the rate of return for these firms was then compared to those firms contained in the three smaller asset size categories containing some observations. The unweighted average difference between large firm rate of return, R_L, and small firm rate of return, R_S, compared with industry concentration is shown below. This table is consistent with the text tables.

C_{63}	$R_L - R_S$
0–20%	6.4%
20–30	9.4
30–40	7.0

40–50	7.0
50–60	12.8
over 60	14.0

(3) The efficiency argument suggests that for a given degree of industry concentration, measured by the four firm concentration ratio, the greater the difference between the sizes of the largest firms and the sizes of the smallest firms, the larger will be the disparity between R_4 and R_1. A linear regression of $R_4 - R_1$ on C_{63} and the average size of firms in the R_4 class yields a positive but not highly significant coefficient for the variable 'average asset size of firms in the R_4 class.' Also, there was a small reduction in the significance of the coefficient of C_{63}.

8 An Evolutionary Theory of Economic Change

Richard R. Nelson and Sidney G. Winter

1. Skills as Programs

A variety of terms have been used in the literature of social science to denote a smooth sequence of behavior that functions, in some sense, as an effective unit. 'Skill' is obviously one such; there is, in particular, a substantial psychological literature relating to skills and skill learning. The terms 'plan,' 'script,' 'habit,' 'routine,' and 'program' have also been used to name either the same concept or a very closely related one. But there are obvious differences in connotation among these terms, and exploration of these various connotations can be informative.

To think of skills as programs is to evoke the image of a computer program. Clearly, the development of the modern electronic computer and its associated software has had an important and widely diffused influence on theoretical thinking about the phenomena that concern us here.[1] Computer programs that simulate complex, patterned behaviors have been developed over a wide range of human and organizational activity. These efforts have shown, above all, that the logical processes of a digital computer can mimic very 'skillful' and 'intelligent' behaviors, at least in the sense of providing a sufficient account of numerous observable aspects of such behavior. Here, however, we will not review specific examples of this sort of research, but will consider only the broad parallels between skills and (computer) programs.

The following features of computer programs are analogous to, and instructive regarding, corresponding features of human skills. First, a program functions as a unit, and its execution is ordinarily a highly complex performance relative to the actions required to initiate the performance. Second, although loops and 'go to' statements and conditional branching statements complicate the picture, the basic organization scheme of a program is serial. There is a beginning and an end (or at least there is supposed to be an end). Also, resumption following an unplanned interruption of program execution is often problematic, and it is easier to start over from the beginning than it is to complete the partial performance. Third, considering that it is performed by an automaton, it is clear that the execution of a computer program is literally 'automatic.' Finally, the speed and accuracy with which an appropriately programmed computer accomplishes its task are often considered impressive. One standard of 'impressiveness' may be human performance on the same task, but perhaps a more useful standard from the point of view of the informativeness of the analogy would be the performance that could be achieved using the computer but not the program—that is, by directly commanding each individual step.

The points about skills implied in the above statements about programs are largely self-evident, but some brief elaboration may be useful. As regards 'functioning as a unit,' it may be noted that, for both programs and skills, there are recognizable 'units' at various levels of organization. Larger units are organized complexes of smaller ones, in which the latter may nevertheless retain some individuality. Thus, for even a moderately proficient touch-typist, the typing of words like 'the,' 'and,' 'here,' 'in,' and 'as' is executable at a stroke, while 'sincerely yours' is both a unit and a two-unit complex. Probably very few typists have fingers for which 'anti-disestablishmentarianism' is a familiar rhythm; nevertheless, a skilled typist will break that word into familiar units and thereby execute it much more quickly than a novice can. Typing skill also serves to illustrate the point about serial organization—essentially, that the order in which component units of a skill are executed is a significant fact about the structure of the skill itself. A typist who can rattle off 'through' without a thought is likely to have to slow down and pay attention to type 'hguorht,' or even 'ughthro.'

Skilled human performance is automatic in the sense that most of the details are executed without conscious volition. Indeed, a welcome precursor of success in an effort to acquire a new skill is the diminishing need to attend to the details. And it is a familiar fact that attempting to attend to the details often has a disruptive effect: in many competitive situations in athletics, the arts, and other spheres, success depends importantly on the ability of the performer to 'stay loose' and 'not clutch'—that is, to resist the pressures that might cause destructive attention to intrude into the details of the performance.[2] It is not uncommon for a performer who is particularly noted for this ability to be compared, approvingly, to a computer or other machine.

Although 'impressiveness' is obviously a matter of degree and relative to expectation, only the most phlegmatic can escape being impressed, at some point, by a skillful performance. Indeed, 'world class' performances in a variety of intellectual, artistic, and athletic pursuits often fall in the range of the 'awesome' rather than that of the merely impressive. In such cases, of course, one is led to speculate about the role that the basic mental and physical equipment of the performer plays in high skill. For this reason, it is perhaps more relevant to our concerns to consider the reaction of the novice to the moderately skilled tennis player, skier, pianist, or solver of differential equations. At least for an observer unjaded by exposure to superstars, performances made possible by a few years of lessons and regular practice are often highly impressive—and depressing, because illustrative of a goal that seems unattainable. This gap between a skilled performer and a novice with the same 'basic equipment' is the analogue of the difference between having the computer and also the right program for the task, and having the computer only.

2. Skills and Tacit Knowing

The late scientist-philosopher Michael Polanyi wrote extensively of the central place in the general scheme of human knowledge occupied by knowledge that cannot be articulated—tacit knowledge. On the simple observation 'We know more than we can tell,' Polanyi built an entire philosophical system (Polanyi, 1967, p. 4). Though the full import of 'tacit knowing' in Polanyi's philosophy can only be hinted at by examples of what would ordinarily be called 'skills,' such examples do provide familiar and compelling illustrations of phenomena of broad significance. In fact, in Polanyi's *Personal Knowledge* (1962), the discussion of skills (ch. 4) plays a role analogous to our own discussion here. It provides a useful perspective on other realms of knowledge—in his case, that of scientific knowledge; in ours, that of organizational capability.

To be able to do something, and at the same time be unable to explain how it is done, is more than a logical possibility—it is a common situation. Polanyi offers a good example early in his discussion of skills: 'I shall take as my clue for this investigation the well-known fact *that the aim of a skillful performance is achieved by the observance of a set of rules which are not known as such to the person following them.* For example, the decisive factor by which the swimmer keeps himself afloat is the manner by which he regulates his respiration; he keeps his bouyancy at an increased level by refraining from emptying his lungs when breathing out and by inflating them more than usual when breathing in; yet this is not generally known to swimmers' (Polanyi, 1962, p. 49).

The difficulty of explaining the basis of a skilled performance comes to the fore in the teaching or learning of skills. Polanyi's swimming example suggests that in some cases the difficulty may arise from the fact that the 'instructor' is quite unaware of the key principles, and that he actually serves less to instruct than to detect and reward randomly occurring improvements in performance. In other cases, the instructor may be able, or at least be subjectively confident that he is able, to explain the matter in detail. But the detailed instruction offered typically consists of a list of subskills to be executed in sequence, and the instructions neither convey the ability to perform the subskills with requisite efficiency nor assure the smooth integration of those subskills into the main skill. This point is emphasized by Miller, Galanter, and Pribam, commenting on a description of how to land an airplane: 'When skillfully elaborated and executed it will serve to get pilot and craft safely back to earth. It is a short paragraph and could be memorized in a few minutes, but it is doubtful whether the person who memorized it could land a plane, even under ideal weather conditions. In fact, it seems likely that someone could learn all the individual acts that are required in order to execute the Plan, and still be unable to land successfully. The separate motions, the separate parts of the Plan, must be fused together to form a skilled performance. Given the description of what he is supposed to do, the student still faces the major task of learning how to do it' (Miller, Galanter, and Pribam, 1960, pp. 82–83).

Instruction in a skill typically consists in large part of the imposition of a discipline of practice, a portion of which is supervised by the instructor. Verbal instruction is included, but is predominantly in the form of critique of practice. Illustration by the instructor and (attempted) imitation by the learner is often employed as an alternative mode to verbal instruction and critique. As Miller et al. indicate, verbal instruction by itself—the information in the 'how-to-do-it' book—provides only a starting point at best for the acquisition of the skill. Possession of such a book—the articulable portion of the knowledge involved—may be indicative of ambition to learn, but it certainly does not certify possession of the skill.

The limitations of verbal instruction are even more apparent when the learner is attempting to reacquire a skill that has become rusty. Only in extreme cases does the how-to-do-it book prove useful in the reacquisition of a rusty skill. The remnant of the skill itself, lying latent in the brain, is typically more helpful as a restarting point than any collection of more words could be. What is needed is renewed practice and constructive criticism, not the beginner's handbook.

These propositions do not relate only to psychomotor skills. With minor modification, they extend to the realm of specific cognitive skills such as facility in mathematical manipulation of a particular type, the ability to solve the theoretical exercises characteristic of a certain area and method of scientific inquiry, or the ability to generate good solutions to complex production scheduling problems. The manipulation of equations in elementary algebra will serve as an example. Clearly, the axioms of the real number system together with a relatively short list of problem-solving heuristics (like 'isolate the unknown') do constitute, in a sense, an articulated account of the skill involved. Equally clearly, the skilled manipulator in action has little or no conscious awareness of this articulated characterization of his activity. He does not think 'distributive law—rearrange terms—factor out X' and so on, but simply 'perceives' productive transformations of the expression and carries them out, often making several transformations at once in the course of rewriting the expression. There is, in Polanyi's terms, only 'subsidiary awareness' of the rules being employed, whereas there is 'focal awareness' of the expression manipulated.

It seems clear that the 'tacitness' of a skill, or rather of the knowledge underlying a skill, is a matter of degree. Words are probably a more effective vehicle for communicating the skills of elementary algebra than for those of carpentry, and more effective for carpentry than for gymnastic stunts. Also, a trait that distinguishes a good instructor is the ability to discover introspectively, and then articulate for the student, much of the knowledge that ordinarily remains tacit. The same knowledge, apparently, is more tacit for some people than for others. Incentives, too, clearly matter: when circumstances place a great premium on effective articulation, remarkable things can sometimes be accomplished. For example, it has been established in occasional emergency situations that it is not impossible to convey by radioed verbal commands enough information on how to fly a small plane so that a person who lacks a pilot's skills can bring the plane in for a landing.[3]

This chapter presents an alternative to orthodoxy's view of organizational behavior as optimal choice from a sharply defined set of capabilities. Our view of organizational behavior has been molded by the contributions of a number of organization theorists and economists—March and Simon, Allison, Gouldner, Perrow, Doeringer and Piore, Williamson, Schumpeter, and others. What is distinctive about our treatment of organizations derives first of all from its place in our broader evolutionary framework; this accounts in particular for the attention we devote to the nature and sources of continuity in the behavioral patterns of an individual organization. Second, the analysis here builds upon that of the previous chapter and exploits the parallels between individual skills and organizational routines. Relatedly, the influence of Michael Polanyi (not usually counted as an organization theorist) is strong in this chapter, though less explicit than in the previous one.

3. Routine as Organizational Memory

It is easy enough to suggest that a plausible answer to the question 'Where does the knowledge reside?' is 'In the organization's memory.' But where and what is the memory of an organization? We propose that the routinization of activity in an organization constitutes the most important form of storage of the organization's specific operational knowledge. Basically, we claim that organizations *remember* by *doing*—although there are some important qualifications and elaborations.

The idea that organizations 'remember' a routine largely by exercising it is much like the idea than an individual remembers skills by exercising them. The point that remembering is achieved largely through exercise, and could not be assured totally through written records or other formal filing devices, does not deny that firms keep formal memories and that these formal memories play an important role. But there must be much more to organizational memory than formal records. Further, cost considerations make 'doing' the dominant mode of information storage even in many cases where formal records could in principle be kept.

To see how exercise of a routine serves as parsimonious organizational memory, consider an organization in fully routine operation and ask what really needs to be remembered, given that such a state has been achieved. Under such a regime, the situations of individual members and of the organization as a whole contain no significant novelties: the situations confronted replicate ones that were confronted the previous day (or week, month, or year) and are handled in the same way. The scope of the activity that actually takes place in such a static condition and the operational knowledge involved are extremely restricted. Members perform only a minute fraction of the routines they have in repertoire. The lathe operator and the lathe turn out a few specific parts; there is an indeterminately larger number that they could (after appropriate setup and learning) produce. The operator's skills as truck driver and short-order cook are never drawn upon, and perhaps are unknown to other organization members. Routine operation of the organization as a whole certainly does not require that the lathe operator maintain his skill in cooking bacon and eggs, or in the machining of parts for products that were discontinued three years previously; neither does it require that other members remember that the lathe operator possesses or once possessed these skills. If the same sate of routine operation is expected to continue indefinitely, there is no economic benefit to be anticipated from holding this sort of information in the organization's memory. (As an obvious corollary, if there is a positive cost to storing information, this sort of 'irrelevant' information will tend *not* to be held in memory under the 'equilibrium' condition of continuing routine operation.)

What is required for the organization to continue in routine operation is simply that all members continue to 'know their jobs' as those jobs are defined by the routine. This means, first of all, that they retain in their repertoires all routines actually invoked in the given state of routine operation of the organization.

There is, however, much more to 'knowing one's job' in an organization than merely having the appropriate routines in repertoire. There is also the matter of knowing what routines to perform and when to perform them. For the individual member, this entails the ability to receive and interpret a stream of incoming messages from other members and from the environment. Having received and interpreted a message, the member uses the information contained therein in the selection and performance of an appropriate routine from his own repertoire. (This may, of course, be merely a 'relay message' routine, or even a 'file and forget' routine.)

The overall picture of an organization in routine operation can now be drawn. A flow of messages comes into the organization from the external environment and from clocks and calendars. The organization members receiving these messages interpret them as calling for the performance of routines from their repertoires. These performances include ones that would be thought of as directly productive—such as unloading the truck that has arrived at the loading dock—and others of a clerical or information-processing nature—such as routing a customer's inquiry or order to the appropriate point in the organization. Either as an incidental consequence of other sorts of action or as deliberate acts of communication, the performance of routines by each organization member generates a stream of messages to others. These messages in turn are interpreted as calling for particular performances by their recipients, which generate other performances, messages, interpretations, and so on. At any given time, organization members are responding to messages originating from other members as well as from the environment; the above description of the process as starting with information input from external sources or timekeeping devices is merely an expositional convenience. There is, indeed, an internal equilibrium 'circular flow' of information in an organization in routine operation, but it is a flow that is continuously primed by external message sources and timekeeping devices.

For such a system to accomplish something productive, such as building computers or carrying passengers between airports or teaching children to read and write, some highly specific conditions must be satisfied, different in each particular case. The specific features that account for the ability of a particular organization to accomplish particular things are reflected, first of all, in the character of the collection of individual members' repertoires. Airlines are the sorts of organizations that have pilots as members, while schools have teachers. The capabilities of a particular sort of organization are similarly associated with the possession of particular collections of specialized plant and equipment, and the repertoires of organization members include the ability to operate that plant and equipment. Finally, of course, the actual exercise of productive capability requires that there be something upon which to exercise it—some computer components to assemble, or passengers to carry, or children to teach. These are the considerations recognized in the 'list of ingredients' level of discussion of productive capability, which is standard in economic analysis. There is also a 'recipe' level of discussion, at which 'technologies' are described in terms of the principles that underlie them and the character and sequencing of the subtasks that must be performed to get the desired result. This is the province of engineers and other technologists, and to some extent of designers and production managers.

But just as an individual member does not come to know his job merely by mastering the required routines in the repertoire, so an organization does not become capable of an actual productive performance merely by acquiring all the 'ingredients,' even if it also has the 'recipe.' What is central to a productive organizational performance is coordination; what is central to coordination is that individual members, knowing their jobs, correctly interpret and respond to the messages they receive. The interpretations that members give to messages are the mechanism that picks out, from a vast array of possibilities consistent with the roster of member repertoires, a collection of individual member performances that actually constitute a productive performance for the organization as a whole.[4] To the extent that the description above is valid, skills, organization, and 'technology' are intimately intertwined in a functioning routine, and it is difficult to say exactly where one aspect ends and another begins. This is another way of arguing that 'blueprints' are only a small part of what needs to be in an organizational memory in order that production proceed effectively. Furthermore, once the set of routines is in memory by virtue of use, blueprints may not be necessary save, perhaps, as a checkpoint to assess what might be wrong when the routine breaks down.

Given this picture, it is easy to see the relationship between routine operation and organizational memory—or, alternatively, to identify the routinization of activity as the 'locus' of operational knowledge in an organization. Information is actually stored primarily in the memories of the members of the organization, in which reside all the knowledge, articulable and tacit, that constitutes their individual skills and routines, the generalized language competence and the specific command of the organizational dialect, and, above all, the associations that link the incoming messages to the specific performances that they call for. In the sense that the memories of individual members do store so much of the information required for the performance of organizational routines, there is substantial truth in the proposition that the knowledge an organization possesses is reducible to the knowledge of its individual members. This is the perspective that one is led to emphasize if one is committed to the view that 'knowing' is something that only humans can do.

But the knowledge stored in human memories is meaningful and effective only in some context, and for knowledge exercised in an organizational role that context is an organizational context. It typically includes, first, a variety of forms of external memory—files, message boards, manuals, computer memories, magnetic tapes—that complement and support individual memories but that are maintained in large part as a routine organizational function. One might, therefore, want to say that they are part of organizational memory rather than an information storage activity of individual members. Second, the context includes the physical state of equipment and of the work environment generally. Performance of an organizational memory function is in part implicit in the simple fact that equipment and structures are relatively durable: they and the general state of the work environment do not undergo radical and discontinuous change. A fire or severe storm may break the continuity. The destruction caused by such an event is informational as well as physical, for there is a disruption of the accustomed interpretive context for the information possessed by human members. One might therefore be tempted to say that an organization 'remembers' in part by keeping—and to the extent that it succeeds in keeping—its equipment, structures, and work environment in some degree of order and repair. Finally, and most important, the context of the information possessed by an individual member is established by the information possessed by all other members. Without the crane operator's ability to interpret the hand signal for 'down a little more' and to lower the hook accordingly, the abilities to perceive the need for the signal and to generate it are meaningless. To view organizational memory as reducible to individual member memories is to overlook, or undervalue, the linking of those individual memories by shared experiences in the past, experiences that have established the extremely detailed and specific communication system that underlies routine performance.

4. Routine as Target: Control, Replication, and Imitation

So far, we have emphasized that a state of routine operation in an organization is in many ways self-sustaining. Judging by the preceding sections, an organization might be expected to encounter difficulty in departing from its prevailing routines, but it should have no trouble in conforming to them. Although this generalization is more than half of the story and is a basic assumption of our evolutionary models, it is subject to important qualification. Just keeping an existing routine running smoothly can be difficult. When this is the case, the routine (in its smoothly functioning version) takes on the quality of a norm or target, and managers concern themselves with trying to deal with actual or threatened disruptions of the routine. That is, they try to keep the routine under control.

4.1 Control

An organization is not a perpetual motion machine; it is an open system that survives through some form of exchange with its environment. Even its most durable machines and oldest hands undergo change with the passage of time and through the organizational process itself, and ultimately are replaced. On a much shorter time scale, current inputs of various kinds flow in, and outputs flow out. The organization's routine, considered as an abstract 'way of doing things,' is an order that can persist only if it is imposed on a continually changing set of specific resources. Some part of this task of imposing the routine's order on new resources is itself handled routinely; another part is dealt with by *ad hoc* problem-solving efforts. Either the routinized or the *ad hoc* part of the task may fail to be accomplished if the environment does not cooperate— for example, if it fails to yield, on the usual terms, the resources that are required.

A major part of the control problem is related, directly or indirectly, to the fact that productive inputs are heterogeneous. The firm itself creates distinctions among inputs in the course of 'imposing the routine's order' upon them; it buys a standard type of machine in the market and bolts it to the floor in a particular location in the shop, and it hires a machinist and familiarizes him with the particular capabilities and layout of its equipment and the tasks that are typically performed. Further differentiation occurs incidental to the input's cumulative experience with the idiosyncratic environment of the firm; the machine suffers particular wear patterns and the machinist particular patterns of frustration with his supervisor. But of course the firm also confronts the fact that different units of the 'same' input may have distinctive characteristics when they are offered to the firm for purchase, and that the entire distribution of characteristics displayed by different units offered concurrently may itself be changing over time. This prepurchase heterogeneity in the market complicates the problem of postpurchase modification, since the same treatment applied to different units will not necessarily produce the same result. Finally, because machines and workers may pass through the market again after a stay in a firm, the modifications resulting from experience in firms contribute to heterogeneity in the market.

4.2 Replication

The axiom of *additivity* is fundamental in orthodox production theory. It implies, among other things, that any feasible pattern of productive activity can be faultlessly replicated: an exact doubling of output per unit time is accomplished by an exact doubling of input. In concrete terms, the claim advanced in this proposition is captured by the image of a plant on a particular site producing a particular output mix in a particular way; on an identical site elsewhere, an identical plant is constructed and produces the identical output mix in the identical way. Or, as F. H. Hahn put it, 'If two identical entrepreneurs set up two identical plants, with an identical labor force, to produce an identical commodity x, then the two together will produce twice the amount of x that could be produced by one alone' (Hahn, 1949, p. 135).

So stated, the proposition seems to have the compelling quality of the answer to a very elementary arithmetic problem. Presumably, the posit of identical entrepreneurs is supposed to entail an identity of productive technique, and the identical plants are not just identical in themselves, but situated in identical environments. After suitable amplification of this sort, the claim may be regarded as a simple tautology or perhaps as an assertion of the universal validity of physical law.

The question is whether the proposition says anything that is helpful in interpreting economic reality. For it to do so, the terms 'identical entrepreneurs,' 'identical plants,' and 'identical labor force' must have empirical counterparts at least in the sense that they describe limiting cases that are often approached in real situations. In the context of orthodox thought, the idea that these connections to reality exist is supported by: (1) a habit of taking the idea of homogeneous input categories seriously, so that the 'identical labor force' assumption is not blatantly contrafactual; (2) a propensity to think of individual entrepreneurs as the repositories of productive knowledge, so that positing 'identical entrepreneurs' assumes identity of productive knowledge; and (3) a tendency to regard productive knowledge as articulable and free of idiosyncratic elements, so that the supposition of 'identical entrepreneurs' does not relate to an exceedingly remote happenstance.

In our evolutionary models, we make the same assumption that perfect replication is possible, with a similar image in mind of a second plant identical to the first and employing identical routines.[5] However, our interpretation of the assumption is quite different from the orthodox one, and our commitment to it considerably less deep. A basic conceptual distinction is that we think of replication as being a costly, time-consuming process of copying an *existing* pattern of productive activity. Though in our modeling we abstract from the costs and make the simplest assumption about the time required, this is still a very different concept from the orthodox one, which is concerned entirely with the structure of *ex ante* possibilities. To put it another way, our assumption relates to what can be accomplished starting from the status quo of a functioning routine, whereas the long-run orthodox theory to which the additivity axiom relates has no notion of a status quo at all. Further, we regard the feasibility of close (let alone perfect) replication as being quite problematic—more problematic than the feasibility of continuation through time of the existing routine, which is itself no foregone conclusion, as the above discussion points out. As an initial perspective on the problem, we would not recommend the Hahn tautology, but the following account from Polanyi: 'The attempt to analyze scientifically the established industrial arts has everywhere led to similar results. Indeed, even in modern industries the indefinable knowledge is still an essential part of technology. I have myself watched in Hungary a new, imported machine for blowing electric lamp bulbs, the exact counterpart of which was operating successfully in Germany, failing for a whole year to produce a single flawless bulb' (Polanyi, 1962, p. 52).

The point emphasized by evolutionary theory is that a firm with an established routine possesses resources on which it can draw very helpfully in the difficult task of attempting to apply that routine on a larger scale. Because the creation of productive organizations is *not* a matter of implementing fully explicit blueprints by purchasing homogeneous inputs on anonymous markets, a firm that is already successful in a given activity is a particularly good candidate for being successful with new capacity of the same sort. The replication assumption in evolutionary models is intended primarily to reflect the advantages that favor the going concern attempting to do more of the same, as contrasted with the difficulties that it would encounter in doing something else or that others would encounter in trying to copy its success.

To understand the nature of these advantages, it is helpful first of all to consider the similarities between replication and control, and the deeper connections to the problem of organizational memory. In replicating an existing routine, the firm seeks to impose that routine's order on an entire new set of specific inputs. That task is a magnified version of one for which the firm already possesses routinized arrangements. For example, its existing personnel and training operations have the capability to 'select and modify' the sorts of employees the routine requires. By diverting these existing capabilities at least in part to the tasks associated with the new facility, it can avoid difficulties that would be very likely to arise if the manning of that new facility were accomplished by an equally new and inexperienced personnel operation. The new plant will ultimately need its own personnel department (at least if 'replication' is taken literally), but the new production system does not have to be hampered by the early mistakes of a new personnel department that may be learning to operate in a novel labor market environment. And a functioning production system that is effective enough to detect mistakes by the new personnel department can then help that department to learn its job.

More generally, the existing routine serves as a template for the new one. The use of the template makes possible a relatively precise copying of a functioning system that is far too large and complex to be comprehended by a single person. It is not necessary for there to be a central file that contains an articulate account of how the whole thing is done. Rather, for each organizational role that is a unique storage point for important and idiosyncratic organizational knowledge, it is necessary that the individual who will occupy that role in the new plant acquire the knowledge required for its performance. This may be accomplished by having that individual observe or be actively trained by the incumbent of that role in the old system, or by transferring the incumbent to the new system and leaving his trained successor in the old one. The collection of new role occupants thus created will make a coordinated, routinely functioning productive organization of the new facility, because the roles were coordinated in the old one—provided that the copying of the individual roles is accurate enough.

Of course, the process described will in general impose some costs in terms of the functioning of the old plant. It is unlikely that there will be enough slack resources available for training new personnel or for actually performing, temporarily, some functions in the new plant. For the replication story to make economic sense, the benefits obtained must exceed or be expected to exceed these costs. This issue is basically one of investment analysis. If the old plant is enjoying a *temporary* period of high prosperity, to be followed by normal or low profits, the opportunity costs of replication may indeed be excessive.[6] The knowledge transfer must make it possible to capture a flow of rents in the new plant that lasts long enough to compensate, in present value terms, the loss of rents in the old plant. The likelihood of this sort of pattern is obviously enhanced to the extent that a large knowledge transfer can be carried out with only small sacrifices in the old plant. Here it is relevant that the costs of a small number of anticipated departures or absences from key positions in the old plant are likely to be small, since such isolated gaps pose just the sort of problem that the control system routinely handles. On the other hand, the value of only a few people who know what they are doing may be enormous in providing the basic matrix of the routine in the new plant. That is, there are likely to be diminishing returns to experienced personnel, in terms of learning costs saved, in both plants. The transfer of a small number of experienced personnel from the old, predominantly experienced plant to the new, predominantly inexperienced one saves a lot of learning costs in the latter and incurs only small ones in the former. Finally, because of imbalances arising from indivisibilities or for other reasons, there may be some resources in the old plant that are actually idle and can be costlessly applied to the replication effort or transferred to the new plant.

There are some potential obstacles to replication that may be difficult to overcome even at very high cost. Some employees at the old plant may be exercising complex skills with large tacit components, acquired through years of experience in the firm. Others may have skills of lesser complexity and tacitness, but be very poor at teaching those skills to someone else—doing and teaching are, after all, different. Some members may for various reasons be unwilling to cooperate in the process of transferring their segment of the memory contents to someone else; they may, for example, be unwilling to disclose how easy their job really is, or the extent of the shortcuts they take in doing it.[7] Finally, personal relationships may be an important factor, particularly in the structure and stability of the truce that the existing routine represents. The personnel department is not likely to be up to the challenge of locating a suitably matched *set* of new role occupants who can be relied upon to maintain the same sort of truce. For these reasons and more, the template provided by the existing routine may not yield a good copy. There will be some mutation of the routine as it is transferred to the new plant.

Of course, perfect replication is no more of an ultimate objective than perfect control. What matters is not that the plant be the same, but that it work with overall efficiency comparable to the old one.

4.3 Imitation

As a final example of a routine serving as a target, let us consider the case in which the target is a routine of some other firm. The interest in this sort of situation arises, of course, because it often happens that a firm observes that some other firm is doing things that it would like to be able to do—specifically, making more money by producing a better product or producing a standard product more cheaply. The envious firm then attempts to duplicate this imperfectly observed success. We will consider here only the case in which the imitatee is not cooperating with the imitation effort, and will assume that non-cooperation implies, at a minimum, that the imitator's personnel cannot directly observe what goes on in the imitatee's plant.[8]

What distinguishes this situation from replication is the fact that the target routine is not in any substantial sense available as a template. When problems arise in the copy, it is not possible to resolve them by closer scrutiny of the original. This implies that the copy is, at best, likely to constitute a substantial mutation of the original, embodying different responses to a large number of the specific challenges posed by the overall production problem. However, the imitator is not directly concerned with creating a good likeness, but with achieving an economic success—preferably, an economic success at least equal to that of the original. Differences of detail that are economically of no great consequence are perfectly acceptable.

By this economically relevant criterion, the prospects for successful imitation vary dramatically from one situation to another. At one extreme, the production in question may be a novel combination of highly standardized technological elements. If so, close scrutiny of the product itself—'reverse engineering'—may permit the identification of those elements and the nature of their combination, and this may suffice for an economically successful imitation. Indeed, even vague rumors about the nature of the product may suffice, perhaps permitting the copy to hit the market almost as soon as the original. At the other extreme, the target routine may involve so much idiosyncratic and 'impacted' tacit knowledge that even successful replication is highly problematic, let alone imitation from a distance.

In the wide range of intermediate cases, the imitator's basic tactic is to follow the example of a replicator wherever possible (and not too expensive), and to fill in the remaining gaps by independent effort. One important application of this tactic is to try to hire away from the imitatee those employees that the imitatee would reasonably want to transfer to a new plant in an attempt to replicate the existing one. Another is to obtain, by whatever means may be available, indirect clues to the nature of the target routine.

An imitator working with an extremely sparse set of clues about the details of the imitatee's performance might as well adopt the more prestigious title of 'innovator,' since most of the problem is really being solved independently. However, the knowledge that a problem *has* a solution does provide an incentive for persistence in efforts that might otherwise be abandoned.

5. Routines and Skills: Parallels

As we observed at the start of the previous chapter, understanding of individual skills informs understanding of organizational behavior in two ways. First, because individuals exercise skills in their roles as organization members, the characteristics of organizational capabilities are directly affected by the characteristics of individual skilled behavior. We have noted some of these connections. For example, an organization's capabilities require the exercise of individual skills that may involve a large component of tacit knowledge; this directly implies limits on the extent to which the organization's capabilities can themselves be articulated, and there are attendant implications for the character of the replication task. Then, too, the inflexibility of behavior displayed by large organizations is attributable in part to the fact that individual skills become rusty when not exercised; it is therefore hard for an organization to hold in memory a coordinated response to contingencies that arise only rarely.

Here we make explicit the other sort of contribution that understanding of individual skills makes to understanding of organizational functioning: the contribution at the level of metaphor. Routines are the skills of an organization. The performance of an organizational routine involves the effective integration of a number of component subroutines (themselves further reducible), and is ordinarily accomplished without 'conscious awareness'—that is, without requiring the attention of top management. This sort of decentralization in organizational functioning parallels the skilled individual's ability to perform without attending to the details. A routine may involve extensive direct interactions with the organization's environment and the making of numerous 'choices' that are contingent both upon the state of the environment and the state of the organization itself, but these choices involve no process of deliberation by top management. The intervention of top management in the detailed functioning of lower levels is ordinarily symptomatic of an attempt to modify routine or of difficulties with the functioning of existing routines—just as conscious awareness of detail and attempts at articulation are symptomatic of new learning or of trouble in the case of individual skills.

In a number of respects, organizational behavior seems to be subject to magnified versions of problems and pathologies that afflict individual skilled behavior. The scale and complexity of a large organization make impossible the degree of centralization of control represented by the brain of an individual human being. This relative weakness of centralized analysis and control in organizations, when compared to individuals, is the obvious explanation for the relative severity of the difficulties that organizations encounter in areas where centralization is for some reason important. Thus, for example, we noted that limits on articulation in the case of individual skills derive partly from the 'whole versus parts' problem of reconciling an exhaustive account of details with a coherent view of the whole. Much more severe limits on the articulation of organizational knowledge arise from the same cause, because although attending to details is something that can be shared and decentralized, the task of achieving a coherent view of the whole is not. Similarly, improvisation of a coordinated response from a system requires centralized control of the system. Organizations are poor at improvising coordinated responses to novel situations; an individual lacking skills appropriate to the situation may respond awkwardly, but an organization lacking appropriate routines may not respond at all.

Organizations can get a great deal accomplished that they do not know how to do, by drawing on the capabilities of other individuals and organizations. In doing so, however, they exercise planning routines that involve the manipulation of symbols representing highly complex entities. Like individuals, organizations may make ineffective use of the array of capabilities available in their environments, or be victimized by hucksters, because of limitations on their planning vocabulary—particularly when they do not themselves possess even the rudiments of the capabilities they seek to acquire.

The basic metaphor can be elaborated and extended in a number of other directions, but we will leave these byways unexplored. The important contribution of the metaphor is the insight it provides into the role of bounded rationality in organizational behavior. We observed in our discussion of individual skills that bounded rationality imposes a tradeoff between capability and deliberate choice. That tradeoff exists for organizations as well, but the relative weakness of centralized control in an organization makes the terms of the tradeoff much less favorable to deliberate choice. One cannot infer from the fact that an organization functions smoothly and successfully in a particular range of observed environments that it is a rational and 'intelligent' organism that will cope successfully with novel challenges. If anything, one should expect environmental change to make manifest the sacrifice of flexibility that is the price paid for highly effective capabilities of limited scope.

Notes

1. For discussions of the influence of cybernetic theory and computer modeling on psychology, see Miller, Galanter, and Pribam (1960, ch. 3) and Newell and Simon (1972, historical addendum, esp. pp. 878–882).
2. Of course, the skilled performer must also avoid the opposite error of being too relaxed and 'losing his concentration.' But the concentration required is on the objective of the performance at each moment, not on the details of the procedure.
3. This observation runs somewhat contrary to the statement of Miller, Galanter, and Pribam quoted above. But it is clear that a pilot who entirely lacks tacit knowledge of how to land is a pilot with whom one would prefer not to ride.
4. We have passed over here the problem of what makes the organization member *willing* to respond appropriately to a message he receives and correctly interprets. This issue is addressed in the following section.
5. We will limit our discussion of replication to the simple case of establishing the same routine in a plant identical to the original. Some of the same issues arise in almost any case of capacity expansion; a typical situation is that capacity is increased

by a partial replication that relaxes the constraint imposed by a particular class of input services. However, partial replications involve some additional complications that we do not treat here.

6. When long-run prospects are favorable but current profits are also high, it can happen that constructing a new plant *de novo* is preferable to replication involving current opportunity costs, even though replication is absolutely profitable and would be the preferred mode of expansion under less favorable conditions.

7. The question of the incentives of organization members to disclose idiosyncratic information of importance to the organization's functioning is addressed by Williamson under the rubric 'information impactedness' (Williamson, 1975, ch. 4).

8. There are cases intermediate between the categories of 'replication' and 'imitation'—cases of attempted near-replication in environments very different from the original one, or of imitation with the active support of the firm being imitated. These are usually addressed under the heading of 'transfer of technology.' Our own thinking in this general area has benefited particularly from the work on technology transfer of Hall and Johnson (1967) and Teece (1977).

References

Hahn, F. H. 1949. 'Proportionality, Divisibility and Economies of Scale: Comment.' *Quarterly Journal of Economics* 63: 131–137.

Hall, G. R., and R. E. Johnson. 1967. *Aircraft Co-Production and Procurement Strategy.* Santa Monica: RAND Corporation.

Miller, G. A., E. Galanter, and K. H. Pribam. 1960. *Plans and the Structure of Behaviour.*

Newell, A., and H. A. Simon. 1972. *Human Problem Solving.* Englewood Cliffs, N.J.: Prentice-Hall.

Polanyi, M. 1962. *Personal Knowledge: Towards a Post-Critical Philosophy.* New York: Harper Torchbooks.

—— 1967. *The Tacit Dimension.* Garden City, N.Y.: Doubleday Anchor.

Teece, D. J. 1977. 'Technology Transfer by Multinational Firms: The Resource Cost of Transferring Technological Know-How.' *Economic Journal* 87: 242–261.

Williamson, O. E. 1975. *Markets and Hierarchies: Analysis and Antitrust Implications.* New York: Free Press.

III. THE RESOURCE-BASED APPROACH

9 Economies of Scope and the Scope of the Enterprise

David J. Teece

1. Introduction

Explaining the scope of activities pursued by the modern business enterprise is clearly central to our understanding of the organization of industry. Yet, as Ronald Coase points out, the received theory of industrial organization is unable to explain why General Motors is not a dominant factor in the coal business or why A & P does not manufacture airplanes (Coase (1972, p. 67)). Nor does the received theory explain why aircraft manufacturers are now producing missiles and space vehicles, why Union Oil is producing energy from geothermal sources, or why Exxon is looking for uranium. One reason for this neglect is suggested by Nelson's observation that microeconomics analysis views the enterprise as little more than a black box, and the distribution of economic activity between markets and firms is taken as datum (Nelson (1972, p. 37)). While sometimes it suffices to take institutions as pre-existing entities and model economic phenomena in familiar demand and cost curve terms, there are other circumstances where it is instructive to begin with more elemental units of analysis. Firms, after all, do not come in predetermined shapes, and neither do markets. Rather, 'both evolve in active juxtaposition with one another, the object being to reach a complementary configuration that economizes on (production and) transactions costs' (Williamson (1978)).

The purpose of this paper is to explore some comparative institutional considerations which surround the scope of the business activities engaged in by the modern business enterprise. Specifically, the paper explores an efficiency rationale of corporate diversification.[1] It turns out that the theoretical framework developed by Williamson to explain vertical integration (Williamson (1975, ch. 5)) can be extended readily to explore multiproduct diversification. This is because the principal differences between vertical integration and

David Teece

diversification relate simply to the types of transactions being internalized. Whereas vertical integration involves internalizing the supply of tangible inputs (such as components and raw materials) to a single production process, the integration of interest here involves internalization of the supply of knowhow and other inputs common to two or more production processes. It turns out that diversification can represent a mechanism for capturing integration economies associated with the simultaneous supply of inputs common to a number of production processes geared to distinct final product markets.

2. Economies of Scope and Diversification

Efforts have recently been made to formulate an efficiency-based theory of the multiproduct firm. These endeavors rest upon specifying cost functions which exhibit economies of scope. Economies of scope exist when for all outputs y_1 and y_2, the cost of joint production is less than the cost of producing each output separately[2] (Panzar and Willig (1975)). That is, it is the condition, for all y_1 and y_2,

$$c(y_1, y_2) < c(y_1, 0) + c(0, y_2).$$

This is illustrated in Fig. 1. According to Panzar and Willig (1975 p. 3), 'it is clear that the presence of economies of scope will give rise to multiproduct firms', and that 'with economies of scope, joint production of two goods by one enterprise is less costly than the combined costs of production of two specialty firms' (Willig (1979, p. 346)).

The analysis to be engaged here indicates that the Panzar and Willig conclusions are too strong. Economies of scope provide neither a necessary nor a sufficient condition for cost savings to be achieved by merging specialized firms. Even if the technology displays scope economies the joint production of two goods by two firms need not be more costly than production of the two goods by one enterprise. This can be readily established by counterexample.[3] Conclusions about the appropriate boundaries of the firm cannot be drawn simply by examining the nature of the underlying cost function.[4] Just as technological interdependency between successive stages of a production process do not explain vertical integration (Williamson (1975, ch. 5)) nor do scope economies explain the multiproduct firm. At least, that is the proposition advanced here.

A sensitive treatment of the organizational issues involved when the cost function displays economies of scope would indicate that the origin of the

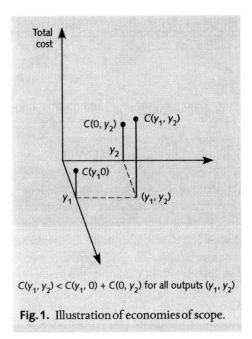

$C(y_1, y_2) < C(y_1, 0) + C(0, y_2)$ for all outputs (y_1, y_2)

Fig. 1. Illustration of economies of scope.

scope economies must first be identified. As a general matter, 'economies of scope arise from inputs that are shared, or utilized jointly without complete congestion. The shared factor may be imperfectly divisible, so that the manufacture of a subset of the goods leaves excess capacity in some stage of production, or some human or physical capital may be a public input which, when purchased for use in one production process, is then freely available to another' (Willig (1979, p. 346)). I submit that the facility with which the common input or its services can be traded across markets will determine whether economies of scope will require the enterprise to be multiproduct in its scope. Where such trading is difficult, and intrafirm governance is superior, then the organizational implications suggested by Panzar and Willig will go through. Only two classes of common inputs can be readily identified where the Panzar and Willig presumption of market failure appears to hold. The common inputs in question are knowhow and specialized and indivisible physical assets. Yet even here, market processes are often sustained. The remainder of this paper seeks to identify the circumstances under which markets for these inputs may break down and where intrafirm transfer is called for. A more tightly circumscribed theory of multiproduct enterprise is suggested. Some illustrations are presented.

3. Knowhow

A principal feature of the modern business enterprise is that it is an organizational entity possessing knowhow. To the extent that knowhow has generic attributes, it represents a shared input which can find a variety of end product applications. Knowhow may also display some of the characteristics of a public good in that it can sometimes be used in many different non-competing applications without its value in any one application being substantially impaired. Furthermore, the marginal cost of employing knowhow in a different endeavor is likely to be much less than its average cost of production and dissemination (transfer). Accordingly, although knowhow is not a pure public good,[5] the transfer of proprietary information to alternative activities is likely to generate scope economies if organizational modes can be discovered to conduct the transfer at low cost. In this regard, the relative efficiency properties of markets and internal organization need to be assessed. If reliance on market processes is surrounded by special difficulties—and hence costs—internal organization, and in particular multiproduct enterprise, may be preferred.

An examination of the properties of information markets readily leads to the identification of several difficulties. They can be summarized in terms of (1) recognition, (2) disclosure and (3) team organization. Thus consider a firm which has accumulated knowhow which can potentially find application in fields of industrial activity beyond its existing markets. If there are other firms in the economy which can apply this knowhow with profit, then according to received microtheory, trading will ensue until Pareto Optimality conditions are satisfied. Or, as Calabresi has put it, 'if one assumes rationality, no transactions costs, and no legal impediments to bargaining, all misallocations of resources would be fully cured in the market by bargains' (Calabresi (1968)). However, one cannot in general expect this happy result in the market for proprietary knowhow. Not only are there high costs associated with obtaining the requisite information but there are also organizational and strategic impediments associated with using the market to effectuate transfer.

Consider, to begin with, the information requirements associated with using markets. In order to carry out a market transaction it is necessary to discover who it is that one wishes to deal with, to inform people that one wishes to deal and on what terms, to conduct negotiations leading up to the bargain, to draw up the contract, to undertake the inspection needed to make sure that the terms of the contract are being observed, and so on (Coase (1960, p. 15)). Furthermore, the opportunity for trading must be identified. As Kirzner (1973, pp. 215–216) has explained:

for an exchange transaction to be completed it is not sufficient merely that the conditions for exchange which prospectively will be mutually beneficial be present: it is necessary also that each participant be aware of his opportunity to gain through exchange. . . . It is usually assumed . . . that where scope for (mutually beneficial) exchange is present, exchange will in fact occur. . . . In fact of course exchange may fail to occur because knowledge is imperfect, in spite of conditions for mutually profitable exchange.

The transactional difficulties identified by Kirzner are especially compelling when the commodity in question is proprietary information, be it of a technological or managerial kind. This is because the protection of the ownership of technological knowhow often requires suppressing information on exchange possibilities. By its very nature, industrial R & D requires disguising and concealing the activities and outcomes of the R & D establishment. As Marquis and Allen (1966, p. 1055) point out, industrial laboratories, with their strong mission orientation, must

cut themselves off from interaction beyond the organizational perimeter. This is to a large degree intentional. The competitive environment in which they operate necessitates control over the outflow of messages. The industrial technologist or scientist is thereby essentially cut off from free interaction with his colleagues outside of the organization.

Except as production or marketing specialists within the firm perceive the transfer opportunity, transfer may fail by reason of non-recognition—which of course, is a manifestation of bounded rationality.

Even where the possessor of the technology recognizes the opportunity, market exchange may break down because of the problems of disclosing value to buyers in a way that is both convincing and does not destroy the basis for exchange. A very severe information impactedness problem exists, on which account the less informed party (in this instance the buyer) must be wary of opportunistic representations by the seller. If, moreover, there is insufficient disclosure, including veracity checks thereon, to assure the buyer that the information possesses great value, the 'fundamental paradox' of information arises: 'its value for the purchaser is not known until he has the information, but then he has in effect acquired it without cost' (Arrow (1971, p. 152)).

Suppose that recognition is no problem, that buyers concede value, and are prepared to pay for information in the seller's possession. Occasionally that may suffice. The formula for a chemical compound or the blue prints for a special device may be all that is needed to effect the transfer. However, more is frequently needed. Knowhow has a strong learning-by-doing character, and it may be essential that human capital in an effective team configuration accompany the transfer.[6] Sometimes this can be effected through a one-time contract (a knowhow agreement) to provide a 'consulting team' to assist start-up. Although such contracts will be highly incomplete, and the failure to reach a comprehensive agreement may give rise to dissatisfaction during execution, this may be an unavoidable, which is to say irremediable, result. Plainly, integration (diversification) is an extreme response to the needs of a one-time exchange. In the absence of a superior organizational alternative, reliance on market mechanisms is thus likely to prevail.

Where a succession of proprietary exchanges seems desirable, reliance on repeated contracting is less clearly warranted. Unfettered two-way communication is needed not only to promote the recognition and disclosure of opportunities for information transfer but also to facilitate the execution of the actual transfer itself. The parties in these circumstances are joined in a small numbers trading relation and, as discussed by Williamson, such contracting may be shot through with hazards for both parties (Williamson (1975, 1979)). The seller is exposed to hazards such as the possibility that the buyer will employ the knowhow in subtle ways not covered by the contract, or the buyer might 'leap frog' the licensor's technology and become an unexpected competitive threat in third markets. The buyer is exposed to hazards such as the seller asserting that the technology has superior performance or cost reducing characteristics than is actually the case; or the seller might render promised transfer assistance in a perfunctory fashion. While bonding or the execution of performance guarantees can minimize these hazards, they need not be eliminated since costly haggling might ensue when measurement of the performance characteristics of the technology is open to some ambiguity. Furthermore, when a lateral transfer is contemplated and the technology has not therefore been previously commercialized by either party in the new application, the execution of performance guarantees is likely to be especially hazardous to the seller because of the uncertainties involved (Teece (1977)). In addition, if a new application of a generic technology is contemplated, recurrent exchange and continuous contact between buyer and seller will be needed. These requirements will be extremely difficult to specify ex ante. Hence, when the continuous exchange of proprietary knowhow between the transferor and transferee is needed, and where the end use application of the knowledge is idiosyncratic in the sense that it has not been accomplished previously by the transferor, it appears that something more than a classical market contracting structure is required. As Williamson (1979, p. 250) notes 'The nonstandardized nature of (these) transactions makes primary reliance on market governance hazardous, while their recurrent nature permits the cost of the specialized governance structure to be recovered'. What Williamson refers to as 'relational contracting' is the solution: this can take the form of bilateral governance, where the autonomy of the parties is maintained; or unified structures, where the transaction is removed from the market and organized within the firm subject to an authority relation (Williamson (1979, p. 250)). Bilateral governance involves the use of what

Williamson has labelled 'obligational contracting' (Wachter and Williamson (1978), Williamson (1979)). Exchange is conducted between independent firms under obligational arrangements, where both parties realize the paramount importance of maintaining an amicable relationship as overriding any possible short-run gains either might be able to achieve. But as transactions become progressively more idiosyncratic, obligational contracting may also fail, and internal organization (intrafirm transfer) is the more efficient organizational mode. The intrafirm transfer of knowhow avoids the need for repeated negotiations and ameliorates the hazards of opportunism. Better disclosure, easier agreement, better governance, and therefore more effective execution of knowhow transfer are likely to result. Here lies an incentive for enterprise diversification.

The above arguments are quite general and extend to the transfer of many different kinds of proprietary knowhow. Besides technological knowhow, the transfer of managerial (including organizational) knowhow, and goodwill (including brand loyalty) represent types of assets for which market transfer mechanisms may falter, and for which the relative efficiency of intrafirm as against interfirm trading is indicated.

Figs. 2 and 3 attempt to summarize the essential dimensions of the above arguments. The matrix in Fig. 2 identifies some illustrative knowhow

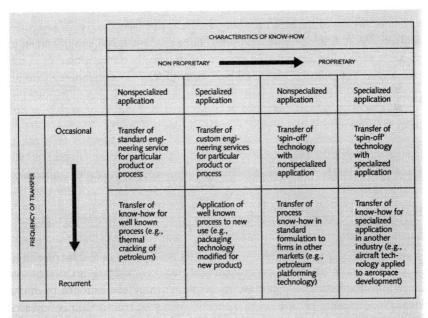

Fig. 2. Illustrative knowhow transactions.

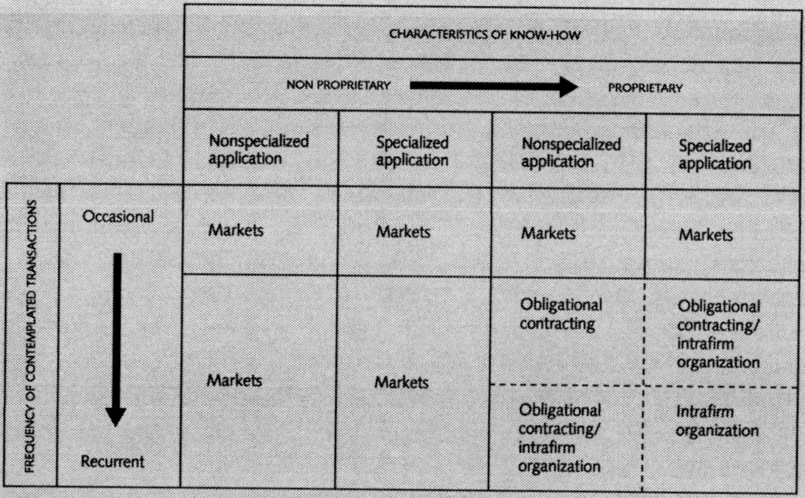

		CHARACTERISTICS OF KNOW-HOW			
		NON PROPRIETARY ⟶ PROPRIETARY			
		Nonspecialized application	Specialized application	Nonspecialized application	Specialized application
FREQUENCY OF CONTEMPLATED TRANSACTIONS	Occasional	Markets	Markets	Markets	Markets
	Recurrent	Markets	Markets	Obligational contracting / Obligational contracting/ intrafirm organization	Obligational contracting/ intrafirm organization / Intrafirm organization

Fig. 3. Some elements of organizational design.

transactions for which governance structures need to be designed. The match of governance structures with transactions which economizes on transactions costs and facilitates efficient knowhow transfer is displayed in Fig. 2. Suggested by Williamson (1979, pp. 247, 253) these figures are a gross simplification of the real world, which cannot of course be so neatly categorized. Still, the figures serve to identify key considerations likely to determine whether multiproduct organizations will be needed to facilitate the efficient utilization of knowhow which is to become an input into a number of different production processes.

4. Indivisibilities: Market Failure Considerations

An indivisible asset, or any asset which yields scale economies, can similarly provide the foundation for scope economies if it serves as an input into two or more production processes. At least two types of indivisibilities can be distinguished (Williamson (1975, p. 42)). The first type involves the utilization of a physical asset. Larger scale units, if they are utilized at design capacity, permit lower average costs to be realized. Whenever this kind of indivisibility exists, and whenever the indivisible asset can serve as a common input into two or more production processes, joint production will produce economies of scope. Thus if a machine used to stamp automobile bodies displays economies of scale, and these economies are not exhausted over the range of the market, and if the stamping facility can also be used to stamp truck bodies, then economies of scope will exist in the stamping of both automobiles and light trucks. The second type of indivisibility involves the indivisibilities associated with information, an indivisibility that was explicitly discussed above with respect to knowhow. Radner (1970, p. 457) observes that 'the acquisition of information often involves a "set up cost" i.e., the resources needed to obtain the information may be independent of the production process in which the information is used'. The set up cost to which Radner refers might be the cost of R & D, or it may simply be the cost of collecting information on a phenomenon of interest. Since the discussion in section 3 above has focussed on the organizational implications of scope economies based on the sharing of information (knowhow), the discussion here will focus on the organizational implications of scope economies based on the sharing of a specialized physical asset.

Clearly, the realization of scope economies based on the sharing of a specialized asset does not imply, as a technological imperative, that the relevant products must be produced within a multi-product enterprise. In the absence of transactional difficulties, there is nothing to prevent one individual or firm from procuring the physical asset in the requisite size to realize the economies in question and contracting to supply the services of this asset to other individuals or firms. All parties could be independent, yet scope economies could be fully realized. In the above example, the automobile manufacturer could own the stamping facility and the truck manufacturer could contract with the automobile manufacturer to have the requisite number of truck bodies stamped in the automobile manufacturer's facility. Alternatively, a third firm could own the stamping facility and contract its services to both the manufacturers of automobiles and the manufacturers of trucks.

However, it is not difficult to identify transactional difficulties that attend market exchange in these circumstances. Consider indivisible physical assets common to two or more production processes. While in many cases markets can be expected to work quite well as devices for selling the services of assets subject to indivisibilities, there are circumstances where transactional difficulties and hence market failure is to be expected. If the fixed asset is highly specialized, and if the number of leasors or leasees is quite small, then markets for the services of the fixed assets may be extremely thin. Bilateral monopoly situations can then arise in which potential leasees may attempt to extract the quasi rents associated with the utilization of the leasor's fixed and specialized asset (Williamson (1975, 1979), Teece (1976), Klein, Crawford and Alchian

(1978)). In order to avoid these hazards intrafirm trading—that is multiproduct diversification—can be engaged. Internal trading changes the incentives of the parties and enables the firm to bring managerial control devices to bear on the transaction, thereby attenuating costly haggling and disruptions and other manifestations of non-cooperative behavior. Exchange can then proceed at lower cost and with higher returns to the participants.

Diversification offers similar advantages with respect to the indivisibilities associated with information. Because of the reasons identified in section 3 above, markets for information are often shot through with hazards, and internal organization has efficiency properties which markets cannot always replicate.

5. Limits to Diversification Economies

Scope economies obtained via diversification are clearly circumscribed. If they are based upon the transfer of knowhow into different markets, then while the value of the knowhow may not be impaired by repeated transfer, the costs of accessing it may increase if the simultaneous transfer of the information to a number of different applications is attempted. This is simply because of a congestion factor which may attend the transfer process. As mentioned above, knowhow is generally not embodied in blueprints alone; the human factor is critically important. Accordingly, as the demands for sharing knowhow increase, bottlenecks in the form of over-extended scientists, engineers, and manufacturing/marketing personnel can be anticipated. Congestion associated with accessing common inputs will thus clearly limit the amount of diversification which can be profitably engaged. However, if the transfers are arranged so that they occur in a sequential fashion, then the limits imposed by congestion are relieved, at least in part (Teece (1977)). Of course, control loss considerations may eventually come into play, as they do with any large organization, but the establishment of a decentralized divisionalized 'M-form' structure is likely to keep control loss problems to the very minimum. In this regard it is important to note that diversification based on scope economies does not represent abandonment of specialization economies in favor of amorphous growth. It is simply that the firm's comparative advantage is defined not in terms of products but in terms of capabilities. The firm is seen as establishing a specialized knowhow or asset base from which it extends its operations in response to competitive conditions.

Just as scope economies associated with the sharing of proprietary knowhow will eventually be exhausted, so too will the scope economies associated with sharing an indivisible specialized asset. When the indivisible asset is fully utilized, no further gains from additional diversification are to be expected. In this regard it is apparent that the exogenous growth of the market will circumscribe the scope economies obtainable from sharing an indivisible specialized asset.

6. Public Policy Implications

Since diversification is a salient characteristic of the modern enterprise, the efficiency with which firms allocate resources internally in contrast to how they might have been allocated by the market becomes a topic of considerable importance. Yet there have been few attempts to examine the internal efficiency properties of the diversified enterprise. Much of the attention has gone to examining relationships between diversification, growth, and competition (Gort (1962), Berry (1975), Utton (1979)).

Recent developments in the theory of scale and scope economies and interproduct complementarities have sharpened understanding of some of the fundamental concepts involved in multiproduct production. However, this literature is seriously flawed insofar as it attempts to derive organizational implications directly from industry cost functions. Economies of scope are neither necessary nor a sufficient condition for cost savings to be achieved by merging specialized firms. But if economies of scope are costly to capture because of the transactional difficulties surrounding the sharing of a common input, then multiproduct organization is likely to yield compelling efficiencies.

Accordingly, if public policy towards the business enterprise is to be fashioned with efficiency as the objective, then it is necessary to consider transactions cost as well as technological issues. Proposals for the divestiture or amalgamation of industries requires a sensitive treatment of both technological and transactions costs considerations. Empirical studies of the kind proposed by Baumol and Braunstein do not suffice (Baumol and Braunstein (1977)) if delineating organizational boundaries for the business enterprise is the issue at hand. The implications for antitrust policy are quite clear. The courts must be sensitive to transactions cost as well as technological issues.

7. Conclusion

By engaging transactions costs analysis in the fashion suggested by Williamson, the relationships between economies of scope and the scope of the enterprise

David Teece

have been clarified. The basic conclusion is that economies of scope do not provide a sufficient raison d'être for multiproduct firms. There are likely to be numerous instances where economies of scope can be captured by an economy of specialized firms contracting in the marketplace for the supply of common inputs. Nevertheless, there are important instances where multiproduct firms will be needed to capture scope economies. Two circumstances were examined in some detail: (1) where the production of two or more products depends upon the same proprietary knowhow base and recurrent exchange is called for, and (2) when a specialized indivisible asset is a common input into the production of two or more products. Under circumstances (1) and (2), integration (that is, multiproduct organization) is likely to be an efficient mode of organization.

Notes

I am grateful for the helpful comments of Armen Alchian, Henry Armour, Victor Goldberg, Nicholas Gonedes, Sanford Grossman, Albert Hirschman, Benjamin Klein, Charles Plosser and James Rosse. A special intellectual debt is owed to Oliver Williamson, whose seminal writings on the economies of internal organization have had a pervasive influence on the development of this paper.

1. Following Gort (1960, p. 9), diversification is defined as 'an increase in the heterogeneity of output from the point of view of the number of markets served by that output'.
2. More formally, consider a set of products indexed by the numbers in the set $N = (1, 2, \ldots, n)$, with the technology for producing the goods in N being represented by the cost function, $c(x_1, \ldots, x_n)$, which gives the minimal cost of the joint production of the quantities $x_1, \ldots, x_n$ of good $1, \ldots, n$ respectively. There are economies of scope in the production of the set of commodities N if the cost of jointly producing these goods is less than the sum of stand-alone production costs. For example, with $N = (1, 2)$, economies of scope mean that $c(x_1, x_2) < c(x_1, 0) + c(0, x_2)$ for $x > 0$.
3. Consider mixed farming. Orchardists must have space between fruit trees in order to facilitate adequate growth of the trees and the movement of farm machinery between the trees. This land can, however, be planted in grass, and sheep may graze to advantage in the intervening pasture. Economies of scope are clearly realized (land is the common input) but the organizational implications are not as sharp as Panzar and Willig's paradigm would suggest. Rather than producing both fruit and sheep, the orchardist can lease the pasture to a sheep farmer. The scope economies in sheep farming and fruit production are realized, but the single product focus of the sheep farmer and the orchardist are preserved. Clearly, market contracts can be used to undo the organization implications which Panzar and Willig impute to the cost function.

4. The cost function summarizes all economically relevant information about the production technology of the firm. But, as commonly interpreted, it does not summarize the firm's organizational technology. To assert otherwise would involve assuming rather than deducing the conditions for efficient multiproduct organization.

5. This is because the value of information often declines with its dissemination and it cannot be transferred at zero marginal cost.

6. Over the years an individual may learn a piece of the company puzzle exceptionally well and he may even understand how the piece fits into the entire puzzle. But he may not know enough about the other pieces to reproduce the entire puzzle (Lieberstein (1979)).

References

Armour, H. and D. Teece, 1978. Organizational structure and economic performance: A test of the multidivisional hypothesis. The Bell Journal of Economics, Spring.

Arrow, K., 1971, Essays in the theory of risk bearing (Markham, Chicago, IL).

Baumol, W. and Y. Braunstein, 1977, Empirical study of scale economies and production complementarity: The case of journal publication. Journal of Political Economy. Oct.

Berry, C., 1975, Corporate growth and diversification (Princeton University Press, Princeton, NJ).

Calabresi, G., 1968, Transactions costs, resources allocation, and liability rules: A comment, Journal of Law and Economics, April.

Chandler, A., 1977, The visible hand (Harvard University Press, Cambridge, MA).

Coase, R., 1960, The problem of social cost, Journal of Law and Economics, Oct.

Coase, R., 1972, Industrial organization: A proposal for research, in: V. R. Fuchs, ed., Policy issues and research opportunities in industrial organization (National Bureau of Economic Research, New York).

Gort, M., 1962, Diversification and integration in American industry (Princeton University Press, Princeton, NJ).

Grabowski, H. and D. Mueller, 1975, Life cycle effects of corporate returns on retentions, Review of Economics and Statistics, Nov.

Kirzner, I., 1973, Competition and entrepreneurship (University of Chicago Press, Chicago, IL).

Klein, B., R. G. Crawford and A. A. Alchian, 1978, Vertical integration, appropriable rents, and the competitive contracting process, Journal of Law and Economics XXI, no. 2, Oct., 297–326.

Lieberstein, S. H., 1979, Who owns what is in your head (Hawthorn Publishers, New York).

Marquis, D. and T. Allen, 1966, Communication patterns in applied technology, American Psychologist 21.

Mueller, D., 1972, A life cycle theory of the firm, Journal of Industrial Economics, July.

Nelson, R. R., 1959, The simple analytics of basic scientific research, Journal of Political Economy, June.

Nelson, R. R., 1972, Issues and suggestions for the study of industrial organization in a regime of rapid technical change, in: V. Fuchs, ed., Policy issues and research opportunities in industrial organization (National Bureau of Economic Research, New York).

Panzar, J. and R. Willig, 1975, Economies of scale and economies of scope in multi-output production, Unpublished Working Paper.

Penrose, E., 1959, The theory of the growth of the firm (John Wiley, New York).

Radner, R., 1970, Problems in the theory of markets under uncertainty, American Economic Review, May.

Teece, D., 1976, Vertical integration and vertical divestiture in the U.S. petroleum industry (Stanford University Institute for Energy Studies, Stanford, CA).

Teece, D., 1977, Technology transfer by multinational firms: The resource cost of transferring technological knowhow, Economic Journal 87, June.

Teece, D. and H. Armour, 1977, Innovation & divestiture in the U.S. oil industry, in: D. Teece, ed., R & D in energy: Implications of petroleum industry reorganization (Stanford University Institute for Energy Studies, Stanford, CA).

Utton, M., 1979, Diversification and competition (Cambridge University Press, Cambridge).

Wachter, M. and O. Williamson, 1978, Obligational markets and the mechanics of inflation, Bell Journal of Economics.

Weston, J. F. and S. K. Mansinghka, 1971, Tests of the efficiency performance of conglomerate firms, Journal of Finance, Sept.

Williamson, O. E., 1975, Markets and hierarchies: Analysis and antitrust implications (Free Press, New York).

Williamson, O. E., 1979, Transactions-cost economies: The governance of contractual relations, Journal of Law and Economics, Oct.

Willig, R., 1979, Multiproduct technology and market structure, American Economic Review, May.

A Resource-Based View of the Firm

Birger Wernerfelt

1. Introduction

For the firm, resources and products are two sides of the same coin. Most products require the services of several resources and most resources can be used in several products. By specifying the size of the firm's activity in different product markets, it is possible to infer the minimum necessary resource commitments. Conversely, by specifying a resource profile for a firm, it is possible to find the optimal product-market activities.

Both perspectives on the firm are reflected in the literature on strategic management. The traditional concept of strategy (Andrews, 1971) is phrased in terms of the resource position (strengths and weaknesses) of the firm, whereas most of our formal economic tools operate on the product-market side. While these two perspectives should ultimately yield the same insights, one might expect these insights to come with differing ease, depending on the perspective taken.

The purpose of this paper is to develop some simple economic tools for analysing a firm's resource position and to look at some strategic options suggested by this analysis. This will apply, in particular, to the relationship between profitability and resources, as well as ways to manage the firm's resource position over time.

Looking at economic units in terms of their resource endowments has a long tradition in economics. The analysis is typically confined, however, to categories such as labour, capital, and perhaps land. The idea of looking at firms as a broader set of resources goes back to the seminal work of Penrose (1959), but, apart from Rubin (1973), has received relatively little formal attention. The reason, no doubt, is the unpleasant properties (for modelling purposes) of some key examples of resources, such as technological skills. The mathematics used by economists typically require that resources exhibit declining returns to scale, as in the traditional theory of factor demand. By virtue of analysing this type of resource, the economic theory of factor demand becomes a special case of the theory put forward in this paper. By dealing with the financial resources of the firm, the product portfolio theories in a sense become another special case of the theory discussed below. Also, the idea that multiproduct firms benefit from non-financial linkages such as joint costs, is an old but largely neglected part of economics. Recently it has, however, received renewed attention, mainly through the formalization of the economies of scope concept (see e.g. Panzar and Willig, 1981).

It turns out that the resource perspective provides a basis for addressing some key issues in the formulation of strategy for diversified firms, such as:

(a) On which of the firm's current resources should diversification be based?
(b) Which resources should be developed through diversification?
(c) In what sequence and into what markets should diversification take place?
(d) What types of firms will it be desirable for this particular firm to acquire?

Specifically, the following propositions will be argued:

1. Looking at firms in terms of their resources leads to different immediate insights than the traditional product perspective. In particular, diversified firms are seen in a new light.
2. One can identify types of resources which can lead to high profits. In analogy to entry barriers, these are associated with what we will call resource position barriers.
3. Strategy for a bigger firm involves striking a balance between the exploitation of existing resources and the development of new ones. In analogy to the growth-share matrix, this can be visualized in what we will call a resource-product matrix.
4. An acquisition can be seen as a purchase of a bundle of resources in a highly imperfect market. By basing the purchase on a rare resource, one can *ceteris paribus* maximize this imperfection and one's chances of buying cheap and getting good returns.

In the next section the simple economics of different types of resources will be examined and the results will be applied to the characteristics of attractive, high profit yielding, resources. Then the analysis is confined to a particular type of resource and some strategies for managing a firm's resource position over time will be looked at.

2. Resources and Profitability

By a resource is meant anything which could be thought of as a strength or weakness of a given firm. More formally, a firm's resources at a given time could be defined as those (tangible and intangible) assets which are tied semi-permanently to the firm (see Caves, 1980). Examples of resources are: brand names, in-house knowledge of technology, employment of skilled personnel, trade contacts, machinery, efficient procedures, capital, etc. In this section, we will ask the question: 'Under what circumstances will a resource lead to high returns over longer periods of time?'

For purposes of analysis, Porter's five competitive forces (Porter, 1980) will be used, although these were originally intended as tools for analysis of products only.

2.1 General Effects

This heading will cover the bargaining power of suppliers and buyers as well as the threat posed by substitute resources.

If the *production of a resource itself or of one of its critical inputs* is controlled by a monopolistic group, it will, *ceteris paribus*, diminish the returns available to the users of the resource. A patent holder, for example, appropriates part of the profits of his licence holders. On a smaller scale, a good advertising agency will be able to take a share of the image builders' (customers') profit.

An equally bad situation can occur on the output side if the *products resulting from use of the resource can be sold only in monopolistic markets*. If a subcontractor develops a machine which is fully idiosyncratic to one customer, he will stand to gain less than if the machine has more buyers.

Finally, the *availability of substitute resources* will tend to depress returns to the holders of a given resource. A recent example is provided by the way electronic and hydraulic skills have eroded the payoffs to electrical and mechanical skills.

2.2 First Mover Advantages—Resource Position Barriers

In some cases, a holder of a resource is *able to maintain a relative position* vis-à-vis *other holders and third persons, as long as these act rationally*. That is, the fact that someone already has the resource affects the costs and/or revenues of later acquirers adversely. In these situations the holder can be said to enjoy the protection of a resource position barrier. Defined in this way, resource position barriers are thus only partially analogous to entry barriers, since they also contain the mechanisms which make an advantage over another resource holder defensible. (Entry barriers in the traditional market context deal only with the situation between incumbents and potential entrants, not with the situation among the incumbents.) Just like entry barriers, resource position barriers do, however, indicate a potential for high returns, since one competitor will have an advantage.

Note that this (resource-based) concept in some sense supersedes the traditional (product-based) entry barrier concept, but in another sense does not:

(a) If a firm has entry barriers towards newcomers in market A, which shares the use of a resource with market B, then another firm which is strong in B might have a cost advantage there and enter A in that way.

(b) If the firm has a resource position barrier in resource α, which is used in market A, it might still survive the collapse of A if it could use α somewhere else.

On the other hand, for a resource position barrier to be valuable, it should translate into an entry barrier in at least one market.

So, an *entry barrier without a resource position barrier leaves the firm vulnerable to diversifying entrants, whereas a resource position barrier without an entry barrier leaves the firm unable to exploit the barrier.* There is thus a nice duality between the two concepts, corresponding to the duality between products and resources.

2.3 Attractive Resources

It is possible to identify classes of resources for which resource position barriers can be built up. By their nature, these barriers are often self-reproducing; that is a firm which at a given time, finds itself in some sense ahead of others may use these barriers to cement that lead. It is the properties of the resources and their mode of acquisition which allow this to be done. *What a firm wants is to create a situation where its own resource position directly or indirectly makes it more difficult for others to catch up.* To analyse a resource for a general potential for high returns, one has to look at the ways in which a firm with a strong position can influence the acquisition costs or the user revenues of a firm with a weaker position.

Let us apply this to a few examples.

Machine Capacity

It is well known that production processes with decreasing returns to scale cannot yield high returns if they can be bought in open markets. On the other hand, economies of scale in the use of resources are the prime example of product entry barriers (Spence, 1979). From the resource perspective, the product entry barrier translates into a resource position barrier, since it will be irrational for entrants to buy the resource necessary to compete in a market where excess capacity would lead to cut-throat competition and low returns. So, in this case, the resource position barrier operates through lower expected revenues for prospective acquirers.

Customer Loyalty

In this case the nature of the market for the resource generates the resource position barrier. It is much easier to pioneer a position than to replace someone else who already has it (see Ries and Trout, 1981). Here, later buyers will have to pay higher prices than earlier buyers. Related examples are the first mover advantages in government contacts, access to raw materials, etc.

Production Experience

As is well known, if the leader executes the experience curve strategy correctly, then later resource producers have to get their experience in an uphill battle with earlier producers who have lower costs. Ideally, later acquirers should pay more for the experience and expect lower returns from it (Boston Consulting Group, 1972). On the other hand, if experience leaks from the early movers to later movers, the effect is to reduce the costs of the latter, so that we might approach the case of an unpatented idea for which no sustainable first mover advantage exists. This is the case, for example, with many production systems and procedures.

Technologial Leads

Here again, two counteracting effects are at work. On the one hand, a technological lead will allow the firm higher returns, and thus enable it to keep better people in a more stimulating setting so that the organization can develop and calibrate more advanced ideas than followers. The followers, on the other hand, will often find the reinvention of your ideas easier than you found the original invention. So you need to keep growing your technological capability in order to protect your position. This should, however, be feasible if you use your high current returns to feed R & D. A good analogy is a high tree in a low forest; since it will get more sun, it will grow faster and stay taller.

In general, one should keep in mind that most resources can be used in several products. As a result, a given resource position barrier will often have consequences for several products, each yielding part of the resulting return.

A resource such as managerial skills, which could be analysed much like technological leads above, is a good example of this.

The general attractiveness of a resource, understood as its capacity to support a resource position barrier, is only a necessary, not a sufficient, condition for a given firm to be interested in it. If everyone goes for the potentially attractive resources and only a few can 'win' in each, firms will lose unless they pick their fights well. So firms need to find those resources which can sustain a resource position barrier, but in which no one currently has one, and where they have a good chance of being among the few who succeed in building one. They have to look at resources which combine well with what they already have and in which they are likely to face only a few competitive acquirers.

2.4 Mergers and Acquisitions

Mergers and acquisitions provide an opportunity to trade otherwise non-marketable resources and to buy or sell resources in bundles. Through this vehicle one can, for example, sell an image or buy a combination of technological capabilities and contacts in a given set of markets. As is well known, this is a very imperfect market with few buyers and targets, and yet with a low degree of transparency owing to the heterogeneity of both buyers and targets. A key implication of the latter is that a given target will have different values for different buyers, with particularly big variance among those who can obtain some sort of fit (synergy) between their resources and those of the target.

Because of the extreme difficulties of investigating (often discreetly):

(a) what resources a given target has
(b) which of those the firm can effectively take advantage of
(c) what the cost of doing so will be
(d) what the firm could pay for them

prospective buyers often limit their search to targets which satisfy certain simple criteria. A resource-based set of acquisition strategies (Salter and Weinhold, 1980) is:

(i) related supplementary (get more of those resources you already have)
(ii) related complementary (get resources which combine effectively with those you already have).

Other acquisition strategies are more product-oriented and tend to focus on the firm's ability to enter (and dominate) attractive markets.

Let us here focus on the purchase of resource bundles, taking as given the profitability of using different combinations. In this perspective, one's chance of maximizing market imperfection and perhaps getting a cheap buy would be greatest if one tried to build on one's most unusual resource or resource position. Doing so should make it possible to get into buying situations with relatively little competition, but also with relatively few targets. Although, in theory, it would be best to be the sole suitable buyer of a lot of identical targets, even a bilateral monopoly situation would be better than a game with several identical buyers and sellers. Especially since the latter situation will most likely lead one into heavier competition in the race to build resource position barriers after the acquisitions have taken place.

3. Dynamic Resource Management: An Example

In the previous section, several situations in which firms could get high returns from individual resources were examined. In general, a first mover advantage in an attractive resource should yield high returns in the markets where the resource in question is dominating. This theory will now be applied to a particular type of resource, the experience type, produced jointly with products. Finally, some ways in which a firm can grow its pool of such resources, will be investigated.

MARKET / RESOURCE	I	II	III	IV	V
A					
B					
C					
D					

Fig. 1. Resource–product matrix.

Birger Wernerfelt

3.1 The Resource-Product Matrix

The analysis will be conducted through what could be called a resource-product matrix, in which the checked entries indicate the importance of a resource in a product and vice versa (see Fig. 1).

This matrix, which is a close cousin of the growth-share matrix, could be made more informative by replacing the checks with one (or two) numbers, indicating the relative importance of resources in products or (and) vice versa. As will be seen, even the simple form above is, however, a very powerful tool. Below it will be used to illustrate several different patterns of resource development.

3.2 Sequential Entry

The use of a single resource in several businesses is the diversification pattern most often considered in business policy (Andrews, 1971). A typical example is provided by BIC's (BIC, 1974) use of their mass marketing skills, which proved critical in pens, lighters and razors, but insufficient in pantihose. Attempts to base firms on a single strong technology also fall into this category. Several consulting firms market concepts which exploit this growth pattern (e.g. the 'shared experience' of the Boston Consulting Group and the 'activity analysis' of Braxton Associates).

Although the general idea is to expand your position in a single resource, it is not always optimal to go full force in several markets simultaneously even with experience curve effects. Quite often, it is better to develop the resource in one market and then to enter other markets from a position of strength. An example is BIC, which entered the markets for pens, lighters and razors sequentially. This *sequential entry* strategy (an idea going back to John Stuart Mill, and his writings on infant industry protection), is also often followed by firms when they go international, as illustrated in Fig. 2, where the firm develops production skills before going international.

To demonstrate the feasibility of this, we can look at a simple mathematical model. (A more elaborate formalization can be found in Bardhan, 1971.) A firm can operate in two markets, A and B, which are such that it takes a_I hours to process I to produce a unit of product A, whereas it takes b_I and b_{II} hours of processes I and II, respectively, to produce a unit of product B. Assume process II skills to be available in a perfect market, whereas process I skills can be developed via experience curve effects. So, skills in process I are the attractive resource. Finally, look at the firm as having a two-period time horizon and consider the wisdom of developing process I skills in market A before market B is entered.

124

RESOURCE / MARKET	Production skills	International contacts	III	IV	Domestic contacts
Domestic	X				X
International	X	X			
C		X		X	
D				X	X

Fig. 2. Sequential entry.

In the following, all parameters are assumed positive and subscripts A, B, I, II, 1, 2, refer to the markets, processes, and periods so named.

The demand curves are assumed to be constant over the two periods and linear so that the quantity sold is a linear function of the price charged. This can be written as:

$$A_i = \theta_A - P_A \phi_A, \quad i = 1, 2$$

$$B_i = \theta_B - P_B \phi_B, \quad i = 1, 2$$

where θ_A and θ_B are the volumes 'sold' at zero price and ϕ_A and ϕ_B the decline in volume per unit price increase.

Variable costs are assumed to be zero and fixed costs, C, of selling above zero outputs are in period I composed of a constant cost of operating each process. In period 2, process I costs are, however, lowered by η_A and η_B for each hour the process was used in period 1. So we get:

$$C_{A1} = \gamma_{A1}, \qquad\qquad\qquad\qquad\quad \text{if } A_1 > 0$$

$$C_{A2} = \gamma_{A2} - \eta_{A1}\left(a_I A_1 + b_I B_1\right), \qquad \text{if } A_2 > 0$$

$$C_{B1} = \gamma_{B1} + \gamma_{BU}, \qquad\qquad\qquad\; \text{if } B_1 > 0$$

$$C_{B2} = \gamma_{B1} - \eta_{B1}\left(a_I A_1 + b_I B_1\right) + \gamma_{BII}, \quad \text{if } B_2 > 0$$

The simple linear version of the experience curve is chosen for analytical convenience and is in no way crucial to the qualitative results below.

If the firm tries to maximize the total profit over the two periods, the objective is to maximize:

$$\left(P_{A1}A_1 - C_{A1}\right) + \left(P_{A2}A_2 - C_{A2}\right) + \left(P_{B1}B_1 - C_{B1}\right) + \left(P_{B2}B_2 - C_{B2}\right)$$

By inserting the above equations, differentiating with respect to P_{A1}, P_{A2}, P_{B1}, P_{B2}, and using the first order conditions, we find that, if all outputs are positive, the optimal levels are

$$A_1^*\left(P_{A1}^*\right) = \frac{1}{2}\left[\theta_A + \phi_A a_1\left(\eta_{A1} + \eta_{B1}\right)\right], \quad \text{where } \eta_{B1} = 0 \text{ if } B_2 = 0$$

$$A_2^*\left(P_{A2}^*\right) = \frac{1}{2}\theta_A$$

$$B_1^*\left(P_{B1}^*\right) = \frac{1}{2}\left[\theta_B + \phi_B b_1\left(\eta_{A1} + \eta_{B1}\right)\right]$$

$$B_2^*\left(P_{B2}^*\right) = \frac{1}{2}\theta_B.$$

By inserting $(A_1^*, A_2^*, B_1^*, B_2^*)$, $(A_1^*, A_2^*, 0, B_2^*)$ and $(A_1^*, A_2^*, 0, 0)$ in the maximant, one can find the conditions under which it is optimal to enter market B only in the second period. These conditions are:

$$\theta_B b_1\left(\eta_{A1} + \eta_{B1}\right) + \frac{1}{4}\left[\theta_B \phi_B^{-1} - b_1\left(\eta_{A1} + \eta_{B1}\right)\right]^2 \phi_B < \gamma_{BI} + \gamma_{BII}$$

$$< \frac{1}{4}\theta_B^2 \phi_B^{-1} + \frac{1}{2}\theta_A \eta_{BI} a_1 + \frac{1}{2}\phi_A a_1^2 \eta_{BI}\left(\eta_{AI} + \frac{1}{2}\eta_{BI}\right).$$

So sequential entry tends to be better when

(a) market A is big relative to market B (θ_A is large, θ_B is small)
(b) product B only uses a little of I (b_1 is small)
(c) product A uses a lot of I (a_1 is large).

Although the effect here is generated through an experience curve type of argument, a little reflection will reveal that other instances of resources produced jointly with products can also have the same effect. An example of this is brand loyalty in connection with economies of scale in process I, which will mean that a big A_1 guarantees sales and thus low costs of process I in period 2.

3.3 Exploit and Develop

If you push the example from Fig. 2 a little further, you could look at the fifth resource, 'domestic contacts', as supporting the buildup of the first, 'production skills' through joint cost effects. This could in turn be used to support the acquisition of 'international contacts' etc. (see Fig. 3).

RESOURCE / MARKET	Production skills	International contacts	III	Project management	Domestic contacts
Domestic	X ←				────── X
International	X ────→ X				
Turn Key		X ────────→ X			
D			X		X

Fig. 3. Exploit and develop.

The close analogy to the product portfolio theory (Henderson, 1979), where strong products in a firm's growth-share matrix supply weak ones with cash, again underscores the duality between the product and the resource perspectives on the firm. Since one often would expect businesses to be related in more ways than financially, the joint cost subsidy from resource relation may be a more potent tool than product to product cash subsidy. Looking at diversified firms as portfolios of resources rather than portfolios of products gives a different and perhaps richer perspective on their growth prospects. Again, optimal management of a resource portfolio is in theory the same as optimal management of a product portfolio, but the two frameworks may highlight different growth avenues.

In the framework above, the optimal growth of the firm involves a balance between exploitation of existing resources and development of new ones (Penrose, 1959; Rubin, 1973; Wernerfelt, 1977). Even in an uncertain setting, this does not necessarily make versatile (multibusiness) resources more attractive than more specialized resources. The reason for this is that although versatile resources give more options, one would expect more and bigger competition in them.

3.4 Stepping Stones

In the management of a resource portfolio, candidates for product or resource diversification must be evaluated in terms of their short-term balance effects (as in the product portfolio) and also in terms of their long-term capacity to function as *stepping stones* to further expansion. This ingenious strategy was attributed to the Japanese by *Business Week* (1981). Briefly, the idea is, that to enter the computer industry, it is necessary to first develop related skills in chips, an industry into which the Japanese could enter more easily, since they already possessed some of the required skills. Figure 4 illustrates this pattern.

4. Conclusion

This paper has attempted to look at firms in terms of their resources rather than in terms of their products. It was conjectured that this perspective would throw a different light on strategic options, especially those open to diversified firms.

Resource position barriers were defined as partially analogous to entry barriers. On the basis of this definition, one can sketch a picture of firms as trying to develop such barriers, perhaps through products in which already strong resources support less strong ones. This mechanism is again exploited in the resource-product matrix, which is somewhat analogous to the growth-share matrix and allows us to consider different growth paths. It should be kept in mind that the theory in the last section considered only resources of the type which are produced jointly with products. Growth strategies for other types of

RESOURCE / MARKET	Mass assembly	Consumer marketing	III	IV	Electronics technology
Chips	X				X
Stereosets	X	X			
C		X		X	
Computers			X		X

Fig. 4. Stepping stone.

resources have yet to be developed. The only general statement made about growth strategy is that in some sense it involves striking a balance between the exploitation of existing resources and the development of new ones.

The paper is meant only as a first cut at a huge can of worms. Apart from the obvious need to look at growth strategies for other types of resources, much more research needs to be done on the implementability of the strategies suggested. Nothing is known, for example, about the practical difficulties involved in identifying resources (products are easy to identify), nor about to what extent one in practice can combine capabilities across operating divisions, or about how one can set up a structure and systems which can help a firm execute these strategies.

The new focus on technology in strategy, the increasing tendency for firms to define themselves in terms of technologies, and the setting up of cross-divisional strategic organizations (Texas Instruments, 1971), technology groups, and arenas (General Electric, 1981) seem to indicate that objectives like the above are strived for, although perhaps implicitly, in several firms.

Note

This paper benefitted from comments by George Bittlingmayer, Cynthia Montgomery and two anonymous referees.

References

Andrews, K. *The Concept of Corporate Strategy*, Dow Jones-Irwin, Homewood, Ill., 1971.

Bardhan, P. K. 'On optimum subsidy to a learning industry: an aspect of the theory of infant-industry protection', *International Economic Review*, 12, 1971, pp. 54–70.

BIC Pen Corporation (A). *Intercollegiate Case Clearing House*, 1-374-305, 1974.

Boston Consulting Group. *Perspectives on Experience*, Boston Consulting Group, Boston, 1972.

Business Week, 14 December 1981.

Caves, R. E. 'Industrial organization, corporate strategy and structure', *Journal of Economic Literature*, 58, 1980, pp. 64–92.

General Electric—Strategic Position. Intercollegiate Case Clearing House, 1-381-174, 1981.

Henderson, B. D. *Henderson on Corporate Strategy*, Abt Books, Cambridge, Mass., 1979.

Panzar, J. C. and R. D. Willig. 'Economies of scope', *American Economic Review*, 71 (2), 1981, pp. 268–272.

Penrose, E. G. *The Theory of the Growth of the Firm*, Wiley, New York, 1959.

Birger Wernerfelt

Porter, M. E. *Competitive Strategy*, Free Press, New York, 1980.

Ries, A. and J. Trout. *Positioning: The Battle for Your Mind*, McGraw-Hill, New York, 1981.

Rubin, P. H. 'The expansion of firms', *Journal of Political Economy*, **81**, 1973, pp. 936–949.

Salter, M. and W. Weinhold. *Diversification by Acquisition*, Free Press, New York, 1980.

Spence, A. M. 'Investment strategy and growth in a new market', *Bell Journal of Economics*, **10**, 1979, pp. 1–19.

Texas Instruments—Management Systems. *Intercollegiate Case Clearing House*, 9-172-054, 1971.

Wernerfelt, B. 'An information based theory of microeconomics and its consequences for corporate strategy', *Unpublished Dissertation*, Harvard University, Graduate School of Business Administration, 1977.

11 Towards a Strategic Theory of the Firm

Richard P. Rumelt

I consider myself a mainstream researcher in the field of business policy, and the ideas I want to describe in this paper concern the foundations of a theory of business strategy that is rooted in economics. But is such a paper, whatever its merits, really appropriate at a conference entitled 'Non-traditional Approaches to Policy Research'? Surprisingly, it is. The use of economic theory to model and explicate business strategy, as it is understood within the field of business policy, is distinctly non-traditional.

To the uninitiated, it appears obvious that the study of business strategy must rest on the bedrock foundations of the economist's model of the firm and the theory of industrial organization. Nevertheless, until very recently, there has been a virtually complete absence of any intersection between business policy and economic theory. Few attempted a cross-fertilization between these fields; most who did reported results barren of much interest. This state of affairs did not reflect the unwillingness of policy researchers to learn economics. Rather, it came about because the neoclassical theory of the firm was created by assuming away the very existence of those phenomena that most concern students of business policy. It was sustained by the mainstream micro-economist's commitment to the position that the theory of the firm not be required to describe the actual behavior of firms.

This situation is beginning to change. The pioneering insights of Coase, Simon, and Stigler set in motion forces that are undermining the neoclassical theory.[1] Recent work by Williamson, Porter, Spence, and others demonstrates that economic concepts can model and describe strategic phenomena.[2] In this paper I want to look closely at this new confluence and suggest the outlines of a 'strategic' theory of the firm.

1. Business Policy and Neoclassical Theory

Business policy is concerned with those aspects of general management that have material effects on the survival and success of business enterprises. For about twenty years the central organizing concept in this field has been *strategy*. The concept is empirical rather than theoretical, having its roots in numerous field studies of business firms and the historical analysis of the evolution of business enterprises. In essence, the concept is that a firm's competitive position is defined by a bundle of unique resources and relationships and that the task of general management is to adjust and renew these resources and relationships as time, competition, and change erode their value. This way of looking at the firm is *not* a theory; it is a set of constructs that have proved useful in describing and summarizing the empirical studies of firm behavior that form the core of the business policy literature. Simply put, these broad empirical observations are:

1. The general managers of firms make choices, and some of these choices are considerably more important (having more impact on performance) than others.
2. Strategic choices are not necessarily explicit but may be characterized by infrequency, uncertainty, the irreversibility of commitments, and multifunctional scope, and they are usually nonrecurring.
3. The most critical strategic choices exhibited by a firm are those concerned with the selection of the product-market areas or segments in which the firm will compete and the basic approach to those businesses.
4. Similar firms facing similar strategic problems may respond differently.
5. Firms in the same industry compete with substantially different bundles of resources using disparate approaches. These firms differ because of differing histories of strategic choice and performance and because managements appear to seek asymmetric competitive positions.

What makes these apparently innocuous observations worth repeating is that they either contradict or stand completely outside the neoclassical theory of the firm and the standard models used in industrial organization.[3] For example, Cohen and Cyert's treatment of the theory of the firm begins this way:

This book concentrates on the most significant institution in our economic system—the business firm—and the most important function of our economic system—resource allocation. It is impossible to have a clear understanding of the functioning of the modern American society without knowing a great deal about the firm and the role it plays in the economy's resource allocation process.[4]

Nevertheless, in the following four hundred pages of this well-written text, few real firms are mentioned and no model is discussed in which the firm's choice problem is anything other than the selection of a price or level of output for a homogeneous product with known production and demand functions. Monopolistic competition is discussed but rejected on theoretical and empirical grounds.

The problem with the neoclassical theory is that it is not really a theory of the firm. The existence of the firm is actually problematic within the axiomatic framework of the theory and must be justified by reference to entrepreneurship as a fixed factor. What the theory actually deals with is the workings of the price system in a setting in which nothing but prices need be known. It is a powerful intellectual achievement, but that power was obtained by assuming away such phenomena as (1) transaction costs, (2) limits on rationality, (3) technological uncertainty, (4) constraints on factor mobility, (5) limits on information availability, (6) markets in which price conveys quality information, (7) consumer or producer learning, and (8) dishonest and/or foolish behavior.

In fact, many of the assumptions embodied in the neoclassical theory are only now coming to light as specialized models of markets are being investigated. One interesting example is Spence's discussion of signaling equilibria,[5] in which it is sensible to invest in otherwise useless activities in order to signal quality differentials. Another is Diamond's observation that the introduction of a small consumer search cost into a retail market model drastically alters the nature of the equilibrium.[6]

The situation with regard to industrial organization has been only marginally better. Within industrial organization there is a subschool which, like business policy, has recorded and commented on a wide variety of real-world business behavior. However, the theoretical structure of the field has never encompassed that richness. The traditional model of industry in industrial organization is taken from oligopoly theory[7] and remains that of identical firms or firms that are homogeneous but for scale. The effect of this modeling assumption has been to reduce the study of industrial competition to the study of relative scale, all other differences being ignored.

Industries differ, in the standard view, according to the degree of concentration, the presence of scale economies, and the degree of product differentiation or nonprice competition. Scale economies and product differentiation are viewed, in this framework, as properties of an industry rather than as the results achieved by firms and both are identified as barriers to entry, creating economic rents (profits that do not attract new production).

By taking the industry as the unit of analysis, industrial organization has largely ignored the theory and evidence of intra-industry differences among firms. Thus, while great efforts have gone toward explaining interindustry differences in the rate of return, it can be easily shown that the dispersion in the characteristic long-term rates of return of firms within industries is five to eight times as large as the variance in returns across industries.[8]

What has caused this mismatch between the concept of strategy and neoclassical theory? To say that the economic models are not 'realistic' would be true, but unfair and beside the point. All models in the social sciences are unrealistic; good models are specialized and simple, generating descriptions of the phenomena of interest with the fewest necessary constructs and assumptions. This mismatch arises because policy researchers and economists have been interested in substantially different phenomena. The central concerns of business policy are the observed heterogeneity of firms and the firm's choice of product-market commitments. By contrast, the basic phenomena of interest in neoclassical theory is the functioning of the price system under norms of decentralized decision making.

In the language of economics, the chief concern of business policy researchers has not been static profit maximization[9] but profit seeking through corporate entrepreneurship and with the empirical observation that corporate entrepreneurship is intimately connected with the appearance and adjustment of unique and idiosyncratic resources. This view of corporate behavior is most closely associated with Schumpeter's vision of competition as the process of 'creative destruction' rather than as a static equilibrium condition.[10] As Nelson and Winter have noted:

The core ideas of Schumpeterian theory are of course quite different from those of neoclassical theory. For Schumpeter the most important firms are those that serve as the vehicles for action of the real drivers of the system—the innovating entrepreneurs . . . The competitive environment within which firms operate is one of struggle and motion. It is a dynamic selection environment, not an equilibrium one. The essential forces of growth are innovation and selection, with augmentation of capital stocks more or less tied to these processes.[11]

Thus the concepts of entrepreneurship and resource heterogeneity, so central to business strategy, have been either omitted or taken as preexisting givens in neoclassical theory. Entrepreneurship is normally omitted because it has become by definition the repository of nonneoclassical phenomena. Entrepreneurs are seen to possess special information, to be unique, to create pure profit, and to act as the essential indivisibilities governing the size distribution of firms. Similarly, resource heterogeneity is taken to be an exogenous property of the physical world rather than an endogenous creation of economic actors. *Their omission has obscured the close logical connections between these constructs.* Without resource heterogeneity (and the equivalent of property rights to unique resources), there is little incentive for investing in the risky exploration of new methods and the search for new value. Given uncertainty, the *ex post* results of entrepreneurial activity will necessarily be resource heterogeneity. At the most primitive level, firms may simply differ in the relative efficiency with which they extract or process homogeneous goods. However, in the absence of perfect intermediate markets for these goods, firms will have incentives to integrate. Thus is born the *strategic* firm, characterized by a bundle of linked and idiosyncratic resources and resource conversion activities.

What accounts for the neglect of these important phenomena? Nordhaus and Tobin have argued that the problem is one of modeling:[12]

> Many economists agree with the broad outlines of Schumpeter's vision of capitalist development, which is a far cry from growth models made nowadays in either Cambridge, Mass. or Cambridge, England. But visions of that kind have yet to be transformed into theory that can be applied to everyday analytic and empirical work.[13]

I agree that there are substantial difficulties in creating formal models of Schumpeterian rivalry, but I do not see them as insurmountable. There may be, however, another factor deterring economists from such efforts—determining the welfare implications of Schumpeterian rivalry is markedly more difficult than modeling it. This implies that policy researchers, who are only secondarily concerned with the technical welfare implications of competitive activity, may well have a comparative advantage at producing descriptive theory in this area.

2. Uncertain Imitability and Ambiguity

This section describes a simple theory of rivalry under conditions of causal ambiguity. I and my colleague Steven Lippman have named the theory and modeling concept it embodies 'uncertain imitability.' We model entrepreneurship as the production of new production functions and generate firm heterogeneity as an outcome rather than as a given. The treatment here is only a rough sketch of the more complete theory, and interested readers are directed to the source.[14]

In neoclassical theory firms entering industries or undertaking substantial expansion efforts select their production functions from a known bundle of technological possibilities. Thus imitative attempts tend to equilibrate firm efficiencies, and long-term differences in profitability signal failures in either product or factor markets. But suppose that there exists an irreducible uncertainty connected with the creation (or production) of a new production function. Then the efficiencies achieved by entrants or major expansion programs will vary. Furthermore, if there is a nonrecoverable cost associated with such entrepreneurial activities, rational actors will stop short of seeking to imitate the best extant firm. Thus the ambiguity that generates the initial heterogeneity will also act to block its homogenization through imitation.

Uncertainty in the creation of new production functions is most likely to come about because there is ambiguity as to what the factors of production actually are and as to how they interact. The standard neoclassical assumption is that there is a finite set of known factors of production and that their marginal productivities can be discerned. However, if the precise reasons for success or failure cannot be determined, even after the event has occurred, there is causal ambiguity and it is impossible to produce an unambiguous list of the factors of production, much less measure their marginal contributions.

In order to model this situation, assume that a market exists for a homogeneous product. There is a known demand function and any entrant into the industry obtains a cost function $C(q,b)$ which is U shaped in q, the rate of output. The parameter b is a measure of relative efficiency and larger values of b imply lower unit costs. Each firm, once it is in the industry, acts as a profit-maximizing price taker. By adjusting output so that marginal cost equals the market price p, a firm with efficiency b obtains a level of profits $y(b,p)$.

If $C(q,b)$ exhibits fixed costs, firms may display negative profits when the market price falls below some level. Define $h(p)$ as the value of b that just allows the firm to break even at a market price p. Thus $y(h(p),p) = 0$, and if $b < h(p)$, the firm cannot make positive profits and is forced to withdraw from the industry.

Now assume that each entrant into the industry must pay a nonrecoverable 'entry fee' K and then receives a cost function $C(q,b)$ in which b is a realization of a random variable X with cumulative distribution F and density f. Intuitively, it should be clear that firms will enter the industry and display a variety of efficiencies. As entry continues, the price will fall, forcing some firms that have received 'poor' cost functions (low b's) out of the industry. Finally, the industry will reach a state that deters further rational entry attempts. In a sense, the final free-entry equilibrium is achieved through processes of variation and selection rather than neoclassical resource flows. In it, firms display a range of efficiencies and the most efficient display stable persistent rents.

In general it is quite difficult to characterize the final equilibrium in that the optimal entry strategy depends in detail upon the mix of extant firms at each point. For simplicity, I will assume that each entrant has a negligible independent impact on the market price.[15] Now define $V(p)$ as the expected value of entry when the prospective entrant faces an *unchanging* price p. Taking the discount rate to be r, we have

$$V(p) = -K + (1/r)y(x,p)dF(x). \qquad (1)$$
$$h(p)$$

For p sufficiently small, $V(p) < 0$ and entry is blocked—even the guarantee of a fixed price being insufficient to make entry attractive. Because V increases in p, there is a unique price $p^\star$ that solves $V(p) = 0$, and atomism ensures that the final entry-blocking equilibrium price will only be infinitesimally less than $p^\star$. Each prospective entrant can therefore expect to receive at least $V(p^\star)$ and entry will proceed as long as $p > p^\star$.

When the price is $p^\star$, the minimum b necessary for survival is $b^\star = h(p^\star)$. Firms in the final equilibrium will be those that received values of b greater than $b^\star$. Thus the probability P_s that an entrant will survive the selection process and be a member of the final equilibrium is

$$P_s = 1 - F(b^\star). \qquad (2)$$

The distribution F_s of survivor's b's is $F(x)/P_s$ for $x > b^\star$ and zero otherwise. Survivors of the selection process earn profits $y_s(b,p^\star)$ in perpetuity and the expected level of survivor's profit is

$$Ey_s = \frac{1}{P_s} \int_{b^\star}^{\infty} y(x, P^\star) dF(x). \qquad (3)$$

Combining (1) with (3) and the condition $V(p^\star) = 0$ gives

$$Ey_s = rK/P_s \qquad (4)$$

and defining survivors' rents as $R_s = Ey_s - rK$ reveals that

$$R_s = rK(1 - P_s)/P_s \qquad (5)$$

From (5) it is clear that the average survivor (and the industry as a whole) displays positive economic profits in equilibrium despite price-taking behavior and free entry. These rents are created by the failure of other firms to survive: if $P_s = 1$, then $R_s = 0$. More precisely, for each survivor there are $(1 - P_s)/P_s$ firms that fail to survive, each suffering a loss K. Consequently the net expected profit from an entry attempt is zero, and the survivor's rents exactly balance the failure's losses.

Another way of looking at (5) is that selection pressure ensures that the 'average' entrepreneur will earn below-average profits. Indeed, if P_s is low enough, the mean of X will fall below $b^\star$ and the average entry attempt will not only earn poor profits but fail to survive.

In this equilibrium the extant firms have been selected for their unusual efficiency at production, and no outsider can expect to beat them at their own game. This result does not depend upon scale economies or sunk costs. Rather, it is the natural

Richard Rumelt

consequence of a nonneoclassical selection-based equilibrium. In the language of business policy, the more-efficient firms have 'created' or discovered unique skills and strengths and will maximize their values by seeking other areas of activity wherein these special skills may also be of value.

What are the implications of increased riskiness? Figure 1 shows the shape of $y_s(b,p^*)$. Note that if y_s is not convex in b for $b > b^*$, it is always possible to find a monotone function $b \to b_1$ together with its associated distribution and density functions, such that $y_s(b_1,p)$ is convex. This means that it is the riskiness of y rather than b that carries economic meaning. For simplicity, assume that the parameterization of $C(q,b)$ is chosen so that $y_s(b,p^*)$ is linear in b for $b > b^*$.

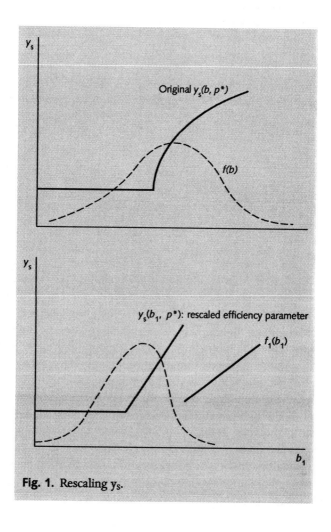

Fig. 1. Rescaling y_s.

138

Given y_s convex in b, it can be seen from (1) that mean-preserving increases in the spread of F (or increases in variance) will tend to *decrease* the equilibrium price p^*. Equivalently, were such a pure increase in riskiness available privately to a prospective entrant, it would *increase* the expected value of that entry attempt. This 'risk-loving' behavior also occurs in the case of call options; *ceteris paribus*, the owner of a call option prefers mean-preserving increases in risk to decreases. The principle also applies to the levered firm, a mean-preserving increase in risk shifting wealth from bondholders to stockholders.

3. A Theory of Firm Size

The relationship between riskiness and private value has interesting implications for the optimal scope of entrepreneurial firms or risky projects. To begin, notice that irreversibly combining two separate entry attempts (paying $2K$ and receiving costs $C(b_1,q_1) + C(b_2,q_2)$) is never attractive. Intuitively, the relative draws from F are independent so that the relative riskiness has decreased, making the expected value of entry negative. Irreversibly combining two entry attempts would only be efficient if the draws from F could be guaranteed to be completely correlated. These considerations suggest that the entrepreneur's problem is not only to decide whether or not to enter but also to assemble the appropriate mix of assets for the attempt.

Which activities should the entrepreneur combine? The general answer is, *Those that will exhibit strongly dependent postentry efficiencies.* Given a bundle of activities with total postentry efficiency determined by the random variable X, adding new activities that involve sunk costs can never be profitable if their efficiencies are uncorrelated with X. Thus new activities are added until the point where further additions would not add sufficiently large expected profits or profit variance to justify the added sunk capital.

Note that this logic is opposite to that underlying diversification. Here the entrepreneur's objective is not to reduce risk, as the expected level of efficiency provides an inadequate return. Rather, the entrepreneur is attempting to concentrate only on those activities that are closely connected with success or failure in the market. Adding extraneous activities not only produces an unnecessary increase in the costs of failure but also may obscure important information regarding the success of the main endeavor.

Interestingly, *this perspective provides a theory of firm size that does not depend upon diseconomies of scale or control loss and is only tangentially related to the notion of a fixed entrepreneurial factor.* In addition, it explains why diversification, which reduces the risk of bankruptcy, is rarely undertaken by those facing the greatest risk—entrepreneurs entering or creating new markets.

4. Selection, Adaptation, and Isolating Mechanisms

Given uncertain imitability, in equilibrium the average firm earns positive economic profit and is more efficient at what it is doing than a new entrant should expect to be. Were this not true, entry would proceed until it was true. If the equilibrium is permeated by heterogeneous firms with evolved local advantages, there are a number of immediate implications. Among the most straightforward are these:

1. New entry activity will essentially be a function of market growth rather than industry profitability. High levels of profitability in stable markets may well signal incumbents possessing difficult-to-imitate skills and deter entry.
2. Firms that are successful in one endeavor will tend to seek out related activities in which their revealed special competences are useful.[16] Hence profitability and growth will be correlated even when the effects of demand pull are controlled.
3. If the basis for success in a market shifts to a new function, firms that have been successful in the past may now be at a disadvantage relative to outside firms possessing demonstrated skills related to the new required competence.

In industrial organization theory a barrier to entry exists when a prospective entrant is at a disadvantage relative to an incumbent.[17] In an important paper, Caves and Porter extend the entry barrier concept by defining *mobility barriers* as asymmetries among firms within industries that act to limit differential expansion and the equalization of profit rates.[18] Their emphasis on heterogeneity deserves special attention:

Limits on entry and limits on mobility remain stubbornly immiscible as long as we stick to conventional thinking about cost functions and intra-industry differences among firms. The conventional approach takes firms within an industry as identical in all economically important respects except for their size. Then cost conditions either define an optimal scale for the firm, leaving no explanation why size should change, or render scale indeterminate, providing no clue as to what could deter infinitesimal changes in a firm's scale. . . . The key to conjoining barriers to entry to a more general theory of interscale mobility of firms is the hypothesis that sellers within an industry are likely to differ systematically in traits other than size.[19]

In Caves and Porter's view, industries can be broken into *groups* of firms that exhibit distinct characteristics (e.g., broad-line vs. specialist). Mobility barriers both define these groups and are reinforced by the strategic activities of group members. The group concept is frequently all that is needed, but there is no theoretical reason to limit mobility barriers to groups of firms. I shall therefore use the term *isolating mechanism* to refer to phenomena that limit the *ex post* equilibration of rents among individual firms.

In the pure theory of uncertain imitability, the isolating mechanism is causal ambiguity. The inability of economic agents to fully understand the causes of efficiency differences limits competition by entry or imitation. However, many other isolating mechanisms exist. For example, mineral rights laws convert the results of risky exploration investments into *ex ante* uncertain but *ex post* persistent streams of rent. Similarly, patents, trademarks, reputation, and brand image serve to limit second-mover imitation of first-mover success. These and other important isolating mechanisms are listed in Table 1.

The importance of isolating mechanisms in business strategy is that they are the phenomena that make competitive positions stable and defensible. Many of them appear as first-mover advantages. For example, the first firm to commit idiosyncratic capital to serving a small market segment may gain a stable position serving that segment. From an equilibrium perspective, such events are inherently uncertain. That is, the existence of the market may have been problematic, the technology may have been uncertain, the information necessary to make the early move may have been unpredictably distributed, or by first-mover we may simply mean the first successful mover.

Although isolating mechanisms provide (*ex post*) stable streams of rent, the opportunities to create, 'jump behind,' or otherwise exploit them must arise from unexpected changes. Without uncertainty there is no wedge between the *ex ante* price of an asset or market position and its *ex post* value. It is the juxtaposition of isolating mechanisms with uncertainty that permits the modeling of heterogeneity in an equilibrium framework.

Table 1. Elements of strategic position

Sources of Potential Rents	Isolating Mechanisms
Changes in technology	Causal ambiguity
Changes in relative prices	Specialized assets
Changes in consumer tastes	Switching and search costs
Changes in law, tax, and regulation	Consumer and producer learning
Discoveries and inventions	Team-embodied skills
	Unique resources
	Special information
	Patents and trademarks
	Reputation and image
	Legal restrictions on entry

Table 1 emphasizes this point by also showing the important sources of potential rents. They are essentially unexpected changes in the environment. Thus Table 1 presents a simple theory of strategy: *a firm's strategy may be explained in terms of the unexpected events that created (or will create) potential rents together with the isolating mechanisms that (will) act to preserve them.* If either element of the explanation is missing, the analysis is inadequate.

....

5. Implications for Normative Theory

Are there normative implications of this view of strategy or does it place the fortunes of the firm in the hands of exogenous events and impersonal isolating mechanisms? My view is that there are very real normative implications and they can be based on much sounder theory than much of the currently popular prescription.

First, it should be clear that a firm's stability and profitability fundamentally depend upon entrepreneurial activity. There cannot be a simple algorithm for creating wealth. Still, it is true that some ways of approaching the problem of strategy will be more fruitful than others. In particular, these points deserve emphasis:

1. The opportunities for strategic change occur infrequently, and their timing is largely beyond the control of management. The chance to substantially improve one's competitive position does not arise out of pricing or advertising tactics, but the recognition of change in some underlying factor.
2. Unexpected events may change the distribution of sales and profits within an industry, acting as windfall gains and losses to incumbents. It is vital that management recognize and take full advantage of these events. The routine component of strategy formulation is the constant search for ways in which the firm's unique resources can be redeployed in changing circumstances.
3. More fundamental shocks act to change the very structure of the industry, altering the nature and magnitudes of the isolating mechanisms at work. Examples of such events are airline deregulation, the advent of small computers, and the impact of oil prices on the world automobile market. In such situations it is usually unclear what the eventual structure of the industry will be. Firms that are lucky or insightful enough to make early commitments to what turn out to be defensible positions can be stunningly suc-

cessful. The implication is that a developmental theory of industry structure would be of significant value.

4. A critical strategic question in a growth industry is the shape of the final equilibrium. When industry growth is rapid, profit rates are normally quite high, but reinvestment rates that are even higher work to produce net negative cash flows. If firms misjudged the strength of isolating mechanisms in the final equilibrium, the slowing of growth will bring profit rates to below-normal rates; the industry will have functioned as a cash trap. Theory and empirical work on this issue would have obvious normative value.

5. If opportunities for significant shifts in strategic position are infrequent, and if isolating mechanisms create defensible positions, it follows that many firms can ignore strategy for long periods of time and still appear profitable. As a corollary, high levels of profitability are not necessarily an indicator of good management. If a strategic position is strong enough, even fools can churn out good results (for a while).

6. Because strategic opportunities are by definition uncertain and connected to the possession of unique information or resources, strategy analysis must be situational. Just as there is no algorithm for creating wealth, strategic prescriptions that apply to broad classes of firms can only aid in avoiding mistakes, not in attaining advantage.

7. Because isolating mechanisms act to protect the first successful mover, speed is critical despite (and, in fact, because of) high levels of ambiguity. Good strategy is not necessarily enacted with a high level of initial confidence, although general management may appear confident in order to spur action. If firms wait until the proper method entering a market or producing a product is fully understood it will normally be too late to take advantage of the information.

---

6. Conclusions

The thesis presented in this paper is that it is both possible and fruitful to attempt formal modeling of Schumpeterian, or strategic, competition. One way this can be done is to model entrepreneurs as rational maximizers with bounded knowledge, making explicit the fact that our causal models of the physical and social worlds are incomplete and frequently in error. The model of uncertain imitability is an example of this approach.

By viewing strategy as entrepreneurship that both depends upon and creates interfirm heterogeneity, I have generated a number of propositions concerning the behavior of populations of firms. I have also drawn implications for normative theory. In particular, the area in which progress would be most valuable appears to be the creation of a developmental model of industry structure.

Notes

1. Ronald Coase, 'The Nature of the Firm,' *Economics*, 4 (November 1937), 386–405; H. A. Simon, *Administrative Behavior*, 2nd ed. (New York: Macmillan, 1961); and George J. Stigler, 'The Economics of Information,' *Journal of Political Economy*, 69 (June 1961), pp. 213–25.
2. Oliver E. Williamson, *Markets and Hierarchies: Analysis and Antitrust implications* (New York: Free Press, 1975); Michael E. Porter, *Competitive Strategy* (New York: Free Press, 1980), and A. M. Spence, 'Investment, Strategy, and Growth in a New Market,' *Bell Journal of Economics*, 10 (Spring 1979).
3. They also contradict the environmental determinism viewpoint in organizational sociology. It is an intriguing example of disciplinary chauvinsim that organization sociologists tend to attribute the straightforward notion that senior management's choices influence the selection of an organization's tasks and internal structure to Child's strong reminder on this point. See John Child, 'Organization Structure, Environment and Performance—The Role of Strategic Choice,' *Sociology*, 6 (January 1972), pp. 1–22.
4. Kalman J. Cohen and Richard M. Cyert, *Theory of the Firm: Resource Allocation in a Market Economy* (Englewood Cliffs, N.J.: Prentice-Hall, 1965), p. 3.
5. A. M. Spence, *Market Signaling: Informational Transfer in Hiring and Related Processes* (Cambridge, Mass.: Harvard University Press, 1974).
6. Peter A. Diamond, 'A Model of Price Adjustment,' *Journal of Economic Theory*, 3 (1971), pp. 156–68.
7. In this regard it is important to note that oligopoly theory, far from providing a predictive model of firm behavior, represents the 'edge' of economics in that a profit-maximizing assumption fails to define behavior. Oligopoly models are constructed by first assuming a pattern of behavior and then deducing the form of the resultant equilibrium, if one exists.
8. See R. P. Rumelt, 'How Important Is Industry in Explaining Firm Profitability?' U.C.L.A., 1981.
9. The standard attack on the neoclassical theory has centered on the assumption of profit maximization. According to the behavioral theory of the firm explicated by Cyert and March, managers are only intendedly rational. Bounds on their information-processing capacities prevent firms from acting as true profit maximizers. Baumol's somewhat different argument is that the quantity corporations act to maximize is not really profits but sales (or growth, or some measure of manager's welfare). Current fashion terms these adjustments to the neoclassical model as highlighting information costs, computation costs, and agency problems. See

Richard M. Cyert and James G. March, *A Behavioral Theory of the Firm* (Englewood Cliffs, N.J.: Prentice-Hall, 1963); and William J. Baumol, *Business Behavior, Value and Growth* (New York: Macmillan, 1959).

10. J. A. Schumpeter, *The Theory of Economic Development* (Cambridge, Mass.: Harvard University Press, 1934; original publication 1911).

11. R. R. Nelson, and S. G. Winter, 'Neoclassical vs. Evolutionary Theories of Economic Growth: Critique and Prospectus,' *Economic Journal*, 84 (December 1974), p. 890.

12. W. Nordhaus, and J. Tobin, 'Is Growth Obsolete?' in *Economic Research: Retrospect and Prospect, Economic Growth*, Ed. R. Gordon (New York: National Bureau of Economic Resarch, 1972), p. 2.

13. Also quoted in Nelson and Winter, 'Neoclassical vs. Evolutionary Theories,' p. 889.

14. S. A. Lippman, and R. P. Rumelt, 'Uncertain Imitability: An Analysis of Interfirm Differences in Efficiency under Competition,' *Bell Journal of Economics*, 13 (1982), pp. 418–38.

15. The nonatomistic free-entry equilibrium can be characterized if firms do not drop out of the industry. This result is obtained if fixed costs are zero, sunk, or scaled with the rest of the firm. With this specification, entry produces a renewal process in total industry capacity. For details, see Lippman and Rumelt, 'Uncertain Imitability.'

16. Strictly speaking, a resource or competence will be fully utilized in one sphere of activity if it is a factor of production for a perfect commodity. However, if firm size is limited by differentiation, segmentation, and other exogenous sources of declining marginal revenue, unique factors may not be fully utilized in a single activity.

17. Defining an entry barrier precisely is no simple task. Perhaps the most straightforward approach is to define it by its results—persistent surplus profits that do not induce entry. Stigler suggests that entry barriers exist when entrants would bear costs not borne by incumbents. This definition neatly separates the impact of scale economies, which are available to any producer, from sunk costs (idiosyncratic investment), which must enter into the entrant's prospective cost calculations but not those of the incumbent. See George J. Stigler, *The Organization of Industry* (Homewood, Ill.: Richard D. Irwin, 1968).

18. R. E. Caves, and M. E. Porter, 'From Entry Barriers to Mobility Barriers: Conjectural Decisions and Contrived Deterrence to New Competition,' *Quarterly Journal of Economics*, May 1977, pp. 241–61.

19. Ibid., p. 250.

12 Strategic Factor Markets: Expectations, Luck, and Business Strategy

Jay B. Barney

1. Introduction

Research on corporate growth through acquisitions and mergers suggests the existence of markets for buying and selling companies (Porter 1980, p. 350; Schall 1972; Mossin 1973; Copeland and Weston 1979). Most empirical evidence seems to suggest that these markets are reasonably competitive. That is, the price an acquiring firm will generally have to pay to acquire a firm in these markets is approximately equal to the discounted present value of the acquired firm (Mandelkar 1974; Halpern 1973; Ellert 1976). Indeed, if above normal returns accrue to anyone in markets for companies, research seems to suggest that they will most likely go to the stockholders of the acquired, rather than the acquiring firms (Porter 1980, p. 352; Ellert 1976).

To suggest that, on average, acquiring firms cannot expect above normal returns from their investments in corporate acquisitions is not the same as suggesting that no firms ever experience such returns. Indeed, to the extent that imperfect competition in these markets exists or can be created, acquiring firms may be able to obtain such returns. Porter (1980, pp. 353–354) has isolated several such competitive imperfections.

From a broader perspective, markets for companies are just one example of strategic factor markets. Whenever the implementation of a strategy requires the acquisition of resources, a strategic factor market develops. These markets are where firms buy and sell the resources necessary to implement their strategies (Hirshleifer 1980). In the case of markets for companies, firms wishing to implement a strategy of product diversification may decide to do so by acquiring other firms. In this sense, because an acquired firm is the resource required to implement a firm's diversification strategy, the market for companies is a strategic factor market.

All strategies that require the acquisition of resources for implementation have strategic factor markets associated with them. Thus, for the strategy of being a low cost producer, a resource necessary for implementation may include, among other resources, large market share (Henderson 1979), and a relevant strategic factor market may be the market for market share (Rumelt and Wensley 1981). For a strategy of low volume, high margin sales (Porter 1980), a relevant resource may be a quality reputation, and a relevant strategic factor market may be the market for corporate reputations (Klein, Crawford, and Alchian 1978). For a strategy of being a product innovator, a relevant resource might be research and development skill (Thompson and Strickland 1980), and relevant strategic factor markets may include the labor market for research scientists (Hirshleifer 1980). For most strategies, management skill will be a resource required for successful implementation (Porter 1980). Thus, in this sense, managerial and other labor markets can also be strategic factor markets.

The existence of strategic factor markets has important implications for returns to product market strategies implemented by firms, for the size of the returns to product market strategies will depend on the cost of the resources necessary to implement them. And the cost of these resources will depend on the competitive characteristics of the relevant strategic factor markets. If strategic factor markets are perfectly competitive, then the full value of product market strategies will be anticipated when the resources necessary to implement these strategies are acquired, and firms will only be able to obtain normal returns from acquiring strategic resources and implementing strategies. Firms can only obtain greater than normal returns from implementing their product market strategies when the cost of resources to implement those strategies is significantly less than their economic value, i.e., when firms create or exploit competitive imperfections in strategic factor markets.

From a normative point of view, the existence of strategic factor markets suggests the importance of developing a conceptual framework that firms can use to anticipate and exploit competitive imperfections in strategic factor markets. Such a framework would assist firms in choosing high return product market strategies to implement. The primary objective of this paper is to begin to develop such a conceptual framework.

We develop our discussion of the competitive implications of strategic factor markets in two parts. In the first part, we argue that firms that wish to obtain expected above normal returns from implementing product market strategies must be consistently better informed concerning the future value of those strategies than other firms acting in the same strategic factor markets. We also argue that other apparent sources of advantage in strategy implementation are, in fact, either a manifestation of these special insights into the future value of strategies, or a manifestation of a firm's good fortune and luck. In the second part of the paper, we outline some ways that firms can become better informed about the future value of strategies being implemented, including through the analysis of a firm's competitive environment and through the analysis of its unique skills and capabilities. We conclude that environmental analysis, by itself, cannot create the required unique insights, while in some circumstances, the analysis of a firm's unique skills and capabilities can. In a final section, our arguments are summarized and some of their implications for the practice and theory of strategy are discussed.

2. Competitive Imperfections in Strategic Factor Markets

2.1 Perfect Strategic Factor Market Competition

When firms seeking to acquire resources to implement a strategy (strategizers) and firms who currently own or control these resources (controllers) have exactly the same, and perfectly accurate, expectations about the future value of product market strategies before they are actually implemented, then the price of the resources needed to implement these strategies will approximately equal their value once they are actually implemented. This is a conclusion of normal returns consistent with all perfect information models of competition where no competitive uncertainty exists (Hirshleifer 1980). Under these perfect expectation conditions, controllers will never sell their resources if the full value of those resources is not reflected in their price, nor will strategizers pay a price for a resource greater than its value in actually implementing a strategy. In such markets, all pure profits that could have been had when the strategy in question was implemented will be anticipated and competed away.

2.2 Expectations in Strategic Factor Markets

These perfect competition dynamics, and the normal returns from implementing strategies they imply, depend, of course, on the very strong assumption that all strategizer and controller firms have the same, and perfectly accurate, expectations concerning the future value of strategies. This is a condition that is not likely to exist very often in real strategic factor markets. More commonly, different firms in these markets will have different expectations about the future value of a strategy. These differences reflect uncertainty in the competitive environments facing firms. Because of these differences, some firm expectations will be more accurate than others, although firms will typically not know, with certainty, ahead of time how accurate their expectations are. When different firms have different expectations concerning the future value of a strategy, it will often be possible for some strategizing firms to obtain above normal returns from acquiring the resources necessary to implement a product market strategy, and then implementing that strategy.

Consider first the return potential of a firm that has more accurate expectations concerning the future value of a particular strategy than other firms. Two likely possibilities exist. On the one hand, several other firms might overestimate a strategy's return potential. This overestimation will typically lead to strategic factor market entry, competition, and the setting of a price for the relevant strategic resource *greater* than the actual value of that resource when it is used to implement a strategy. In this situation, firms with more accurate expectations concerning the return potential of a strategy will usually not enter the strategic factor market, for they will believe that in doing so they will probably sustain an economic loss by paying more for a strategic resource than that resource is worth in implementing a strategy. Thus, in the long run, firms with more accurate expectations will usually be able to avoid economic losses associated with buying overpriced strategic resources. Firms that do acquire these overpriced resources suffer from the 'winner's curse,' i.e., the fact that they successfully acquire the resources in question suggests that they overbid (Bazerman and Samuelson 1983).

The second possibility facing firms with more accurate expectations is that other firms, rather than overestimating the return potential of a strategy, might underestimate that strategy's true future value. Entry and competition in the strategic factor market would, in this case, typically lead to a strategic resource price less than the actual future value of the strategy. In this situation, firms with more accurate expectations about the future value of the strategy in question will enter the strategic factor market and will pay the same for the relevant strategic resource as firms with less accurate (i.e., pessimistic) expectations. Firms with more accurate expectations will not be able to buy the relevant resource for less because of the inaccurate expectations held by ill-informed controllers and strategizers. And firms with more accurate expectations will certainly not want to buy these resources for more. As strategies are implemented, equal above normal returns will accrue to all those firms that acquired the resource and implemented the strategy, the well informed and ill-informed alike.

Thus, on the one hand, firms with more accurate expectations concerning the future value of a strategy can avoid economic losses due to the optimistic expectations of other firms. On the other hand, these firms will also be able to anticipate and exploit any opportunities for above normal returns in strategic factor markets when they exist. Thus, by avoiding losses and exploiting profit opportunities, these firms, over the long run, can expect to perform better than firms with less accurate expectations about the future value of strategies.

Despite the advantages of having a superior understanding of a strategy's return potential when acquiring the resources necessary to implement that strategy, firms without this superior insight can still obtain above normal returns when acquiring resources to implement strategies. This can occur when several of these firms underestimate the return potential of a strategy. Because of this underestimation, the price of the resources necessary to implement a strategy will be less than the actual future value of the strategy. In this sense, these firms are able to buy a strategy generated cash flow for less than the value of that cash flow. This is one definition of an above normal return. However, this above normal return must be a manifestation of these firms' good fortune and luck, for the price of the strategic resource acquired was based on expectations about the return potential of that strategy. Returns greater than what were expected are, by definition, unexpected. Unexpected superior economic returns are just that, unexpected, a surprise, and a manifestation of a firm's good luck, not of its ability to accurately anticipate the future value of a strategy.

Even well-informed firms can be lucky in this manner. Whenever *actual* returns to a strategy are greater than *expected* returns, the resulting difference is a manifestation of a firm's unexpected good fortune. The more accurate a firm's expectations about a strategy's return potential, the less of a role luck will play in generating above normal returns. In the extreme, though probably very rare, case where a firm knows with certainty the return potential of a strategy before that strategy is implemented, there can be no unexpected returns to that firm from implementing strategies, and thus no financial surprises. However, to the extent that a firm has less than perfect expectations, luck can play a role in determining a firm's returns to implementing its strategies.

2.3 Other Apparent Competitive Imperfections

Firms with consistently more accurate expectations concerning the return potential of strategies they are implementing can expect to enjoy higher returns from implementing their strategies over the long run. In this sense, differences in firm expectations constitute a strategic factor market competitive imperfection.

Some have suggested that other differences between firms, besides differences in firm expectations, can create competitive imperfections in strategic factor markets. These firm differences, it is thought, can prevent certain firms from implementing strategies that other firms can implement. However, close analysis of these other differences between firms suggests that, to the extent that they constitute competitive imperfections in strategic factor markets, they are actually a manifestation of different expectations firms hold about the future value of strategies being implemented. In this sense, differences in firm expectations are the central source of above normal returns from acquiring resources from strategic factor markets to implement product market strategies. To see how other firm differences that can apparently give firms competitive advantages in strategic factor markets are actually manifestations of differences in firm expectations, consider the following examples.

Lack of Separation

It has been suggested that a competitive imperfection in a strategic factor market exists when a small number of firms seeking to implement a strategy already control all the resources necessary to implement it (Thompson and Strickland 1980). In this setting, these firms do not need to buy the resources necessary to implement a strategy, and thus apparently stand in some competitive advantage. An example of this lack of separation might include a uniquely well-managed firm seeking to implement a low cost manufacturing strategy. Such a firm already controls most, if not all, the resources necessary to implement such a strategy and thus is at an advantage compared to firms that would have to improve their efficiency in order to implement such a strategy (Porter 1980). However, from another point of view, whether or not a lack of separation between strategizers and controllers of this type is a competitive imperfection depends on the expectational characteristics of earlier strategic factor markets.

Firms begin their history with a relatively small endowment of strategy relevant resources (Lippman and Rumelt 1982; Kimberly and Miles 1981). Most resources for implementing strategies must be acquired from a firm's environment at some point in a firm's history (Pfeffer and Salancik 1978; Hannan and Freeman 1977). Once acquired, they can be combined and recombined in a variety of ways to implement different strategies. It certainly may be the case that a firm, some time ago, acquired the resources necessary to implement some strategy that it would now like to implement. If the value of these resources in their current strategic use was anticipated by strategizers and controllers at the time it was originally acquired, then these resources would have been priced at a competitive level. Thus, no competitive imperfection currently exists, even though the firm controls all the resources necessary to implement a strategy, because these resources were competitively priced in a previous strategic factor market.

If, as seems more likely, the resource was acquired for one purpose, and only recently did its value in implementing another strategy become known, then its current value was unanticipated when the resource was acquired. That is, this original strategic factor market was imperfectly competitive because of imperfect expectations held by firms at that time. Thus, any current above normal returns to a firm because it controls all the resources necessary to implement a strategy are attributable to this prior imperfectly competitive strategic factor market. From our previous discussion of expectations in such markets, we can conclude that either the firm in question had more accurate expectations about the ultimate value of these strategic resources when they were acquired, or that this firm did not expect these current advantages when the resources were acquired, in which case its current above normal returns from implementing a strategy are a manifestation of its good luck.

Uniqueness

Others have argued that when only one firm can implement a strategy, then a strategic factor market competitive imperfection exists. Such a firm may have a unique history or constellation of other assets, and thus may uniquely be able to pursue a strategy. IBM, for example, has a very large installed base of users that allows it to implement strategies that cannot be implemented by firms, like Honeywell and Burroughs, without such a base (Peters and Waterman 1982). In such settings, competitive dynamics cannot unfold, and uniquely strategizing firms could obtain above normal performance from acquiring strategic resources and implementing strategies.

However, as before, a firm's uniqueness is actually a manifestation of the expectational attributes of a previous strategic factor market. The key issues become, how did the strategizing firm obtain the unique assets that allow it to develop the unique strategy it is implementing, what price did this firm have to pay for these assets, and what price must potential strategizers pay in order to reproduce this set of organizational assets so that they can enter and create a competitive strategic factor market? If the current value of 'unique' resources in implementing a strategy was anticipated at the time those resources were acquired, then they would have been competitively priced, and any anticipated above normal returns would have been competed away. Thus, any current above normal returns enjoyed by a firm because of its ability to uniquely implement a strategy must either be a reflection of that firm's more accurate expectations of the value of that resource when it was acquired or, if the firm had no special expectations concerning the value of the resource when it was acquired, these above normal returns are a manifestation of a firm's good fortune and luck.

Lack of Entry

Another source of an apparent competitive imperfection in a strategic factor market exists when firms that could enter such a market by becoming strategizers do not do so. This lack of entry, however, like separation and uniqueness, is actually a special case of the expectations firms hold about the future value of strategies. Lack of entry might occur for one of at least three reasons. First, firms that, in principle, could enter, might not because they are not attempting to act in a profit maximizing manner. Second, potential strategizers may not have sufficient financial strength to enter a strategic factor market and compete for strategic resource. Finally, firms that, in principle, could enter, may not know how to, for they may not understand the return generating characteristics of the strategies that current strategizers are implementing. We will consider each of these possibilities in order.

Profit Maximizing

While certain examples of firms in strategic factor markets not behaving in profit maximizing ways can be cited (Porter 1980, p. 354), overall this is probably a rare event. Usually, firms do not knowingly abandon profit maximizing behavior (Hirshleifer 1980), although firms can be mistaken in their expectations about the potential value of a strategy (Roll 1985). These incorrect expectations could lead them to fail to enter a strategic factor market when more correct expectations would suggest that entry was appropriate. But this lack of entry is typically due to a firm's imperfect expectations about the true value of a strategy, not the abandonment of profit maximizing behavior (Roll 1985).

Financial Strength

Another apparent strategic factor market competitive imperfection exists when only a few firms have enough financial backing to enter a strategic factor market and attempt to acquire the resources needed to implement a product market strategy. Because only a few firms are competing for the relevant strategic resources, perfect competition dynamics are less likely to unfold, and it may be possible to obtain above normal economic returns from using the acquired resources to implement a strategy. IBM may, once again, be an example of a firm with this type of financial advantage, for its vast financial resources allow it to engage in strategic behaviors not possible for smaller firms.

However, even such large differences in financial strength typically reflect expectational differences in strategic factor markets rather than differences between the financial strengths of firms, per se. Two ways in which differences in financial strength represent these differences in firm expectations are considered below.

First, in some circumstances, the actual future value of a given strategy may be the same for whatever firm implements it. In this case, if capital markets are efficient and well informed concerning the actual future value of a strategy, then funds will flow to firms wishing to enter a strategic factor market with anticipated above normal returns. Sources of capital will recognize the possibility of above normal returns and will provide whatever funds are necessary to ensure that potential strategizers will enter and become actual strategizers (Copeland and Weston, 1979). The same holds true for controllers. In this way, competition within a strategic factor market will grow, and any anticipated pure profit will approach zero. This entry will only *not* occur if capital sources are underinformed about the possibility that firms can obtain above normal returns from acquiring resources to implement a strategy. In this situation, potential strategizers and controllers would not be able to obtain adequate financial backing from underinformed sources of capital to enter into the strategic factor market. This lack of entry creates the possibility of pure profits for firms that do enter.

However, when are capital sources likely to be underinformed concerning the anticipated returns from implementing a strategy? If potential strategizers and controllers are as well informed as actual strategizers and controllers, then it seems likely that the relevant information needed to generate return expectations falls into the general category of 'publicly available information,' and thus would be taken into consideration by capital sources in making funding decisions (Fama 1970; Copeland and Weston 1979). Thus, only when actual strategizers and controllers have expectational advantages over potential strategizers and controllers is it likely that sources of capital will be underinformed. Thus, in this case, the lack of entry into a strategic factor market due to insufficient financial backing is, once again, a reflection of the expectational advantages enjoyed by some firms in a strategic factor market.

In an efficient capital market, when the actual future value of strategies does not depend on which firm implements them, then the inability of firms to attract sufficient financial support to enter and compete for strategic resources must reflect differences in expectations among current and potentially competing firms. However, sometimes a strategy implemented by one firm will have a greater future value than that same strategy implemented by other firms. In this situation, and under the assumption of efficient and well-informed capital markets, capital will flow to high return potential firms, while low return potential firms may not receive such financial backing (Copeland and

Weston 1979). This lack of financial backing may prevent entry, and thus constitute a competitive imperfection in a strategic factor market.

However, when can one firm implementing a strategy obtain higher returns than other firms implementing that same strategy? The answer must be that the higher return firm already controls other strategically relevant assets not controlled by firms with a lower return potential (Chamberlin 1933; Copeland and Weston 1979). Thus, this firm's ability to attract financial backing is a reflection of its unique portfolio of strategically valuable assets and resources, resources not controlled by low return potential firms. In this sense, lack of entry is simply a special case of a firm implementing a unique strategy, and our previous discussion of expectations in strategic factor markets applies here as well. In short, firms with unique resources that give them a higher return potential are either exploiting special insights they had into the future value of those resources when those resources were acquired, or, if they enjoyed no such insights, they are simply enjoying their good fortune.

Lack of Understanding

The final reason entry might not occur is that entrants may not understand the return generating processes underlying a strategy. Firms form their return expectations about specific strategies based on their understanding of the economic return generating processes underlying these strategies, i.e., on their understanding of the cause and effect relations between organizational actions and economic returns (Lippman and Rumelt 1982). Some of this understanding may be of the 'learning by doing' variety (Williamson 1975), and thus not available to potential strategizers and controllers. When potential entrants do not understand the relationship between organizational actions and returns as well as current actors in a strategic factor market, potential entrants are likely to incorrectly estimate the true value of strategies. If they underestimate this value, then these firms will not enter the strategic factor market, even when expectations set with a more complete understanding of a strategy's return generating processes would suggest that entry was appropriate. Again, this lack of entry, and the competitive imperfection that it might create, reflects the different expectations firms have about the return potential of strategies to be implemented.

3. Developing Insights into Strategic Value

Thus far we have argued that, in perfectly competitive strategic factor markets, the cost of the resources necessary to implement a strategy will approximately equal the discounted present value of that strategy once it is implemented. We have also argued that competitive imperfections in this market can give firms opportunities for obtaining above normal returns when implementing strategies, but that the existence of these imperfections depends on different firms having different expectations concerning the future value of a strategy. Other apparent competitive imperfections in strategic factor markets, including lack of separation, uniqueness, and lack of entry, in fact, reflect the expectational characteristics of either current or previous strategic factor markets.

In imperfectly competitive strategic factor markets, firms can obtain above normal returns from acquiring the resources necessary to implement strategies in one or a combination of two ways. First, firms with consistently more accurate expectations about the future value of a strategy than other firms can use these insights to avoid economic losses and obtain economic profits when acquiring resources to implement strategies. Second, firms can obtain above normal returns through luck when they underestimate the true future value of a strategy. Thus, because luck is, by definition, out of a firm's control, an important question for managers becomes, 'How can firms become consistently better informed about the value of strategies they are implementing than any other firms?' Firms that are successful at doing this can, over time, expect to obtain higher returns from implementing strategies than less well-informed firms, although, as always, firms can be lucky.

There are fundamentally two possible sources of the informational advantages necessary to develop consistently more accurate insights into the value of strategies: the analysis of a firm's competitive environment and the analysis of organizational skills and capabilities already controlled by a firm (Barney 1985a,b; Porter 1980; Stevenson 1976; Lenz 1980). We briefly consider each of these possibilities below.

3.1 Environmental Analysis

Of these two sources of insights into the future value of strategies, environmental analysis seems less likely to systematically generate the expectational advantages needed to obtain expected above normal returns. This is because both the methodologies for collecting this information (Porter 1980; Thompson and Strickland 1979) and the conceptual models for analyzing it (e.g., Porter 1980; Henderson 1979) are in the public domain. It will normally be the case that firms applying approximately the same publicly available methodology to the analysis of the same environment will collect about the same information. And these same firms applying publicly available conceptual frameworks to analyze this information will typically come to similar conclusions about the potential of strategies. Thus, analyzing a firm's competitive environment cannot, on average, be expected to generate the expectational advantages that can lead to expected above normal returns in strategic factor markets.

Some would suggest that it is not the availability of these environmental methods of data collection and analysis that is important, but rather the skill with which these methods are applied. More skilled firms can thus generate the required expectational advantages through an analysis of the competitive environment. However, the skills of environmental analysis can be 'rented' from various investment banking and consulting firms, and thus skill advantages in analyzing competitive environments will typically only be temporary.

It may be the case that, in the collection of information concerning the value of a strategy from a firm's competitive environment, a firm might 'stumble' onto some information that gives it an expectational advantage over other firms. However, if such information was obtained through the systematic application of environmental analysis techniques, then other firms besides the firm that has this information would have obtained it, and it would no longer give an advantage. Thus, only if the information was obtained through nonsystematic means can it give a firm expectational advantages. However, such information, because it does not result from the systematic application of environmental analysis methodologies, must be stochastic in origin. Any informational advantages obtained in this manner must reflect a firm's good fortune and luck, not their skill in evaluating the return potential of strategies.

3.2 Organizational Analysis

While firms cannot obtain systematic expectational advantages from an analysis of the competitive characteristics of their environment, it may be possible, under certain conditions, to obtain such advantages by turning inwardly and analyzing information about the assets a firm already controls. Firms will usually enjoy access to this type of information that is not available to other firms. If these assets also have the potential to be used to implement valuable product market strategies, *and* if similar assets are not controlled by large numbers of competing firms, then they can be a source of competitive advantage. Examples of the types of organizational assets that might generate such expectations include special manufacturing know-how (Williamson 1975), unique combinations of business experience in a firm (Chamberlin 1933), and the teamwork of managers in a firm (Alchian and Demsetz 1972). Firms endowed with such organizational skills and abilities can be consistently better informed concerning the true future value of strategies they implement than other firms by exploiting these assets when choosing strategies to implement.

4. Summary and Implications

In summary, firms seeking to obtain above normal returns from implementing product market strategies must have consistently more accurate expectations about the future value of those strategies when acquiring the resources necessary to implement them, although firms can be lucky. Moreover, while it is usually not possible to obtain these advantages through the analysis of a firm's competitive environment, firms can sometimes obtain them when choosing to implement strategies that exploit resources already under their control.

These conclusions have important implications for the practice and theory of strategy. For example, firms that do not look inwardly to exploit resources they already control in choosing strategies can only expect to obtain normal returns from their strategizing efforts. For a strategy of diversification through acquisition, this implies that firms that fail to discover unique synergies between themselves and potential acquisitions, but rather rely only on publicly available information when pricing an acquisition, can only expect normal returns from their acquisition strategies, though these firms might be lucky and acquire a firm with an unanticipated synergy. For a low cost manufacturing strategy, our arguments suggest that firms without any special skills at low cost manufacturing can only expect normal returns from imitating the low cost manufacturing strategies of other firms, while firms with cultural or other advantages in low cost manufacturing, if few other firms have these same advantages, can exploit them to obtain above normal returns from implementing a low cost strategy (Ouchi 1981; Peters and Waterman 1982). Also, firms that currently enjoy above normal returns may do so because of unique insights and abilities they controlled when the strategies generating high current returns were chosen. On the other hand, these firms might also have been lucky. Thus, above normal economic performance may not always be a sign of strategizing and managerial excellence (Peters and Waterman 1982).

Our emphasis on competition for the resources needed to implement strategies differs from much current work in the field of strategy. Much of this research is based on the observation that firms which compete in imperfectly competitive *product* markets enjoy above normal returns (Porter 1980). As a description of the correlation between imperfect product market competition and above normal returns, this research has significant theoretical and empirical support (Hirshleifer 1980). Its implications for managers are less clear. Simply because firms that compete in imperfectly competitive product markets enjoy above normal returns does not necessarily imply that firms that adopt strategies to *create* these product market imperfections will enjoy above normal returns. As we have suggested, this will depend on the competitive characteristics of the markets through which the resources necessary to implement these strategies are acquired, that is, on the competitive characteristics of strategic factor markets.

Note

This work was made possible by a grant from the Office of Naval Research. Additional support was provided by IBM, Westinghouse, the General Electric Foundation, the Alcoa Foundation, the Mellon Foundation, and Amp Inc. Many of these ideas were developed in discussions with Dick Rumelt, Robin Wensley, Bill Ouchi, Barbara Lawrence, Connie Gersick, Bill McKelvey, and the Organizational Economics Seminar at UCLA.

References

Alchian, A. A. and H. Demsetz, 'Production, Information Costs, and Economic Organization,' *Amer. Economic Rev.*, 62 (1972), 777–795.

Barney, J. B., 'Rational Expectations Markets for Strategy Implementation: Asymmetric Expectations, Luck, and the Theory of Strategy,' Unpublished, Graduate School of Management, UCLA, 1985a.

——, 'Strategizing Processes and Returns to Strategizing,' Unpublished, Graduate School of Management, UCLA, 1985b.

Bazerman, M. and W. Samuelson, 'The Winner's Curse: An Empirical Investigation,' *Lecture Notes in Economics and Math. Systems*, 213 (1983), 186–200.

Chamberlin, E. H., *The Theory of Monopolistic Competition*, Harvard University Press, Cambridge, 1933.

Copeland, T. and J. F. Weston, *Financial Theory and Corporate Policy*, Addison-Wesley, Reading, Mass., 1979.

Ellert, J. C., 'Merger, Antitrust Law Enforcement, and Stockholder Returns,' *J. Finance*, (May 1976), 715–732.

Fama, E. F., 'Efficient Capital Markets: A Review of Theory and Empirical Work,' *J. Finance* (May 1970), 383–417.

Halpern, P. J., 'Empirical Estimates of the Amount and Distribution of Gains to Companies in Mergers,' *J. Business* (1973), 554–575.

Hannan, M. T. and J. Freeman, 'The Population Ecology of Organizations,' *Amer. J. Sociology*, 82 (1977), 929–964.

Henderson, B. D., *Henderson on Corporate Strategy*. Mentor, New York, 1979.

Hirshleifer, J., *Price Theory and Applications*. 2nd Ed., Prentice-Hall, Englewood Cliffs, N.J., 1980.

Kimberly, J., R. Miles and Associates (ed.), *Organizational Life Cycles*, Jossey-Bass, San Francisco, 1981.

Klein, B., R. Crawford and A. A. Alchian, 'Vertical Integration, Appropriable Rents, and the Competitive Contracting Process,' *J. Law and Economics*, 21, 2 (1978), 297–326.

Lenz, R. T., 'Strategic Capability: A Concept and Framework for Analysis,' *Acad. Management Rev.*, 5, 2 (1980).

Lippman, S. and R. Rumelt, 'Uncertain Imitability: An Analysis of Interfirm Differences in Efficiency Under Competition,' *Bell J. Economics*, 13 (1982), 418–453.

Mandelker, G., 'Risk and Return: The Case of Merging Firms,' *J. Financial Economics* (1974), 303–335.

Mossin, J., *Theory of Financial Markets*, Prentice-Hall, Englewood Cliffs, N.J., 1973.

Ouchi, W. G., *Theory Z*, Addison-Wesley, Reading, Mass., 1981.

Peters, T. and R. H. Waterman, *In Search of Excellence*, Harper and Row, New York, 1982.

Pfeffer, J. and G. R. Salancik, *The External Control of Organizations: A Resource Dependence Perspective*, Harper and Row, New York, 1978.

Porter, M. E., *Competitive Strategy: Techniques for Analyzing Industries and Competitors*, Free Press, New York, 1980.

Roll, R., 'The Hubris Hypothesis,' Unpublished, Graduate School of Management, UCLA, 1985.

Rumelt, R. and J. R. C. Wensley, 'Market Share and the Rate of Return: Testing the Stochastic Hypothesis,' Unpublished, Graduate School of Management, UCLA, 1981.

Schall, L. D., 'Asset Valuation, Firm Investment, and Firm Diversification,' *J. Business* (1972), 11–28.

Stevenson, H., 'Defining Corporate Strengths and Weaknesses,' *Sloan Management Rev.*, 17, 3 (1976).

Thompson, A. A. and A. J. Strickland, *Strategy Formulation and Implementation*, Business Publications, Dallas, 1980.

Williamson, O. E., *Markets and Hierarchies: Analysis and Antitrust Implications*, Free Press, New York, 1975.

13 Asset Stock Accumulation and Sustainability of Competitive Advantage

Ingemar Dierickx and Karel Cool

Recently, a number of scholars have expressed the concern that much of the strategy literature focuses too narrowly on privileged product market positions as a basis for competitive advantage and above-normal returns (*e.g.*, Gabel 1984; Wernerfelt 1984; Barney 1986). The fact that resource bundles need to be deployed to achieve or protect such privileged product market positions is often overlooked. This creates both analytical and managerial problems. The analytical problem stems from the fact that if a privileged product market position is achieved or protected by the deployment of scarce assets, it is necessary to account for the *opportunity cost* of those assets. Unless the opportunity cost of those scarce assets is properly accounted for, measured returns of product market activities will be inflated. The managerial problem stems from the fact that hidden cross-subsidization, in turn, distorts performance appraisal and capital allocation decisions. In addition, managers often fail to recognize that a bundle of assets, rather than the particular product market combination chosen for its deployment, lies at the heart of their firm's competitive position. In such cases, inadequate attention is given to protecting these assets from being imitated, bid away to competitors, or rendered valueless as a result of substitution by other assets.

A recent statement reflecting this critique is presented by Barney (1986). To help analyze the cost of implementing product market strategies, Barney introduces the concept of a 'strategic factor market' defined as 'a market where the resources necessary to implement a strategy are acquired' (p. 1231). For example, the market for market share is cited as a relevant strategic factor market for implementing a cost leadership strategy. Barney then argues that in the absence of imperfections in strategic factor markets, buyers will not be able to extract superior economic performance from any factor, since the cost of acquiring strategic resources will approximately equal the economic value of those resources once they are used to implement product market strategies. Firms may, however, have different expectations about the future value of a strategic asset. In that case, strategic factor markets are 'imperfectly competitive' (p. 1231). According to Barney, firms may obtain above normal returns only when they have superior information, when they are lucky, or both.[1] It is argued that all other apparent sources of either quasi-rents or market power ultimately boil down to either superior information or luck. The managerial implication drawn is that firms should focus their analysis mainly on their 'unique' skills and resources rather than on the competitive environment.

The purpose of this paper is threefold: (1) to discuss some of the limitations inherent in the concept of 'strategic factor markets', (2) to put forward a complementary framework based on the notion of asset stock accumulation, and (3) to develop guidelines for assessing the sustainability of a firm's competitive advantage.

1. Incomplete vs. Imperfect Factor Markets

While Barney focuses on market 'imperfections', the central question whether all required assets to implement a given strategy are actually traded is not examined. Instead, it is assumed that all required assets can be bought and sold. Granted, many inputs required to implement a strategy may be acquired in corresponding factor markets, and in those cases, the concept proposed by Barney is indeed useful to evaluate the opportunity cost of deploying those assets in product markets. Yet, it is not clear that *all* resources are actually bought and sold. In fact, some of the very examples suggested by Barney cast serious doubt on the universal validity of this assumption. The example of corporate reputations (Barney 1986, p. 1232) is a case in point. Are reputations for quality, for 'toughness' (readiness to retaliate) and so on, really bought in 'the market for corporate reputations'? Can a business school perceived as a teaching institution purchase a reputation for research excellence in a market for 'research institute reputations'? Can a scholar buy his or her reputation for quality work in a strategic factor market?

The implementation of a strategy may require assets which are nonappropriable. Nonappropriability may stem from various sources, such as the absence of well-defined property rights, or 'bookkeeping feasibility' problems (see, *e.g.*, Meade 1952; Bator 1958). Clearly, markets for such assets do not exist. Loyalty of one's dealers or the trust of one's customers cannot be bought. Dealer loyalty must be cultivated, and customers' trust must be earned through a history of honest dealings. As Arrow (1974, p. 23) points out: 'Unfortunately, [trust] is not a commodity which can be bought very easily. If you have to buy it, you already have some doubts about what you've bought. Trust and similar values, loyalty or truth telling, are examples of what the economist would call "externalities". They are goods, they are commodities; they have real, practical economic value; [. . .] But they are not commodities for which trade on the open market is technically possible or even meaningful'.

In addition, the successful implementation of a strategy often requires highly firm-specific assets, as opposed to undifferentiated inputs. Firms may, of course, acquire imperfect substitutes for the desired strategic input factor(s) and adapt them, at a cost, to the specific use it intends. For example, firms do not employ 'generic labor', but people endowed with firm-specific skills and values. 'Generic labor' is rented in the market; firm-specific skills, knowledge and values are accumulated through on the job learning and training. In sum, as Williamson (1979) points out, the idiosyncratic nature of firm-specific assets precludes their tradeability on open markets. Being nontradeable, the firm-specific component is *accumulated* internally.

Under the assumption of complete factor markets, competitors can replicate any asset bundle, and dispose of it at will, merely by purchasing and selling the required components at going market prices. So firms may as well realize the value of their asset bundles through the relevant factor markets instead of deploying them in product markets. Clearly, the assumption that factor markets are complete may not be pushed too far. As Caves (1980, p. 65) pointed out several years ago, 'at least some [factors] are simply not traded on open markets that permit capitalizing their differential qualities into their contract prices. Thus rents that the firm can earn are not entirely passed along to the unique fixed factors responsible for them'.

In sum, firms deploy both tradeable and nontradeable assets. Many inputs required for the implementation of a firm's product market strategy may be bought and sold in corresponding factor markets. The concept proposed by Barney is indeed useful to evaluate the opportunity cost of deploying these assets. However, the deployment of such assets does not entail a sustainable competitive advantage, precisely because they are freely tradeable. Factor markets, however, are not complete. Some factors are simply not traded on open markets. Thus, a complementary framework is required to gauge the sustainability of the stream of quasi rents generated through the deployment of nontradeable assets. The remainder of our paper proposes such a framework, based on the notion of accumulation of asset stocks.[2]

2. Accumulation of Asset Stocks

When an asset is nontradeable, the option to realize its value in a factor market is not available. In order to tap its rent earning potential, the owner of such an asset has to deploy it in product markets where, owing to the factor's non-tradeability, it may remain in fixed supply.[3] Conversely, a firm which does not own a nontradeable asset which it requires for the implementation of its product market strategy is constrained to 'building' this asset.

For example, a reputation for quality may be built (rather than bought) by following a consistent set of production, quality control etc. policies over some period of time. Similarly, a reputation for 'toughness' (readiness to retaliate) is established through a history of aggressive behavior, and so on. The same goes for factors such as firm-specific human capital, dealer loyalty, R&D capability (as opposed to a specific technology), etc. The common element in all of these cases is that the strategic asset is the cumulative result of adhering to a set of consistent policies over a period of time. Put differently, strategic asset *stocks* are *accumulated* by choosing appropriate time paths of *flows* over a period of time.[4]

The fundamental distinction between stocks and flows may be illustrated by the 'bathtub' metaphor: at any moment in time, the stock of water is indicated by the level of water in the tub; it is the cumulative result of flows of water into the tub (through the tap) and out of it (through a leak). In the example of R&D, the amount of water in the tub represents the stock of know-how at a particular moment in time, whereas current R&D spending is represented by the water flowing in through the tap; the fact that know-how depreciates over time is represented by the flow of water leaking through the hole in the tub. A crucial point illustrated by the bathtub metaphor is that *while flows can be adjusted instantaneously, stocks cannot.* It takes a consistent pattern of resource flows to accumulate a desired change in strategic asset stocks.

It follows that a key dimension of strategy formulation may be identified as the task of making appropriate choices about strategic expenditures (advertising spending, R&D outlays, etc.) with a view to accumulating required resources and skills (brand loyalty, technological expertise, etc.). In other words, appropriate time paths of relevant flow variables must be chosen to build required asset stocks. *Critical* or *strategic* asset stocks are those assets which are *nontradeable*, and as will be argued below, *nonimitable* and *nonsubstitutable*.

3. Sustainability of Privileged Asset Positions

Sustainability of a firm's privileged asset position hinges on how easily it can be replicated. If certain assets cannot be bought in factor markets, rivals may either attempt to *imitate* them by accumulating similar asset stocks of their own or they may try to *substitute* them by other assets.

3.1 Imitation of Asset Stocks

Whether imitation of a particular asset stock will be time consuming, costly, or both depends on the relative ease with which rival firms are able to accumulate a similar asset stock of their own. That is, imitability of an asset stock is related to the characteristics of the process by which it may be accumulated. In general, the following characteristics can be identified: *time compression diseconomies, asset mass efficiencies, interconnectedness of asset stocks, asset erosion,* and *causal ambiguity.*[5]

Time Compression Diseconomies

The importance of time compression diseconomies for sustaining competitive advantage is perhaps best illustrated by the following dialogue between a British Lord and his American visitor:

'How come you got such a gorgeous lawn?' 'Well, the quality of the soil is, I dare say, of the utmost importance.' 'No problem.' 'Furthermore, one does need the finest quality seed and fertilizers'. 'Big deal'. 'Of course, daily watering and weekly mowing are jolly important'. 'No sweat, jest leave it to me!'. 'That's it.' 'No kidding?!' 'Oh, absolutely. There is nothing to it, old boy; just keep it up for five centuries'.

In addition, the irresistible Thorstein Veblen would have commented, genuine blue-blooded nobility such as his Lordship's can only be produced through several generations of careful breeding. Clearly, both examples illustrate the importance of time compression diseconomies as a source of early-mover advantages.

Conceptually, time compression diseconomies and the notion of 'strictly convex adjustment costs' in the theory of capital investment to which they are related express the same fundamental mechanism: the 'law of diminishing returns' when one input, *viz.* time, is held constant. For example, MBA students may not accumulate the same stock of knowledge in a one-year program as in a two-year program, even if all inputs other than time are doubled. In the case of R&D, the presence of time compression diseconomies implies that maintaining a given rate of R&D spending over a particular time interval produces a larger increment to the stock of R&D know-how than maintaining twice this rate of R&D spending over half the time interval. Empirically, this does indeed seem to be the case (see, *e.g.*, Scherer 1967; Mansfield 1968).[6] 'Crash' R&D programs, for example, are typically less effective than programs where annual R&D outlays are lower but spread out over a proportionally longer period of time.

Asset Mass Efficiencies

Sustainability will be enhanced to the extent that adding increments to an existing asset stock is facilitated by possessing high levels of that stock. The underlying notion is that 'success breeds success'; historical success translates into favorable initial asset stock positions which in turn facilitate further asset accumulation. For example, firms who already have an important stock of R&D know-how are often in a better position to make further breakthroughs and add to their existing stock of knowledge than firms who have low initial levels of know-how. Similarly, a firm's cumulative sales base may be an important determinant of its current sales. This will be the case when 'word of mouth' increases product awareness, when 'bandwagon effects' influence buying behavior, or when the value of a product or a service increases with the size of the 'network' of adopters (as, *e.g.*, in the market for personal computers, markets for franchises, automobile dealer networks, etc.).

The competitive implication is clear: when asset mass efficiencies are important, building asset stocks starting from low initial levels may be difficult. Difficulties in 'catching up' may be greater still when the asset accumulation process exhibits discontinuities, *i.e.* when critical mass is required. Setting up a dealer network in a new geographic area is a case in point: one of the toughest problems may to establish a beachhead.

Interconnectedness of Asset Stocks

Accumulating increments in an existing stock may depend not just on the level of that stock, but also on the level of *other* stocks. For example, to the extent that new product and process developments find their origin in customer requests or suggestions (Von Hippel 1978), it may be harder to develop technological know-how for firms who do not have an extensive service network. Here, the difficulty of building one stock is related, not to the initial level of that stock, but to the low initial level of another stock which is its complement.

Asset Erosion

As is the case with physical plant and equipment, all asset stocks 'decay' in the absence of adequate 'maintenance' expenditures. R&D know-how depreciates over time because of technological obsolescence; brand awareness erodes because the consumer population is not stationary (existing consumers leave the market, while new consumers enter), consumers forget, etc. The characteristics of the decay process have several managerial implications. There is an important relation between an asset's 'half life' and strategic entry deterrence. To *credibly* deter entry, firms must be *committed* to punitive post entry behavior. Thus, output and advertising policies are not, in general, credible vehicles for entry deterrence, whereas capacity and brand loyalty are. The reason is that the former, pertaining to flow variables, could be adjusted at will should entry occur,[7] whereas the latter, being stock variables cannot. In general, only variables that have the nature of a stock, as opposed to a flow, can carry a credible threat, and the more so, the slower the stock is decaying over time. If the stock is decaying rapidly over time, a credible threat is harder to establish (see, *e.g.*, Eaton and Lipsey 1980).

More generally, higher decay rates weaken the inherent asymmetry between firms having important asset stocks and those having lower asset stock levels. Yet, it is important to note that a firm's dominant position may be sustainable even though its underlying asset base is subject to rapid decay, provided it faces lower 'maintenance' costs. This may be the case when a firm enjoys greater efficiency in asset accumulation due to asset mass efficiencies and/or asset interconnectedness. Conversely, the presence of time compression diseconomies in addition to rapid asset erosion makes it extremely hard to sustain asset stock level asymmetries.

Causal Ambiguity

So far, we have implicitly assumed that the process of accumulation of asset stocks is both deterministic and continuous. These may be reasonable simplifications for some industries, but not for others. In the pharmaceutical industry, for example, the process is better described as stochastic and discontinuous. The underlying process can perhaps be described as a 'jackpot model'. Firms sink R&D flows in projects with highly uncertain outcomes, and only few firms actually 'hit the jackpot' by bringing out highly successful products. The stocks *vs.* flows framework discussed earlier can easily be accommodated to deal with such industries. In fact, the levels of the firm's stocks will determine each firm's probability of success, *i.e.* different firms try their fortunes on different slot machines, the odds of each machine being set by the levels of that firm's relevant asset stocks.

The stochastic nature of the accumulation process may stem from our inability to *identify* some of the relevant variables as well as our inability to *control* them. Indeed, for some asset stocks it may be impossible to fully specify which factors play a role in their accumulation process, even for firms who already own those stocks (Nelson and Winter 1982). Clearly, imitation of those stocks by other firms becomes next to impossible. Causal ambiguity about the process of asset stock accumulation is captured by the notion of 'uncertain imitability' (Lippman and Rumelt 1982), suggesting that sustained performance differences may be found even in perfectly competitive industry settings.

Summarizing, the degree of imitability of a particular asset is determined by the interplay of a number of basic properties which may or may not characterize that asset's accumulation process: *asset mass efficiencies* (the initial level of an asset stock significantly influences the pace of its further accumulation), *time compression diseconomies* (decreasing returns of the fixed factor time), *interconnectedness* (the pace of an asset's accumulation is influenced by the level of other asset stocks), *asset erosion*, and *causal ambiguity* about the accumulation process.

3.2 *Substitution of Asset Stocks*

Even when, for reasons outlined above, imitation is not a major threat, asset stocks may still be vulnerable to *substitution* by *different* asset stocks. The fundamental danger lies in the fact that successful substitution threatens to render the original asset stocks obsolete, typically because they no longer create value to the buyer. The strategy followed by Canon to upset Xerox's dominant position in the low to medium volume copier market provides a good example. Capitalizing on its stock of R&D, Canon was able to 'design service out of the product', thereby substituting superior product design for Xerox's extensive service network. As a result of the substitution process, Xerox's service network became partly obsolete, as the value it created for the buyer had sharply diminished.

....

4. Conclusion

As Barney (1986) correctly points out, firms need to be analyzed from the resource side as well as from the product side: if a privileged product market position is achieved or protected by the deployment of scarce assets, it is necessary to account for the *opportunity cost* of those assets.

Many inputs required to implement a strategy may be acquired in corresponding input markets. In those cases, market prices are indeed useful to evaluate the opportunity cost of deploying those assets in product markets. However, the deployment of such assets does not entail a sustainable competitive advantage, precisely because they are freely tradeable. Factor markets, however, are not complete. Some factors are simply not traded on open markets. Thus, a complementary framework is required to gauge the sustainability of the stream of quasi rents generated through the deployment of nontradeable assets. The proposed framework is based on the notion of *asset stock accumulation*.

The rent earning potential of a nontradeable asset may be tapped by deploying it to product markets. Conversely, nontradeability is required to ensure that the asset, once deployed in a given product market, remains in fixed supply. Competitors who need an asset which is nontradeable are constrained to 'building' it. Asset stocks are 'built' or *accumulated* through a consistent time pattern of expenditures or flows.

Sustainability of a firm's asset position hinges on how easily it can be replicated. If certain assets cannot be bought in factor markets, rivals may either attempt to *imitate* them, by accumulating similar asset stocks of their own, or they may try to *substitute* them by other assets. Imitability depends on the extent to which asset accumulation processes exhibit the following properties: time compression diseconomies, asset mass efficiencies, interconnectedness, asset erosion, and causal ambiguity. Substitution threatens to render the original asset stocks obsolete, because they no longer create value to the buyer. In short, asset stocks are *strategic* to the extent that they are *nontradeable, nonimitable* and *nonsubstitutable*.

Within the framework presented in this paper, a firm's current *strategy* involves choosing *optimal time paths of flows*, whereas its *competitive position* and hence its potential profitability is determined by the level of its *stocks*. Strategic flows enter the current profit equation only in a 'trivial' fashion, viz. on the expenditure side.[8] It follows that attempts to explain performance differences among firms on the basis of current strategic expenditures only are pointless and likely to lead to conflicting results. Thus, the framework has important implications for empirical strategy-performance research. A central objective has been to explain differences in firm performance. That this endeavor has not led to unequivocal results is well known (see, *e.g.*, McGee and Thomas 1986). In our opinion, this is due to a large extent to the lack of attention paid to variable selection in terms of the fundamental distinction between strategic stocks and flows. Research on the performance implications of strategic group membership also illustrates the same basic problem. While some studies found performance differences among strategic groups, others did not find such evidence (see Cool and Schendel 1987 for an overview). Although other factors may contribute to this phenomenon, clearly the failure to distinguish between strategic flow and strategic stock variables to identify strategic groups precludes unequivocal results. It is hoped that this paper will prove useful to further empirical research by suggesting a theoretical framework for variable selection.

Notes

1. Barney's work is one of several contributions emphasizing this point. See, *e.g.*, Alchian (1950), Mancke (1974), Rumelt (1984); for a different view, see, *e.g.*, Caves, Gale and Porter (1977).

2. Of course, Barney's fundamental argument about competition for resources may be extended in a straightforward manner from competition in factor markets to competition in resource accumulation. Thus, our paper should not be read as a prescription for creating competitive advantage. Indeed, it appears logically impossible to formulate a set of rules to systematically create competitive advantage. This issue has been dealt with elsewhere (Barney 1988), and is not the focus of the present paper, which addresses the issue of sustainability of competitive advantage.

3. At least for some time. Nontradeability is a necessary, but not a sufficient condition; see below.

4. The fundamental notion that strategic expenditures should be viewed as investments in (intangible) asset stocks goes back at least 25 years. In a classic paper on advertising, Telser (1961, p. 197) pointed out that '. . . consumers tend to forget brands and continuous advertising is needed to maintain a given rate of sales. Thus, advertising expenditures can be viewed as a capital good that depreciates over time and needs maintenance and repair.' Similarly, 'The annual research and development expenditures of a firm are considered to be investments which add to a firm's stock of knowledge. This stock of knowledge is depreciating over time so that the contribution of older R&D investments becomes less valuable as time passes' (Hall, Griliches and Hausman 1986, p. 265).

5. Note that it is not implied here that all asset accumulation processes exhibit the properties described below. In fact, many do not. It is suggested only that imitability in any particular case is determined by the extent to which asset accumulation processes exhibit these properties.

6. The assumption of time compression diseconomies is also very common in recent theoretical work on R&D. See, *e.g.*, Reinganum (1982).

7. Firms may, however, *contractually commit* themselves to a given output level; in this case contract length becomes critical. See Aghion and Bolton (1987).

8. See, *e.g.*, Arrow and Nerlove (1962), where, in contrast to the earlier Dorfman and Steiner (1954) model, current advertising does not directly enter the firm's demand function, but only indirectly through the accumulated stock of 'goodwill'; the flow of current advertising outlays enters the current profit equation only as a cost.

References

Aghion, P. and P. Bolton, 'Contracts as Barriers to Entry,' *Amer. Economic Rev.* (June 1987), 388–401.

Alchian, A., 'Uncertainty, Evolution, and Economic Theory,' *J. Political Economy* (June 1950), 211–221.

Arrow, K., *The Limits of Organization*, W. W. Norton & Company, New York, 1974.

—— and M. Nerlove, 'Optimal Advertising Policy under Dynamic Conditions,' *Economica* (May 1962), 129–148.

Barney, J., 'Strategic Factor Markets: Expectations, Luck, and Business Strtegy,' *Management Sci.* (October 1986), 1231–1241.

—— 'The Prescriptive Limits of Strategic Management Theory,' Working Paper, Department of Management, Texas A&M University, 1988.

Bator, F., 'The Anatomy of Market Failure,' *Quart. J. Economics* (August 1958), 351–379.

Caves, R., 'Industrial Organization, Corporate Strategy and Structure,' *J. Economic Lit.* (March 1980), 64–92.

—— B. Gale and M. Porter, 'Interfirm Profitability Differences: Comment,' *Quart. J. Economics* (November 1977), 667–676.

Cool, K. and D. Schendel, 'Strategic Group Formation and Performance: The Case of the US Pharmaceutical Industry, 1963–1982,' *Management Sci.* (September 1987), 1102–1124.

Dorfman, R. and P. Steiner, 'Optimal Advertising and Optimal Quality,' *Amer. Economic Rev.* (December 1954), 826–836.

Eaton, B. and R. Lipsey, 'Exit Barriers Are Entry Barriers: The Durability of Capital as a Barrier to Entry,' *Bell J. Economics* (Autumn 1980), 721–729.

Gabel, L., 'The Microfoundations of Competitive Strategy,' Insead Working Paper, October 1984.

Hall, B., Z. Griliches, and J. Hausman, 'Patents and R&D: Is There a Lag?,' *Internat. Economic Rev.* (June 1986), 265–283.

Lippman, S. and R. Rumelt, 'Uncertain Imitability: An Analysis of Interfirm Differences in Efficiency under Competition,' *Bell J. Economics* (Autumn 1982), 418–438.

Mancke, R., 'Causes of Interfirm Profitability Differences: A New Interpretation of the Evidence,' *Quart. J. Economics* (May 1974), pp. 181–193.

Mansfield, E., *The Economics of Technological Change*, W. W. Norton & Company, New York, 1968.

McGee, J. and H. Thomas, 'Strategic Groups: Theory, Research and Taxonomy,' *Strategic Management J.* (March–April 1986), 141–160.

Meade, J., 'External Economies and Diseconomies in a Competitive Situation,' *Economic J.* (March 1952), 56–67.

Nelson, R. and S. Winter, *An Evolutionary Theory of Economic Change*, Harvard University Press, Cambridge, MA, 1982.

Reinganum, J., 'A Dynamic Game of R. and D.: Patient Protection and Competitive Behavior,' *Econometrica* (1982), 671–688.

Rumelt, R., 'Toward a Strategic Theory of the Firm,' in *Competitive Strategic Management*, R. Lamb (Ed.), Prentice Hall, Englewood Cliffs, MD, 1984, 556–570.

Scherer, F., 'Research and Development Resource Allocation under Rivalry,' *Quart. J. Economics* (1967), 367–391.

Telser, L., 'How Much Does It Pay Whom to Advertise?,' *Amer. Economic Rev. (Proc.)* (May 1961), 194–205.

Von Hippel, E., 'Successful Industrial Products from Customer Ideas,' *J. Marketing*, 1 (1978), 39–49.

Wernerfelt, B., 'A Resource-Based View of the Firm,' *Strategic Management J.* (1984), 171–180.

Williamson, O. E., 'Transaction-Cost Economics: The Governance of Contractual Relations,' *J. Law and Economics*, 22, 2 (October 1979), 233–261.

Diversification, Ricardian rents, and Tobin's q

Cynthia A. Montgomery and Birger Wernerfelt

1. Introduction

It is beyond dispute that multimarket firms play a dominant role in modern society. Despite this, economic analysis does not have a great deal to say about firm diversification, and the theory that does exist is largely untested.[1]

The prevailing theory of diversification (e.g., Caves, 1971; Gorecki, 1975; Penrose, 1959; Teece, 1982) is based on excess capacity of productive factors. It argues that failure in the markets for these factors may make diversification an efficient choice, although the factors are expected to lose some efficiency in the transfer. In this article we attempt to extend this theory by considering the heterogeneity of factors that prompts diversification and the profit-maximizing decisions made by diversifying firms.

In Section 2 we discuss the nature of rents and argue that Ricardian rents may be appropriated by owners of inimitable factors, or by their trading partners if relationship-specific investments tie the parties together. After characterizing these factors, in Section 3 we consider different utilization patterns and their profit implications. In general, we assume that application in a firm's current domestic or foreign markets should be the most profitable. If these applications leave excess capacity, however, diversification then becomes a viable choice. At this juncture, the specificity of the factor and the nature of the firm's diversification opportunities become important. In particular, one would expect that the more widely a firm diversifies, the lower will be its average rents. Two points support this argument: first, wider diversification suggests the presence of less specific factors that normally yield less competitive advantage; second, a given factor will lose more value when transferred to markets that are less similar to that in which it originated.

In Section 4 we introduce Tobin's q and show how Ricardian rents will be reflected in this measure of firm performance. Section 5 contains our data and measures. Section 6 gives the empirical results using Tobin's q to test the hypothesis that rents decrease as large firms diversify more widely. A summary and suggestions for future research appear in Section 7.

2. Sources of Ricardian Rents

Firms earn rents for many reasons, and there are several ways to classify such rents. Rents can result from collusive relationships with competitors, from disequilibrium effects (luck), and from unique factors. The last class will be called Ricardian rents and is the focus of this article.[2]

Economic or Ricardian rents are ordinarily thought of as accruing to *owners* of unique factors. A firm could, for example, earn Ricardian rents if it is owned and operated by a good manager,[3] if it owns attractively located land, or if it holds a patent. As highlighted by Lippman and Rumelt (1982), a firm may also earn rents if it owns factors subject to uncertain imitability, such as the rights to a reputable brand name or a reputation for fairness (cf. Kreps, 1984). Although competitors could invest in developing comparable reputations, this may be an uncertain project. In such cases the firm may continue to earn rents although, in principle, the factor is imitable. On the other hand, a firm cannot earn rents just by employing a good manager or taking a license on a brand name since the price of these services will be bid up to the point where all rents accrue to the factor owners.

We suggest that Ricardian rents from the factors a firm owns are only part of the story. Firms also may appropriate substantial rents as trading partners of factor owners, provided that relationship-specific investments tie the parties together.[4] In such cases we shall say that the firm *shares* the factor in question. For example, if a firm employs a team of managers with superadditive productivity, the firm may appropriate some of the rent the team earns because the managers have difficulty marketing themselves as a package.[5] As another example, the firm may employ a manager or use a supplier who makes unanticipated investments that cement the trading relationship by creating switching costs.[6] Because of laws against slavery, this is the only way a publicly held corporation can appropriate rents from human factors.

3. Diversification as a Way to Appropriate Ricardian Rents

Let us now assume that a firm owns or shares a factor that has excess capacity and can be used beyond the firm's current scope. In such circumstances it is important to consider the patterns of utilization that will allow the firm to extract maximum rents.

If the factor is subject to market imperfections, the firm may decide to use the capacity internally instead of selling or renting it in an imperfect factor market. According to standard theory, these circumstances lead to diversification (Williamson, 1985).

To simplify the argument we make four important assumptions. First, we abstract from the indivisibility problem emphasized by Penrose (1959) by assuming that the firm can dispose of excess capacity (sell it at price zero) without affecting the rest of its operations. Second, we do not consider cases where there are natural economies of scope between two industries such that any firm in one industry will participate uniformly in the other. In effect, we shall look at such pairs of industries as a single industry. Third, we concentrate on firms that own or control rent-yielding factors, not firms that lack access to such factors. Fourth, for maximum transparency we conduct the analysis in a static model and evaluate the case of a single diversification move in which a firm with excess capacity of a rent-yielding factor considers a marginal expansion of its scope.[7] While these assumptions abstract from reality, we shall demonstrate that a theory consistent with the data can be built around them.

With respect to a marginal change in the scope of the firm, the givens are a set of factors and a list of markets to which they may be transferred and result in smaller or greater competitive advantages. Let us define that market in which the factor will yield the highest rents as the 'closest.' Further, let us think of the distance to that market as larger to the extent that the critical factors in the market differ from those in the firm's current scope. The more a firm has to diversify, i.e., the farther from its current scope that it must go, *ceteris paribus*, the larger will be the loss in efficiency and the lower will be the competitive advantage conferred by the factor.

Accordingly, if a firm diversifies, it will transfer excess factors to the closest market it can enter. If excess capacity remains, it will enter markets even farther afield, until marginal rents become subnormal. A firm whose opportunity set is such that it must transfer a great deal of excess capacity to a distant market will realize low marginal rents. Therefore, the value of the original set of factors, and thus the total value of the firm, will, *ceteris paribus*, depend negatively on the optimal extent of diversification.

Of course, all things are not equal, and one important way firms' factors may vary is in their specificity. We define less specific factors as those that lose less efficiency as they are applied farther from their origin (see Fig. 1). These factors will normally yield less advantage because they are in wider supply. Our argument here is that many firms have the opportunity to develop factors that apply in many industries (e.g., teams of general managers), whereas fewer firms have natural opportunities to create more specific factors (e.g., teams of biochemists). Because less specific factors normally support wider diversification, their relatively lower value will tend to strengthen the negative relationship between the extent of diversification and average rents.[8]

In summary, given the specificity of a set of factors, the optimal decision for a firm is to apply its excess capacity to the closest entry opportunity. The rent the firm can extract from the move depends on the specificity of the factors and the closeness of the new market. These conditions result in the following stylized relationships:

(a) Firms with less specific factors and nearby entry opportunities will diversify narrowly and extract medium rents on average.
(b) Firms with more specific factors whose closest entry opportunities are in 'nearby' markets will diversify narrowly and extract high rents on average.
(c) Firms with less specific factors that have only quite 'distant' opportunities will diversify widely and extract low rents on average.
(d) Firms with more specific factors and no nearby entry opportunities will not be able to diversify at positive marginal rents. Because the factors are more specific, they should yield high rents in those markets. Further, the fact that these firms do not make additional investments at lower marginal rents will preserve the high average. In sum, these firms are likely to have very high *average returns*, although it is clear that their *total profits* would increase if they had opportunities to diversify.

This reasoning, illustrated in Fig. 2, allows us to predict that as optimal diversification increases, average rents decline.

The prediction that undiversified firms earn the highest average rents is quite sensitive to our assumptions. First, if unused excess capacity imposes a cost on the firm, the analysis of case (d) would have to be modified to net this out. Second, if firms diversify owing to natural economies of scope that affect all participants in their industries, their performance should resemble that of undiversified firms. If this is a common phenomenon in our sample, case (d) will be less exceptional. Third, if a firm owns or controls few or no rent-yielding factors, our conclusions will not apply. Given that our analysis concentrates on very large firms, this third caveat should not be relevant.

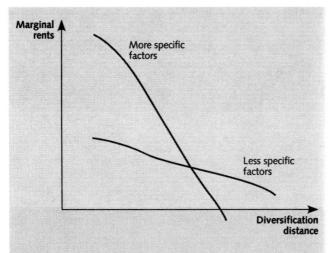

Fig. 1. Hypothesized relationship between diversification distance and marginal rents for different degrees of factor specificity.

4. Tobin's *q* as a Measure of Rents

The use of accounting measures as a proxy for rents has recently come under severe criticism (Benston, 1985; Fisher and McGowan, 1983). In particular, accounting rates of return are distorted by a failure to consider differences in systematic risk, temporary disequilibrium effects, tax laws, and arbitrary accounting conventions. Instead, it is recommended that one rely on the hypothesis of an efficient capital market to get unbiased measures of capitalized rents. For practical purposes, however, pure-capital-market measures capture only changes in firm value, not levels of value. For this reason, our main hypothesis—that more widely diversified firms *ceteris paribus* earn lower rents—cannot easily be tested on pure-capital market data. If the hypothesis is true an efficient capital market will aleady have incorporated the diversification effect in share prices, and later observations would not reveal differential changes in value creation.

For our purposes, Tobin's *q*, defined as the ratio of market value to the replacement cost of the firm, is a more appropriate measure. By combining capital market data with accounting data, *q* implicitly uses the correct risk-adjusted discount rate, imputes equilibrium returns, and minimizes distortions due to tax laws and accounting conventions. Although originally introduced in macroeconomics, these attractive properties have recently given *q* increasing

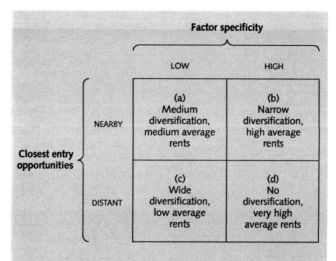

Fig. 2. Hypothesized relationships between specificity of factors in excess capacity, closest entry opportunity, and extracted average rents.

use in industrial organization research (Lindenberg and Ross, 1981; Salinger, 1984; Smirlock et al., 1984). In this article the use of q is especially attractive since firms with different diversification profiles have been found to concentrate in different industries (Caves et al., 1980, chap. 12; Lecraw, 1984). Therefore, to minimize industry-related biases, it is important that we control for systematic risk, disequilibria, tax laws, and accounting conventions that tend to vary much more across industries than within them.

In principle, the numerator in q can be decomposed into the sum of the firm's capitalized income streams. While many decompositions are possible, the literature (Lindenberg and Ross, 1981; Salinger, 1984; Smirlock et al., 1984) suggests that we decompose the market value of the firm into the value of its physical assets, the value of its intangible assets, the capitalized rents from collusive relationships, capitalized Ricardian rents, and, possibly, disequilibrium effects.

As defined, the denominator of q is the replacement cost of a firm's assets. In practice, this has come to mean the replacement value of a firm's physical assets. The extent to which q differs from one is thus a measure of the extent to which the firm's capitalized rents differ from the fair market price of its physical assets.

From this, we can write q as

$$q = M/V_p = 1 + \left(V_I + V_C + V_R + V_E\right)/V_p, \tag{1}$$

where

M = the market value of the firm;
V_p = the (replacement) value of physical assets;
V_I = the value of intangible assets purchased by the firm;
V_C = the value of collusive relationships with competitors;
V_R = the capitalized Ricardian rents; and
V_E = disequilibrium effects.

We estimate (1), using the conventional proxies for V_I, V_C, and V_E, so that we may focus on the relationship between V_R and multimarket activity. This relationship, however, is not straightforward. If we denote d as diversification, s as specificity, and o as opportunities, our theory is that V_R / V_p is an increasing function of s and a decreasing function of d, while d is a decreasing function of s and an increasing function of o. Formally,

$$\frac{V_R}{V_p}\left(s,\, d\right) \tag{2}$$

$$d\left(s,\, o\right). \tag{3}$$

A problem is that s and o are unobserved. We propose to solve this problem by using a set of industry dummies as an instrument for d in

$$\frac{V_R}{V_p}\left(d\right). \tag{4}$$

This amounts to using the average industry-level diversification, rather than each firm's own diversification level, as a proxy for s and o. Given that (2) and (3) are likely to be underspecifed, (4) is of course subject to the usual errors-in-variables problem.

....

5. Data, Measures, and Tests

Lindenberg and Ross (1981) generously shared their estimates of 1976 *q* for a random sample of 246 firms. Trinet/EIS provided 1976 domestic market share data and dollar sales per four-digit SIC code (*EIS Establishment Database*). 1976 replacement cost data are from 10 K's, and foreign sales estimates (available only for 1978) are from the *EIS Directory of Top 1500 Firms*. Industry estimates of marketing expenditures and company sponsored R&D are from the *1976 Line-of-Business Report*, published by the Federal Trade Commission. Four-firm concentration ratios for 1977 and 1972–1977 growth rates per SIC code are from the *1977 Census of Manufactures*. Missing data reduced the sample size to 167.

Cynthia Montgomery and Birger Wernerfelt

From these data we can construct estimates of the following variables:

A_i = firm i's marketing expenditures (sales weighted);[9]
R_i = firm i's R&D (sales weighted);
C_i = concentration in firm i's markets (sales weighted);
G_i = growth of shipments in firm i's markets (sales weighted);
S_i = firm i's market share (sales weighted);
F_i = firm i's foreign sales (in percent); and
V_{pi} = replacement costs of firm i's physical assets.

The diversification measure requires more explanation. Several measures have been used in the literature, and, while they typically correlate very strongly (Caves et al., 1980, p. 201), they still are not the same. In particular, we want to differentiate between more and less similar diversification. While a categorical measure, such as that used by Lecraw (1984), is a possibility, we felt that we would lose too much information with such a procedure. Instead, we chose the 'concentric index' of Caves et al. (1980), given by

$$D_i = \sum_{j=1}^{n} m_{ij} \sum_{l=1}^{n} m_{il} r_{jl},$$

where m_{ij} is the percentage of firm i's sales in industry j, and r_{jl} is zero if j and l have the same three-digit code, one if they have different three-digit codes but identical two-digit codes, and two if they have different two-digit codes.

For instruments for D_i, we use vectors of dummy variables $t_i = (t_{i20}, t_{i21}, \ldots, t_{i39})$, where t_{ij} is one if firm i is active in two-digit industry j, and otherwise zero.[10] The results of King (1966), Farrell (1974), and Livingston (1977) show few variations in returns within (but large variations between) two-digit industries; thus, we do not expect to lose much information by operating at this level of aggregation. Further, an advantage of the aggregation is that it diminishes the endogeneity problem.

From this, we estimate two equations

$$q = \beta_0 + \beta_1 \frac{A}{V_p} + \beta_2 \frac{R}{V_p} + \beta_3 C + \beta_4 S + \beta_5 D + \beta_6 F + \beta_7 G + \varepsilon \tag{5a}$$

$$q = \beta'_0 + \beta'_1 \frac{A}{V_p} + \beta'_2 \frac{R}{V_p} + \beta'_3 C + \beta'_4 S + \beta'_5 \hat{D} + \beta'_6 F + \beta'_7 G + \varepsilon', \tag{5b}$$

where $\hat{D}$ indicates that D is estimated through the instruments.

In these equations β_0 should be roughly one, the value of q under perfect competition, since in that case the other terms will all be zero. The coefficients of purchased intangible assets, β_1 and β_2, correct for the fact that such costs are omitted from the denominator of q. We use the 1976 values of advertising and R&D as measures of the rate at which such assets are purchased. If these rates are constant and we apply depreciation rates of .3 and .1, respectively (as done by Salinger (1984) and originally recommended by Grabowski and Mueller (1978)), the stocks of the intangibles should be 10/3 and 10 times the 1976 inflows. If the value of the stocks is unity, β_1 and β_2 should therefore be roughly 10/3 and 10, respectively.

Predictions about concentration (β_3) and market share (β_4) depend on one's beliefs about the structure-conduct-performance paradigm versus the 'efficient-structure' hypothesis. If the results of Smirlock et al. (1984) extend to our sample, β_3 is unlikely to be significantly different from zero, while we would expect a positive β_4, an indication of Ricardian rents.

On the basis of arguments outlined in Section 3, we clearly expect the coefficient of diversification (β_5) to be negative. The more widely a firm diversifies, the lower will be its average returns.

The coefficient of foreign sales (β_6) is harder to assess. If foreign markets are nearly identical to domestic markets, sales in those markets should have the same effect as higher market share, and β_6 will be positive, which reflects Ricardian rents. On the other hand, if foreign markets differ enough that the firm's factors face significant efficiency losses in the transfer, β_6 will be negative. It is likely that both kinds of markets are represented in our sample, which makes it difficult to predict the sign. A further complication is that foreign assets are outside the requirements of replacement-cost accounting so that q normally will be biased upwards for firms with substantial foreign assets. Finally, we expect the coefficient of industry growth, β_7, which captures disequilibrium effects, to be positive (see also Salinger, 1984).

Because both sides of (5) are divided by V_p, measurement error in this variable induces some problems. We therefore follow Griliches (1981) and take logs, using the $x \approx \log(1 + x)$ approximation, to get

$$\log M = \gamma_0 + \gamma_1 \log V_p + \gamma_2 \frac{A}{V_p} + \gamma_3 \frac{R}{V_p} + \gamma_4 C + \gamma_5 S + \gamma_6 D + \gamma_7 F + \gamma_8 G + e \quad \text{(6a)}$$

$$\log M = \gamma_0' + \gamma_1' \log V_p + \gamma_2' \frac{A}{V_p} + \gamma_3' \frac{R}{V_p} + \gamma_4' C + \gamma_5' S + \gamma_6' \hat{D} + \gamma_7' F + \gamma_8' G + e', \quad \text{(6b)}$$

which we also estimate.

....

6. Results

The first line in Table 1 is equation (5a), the linear form estimated without using instruments for D. Note first that the adjusted R^2 is similar to that of other studies of this type (Salinger, 1984). As expected, the intercept is not significantly different from one, and the coefficients of A/V_p and R/V_p are not significantly different from $10/3$ and 10, respectively.[11] Market share (S) has a positive coefficient, while concentration (C) has a negative effect. These results indicate that large firms in otherwise fragmented industries reap high Ricardian rents, a result that is consistent with the findings of Smirlock et al. (1984). As expected, the coefficient on diversification (D) is negative and significant.[12] As firms diversify more widely, their average rents decline. Let us emphasize that this does not mean that diversification conflicts with value maximization. A firm's marginal investments should still have a q that exceeds one, even where this q is below the average q of the firm's other activities. The coefficient of foreign sales (F) is positive. This would indicate that for most of our firms foreign sales are more similar to domestic sales than to diversification (although it is difficult to evaluate the positive bias alluded to in Section 5). Finally, it is somewhat surprising that industry growth is insignificant, given that Salinger (1984) typically finds this to be the strongest coefficient.

The second line in Table 1 is (5b), the linear form estimated by using the industry dummies as instruments for D. The coefficient of $\hat{D}$ is somewhat larger than that of D, and the adjusted R^2 for this equation is virtually identical to that of (5a). Overall, however, the results are quite similar, which indicates that the possible bias from treating D as exogenous is small.

The third and fourth lines in Table 1 are (6a) and (6b), the logarithmic forms without and with the instruments, respectively. The overall behavior of the model is essentially unchanged, although neither the coefficient of D nor that of $\hat{D}$ is significant in these versions. The positive correlation between D and V_p presumably explains the larger coefficients of diversification in these models.

7. Discussion

Using Tobin's q, we have tested the conjecture that large firms earn decreasing average rents as they diversify more widely. Our findings are consistent with the idea that diversification is prompted by excess capacity in rent-yielding factors that are subject to market failure. More specifically, our results indicate that the farther they must go to use their factors, the lower the marginal rents they extract.

The issue of alternative explanations remains. Focusing on equation (5a), we could explain the negative relationship between market valuation and diversification by other theories. First, as suggested by a referee, there is a possibility

Table 1. Regression results: firm value of extent of diversification[a]

Dependent Variable	I	$\log V_p$	A/V_p	R/V_p	C	S	D	$\hat{D}$	F	G	$\bar{R}^2$
q	.908		2.71	8.98	−.006	1.01	−.145		.417	.007	.293
	(5.88)		(4.70)	(3.36)	(2.44)	(2.35)	(1.97)		(1.84)	(.091)	
q	.888		2.52	9.33	−.006	1.13		−.186	.469	.008	.296
	(5.67)		(4.08)	(3.28)	(2.17)	(2.51)		(2.20)	(1.93)	(.086)	
$\log M$	−.728	1.03	2.23	9.47	−.006	.846	−.035		.273	.024	
	(1.83)	(35.4)	(4.12)	(4.05)	(2.57)	(1.93)	(.538)		(1.32)	(.302)	
$\log M$	−.926	1.05	2.24	9.92	−.005	.714		−.139	.281	.011	
	(2.12)	(32.0)	(3.93)	(3.99)	(2.27)	(1.55)		(1.76)	(1.29)	(.133)	

[a] *t*-statistics in parentheses. $N = 167$ for all equations.

that at some point firms believed that rents from diversification would be gained more easily than history has borne out. As experience and information to the contrary reached the market, stock prices of diversified firms may have fallen to reflect these errors in judgment. Second, Jensen's (1986) 'free-cash-flow' hypothesis implies that firms with available cash undertake diversification against the interests of stockholders. Third, one can offer various agency-theoretic arguments to the effect that firms diversify to overcome severe moral-hazard problems.

The fact that the industry dummies worked so well as instruments for diversification provides an argument against the first and third of these theories. It is eminently reasonable that asset specificity is homogeneous within industries. It is less reasonable that beliefs about the profitability of diversification, and the incidence of specific types of agency problems, should follow industry lines as sharply as our results indicate. The 'free-cash-flow' hypothesis is more difficult to rule out, although it need not be inconsistent with our story. We envision a firm (Section 3) as having a queue of potential diversification opportunities. We argue that a firm, in electing to diversify, will begin with the most profitable opportunities and move toward the least profitable ones. Our expectation is that this process will end when marginal rents become subnormal. In the free-cash-flow view one could expect firms to pursue investments beyond this point.

The study has several limitations. On the theoretical side, we made several simplifying assumptions. In particular, we assumed that disposal of excess capacity is costless and that natural economies of scope, affecting all firms in a pair of industries, do not exist. As discussed in Section 3, these assumptions are important for our prediction about the performance of undiversified firms; without them, one might expect that closely diversified firms may earn even higher average rents. Although more complex theories may highlight other dimensions of the problem, these assumptions allow us to focus on a few key implications of factor heterogeneity and are sufficient to explain the evidence. On the empirical side, it is worth noting that the study pertains only to large, successful firms. As discussed in Section 3, the theory is not expected to extend to small competitive firms. Finally, we would like to reemphasize that both theory and tests refer to average rents, not total profits.

....

Notes

We are grateful to Robert Sartain for research assistance and to Stephen Ross and the Institute for the Study of Business Markets for supplying part of the data used in this study. We benefited from commentary by two anonymous referees and Marvin Lieberman on an earlier draft.

1. See Caves, Porter, and Spence (1980) for some of the most careful work and further references.
2. Lindenberg and Ross (1981), Salinger (1984), and Smirlock, Gilligan, and Marshall (1984) have studied rents resulting from collusive and disequilibrium effects, which will be incorporated in the present analysis as control variables.
3. It is obviously possible to impute the rent of the owner-manager to the person rather than the firm, but this difference is immaterial for our purposes.
4. In related literature Nelson and Winter (1982) stress team effects and von Weizsäcker (1984) analyzes the effects of switching costs.
5. Again, here it is possible to attribute the rents to the ownership of the employment contracts, etc. Such semantic exercises may not be the best way to make progress in this area, however.
6. Switching costs will be contracted for *ex ante*. See Klein Crawford, and Alchian (1978).
7. In cases where the underlying factor is intangible, it often does not obey the law of conservation, and a single instance of excess capacity can lead to several diversification moves. For example, reputations or information may have almost infinite capacity. Even in these instances, however, the basic building block is the individual diversification move.
8. An additional problem for firms with less specific factors is that such factors alone are insufficient to allow the firm to enter industries where more specialized factors are required. Accordingly, one would expect that the industries these firms enter will have a high concentration of firms competing with less specific factors, and no firm will have a major differential advantage.
9. Firm-level estimates for marketing and R&D expenditures are derived by weighing industry-level data, and thus rest on the assumption that a firm's spending per market is approximately equal to the industry average. Direct firm-level estimates were obtained from Compustat for 75 of the 167 firms. These correlated with our estimates at the .811 and .765 level, respectively. On the other hand, the Compustat data lacked surface validity: in addition to the many entries labeled as 'missing,'

a number of observations showed zero-levels of spending, e.g., zero advertising dollars for Chrysler.

10. We are indebted to a referee for suggesting this instrument.
11. In addition, we know from many studies (e.g., Caves et al., 1980) that there is a strong correlation between R&D and diversification. We also estimated the model without R&D, and no significant results changed.
12. In another article (Wernerfelt and Montgomery, 1988), we compared the importance of industry, diversification, and market share effects in explaining q. Industry effects explain 20–30% of the variance, while diversification effects account for roughly 3% and market share is insignificant.

References

Benston, G. J. 'The Validity of Profits-Structure Studies with Particular Reference to the FTC's Line-of-Business Data,' *American Economic Review*, Vol. 75 (1985), pp. 37–67.

Caves, R. E. 'International Corporations: The Industrial Economics of Foreign Investment,' *Economica*, Vol. 38 (1971), pp. 1–27.

——— Porter, M. E. and Spence, A. M. *Competition in the Open Economy*. Cambridge: Harvard University Press, 1980.

Economic Information Systems. *EIS Directory of Top 1500 Companies*. New York: Economic Information Systems, Inc., 1974.

Farrell, J. L., Jr. 'Analyzing Covariance of Returns to Determine Homogeneous Stock Groupings,' *Journal of Business*, Vol. 47 (1974), pp. 186–207.

Federal Trade Commission. *Statistical Report: Annual Line-of-Business Report 1976*. Washington, D.C.: Bureau of Economics, Federal Trade Commission, 1982.

Fisher, F. and McGowan, J. 'On the Misuse of Accounting Rates of Return to Infer Monopoly Profits,' *American Economic Review*, Vol. 73 (1983), pp. 82–97.

Gorecki, P. K. 'An Interindustry Analysis of Diversification in the U.K. Manufacturing Sector,' *Journal of Industrial Economics*, Vol. 24 (1975), pp. 131–146.

Grabowski, H. G. and Mueller, D. C. 'Industrial Research and Development, Intangible Capital Stocks, and Firm Profit Rates,' *Bell Journal of Economics*, Vol. 9 (1978), pp. 328–343.

Griliches, Z. 'Market Value, R&D, and Patents,' *Economics Letters*, Vol. 7 (1981), pp. 183–187.

Jensen, M. C. 'Agency Costs of Free Cash Flow, Corporate Financing, and Takeovers,' *American Economics Review, Papers and Proceedings*, Vol. 76 (1986), pp. 323–329.

King, B. F. 'Market and Industry Factors in Stock Price Behavior,' *Journal of Business*, Vol. 39 (1966), pp. 139–190.

Klein, B., Crawford, R. G., and Alchian, A. A. 'Vertical Integration, Appropriable Rents, and the Competitive Contracting Process,' *Journal of Law and Economics*, Vol. 21 (1978), pp. 297–326.

Cynthia Montgomery and Birger Wernerfelt

Kreps, D. M. 'Corporate Culture and Economic Theory,' Mimeo, Graduate School of Business Administration, Stanford University, 1984.

Lecraw, D. J. 'Diversification Strategy and Performance,' *Journal of Industrial Economics*, Vol. 33 (1984), pp. 179–198.

Lindenberg, E. B. and Ross, S. A. 'Tobin's q Ratio and Industrial Organization,' *Journal of Business*, Vol. 54 (1981), pp. 1–32.

Lippman, S. A. and Rumelt, R. P. 'Uncertain Imitability: An Analysis of Interfirm Differences under Competition,' *Bell Journal of Economics*, Vol. 13 (1982), pp. 418–438.

Livingston, M., 'Industry Movements of Common Stocks,' *Journal of Finance*, Vol. 32 (1977), pp. 861–874.

Nelson, R. R. and Winter, S. G. *An Evolutionary Theory of Economic Change*. Cambridge: Harvard University Press, 1982.

Penrose, E. *The Theory of the Growth of the Firm*. London: Basil Blackwell, 1959.

Salinger, M. A. 'Tobin's q, Unionization, and the Concentration-Profits Relationship,' *RAND Journal of Economics*, Vol. 15 (1984), pp. 159–170.

Smirlock, M., Gilligan, T., and Marshall, W. 'Tobin's q and the Structure-Performance Relationship,' *American Economic Review*, Vol. 74 (1984), pp. 1051–1060.

Teece, D. J. 'An Economic Theory of Multiproduct Firms,' *Journal of Economic Behavior and Organization*, Vol. 3 (1982), pp. 39–63.

von Weizsäcker, C. C. 'The Costs of Substitution,' *Econometrica*, Vol. 52 (1984), pp. 1085–1116.

Wernerfelt, B. and Montgomery, C. A. 'Tobin's q and the Importance of Focus in Firm Performance,' *American Economic Review*, Vol. 78 (1988), pp. 246–250.

Williamson, O. E. *The Economic Institutions of Capitalism*. New York: Free Press, 1985.

15 The Cornerstones of Competitive Advantage: A Resource-Based View

Margaret A. Peteraf

1. Introduction

In recent years, a model of how firms compete, which is unique to the field of strategic management, has begun to emerge. Known as the 'Resource-Based View', it is regarded by some as having momentous potential as a paradigm for our field. Others wonder whether this emergent model provides much additional insight over traditional understandings. Admittedly, resource-based work is consistent with and rooted squarely in the policy research tradition. The notion that firms are fundamentally heterogeneous, in terms of their resources and internal capabilities, has long been at the heart of the field of strategic management. The classic approach to strategy formulation, for example, begins with an appraisal of organizational competencies and resources (Andrews, 1971). Those which are distinctive or superior relative to those of rivals, may become the basis for competitive advantage if they are matched appropriately to environmental opportunities (Andrews, 1971; Thompson and Strickland, 1990).

Those ideas may be thought of as the basic principles upon which resource-based research continues to build. While the model is still in the developmental stage, it has deepened our understanding regarding such topics as how resources are applied and combined, what makes competitive advantage sustainable, the nature of rents, and the origins of heterogeneity.[1] The work of Penrose (1959) is considered a very influential force. Other notable contributions include Lippman and Rumelt (1982), Teece (1980, 1982), Nelson and Winter (1982), Rumelt (1984, 1987), Wernerfelt (1984), Barney (1986, 1991), Dierickx and Cool (1989), Castanias and Helfat (1991), Connor (1991), and

Mahoney and Pandian (1992). This research stream is an impressive one. And while many agree that there is a need for greater rigor and richness of detail, the work that has been done provides a strong foundation and an inspiration for work to come.

In reviewing this work, one encounters numerous strands of research on a series of closely related topics. While each paper offers a distinct contribution, there is also considerable overlap of ideas. To the uninitiated this may be confusing. In part, this is because subtle variations in terminology across papers have made communication more difficult. But in addition, the underlying model seems somewhat disjointed, as if the ideas of these disparate authors have not fully coalesced into an integrated whole. While there is general agreement as to the basic insights of the model, there are small disagreements over minor points.

The purpose of this paper is to develop a general model of resources and firm performance which at once integrates the various strands of research and provides a common ground from which further work can proceed. My aim is to build consensus for a parsimonious model, clarify basic issues, suggest possible implications, and, in so doing, facilitate the continuing dialogue among scholars.

In the first section, a resource-based model of the theoretical conditions which underlie competitive advantage is presented. There are four such conditions, all of which must be met. The first of these is *resource heterogeneity*, from which come Ricardian or monopoly rents. *Ex post limits to competition* are necessary to sustain the rents. *Imperfect resource mobility* ensures that the rents are bound to the firm and shared by it. *Ex ante limits to competition* prevent costs from offsetting the rents. Each of these conditions is described in turn.

The model is intended to aid our theoretical understanding of superior firm performance as well as to inform management practice.

In the final section, some applications and implications of the model are described. In particular, the application of resource-based work to single-business strategy, as well as to multibusiness corporate strategy, in all of its forms, is discussed.

2. A Model of Competitive Advantage

2.1 Heterogeneity

A basic assumption of resource-based work is that the resource bundles and capabilities underlying production are heterogeneous across firms (Barney, 1991).[2] One might describe productive factors in use as having intrinsically differential levels of 'efficiency.' Some are superior to others. Firms endowed with such resources are able to produce more economically and/or better satisfy customer wants.

Heterogeneity implies that firms of varying capabilities are able to compete in the market-place and, at least, breakeven. Firms with marginal resources can only expect to breakeven.[3] Firms with superior resources will earn rents.[4]

Ricardian Rents

Heterogeneity in an industry may reflect the presence of superior productive factors which are in limited supply. They may be fixed factors which cannot be expanded. More often, they are quasi-fixed, in the sense that their supply cannot be expanded rapidly. They are scarce in the sense that they are insufficient to satisfy demand for their services. Thus, inferior resources are brought into production as well.

This is the familiar Ricardian argument.[5] It may be understood most clearly by assuming that firms with superior resources have lower average costs than other firms[6] (see Fig. 1). These low cost firms have somewhat inelastic supply curves, in that they cannot expand output rapidly, regardless of how high the price may be. High prices, however, do induce other less efficient firms to enter the industry. Such firms will enter and produce so long as price exceeds their marginal cost (MC). In equilibrium, industry demand and supply are in balance, high-cost firms breakeven (P = AC), and low-cost firms earn supranormal profits in the form of rents to their scarce resources (P > AC).

Note that this model is consistent with competitive behavior in the product market. Firms are price takers and produce at the point where price equals marginal cost. The high returns of efficient firms cannot be attributed to an artificial restriction of output or to market power. Neither do they depend upon

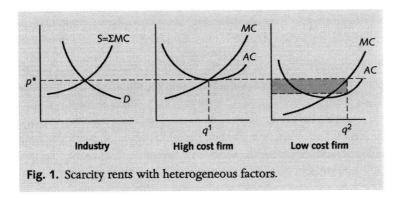

Fig. 1. Scarcity rents with heterogeneous factors.

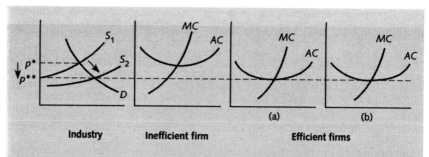

Fig. 2. Imitation (expansion) of low cost firms causes rents to dissipate and high-cost firms to exit.

uniqueness or even rarity in the absolute sense. It is theoretically possible for rents to be earned by a number of equally efficient producers, so long as an efficiency differential remains between them and other producers. What is *key* is that the superior resources remain *limited* in supply. Thus, efficient firms can sustain this type of competitive advantage only if their resources cannot be expanded freely or imitated by other firms.

Consider what happens if this is not so (see Fig. 2). Increased production by additional efficient producers will shift the supply curve out. This will drive down the equilibrium price, forcing marginal firms to leave the market. Remaining firms will produce at the point where price equals both marginal cost and average cost. As a result, rents will be dissipated and only normal returns will be earned by efficient (now homogeneous) producers.

The Ricardian model is often thought of with respect to resources which are strictly fixed in supply. But it may be applied as well to quasi-fixed resources, which are of much greater importance. These are resources which, while limited in the short run, may be renewed and expanded incrementally within the firm that utilizes them.[7] Utilization of such resources may in fact augment them.

Prahalad and Hamel (1990) describe how core competencies, particularly those which involve collective learning and are knowledge-based, are enhanced as they are applied. Such resources may provide both the basis and the direction for the growth of the firm itself. For example, there may be a natural trajectory embedded in a firm's knowledge base.[8] Current capabilities may both impel and constrain future learning and investment activity.[9] Incremental growth and renewal of such limited resources, however, is not inconsistent with a Ricardian view of rent and competitive advantage.

Monopoly Rents

The condition of heterogeneity is equally consistent with models of market power and monopoly rents as it is with the Ricardian story. What distinguishes monopoly profits from Ricardian rents is that monopoly profits result from a deliberate restriction of output rather than an inherent scarcity of resource supply.

In monopoly models, heterogeneity may result from spatial competition or product differentiation.[10] It may reflect uniqueness and localized monopoly. It may be due to the presence of intra-industry mobility barriers which differentiate groups of firms from one another (Caves and Porter, 1977). It may entail size advantages and irreversible commitments or other first mover advantages.[11] There are numerous such models. What they all have in common is the supposition that firms in favorable positions face downward sloping demand curves. These firms then maximize profits by consciously restricting their output relative to competitive levels. These are models of market power. Unlike Ricardian models, many are 'strategic' in that firms take into account the behavior and relative position of their rivals.

Apparently homogeneous firms may also earn monopoly rents. Cournot behavior exhibited by identical rivals, for example, may yield prices in excess of marginal costs. So may collusive behavior, tacit or otherwise. But these kinds of behaviors are facilitated by fewness of numbers and therefore depend on barriers to entry. Asymmetries must exist between incumbent firms and potential entrants. In this case, the heterogeneity occurs across these two groups of firms.

2.2 Ex Post Limits to Competition

Regardless of the nature of the rents, sustained competitive advantage requires that the condition of heterogeneity be preserved. If the heterogeneity is a short-lived phenomenon, the rents will likewise be fleeting. Since strategists are primarily concerned with rents over a longer term, the condition of heterogeneity must be relatively durable to add value. This will be the case only if there are in place *ex post* limits to competition as well. By this I mean that *subsequent* to a firm's gaining a superior position and earning rents, there must be forces which limit competition for those rents. Competition may dissipate rents by increasing the supply of scarce resources. Alternatively, it might undermine a monopolist's (or oligopolist's) attempts to restrict output. Fig. 2 illustrates how *ex post* competition makes the industry supply curve more elastic and erodes Ricardian rents. *Ex post* competition erodes monopoly rents as well, by increasing output or by making individual demand curves more elastic.

Resource-based work has focused on two critical factors which limit *ex post* competition: imperfect imitability and imperfect substitutability.[12] Substitutes reduce rents by making the demand curves of monopolists or oligopolists more elastic. This is one of Porter's (1980) classic 'five forces.' Much greater attention, however, has been given to the condition of imperfect imitability.

Rumelt (1984) coined the term 'isolating mechanisms' to refer to phenomena which protect individual firms from imitation and preserve their rent streams. These include property rights to scarce resources and various quasi-rights in the form of lags, information asymmetries, and frictions which impede imitative competition (Rumelt, 1987). Of particular interest is the notion of causal ambiguity (Lippman and Rumelt, 1982). This refers to uncertainty regarding the causes of efficiency differences among firms. Causal ambiguity prevents would-be-imitators from knowing exactly what to imitate or how to go about it. Coupled with nonrecoverable costs, such uncertainty may limit imitative activity, thus preserving the condition of heterogeneity.

Other isolating mechanisms include producer learning, buyer switching costs, reputation, buyer search costs, channel crowding, and economies of scale when specialized assets are required (Rumelt, 1987).[13]

Rumelt (1984) describes isolating mechanisms as an analog of Caves and Porter's (1977) mobility barriers, which are themselves an extension of Bain's (1956) concept of entry barriers.[14] Mobility barriers, however, serve to isolate groups of similar firms in a heterogeneous industry, while entry barriers isolate industry participants from potential entrants.

Yao (1988) has distilled a set of factors more basic than the list of entry barriers suggested by Porter (1980) and Bain (1956). He contends that failures of the competitive market are due more fundamentally to production economies and sunk costs, transaction costs, and imperfect information.

Ghemawat (1986) suggests a different categorization, with more of a firm than a market orientation. He argues that inimitable positions derive from size advantages, preferred access to either resources or customers, and/or restrictions on competitors' options.

Dierickx and Cool (1989) offer a unique perspective on the topic of limits to imitation. They focus on factors which prevent the imitation of valuable but nontradeable asset stocks. They maintain that how imitable an asset is depends upon the nature of the process by which it was accumulated. They identify the following characteristics as serving to impede imitation: time compression diseconomies, asset mass efficiencies, interconnectedness of asset stocks, asset erosion, and causal ambiguity.

Dierickx and Cool's (1989) paper is a particularly important piece of work because it focuses precisely on those kinds of resources and capabilities which are of central concern to resource-based theory: nontradeable assets which develop and accumulate within the firm. Such assets tend to defy imitation because they have a strong tacit dimension and are socially complex. They are born of organizational skill and corporate learning. Their development is 'path dependent' in the sense that it is contingent upon preceding levels of learning, investment, asset stocks, and development activity.[15] For such assets, history matters. Would-be-imitators are thwarted by the difficulty of discovering and repeating the developmental process and by the considerable lag involved. Importantly, assets of this nature are also immobile and thus bound to the firm. Factor immobility, or imperfect mobility is another key requirement for sustainable advantage.

2.3 Imperfect Mobility

Resources are perfectly immobile if they cannot be traded. Dierickx and Cool (1989) discuss several examples of this sort. Resources for which property rights are not well defined or with 'bookkeeping feasibility' problems fall into this category (Dierickx and Cool, 1989; Meade, 1952; Bator, 1958). So do resources which are idiosyncratic to the extent that they have no other use outside the firm. (See Williamson, 1979.)

Other kinds of resources may be described as imperfectly mobile. These are resources which are tradeable but more valuable within the firm that currently employs them than they would be in other employ. Resources are imperfectly mobile when they are somewhat specialized to firm-specific needs.[16]

Montgomery and Wernerfelt (1988) use the concept of switching costs to discuss how firm-specific investments may cement the trading relationship between a firm and the owners of factors employed by the firm. These investments by the resource owners may be regarded as a sunk cost (nonrecoverable cost) which may inhibit the factor's exit from a firm. These costs give the firm a greater claim on the resource in question.

Cospecialized assets may be another case in point (Teece, 1986). These are assets which must be used in conjunction with one another or which have higher economic value when employed together. To the extent that they have no other equivalent uses (they are transaction specific) and to the extent that at least one of the assets is firm-specific, their mobility is limited.

Other resources may be imperfectly mobile simply because the transactions costs associated with their transfer are exceedingly high (Williamson, 1975; Rumelt, 1987).

Because immobile or imperfectly mobile resources are nontradeable or less valuable to other users, they cannot be bid away readily from their employer. They remain bound to the firm and available for use over the long run. Thus, they can be a source of sustained advantage.[17] Furthermore, the opportunity cost of their use is significantly less than their value to the present employer.

This is an important point and one which will be developed further in the next section. It implies that any Ricardian or monopoly rents generated by the asset will not be offset entirely by accounting for the asset's opportunity cost.

I use opportunity cost, here, in a sense slightly different from the conventional use of the term. Conventionally, it refers to the value of a resource in its next best use. Here, I mean it to refer to the value of the resource to its second-highest valuing potential-user. (See Klein, Crawford, and Alchian, 1978.) The use to which the potential user may wish to put it may be exactly the same.

This difference between the value of a resource to a firm and its opportunity cost is also a form of rent. Pareto rents, also called quasi-rents, are the excess of an asset's value over its salvage value or its value in its next best *use*. Following Klein *et al.* (1978), I use the term 'appropriable quasi-rents' or 'A-Q rents' to refer to the excess of an asset's value over its value to the second-highest valuing potential user or bidder for the resource. Klein *et al.* (1978) demonstrate that it is entirely possible for a resource to generate A-Q rents in the absence of either Ricardian or monopoly rents. Resources need not be rare or inimitable for them to be differentially valuable to possible users. Thus the presence of A-Q rents is not a sufficient indicator of competitive advantage. There must be monopoly or Ricardian rents generated as well.

A-Q rents are appropriable in the sense that they need not be paid out to the resource for the user to retain its services (Klein *et al.*, 1978). Were the user to appropriate the whole of the A-Q rents, the resource could earn no more elsewhere.[18]

It may be more accurate, however, to recognize that the rents will be shared between the factor owners and the firm employing them. First, one might as easily view the firm as tied to the use of specialized factors, since it cannot substitute generic factors at equal cost. This implies that the situation might be characterized best as a bilateral monopoly, in which the distribution of rents is indeterminate. Secondly, it should be recognized that the rents are in fact *jointly* produced and are as much due to the firm as to the factor. A specialized factor cannot be so productive apart from the firm. Therefore, its super-productivity is attributable as much to the context and other elements of the firm as to the factor itself. The firm and the factor are, in essence, a team. Caves (1980) states that rents are not entirely passed on to factors which are not traded on the open market. In a similar vein, Rumelt (1987) has argued that 'the rent on (specialized) factor(s) is not logically or operationally separable from the profits of the firm' (p. 143).

These two facts—that imperfectly mobile resources will remain available to the firm and that the rents will be shared by the firm—are the key features of imperfect factor mobility (see Wernerfelt, 1989). They, in turn, make imperfect factor mobility a necessary condition for sustainable competitive advantage. In addition, imperfect factor mobility is a particularly important component of the model because such resources are less likely to be imitable than other kinds.[19] Furthermore, the opportunity cost of such assets, as defined above, does not offset the rents. But even together with heterogeneity and *ex post* limits to competition, imperfect factor mobility is not yet sufficient for sustained competitive advantage.

2.4 Ex Ante Limits to Competition

One last condition must be met for a firm to have competitive advantage. There must be *ex ante* limits to competition as well. By this I mean that, prior to any firm's establishing a superior resource position, there must be limited competition for that position. This may be best explained by illustration. Suppose it is perceived, *a priori*, by equally endowed firms that by occupying certain choice locations they can gain an inimitable resource position over their rivals. What will ensue is fierce competition for those locations to the point that the anticipated returns are, in essence, competed away. A superior location could only be a source of above normal returns if some firm had the foresight or good fortune to acquire it in the absence of competition. This is the point brought out by Barney (1986) in arguing that the economic performance of firms depends not only on the returns from their strategies but also on the cost of implementing those strategies. Without imperfections in strategic factor markets, where the resources necessary to implement strategies are acquired, firms can only hope for normal returns. Rumelt (1987) makes a similar point in noting that unless there is a difference between the *ex post* value of a venture and the *ex ante* cost of acquiring the necessary resources, the entrepreneurial rents are zero. Profits come from *ex ante* uncertainty.

While only tradeable resources can be acquired in strategic factor markets, the argument can be extended to immobile and imperfectly mobile resources as well, as both Dierickx and Cool (1989) and Barney (1989) have noted. *Ex ante* competition to develop imperfectly mobile resources, such as the good will of clients, can also dissipate expected returns. While it is less likely that the full value of such resources will be anticipated or that firms will be equally efficient in accumulating such resources, it is important to recognize that imperfect resource mobility is not sufficient unto itself. There must be limits to *ex ante* competition as well.

2.5 The Cornerstones of Competitive Advantage

In sum, four conditions must be met for a firm to enjoy sustained above-normal returns. Resource heterogeneity creates Ricardian or monopoly rents. *Ex post* limits to competition prevent the rents from being competed away. Imperfect factor mobility ensures that valuable factors remain with the firm and that the rents are shared. *Ex ante* limits to competition keep costs from offsetting the rents. The model is summarized in Fig. 3.

This model is intended to highlight the importance of each of these conditions, as distinct from one another, and to explicate the particular role that each plays in creating and sustaining rents. It is not meant to imply, however, that these four conditions are entirely independent of one another. They are, in fact, related conditions.

Heterogeneity is the most basic condition. It is the sine-qua-non of competitive advantage and has long been a fundamental concept of strategic management. For these reasons it deserves special emphasis. The model tells us that heterogeneity is necessary for sustainable advantage, but not sufficient. For

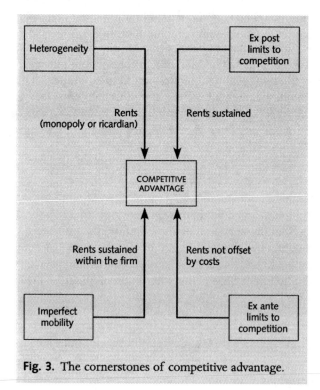

Fig. 3. The cornerstones of competitive advantage.

rents to be sustained, we required *ex post* limits to competition *as well*. One can imagine heterogeneity without *ex post* limits to competition. Firms may have short-lived and unsustainable readily-imitated differences. It takes a greater stretch of the imagination to conceive of *ex post* limits to competition without heterogeneity. (Perhaps a regulator enforcing a pricing cartel among numerous homogeneous trucking firms.) For the most part, *ex post* limits to competition imply heterogeneity, although heterogeneity does not imply *ex post* limits to competition.

Heterogeneity underlies the condition of imperfect mobility as well. Again heterogeneous resources need not be imperfectly mobile. But it is hard to imagine any imperfectly mobile resources which are not also heterogeneous in nature. Resources which are immobile because of their idiosyncratic or firm-specific nature are certainly heterogeneous. Resources which are immobile due to ill-defined property rights or the lack of a market might possibly be homogeneous (pollution rights, for example?) Once again, however, imperfect mobility, for the most part, implies heterogeneity as well.

Finally, it is important to recognize that the productivity of superior resources depends upon the nature of their employment and the skill with which a strategy based on resource superiority is implemented.

3. Applications of the Resource-Based Model

A major contribution of the resource-based model is that it explains long-lived differences in firm profitability that cannot be attributed to differences in industry conditions. Indeed, there is considerable evidence to show that such differences are not well explained by industry participation (Schmalensee, 1985; Mueller, 1986; Wernerfelt and Montgomery, 1988; Hansen and Wernerfelt, 1989; Rumelt, 1991). There is less agreement on the relative magnitude of firm effects, but several studies have indicated that these effects are substantial (Mueller, 1986; Hansen and Wernerfelt, 1989; Rumelt, 1991). The resource-based model is a theoretical complement to this work.

On the practical side, the model may prove useful to managers seeking to understand, preserve, or extend their competitive advantage. While the model itself is freely available to all, its strategic implications depend on a firm's specific resource endowment. Barney (1986) argues that a firm may gain expectational advantages by analyzing information about the assets it already controls.

So long as its assets are imperfectly mobile, inimitable, and nonsubstitutable, other firms will not be able to mimic its strategy. Thus application of the model will not increase competition for available rents. It will only ensure that each firm optimizes the use of its own specialized resources.

Because of its focus on imperfectly mobile resources, for which the transactions cost of market exchange are high, resource-based theory has important implications for corporate strategy and issues regarding the scope of the firm as well as single business strategy. Some applications in each of these areas are discussed in turn.

3.1 Single Business Strategy

At the single business level, the model may help managers differentiate between resources which might support a competitive advantage from other less valuable resources (Barney, 1991). For example, a brilliant, Nobel prize winning scientist may be a unique resource, but unless he has firm-specific ties, his perfect mobility makes him an unlikely source of sustainable advantage. Managers should ask themselves if his productivity has to do, in part, with the specific team of researchers of which he is a part. Does it depend on his relationship with talented managers who are exceptionally adept at managing creativity? Does it depend on the spirit of the workers or the unique culture of the firm?

A resource-based perspective may also help a firm in deciding whether to license a new technology or whether to develop it internally. If the technology is imperfectly mobile in the sense that its potential value cannot be well communicated to others because of the risk of revealing proprietary information, it might best be developed internally. Alternatively, its marketability might depend upon cospecialized assets such as long established relationships with vendors who are reluctant to switch to other suppliers. If the cospecialized assets are held by the firm and are themselves immobile, internal development may still make sense. If the innovation is perfectly mobile, the innovators could do no better than to license the technology.

Decision-making would also be enhanced by considering how imitable the innovation is. If the innovation is no more than a clever and complex assembly of relatively available technologies, then no wall of patents could keep opponents out. Recognizing this vulnerability, a manager might want to think more carefully about the length of the expected entry lag and whether or not there may be some advantage possible due to firm-specific learning or asset mass efficiencies. He might consider trying to use his head start to build other cospecialized resources that are less available (say a reputation for service on the new technology). This might be possible if the secondary resource is time path dependent or if his expectational advantage inhibits competition from developing the secondary resource.

The general point is that by analyzing his resource position, a manager would have a clearer understanding of whether his situation meets necessary conditions for a sustainable advantage. Fewer strategic mistakes would be made. But in addition, it might help him to utilize his expectational advantage in looking ahead.

Amit and Schoemaker (1993) draw upon resource-based theory in developing a behavioral view of strategic assets and offer some prescriptive advice on how to target, develop and deploy them. Wernerfelt (1989) proposes some guidelines to help managers identify their critical resources and decide how to apply them.

In some cases causal ambiguity may make it impossible for a firm to evaluate its resources or even to identify them. (See Lippman and Rumelt, 1982.) While such resources may be the basis for competitive advantage, the causal ambiguity involved leaves little room for strategy. Firms owning the resources have no informational advantage over other firms and little ability to leverage these resources further since there is uncertainty regarding their dimensions and/or their value.

Other resources can more easily be identified as value-creating resources, but their reproduction may be highly uncertain. Resources which are strongly time-path dependent or which are socially complex fit this category. (See Barney, 1991.) While these resources may be *difficult* to reproduce or extend, the firm owning the assets is likely to have a strong advantage in extending them over other firms. In part, this advantage is informational, based on complex and tacit understandings, not easily accessible to outsiders. But also it's because the production of a socially complex resource is likely to require firm specific cospecialized assets which cannot be duplicated in other settings. The resource-based view would help managers to understand that such resources can be an important basis for competitive advantage. And, by highlighting the value of these resources, it might help managers see that, despite the difficulty, they should consider leveraging these resources further.

In sum, this emerging theory may prove to be a paradigm capable of elucidating and integrating research in all areas of strategy. Despite the need for further work, it has already shown itself to be a robust and integrative tool. It has strong implications for single-business strategy, for corporate strategy, for theorists and practitioners alike. Importantly, it is the only theory of corporate scope which is capable of explaining the range of diversification, in all its richness, from related constrained to the conglomerate form. This is the crucial mark of a robust theory of diversification (Teece, 1982). It is an area ripe for research, which has already demonstrated its fruitfulness and deserves the concentrated efforts of this community of scholars.

Notes

I would like to thank Connie Helfat, Yair Aharoni, Kurt Christensen, Joe Mahoney and Ruth Raubitschek, for helpful comments. Raffi Amit, Jay Barney, Anne Huff, Bruce Kogut, Cynthia Montgomery, and Birger Wernerfelt gave me constructive criticism on an earlier version of this paper. I am grateful to David Besanko and Jeff Williams for their encouragement and support. Thanks are due as well to the SMJ editors and reviewers. Remaining errors are my own.

1. This is not meant to suggest that the contributions of resource-based work have been limited to these topics.
2. See Nelson (1991) and Williams (1992) for discussions on why firms are different.
3. In equilibrium, industry demand and supply conditions determine the minimum efficiency level required to breakeven.
4. Earnings in excess of breakeven are called rents, rather than profits, if their existence does not induce new competition.
5. See Ricardo (1817) and Rumelt (1987).
6. Note, however, that superior resources do not necessarily lead to a low cost position. This is simply the most tractable example.
7. See Nelson and Winter (1982) and Wernerfelt (1989).
8. This is a notion attributable to organizational economics. See Teece (1990).
9. See Dosi, Teece, and Winter's (1990) discussion of core capabilities, path dependencies and learning.
10. See Schmalensee (1978).
11. See Ghemawat (1986) and Lieberman and Montgomery (1988). Consider also models of dominant firm behavior.
12. See Barney (1991) and Dierickx and Cool (1989).
13. These topics and other related ones have received much attention in modern industrial organization literature as well.
14. For further discussion, see Mahoney and Pandian (1992).
15. See Barney (1991) and Dosi, Teece, and Winter (1990).
16. Williamson (1985) discusses such assets and their implications for efficient firm boundaries extensively.
17. On the other hand, such assets may make a firm less responsive and flexible in the face of environmental or technological changes which upset a previously held advantage. Specialization is a two-edged sword.
18. Note that, in a multiperiod model, human resources would be reluctant to invest in firm-specific attributes if they expected the firm to appropriate the rents generated.
19. Dierickx and Cool (1989) contend that nontradeability is required to ensure that an asset remains fixed in supply.

References

Amit, R. and P. J. Schoemaker (1993). 'Strategic assets and organizational rent', *Strategic Management Journal*, **14**, pp. 33–46.

Andrews, K. R. (1971). *The Concept of Corporate Strategy*, Irwin, Homewood, IL.

Bain, J. (1956). *Barriers to New Competition*, Harvard University Press, Cambridge, MA.

Barney, J. B. (1986). 'Strategic factor markets: Expectations, luck and business strategy', *Management Science*, **42**, pp. 1231–1241.

Barney, J. B. (1989). 'Asset stocks and sustained competitive advantage: A comment', *Management Science*, **35**, pp. 1511–1513.

Barney, J. B. (1991). 'Firm resources and sustained competitive advantage', *Journal of Management*, **17**, pp. 99–120.

Bater, F. (1958). 'The anatomy of market failure', *Quarterly Journal of Economics*, pp. 301–309.

Castanias, R. and C. Helfat (1991). 'Managerial resources and rents', *Journal of Management*, **17**, pp. 155–171.

Caves, R. E. (1980). 'Industrial organization, corporate strategy and structure', *Journal of Economic Literature*, **18**, pp. 64–92.

Caves, R. E. and M. Porter (1977). 'From entry barriers to mobility barriers: Conjectural decisions and contrived deterrence to new competition', *Quarterly Journal of Economics*, **91**, pp. 241–262.

Connor, K. (1991). 'A historical comparison of resource-based theory and five schools of thought within industrial organization economics: Do we have a new theory of the firm?', *Journal of Management*, **17**, pp. 121–154.

Dierickx, I. and K. Cool. (1989). 'Asset stock accumulation and sustainability of competitive advantage', *Management Science*, **35**, pp. 1504–1511.

Dosi, G., D. Teece, and S. Winter. (1990). 'Toward a theory of corporate coherence: Preliminary remarks', Working paper.

Ghemawat, P. (Sept–Oct 1986). 'Sustainable advantage', *Harvard Business Review*, pp. 53–58.

Hansen, G. and B. Wernerfelt (1989). 'Determinants of firm performance: The relative importance of economic and organizational factors', *Strategic Management Journal*, **10**, pp. 399–411.

Klein, B., R. Crawford, and A. Alchian (1978). 'Vertical integration, appropriable rents, and the competitive contracting process', *Journal of Law and Economics*, **21**, pp. 297–326.

Lieberman, M. and D. Montgomery (1988). 'First mover advantage', *Strategic Management Journal*, **9**, Special issue, pp. 41–58.

Lippman, S. A. and R. P. Rumelt (1982). 'Uncertain imitability: An analysis of interfirm differences in efficiency under competition', *The Bell Journal of Economics*, **13**, pp. 418–438.

Mahoney, J. and J. R. Pandian (1992). 'The resource-based view within the conversation of strategic management', *Strategic Management Journal*, **13**, pp. 363–380.

Meade, J. (1952). 'External economies and diseconomies in a competitive situation', *Economic Journal*, pp. 56–67.

Montgomery, C. A. and B. Wernerfelt (1988). 'Diversification, Ricardian rents, and Tobin's q', *Rand Journal*, pp. 623–632.

Mueller, D. (1986). *Profits in the Long Run*. Cambridge University Press, Cambridge, MA.

Nelson, R. (1991). 'Why do firms differ and how does it matter'. *Strategic Management Journal*, **12**, pp. 61–76.

Nelson, R. R. and S. O. Winter. (1982). *An Evolutionary Theory of Economic Change*, Belknap Press, Cambridge, MA.

Penrose, E. T. (1959). *The Theory of Growth of the Firm*, Basil Blackwell, London.

Porter, M. E. (1980). *Competitive Strategy: Techniques for Analyzing Industries and Competitors*, The Free Press, New York.

Prahalad, C. K. and G. Hamel (May–June 1990). 'The core competence of the corporation', *Harvard Business Review*, pp. 79–91.

Ricardo, D. (1965, Original 1817). *The Principles of Political Economy and Taxation*. Reprinted, J. M. Dent and Son, London.

Rumelt, R. P. (1984). 'Toward a strategic theory of the firm'. In R. Lamb (ed.), *Competitive Strategic Management*, Prentice Hall, Englewood Cliffs, NJ, pp. 556–570.

Rumelt, R. P. (1987). 'Theory, strategy, and entrepreneurship'. In D. Teece, (ed.), *The Competitive Challenge*. Ballinger, Cambridge, MA, pp. 137–158.

Rumelt, R. P. (1991). 'How much does industry matter?', *Strategic Management Journal*, **12**, pp. 167–186.

Schmalensee, R. (1978). 'Entry deterrence in the ready-to-eat breakfast cereal industry', *Bell Journal of Economics*, **9**, pp. 305–327.

Schmalensee, R. (1985). 'Do markets differ much?', *The American Economic Review*, **75**, pp. 341–350.

Teece, D. J. (1980). 'Economies of scope and the scope of the enterprise', *Journal of Economic Behavior and Organization*, **1**, pp. 223–247.

Teece, D. J. (1982). 'Toward an economic theory of the multiproduct firm', *Journal of Economic Behavior and Organization*, **3**, pp. 39–63.

Teece, D. J. (1986). 'Firm boundaries, technological innovation, and strategic management'. In L. G. Thomas, III (ed.), *The Economics of Strategic Planning*, Lexington, Lexington, MA, pp. 187–199.

Teece, D. (1990). 'Contributions and impediments of economic analysis to the study of strategic management'. In J. W. Fredrickson (ed.), *Perspectives on Strategic Management*, Harper Business, New York, pp. 39–80.

Thompson, A. A. and A. J. Strickland (1990). *Strategic Management: Concepts and Cases*, Irwin, Homewood, IL.

Wernerfelt, B. (1984). 'A resource based view of the firm', *Strategic Management Journal*, **5**, pp. 171–180.

Wernerfelt, B. (1989). 'From critical resources to corporate strategy', *Journal of General Management*, **14**, pp. 4–12.

Wernerfelt, B. and C. A. Montgomery (1988). 'Tobin's q and the importance of focus in firm performance', *American Economic Review*, **78**, pp. 246–250.

Williamson, O. (1975). *Markets and Hierarchies*. Free Press, New York.

Williamson, O. E. (1979). 'Transaction-cost economics: The governance of contractual relations', *Journal of Law and Economics*, **22**, pp. 233–261.

Williamson, O. E. (1985). *The Economic Institutions of Capitalism*. Free Press, New York.

Williams, J. (1992). 'Strategy and the search for rents: The evolution of diversity among firms,' Working Paper, Carnegie Mellon University.

Yao, D. (1988). 'Beyond the reach of the invisible hand: Impediments to economic activity, market failures, and profitability, *Strategic Management Journal*, **9**, pp. 59–70.

16 The Resource-Based View Within the Conversation of Strategic Management

Joseph T. Mahoney and J. Rajendran Pandian

McCloskey (1985) persuasively argues that 'good science is good conversation.' The resource-based view is good management science, properly speaking, because it stimulates good conversation within the strategic management field. The resource-based approach (Penrose, 1959; Wernerfelt, 1984) is attracting the attention of a growing number of researchers precisely because the framework encourages a dialogue between scholars from a variety of perspectives. The purpose of this paper is to coalesce and sustain this conversation.

In particular, three major research programs are currently intertwined in the resource-based framework. First, the resource-based view incorporates concepts from mainstream strategy research. Distinctive competencies (Andrews, 1971; Ansoff, 1965; Selznick, 1957) of heterogeneous firms, for example, are a fundamental component of the resource-based view. Moreover, the resource-based theory is concerned with the rate, direction and performance implications of diversification strategy which are areas of considerable focus in the strategy field (Ramanujam and Varadarajan, 1989).

Second, the resource-based approach fits comfortably within the conversation of organizational economics (Barney and Ouchi, 1986). In fact, the resource-based view may arguably be considered a fifth branch of the organizational economics tree of knowledge along with positive agency theory (Eisenhardt, 1989), property rights (Alchian 1984; Coase, 1960), transaction cost economics (Williamson, 1985), and evolutionary economics (Nelson and Winter, 1982).

Third, the resource-based approach is complementary to industrial organization analysis (Caves, 1982; Porter 1980). In particular, we emphasize that the resource-based view contains elements of both the Harvard (Bain, 1968; Mason, 1957) and Chicago (Demsetz, 1982; Stigler, 1968) schools of industrial organization thought. Indeed, Conner (1991) persuasively argues that the resource-based approach both reflects a strong industrial organization approach and is at the same time unique.

The resource-based view not only stimulates conversation within mainstream strategy research, organizational economics and industrial organization research but it also provides a framework for increased discussion between these research perspectives. In this paper we develop our thesis that the resource-based approach presents an opportunity for dialogue and debate between scholars from different research perspectives. Future resource-based studies that give simultaneous attention to these three research programs are suggested.

1. Resource-Based Theory Within the Conversation of Strategy

1.1 Types of Rent

Strategy can be viewed as a 'continuing search for rent' (Bowman, 1974: 47), where rent is defined as return in excess of a resource owner's opportunity costs (Tollison, 1982). A resource may be conveniently classified under a few headings—for example, *land* and equipment, *labor* (including workers' capabilities and knowledge), and *capital* (organizational, tangible and intangible)—but the subdivision of resources may proceed as far as is useful for the problem at hand (Penrose, 1959: 74).[1]

The generation of above-normal rates of return (i.e. rents) is the focus of analysis for competitive advantage (Porter, 1985). In contrast to efficient market theorists, most resource-based theorists insist that short-term (if not long-term) economic rents are possible (Schoemaker, 1990). Several types of rents may be usefully distinguished. First, rents may be achieved by owning a valuable resource that is scarce (Ricardo, 1817). Resources yielding *Ricardian rents* include ownership of valuable land, locational advantages, patents and copyrights. Second, *monopoly rents* may be achieved by government protection or by collusive arrangements when barriers to potential competitors are high (Bain,

1968). Third, *entrepreneurial (Schumpeterian) rent* may be achieved by risk-taking and entrepreneurial insight in an uncertain/complex environment (Cooper, Gimeno-Gascon, and Woo, 1991; Rumelt, 1987; Schumpeter, 1934). Entrepreneurial rents are inherently self-destructive due to diffusion of knowledge (Schoemaker, 1990; Schumpeter, 1950).

Finally, the firm may be able to appropriate rents when resources are firm-specific. The difference between the first-best and second-best use value of a resource—the so-called *quasi-rent*[2] (Klein, Crawford and Alchian, 1978)—is precisely the amount that a firm may appropriate to achieve above-normal returns. Quasi-rents are appropriable from idiosyncratic physical capital, human capital and dedicated assets (Williamson, 1979).

1.2 Sources of Rent

The existence and maintenance of rents depend upon a lack of competition in either acquiring or developing complementary resources. Rents derived from services of durable resources that are relatively important to customers and are simultaneously superior, imperfectly imitable, and imperfectly substitutable, will not be appropriated if they are nontradeable or traded in imperfect factor-markets (Barney, 1991; Dierickx and Cool, 1989; Peteraf, 1990).

The resource-based view incorporates the insights of the early seminal contributions to strategic management in order to explain how firms generate rents. The traditional concept of strategy (Andrews, 1971; Ansoff, 1965) considers the resource position of the firm. A firm selects its strategy to generate rents based upon their resource capabilities. Organizations with the strategic capability to focus and coordinate human effort and the ability to evaluate effectively the resource position of the firm in terms of strengths and weaknesses have a strong basis for competitive advantage (Andrews, 1971). Rent theory allows us to clarify the SWOT framework by identifying exactly what can be real 'strengths' and firm capabilities for strategic advantage. Differences among firms in terms of *information, luck,* and/or *capabilities* enable the firm to generate rents.[3]

The firm's unique capabilities in terms of technical know-how and managerial ability are important sources of heterogeneity that may result in sustained competitive advantage. In particular, distinctive competence and superior organizational routines in one or more of the firm's value-chain functions may enable the firm to generate rents from a resource advantage (Hitt and Ireland, 1985).

1.3 Distinctive Competence is a Function of the Resources Which a Firm Possesses at any Point in Time

Penrose argues that: 'It is the heterogeneity . . . of the productive services available or potentially available from its resources that gives each firm its unique character' (1959: 75). For example, top management in a diversified enterprise can be a significant and distinctive resource if it uniquely contributes to the sustained profitability of the enterprise (Castanias and Helfat, 1991).

A firm may achieve rents not because it has better resources, but rather the firm's distinctive competence involves making better use of its resources (Penrose, 1959: 54).[4] The firm may make better use of human capital by correctly assigning workers to where they have higher productivity in the organization (Tomer, 1987), and the firm may make better allocations of financial capital toward high yield uses (Bower, 1970; Williamson, 1975).

A rich connection among the firm's resources, distinctive competencies and the mental models or 'dominant logic' (Prahalad and Bettis, 1986) of the managerial team drives the diversification process (Ginsberg, 1990; Grant, 1988). Penrose argues that unused productive services of resources 'shape the scope and direction of the search for knowledge' (1959: 77). The services and rents that resources will yield depend upon the dominant logic of the top management team, but the development of the dominant logic of the top managerial team is partly shaped by the resources with which they deal. This notion that the firm's current resources influence managerial perceptions and hence the direction of growth is a cognitive proposition that reinforces the economic rationale that a firm's resource profile will influence the direction of diversification (Wernerfelt, 1984).

1.4 Diversification Strategy and Resources

The resource-based view contributes to the large stream of research on diversification strategy (Ramanujam and Varadarajan, 1989) in four areas: First, the resource-based approach considers the limitations of diversified growth (via internal development and mergers and acquisitions). Second, the resource-based view considers important motivations for diversification. Third, the resource-based approach provides a theoretical perspective for predicting the *direction* of diversification. Fourth, the resource-based view provides a theoretical rationale for predicting superior performance for certain categories of related diversification.

Limits to Growth

Penrose (1959) provides a seminal contribution in the resource-based tradition. Fundamentally, it is the resources of the firm which limit the choice of markets it may enter, and the levels of profits it may expect (Wernerfelt, 1989). Key resource constraints include: (1) shortage of labor or physical inputs, (2) shortage of finance, (3) lack of suitable investment opportunities, and (4) lack of sufficient managerial capacity. Penrose (1959) considers the growth of the firm as limited only in the long-run by its internal management resources.

The total managerial services that a firm requires at a point in time are partly constrained by the necessity to run the firm at its current size, and is partly required to carry out expansionary ventures with respect to new products and expansion generally (Gort, 1962; Hay and Morris, 1979; Marris, 1964). New managerial recruits increase the growth potential of the firm. However, the training of new managers and their integration into the work-force occupy some of the time and effort of existing managers, and thus reduce the managerial services available for expansion. In Penrose's theory 'management (is) both the accelerator and the brake for the growth process' (Starbuck, 1965: 490).

This managerial constraint on the growth rate of the firm, the so-called 'Penrose effect' (Marris, 1963), suggests that fast-growing firms in one period tend to experience slower growth in the next period (Penrose, 1959: 49). Hence, the Penrose effect suggests a negative correlation between growth rates in successive periods (Slater, 1980b). Case studies (Edwards and Townsend, 1961; Penrose, 1960; Richardson, 1964), formal models (Slater, 1980a; Uzawa, 1969), and econometric tests (Shen, 1970) provide support for the Penrose effect. A corollary to the Penrose effect is that a higher interdependence among resources will lower the firm's growth rate (Robinson, 1932).

A Resource-Based Motivation for Growth

In addition to analyzing the limits of the rate of a firm's growth, Penrose (1955, 1959) also examines the motives for expansion. It is rare for all units to be operating at the same speed and capacity, and this phenomenon creates an internal inducement for firm growth. Penrose (1985: 13) presents a *resource approach* arguing that firms are administrative organizations *and* collections of physical, human and intangible assets. Unused productive services from existing resources present a 'jig-saw puzzle' for balancing processes (Penrose, 1959: 70). Excess capacity due to indivisibilities, and cyclical demand, to a large extent drives the diversification process (Caves, 1980; Chandler, 1962).[5] The resource of unused human expertise, in particular, may drive diversification (Farjoun, 1991).

The firm's capability[6] lies upstream from the end-product—it resides in skills, capacities, and a dynamic resource fit which may find a variety of end uses (Caves, 1984; Teece, 1982; Ulrich and Lake, 1990). Excess physical capacity leads to related diversification if the capacity is end-product specific (Chatterjee and Wernerfelt, 1988).

At all times there exist within every firm, pools of unused productive services, and these, together with the changing knowledge of management, create unique productive opportunities for each firm (Chandler, 1977, 1990; Teece, 1980). Penrose argues that there is a 'virtuous circle' (1959: 73) in which the process of growth necessitates specialization but specialization necessitates growth and diversification to fully utilize unused productive services. Thus, *specialization induces diversification*.

Rubin (1973) formally models firms' diversification decisions according to Penrose's theory. Rubin's (1973) dynamic programing model illustrates Penrose's thesis that there is an optimal growth rate for the firm. An optimal growth of the firm involves a balance between exploitation of existing resources and development of new resources (Penrose, 1959; Rubin, 1973; Wernerfelt, 1984).

The Direction of Growth

In addition to providing insights on the *rate* of the growth of the firm, the resource-based approach provides value-added theoretical explanations for the *direction* of a firm's diversification. The direction of a firm's diversification is due to the nature of its available resources and the market opportunities in the environment.

Several econometric studies support the resource-based theory that an enterprise's firm-specific resources serve as the driving force for its diversification strategy. Lemelin (1982) finds that industries assigned to categories of producer goods, consumer convenience goods and consumer nonconvenience goods are more likely to diversify into other industries assigned to the same category. Lemelin (1982) argues that this pattern is consistent with the resource-based hypothesis that firms attempt to transfer intangible capital among related activities.

MacDonald (1985) finds that firms are more likely to enter industries that are related to their primary activities. R&D intensive firms channel their diversification toward R&D intensive industries. R&D expenditure is a reasonably effective proxy for capturing an enterprise's endowment of unique knowledge possessed by individuals and teams within the organization (Caves, 1982). Thus, the diversification pattern that MacDonald (1985) finds may reflect the transfer of shareable idiosyncratic organizational and intangible capital among related activities (Prescott and Visscher, 1980; Williamson, 1985).

Similarly, Stewart, Harris and Carleton (1984) find a very strong positive relationship between the advertising intensity of the acquiring firm's primary industry and the advertising intensity of the acquired firm's primary industry. Advertising expenditure is a reasonably effective proxy for capturing a firm's intangible assets (such as brand name and reputation).

Montgomery and Hariharan (1991) supply further support for the resource-based view that the resource profile of the diversifying firm is critical in predicting the resource characteristics of the destination industry. While previous empirical research, discussed above, assigned firms to their primary industry and studied the relationship between these primary (origin) industries and destination industries, Montgomery and Hariharan (1991) provide a significant contribution by using the FTC Line-of-Business (LB) data to consider the resource profile of diversifying firms. Montgomery and Hariharan (1991) find strong empirical evidence to *reject the hypothesis that the direction of diversification occurs at random*. They find that a firm's competencies and intangible assets in advertising and R&D explain the direction of diversification strategy. The productive services of these resources are a selective force in determining the direction of diversification (Penrose, 1959: 87) and the pattern of reconfigurations, in general (Singh and Chang, 1991).[7]

These empirical studies suggest that firm-specific resources and relatedness of activities are important variables in the diversification process. Companies grow in the directions set by their capabilities and these capabilities slowly expand and change (Penrose, 1959; Richardson, 1972).

Diversification and Performance

It is not our intention to review the vast literature on diversification and performance. Our objective here is simply to state the resource-based logic for the possible association between firm diversification and performance.

The resource-based discussion of the diversification–performance linkage is embedded within the more general question of whether *any* strategy that the firm utilizes makes a difference. There still is an important debate concerning the significance of firm effects as opposed to industry attractiveness effects on performance. While Schmalensee (1985) does not find support for the existence of firm effects, several other studies find significant firm effects (Cubbin and Geroski, 1987; Duhaime and Stimpert, 1991; Hansen and Wernerfelt, 1989; Jacobson, 1988; Mueller, 1977, 1986; Rumelt, 1987, 1991; Scott and Pascoe, 1986; Vasconcellos and Hambrick, 1989; Wernerfelt and Montgomery, 1988). A focus on specific resources rather than strategy types in the merger and acquisition research may better explain firm performance (Harrison, Hitt, Hoskisson and Ireland, 1991).

The preponderance of empirical evidence suggests that firms' strategies may influence their rent stream.

2. Resource-Based Theory Within the Conversation of Organizational Economics

The organizational economics paradigm (Barney and Ouchi, 1986) includes evolutionary economics (Barney 1986b; Nelson and Winter, 1982; Schumpeter, 1950), transaction cost economics (Coase, 1937; Ouchi, 1980; Williamson, 1975); property rights theory (Alchian, 1984; Jones, 1983) and positive agency theory (Eisenhardt, 1989; Jensen and Meckling, 1976). Theorists from these perspectives share the resource-based theorists' dissatisfaction with the neoclassical theory of the firm.

Barney and Ouchi (1986) note that positive microeconomics has been dominated by a research program that emphasizes supply and demand, equilibria, optimization analyses and industry structure. The task of strategic management is to contribute insight concerning the structure-strategy-performance paradigm (Bain, 1968; Porter, 1981; Scherer, 1980) and to get 'inside the black box' by analyzing the 'strategic firm'[8] (Rumelt, 1984). While industrial organization analysis attempts to characterize the behavior of a 'representative firm', the resource-based approach focuses on the key success factors of individual firm behavior to achieve firm-specific advantages by a portfolio of differential core skills and routines, coherence across skills, and unique proprietary know-how (Aharoni and Sticht, 1990; Dosi, Teece and Winter, 1990; Prahalad and Hamel, 1990).

The fundamental paradox of the neoclassical theory of the firm is that the firm need not exist. The neoclassical theory assumes away transaction costs (Williamson, 1975); limits on rationality (Simon, 1976); technological uncertainty (Schumpeter, 1950); consumer or producer learning (Lieberman and Montgomery, 1988) and prices as signals of quality (Spence, 1974). The removal of these 'frictions' leads to the conclusion that prices are no longer sufficient statistics (Koopmans, 1957).[9]

This static equilibrium approach consequently does not address the competitive *process* which is of central concern in strategy (Teece and Winter, 1984). The view of corporate behavior is most closely associated with Schumpeter's vision of competition as a process of 'creative destruction' rather than as a static equilibrium condition (Barney, 1986b; Lippman and Rumelt, 1982; Nelson and Winter, 1982; Phillips, 1971).

The resource-based approach may be framed in a dynamic context. Schumpeterian competition involves carrying out 'new combinations' including new methods of production as well as organizational innovation (Iwai, 1984). This Schumpeterian competition may be translated into the resource-based framework by considering the firm's 'new combinations of resources' (Penrose, 1959: 85) as a means of achieving the goal of sustained competitive advantage (Ghemawat, 1986). Penrose (1959), following Schumpeter (1950), views the competitive process as dynamic involving uncertainty, struggle and disequilibrium. Firms accumulate knowledge as a strategic asset (Winter, 1987) through R&D and learning, some of it incidental to the production process. Indeed, Rumelt combines the Schumpeterian perspective with the resource-based view by suggesting that strategy formulation concerns: 'the constant search for ways in which the firm's unique resources can be redeployed in changing circumstances' (1984: 569).

The resource-based view on distinctive competencies may also be analyzed in an evolutionary context. The firm's distinctive competencies may be defined by the set of substantive rules and routines used by top management. Managers' past decisions and decision rules are the basic genetics which firms possess. Sustainable advantage is thus a history (path) dependent process (Arthur, 1988; Barney, 1991; Nelson and Winter, 1982).

The resource-based approach is also closely aligned with other theories composing the organizational economics paradigm (Barney and Ouchi, 1986). The resource-based view is linked to agency theory because the resource deployment of the firm is influenced by (minimizing) agency costs (Castanias and Helfat, 1991). The resource-based view is linked to property rights since delineated property rights make resources valuable and as resources become more valuable, property rights become more precise (Libecap, 1989). Finally, the resource-based theory is linked to transaction cost theory because resource combinations are influenced by transaction cost economizing (Teece, 1982; Williamson, 1991b).

In the translation of the transaction cost approach into the resource-based approach, a firm is considered both an administrative organization and a pool of productive resources (Penrose, 1959). In planning expansion, the firm considers the active juxtaposition of its own 'inherited' endowment of resources and those that it must obtain from the market in order to carry out its program of activities (Barney, 1991; Caves, 1980).[10] These resource endowments factors are assumed to be semipermanently tied ('sticky') to the firm due to recontracting costs and market imperfections (Teece, 1990; Yao, 1988). Firm-specific resources may result in sustainable performance differences (Hill and Jones, 1989; Oster, 1990; Robins, 1992; Williamson, 1985). The analysis of these resources extends quite naturally to international business competition and cooperation (Collis, 1991; Tallman, 1991).

The resource-based framework views diversification as a response to indivisibilities and market failure (Teece, 1982). The transaction cost, property rights, and positive agency theory literatures provide the theoretical underpinnings for the resource-based approach by analyzing the nature of market failure. Market failure occurs when: there exists private synergy and sunk cost (Baumol, Panzar and Willig, 1982); property rights are ill-defined (Alchian, 1984); externalities are present (Dahlman, 1979); imperfect (asymmetric) information exists (Eisenhardt, 1989, Yao, 1988); and transaction costs are positive (Williamson, 1991a). The result of these market imperfections is that recognition, disclosure, team organization, monitoring and dissipation costs are incurred in contractual exchange (Caves, 1982; Teece, 1982).

While market failure explains the existence of the firm (Coase, 1937), the resource-based view posits *heterogeneous* firms as the outcome of certain types of market failure. Transaction cost analysis (Teece, 1984; Williamson, 1975) suggests that idiosyncratic capital is an important source of market failure and heterogeneity. Unique assets may take the form of human capital (Becker, 1964), physical capital (Klein, Crawford and Alchian, 1978), legal capital (Alchian, 1984; Barzel, 1989), organizational capital and experience (Huff, 1982; Prahalad and Bettis, 1986; Spender, 1989), and intangible capital (Caves, 1982).

The diversification literature, discussed above, emphasizes the role of intangible assets in explaining heterogeneity. Successful firms in most industries possess one or more types of intangible assets—technological know-how, patented process or design, know-how shared among employees, and marketing assets. Intangible assets are often subject to market (transaction cost) failure. Even if the firm can market its intangible assets effectively, it could not disentangle them from the skills and knowledge of the managerial team (Nelson and Winter, 1982). In summary, idiosyncratic physical, human, and intangible resources supply the genetics of firm heterogeneity.

Not only are there substantive areas of overlap between organizational economics and the resource-based view of the firm but there are methodological similarities as well. Fundamentally, the organizational economics paradigm of evolutionary economics, transaction cost theory, positive agency theory and property rights theory attempt to explain the origin, function, evolution, and sustainability of our 'institutions of capitalism' (Williamson, 1985). The resource-based view is expressly concerned with a specific institution, namely, the rent-generating heterogeneous firm and its origin, function, evolution, and sustainability (Barney, 1991; Lippman and Rumelt, 1982; Rumelt, 1984). Debates concerning the validity of the organizational economics methodology (Barney and Ouchi, 1986) need to be seriously analyzed by resource-based scholars.

While the resource-based view is intertwined with the organizational economics literature, a case can be made that the resource-based view is also complementary to the industrial organization structure–conduct–performance paradigm. Valuable resources are often imperfectly imitable and imperfectly substitutable enabling the heterogeneous firm to generate and sustain rents. The *sustainability* of rents is a function of 'barriers to imitation,' which have been a major focus of the industrial organization paradigm considered below.

3. Resource-Based Theory Within the Conversation of Industrial Organization

The resource-based view is complementary to the analytic (Hill, 1988; Karnani, 1984; Schmalensee, 1978) and empirical literature (Dess and Davis, 1984; Grinyer, McKiernan and Yasai-Ardekani, 1988) based on the Bain-Porter framework (Bain, 1968; Porter, 1985). Peteraf (1990) provides a contribution to the resource-based literature by systematically contrasting the classical 'Harvard-school' Porter framework (1980), and the resource-based view of the firm. Peteraf (1990) also contrasts the revisionist 'Chicago-school' (Stigler, 1968) industrial organization view to the resource-based view. The emphasis in this section is on the common ground shared between these 'two systems of belief' (Demsetz, 1974) in industrial organization and the resource-based approach.

While the industrial organization literature focuses externally on the industry and product markets (Phillips and Stevenson, 1974; Tirole, 1988) and the resource-based view focuses internally on the firm and its resources, there is nonetheless a *duality* between the economist's constrained maximization problem of maximizing production given resource constraints and the constrained minimization problem of minimizing resource costs given a desired production level. Wernerfelt (1984) reminds us of this fundamental principle: specifying the enterprise's product mix enables the researcher to specify the minimum necessary resource commitments. Conversely, by specifying a resource profile, for the enterprise, an optimal product-mix profile can be developed. Indeed, the product market and resource market are 'two sides of the same coin' (Wernerfelt, 1984: 171).

The resource-based view correctly suggests that focusing on firm effects is important in developing and combining resources to achieve competitive advantage, but this does not imply that industry product analysis merely yields normal returns. On the contrary, analysis of the environment is still critical since environmental change 'may change the significance of resources to the firm' (Penrose, 1959: 79).

The essential theoretical concept for explaining the *sustainability* of rents in the resource-based framework is 'isolating mechanisms' (Rumelt, 1984). The notion of isolating mechanism (at the firm level of analysis) is an analogue of entry barriers (at the industry level) and mobility barriers at the strategic group level (Caves and Porter, 1977; McGee and Thomas, 1986).[11] In this sense, the resource-based view utilizes a central concept of the structure–strategy–performance paradigm, albeit at a different level of analysis. These isolating mechanisms (barriers to imitation) explain (*ex post*) a stable stream of rents and provide a rationale for intraindustry differences among firms.

Examples of isolating mechanisms (both efficiency and market power) are derived from the resource-based theory, mainstream strategy research, organizational economics and the industrial organization literature (Table 1). It is no

Table 1. Isolating mechanisms

Resource-based view/strategy literature	
Mechanism	Reference
Resource position barriers	Wernerfelt, 1984
Unique or rare resources which are not perfectly mobile	Barney, 1991
Unique managerial talent that is inimitable	Penrose, 1959
Resources with limited strategic substitutability by equivalent assets	Dierickx and Cool, 1989
Valuable, nontradeable or imperfectly tradeable resources	Barney, 1991; Dierickx and Cool, 1989
Distinctive competencies and core competencies that are difficult to replicate	Andrews, 1971; Dosi, Teece, and Winter, 1990
Unique combinations of business experience	Huff, 1982; Prahalad and Bettis, 1986; Spender, 1989
Corporate culture that is valuable, rare and imperfectly imitable due to social complexity, tacit dimensions and path dependency	Barney, 1986a; Fiol, 1991
Culture that is the result of human action but not of human design	Arrow, 1974; Camerer and Vepsalainen, 1988; Hayek, 1978
Invisible assets that by their nature are difficult to imitate	Itami, 1987
Valuable heuristics and processes that are not easily imitated	Schoemaker, 1990
Time compression diseconomies	Dierickx and Cool, 1989
Response lags	Lippman and Rumelt, 1982
Organizational economics literature	
Mechanism	Reference
Schumpeter's resource combinations	Schumpeter, 1934
Management skills and team embodied capabilities	Nelson and Winter, 1982
Organizational innovation that is characterized by a slow diffusion process	Armour and Teece, 1978; Mahajan, Sharma and Bettis, 1988
Unique historical conditions in which firm-specific skills and resource combinations result in path dependencies and heterogeneity over time	Arthur, 1989; Barney, 1991; De Gregori, 1987

Table 1. *Continued*

Resource-based view/strategy literature	
Mechanism	Reference
Uncertain imitability due to bounded rationality and causal ambiguity	Lippman and Rumelt, 1982
Enacted complexity	Schoemaker, 1990
Idiosyncratic assets	Williamson, 1979
The rich connections between ambiguity and uniqueness	Demsetz, 1973
	Reed and DeFillippi, 1990
Co-specialized assets	Teece, 1986, 1987
(high interconnectedness)	Dierickx and Cool, 1989
Organizational capital	Tomer, 1987
Reputation and image	Klein and Leffler, 1981
	Kreps and Wilson, 1982; Kreps, 1990
Consumer trust	Itami, 1987
Private or asymmetric information and knowledge as strategic resources	Barney, 1986c
	Eisenhardt, 1989; Holmstrom, 1979
	Winter, 1988
Resource commitments	Caves, 1984; Ghemawat, 1991
First-mover advantages in acquiring information and other valuable resources that inhibit imitation	Lieberman and Montgomery, 1988
Firm-specific knowledge of buyers, sellers and worker's capabilities	Prescott and Visscher, 1980
Imperfect factor markets	Barney, 1986c
	Wernerfelt and Montgomery, 1986
Ill-defined property rights that result in imperfect mobility of resources	Alchian and Demsetz, 1972
Patents, trademarks, and copyrights	Alchian, 1984

Industrial organization literature	
Mechanism	Reference
Investments that entail high exit barriers and high switching costs	Porter, 1980
High sunk cost investments	Baumol, Panzar and Willig, 1982
Learning and experience curve advantages that are kept proprietary	Lieberman, 1987
	Spence, 1981
Legal restrictions on entry	Stigler, 1968
Economies of scale combined with imperfect capital markets	Bain, 1968

exaggeration to claim that the concept of isolating mechanisms (Rumelt, 1984) is an insightful and unifying concept. The crucial aspect for competitive advantage involves the productive services of rent-generating resources and resource combinations which cannot be easily imitated or substituted.

Although the list of isolating mechanisms is impressive, what is the generalizable insight? A careful examination of the list of isolating mechanisms suggests that absent government intervention, isolating mechanisms exist because of *asset specificity* and *bounded rationality* (Williamson, 1979). Or, put differently, isolating mechanisms are the result of the rich connections between *uniqueness* and *causal ambiguity* (Lippman and Rumelt, 1982). A reasonably comprehensive review of the strategy, organizational economics and industrial organization literature on 'barriers to imitation' reveals the powerful generalizable insights of these two seminal articles.[12]

The resource-based view is closer to the 'Harvard School' Mason-Bain-Porter framework in believing in the *effectiveness* of these isolating mechanisms. The 'Chicago School' view questions whether economies of scale, advertising and R&D expenditure can ever be a barrier to entry or isolating mechanism (Demsetz, 1974, 1982; Kitch, 1983; Stigler, 1968). Many industrial economists take an eclectic view between the two camps (Mancke, 1974; Phillips, 1976; Williamson, 1985).

Peteraf (1990) argues that the resource-based view is closer to the 'Chicago School' in emphasizing efficiency rents rather than monopoly rents. However, this distinction should not be taken too far. As Demsetz notes, there is no reason to suppose that competitive behavior never yields monopoly rents (1973: 3). The resource-based view is closer to the 'Harvard School' in terms of positing *sustainable* rents. This difference is due to the divergent premises of the 'Harvard School' and 'Chicago School' on the effectiveness of isolating mechanisms, as noted above. In short, we argue here that the resource-based approach appears to be generating new intellectual combinations of thought (Conner, 1991). Suggestions for sustaining the conversation are considered below.

4. Discussion and Conclusions

A fully developed theory of the expansion of the firm is a formidable challenge for strategic management research. The theory would involve production theory (Hayes and Wheelwright, 1984), investment theory (Hirshleifer, 1970), portfolio theory (Sharpe, 1970), organizational economics (Barney and Ouchi, 1986; Williamson, 1985), the theory of oligopoly (Friedman, 1983), the theory of international finance (Sodersten, 1980), and so forth. While not claiming to be a comprehensive theory of expansion, the resource-based approach provides an illuminating generalizable theory of the growth of the firm.

As we reflect back on the full set of articles published on, or related to, the resource-based view of the firm, a few value-added areas for research are suggested.

Joseph Mahoney and Rajendran Pandian

4.1 Integrating the Diversification Literature with the Organizational Economics Literature

To be a fruitful comprehensive theory of diversification, the resource-based view must also aid management practice on the choice of *governance structure* (i.e. mergers and acquisitions, internal development, and intermediate modes such as joint ventures). The choice of organizational form is of primary concern in organizational economics (Williamson, 1985). Integration of the emerging resource-based view with organizational economics may provide value-added insights on the implementation of diversification strategy (Chatterjee, 1990b; Lamont and Anderson, 1985; Simmonds, 1990; Yip, 1982).[13] Hybrids and networks involve the coordination of resources across firm boundaries (Borys and Jemison, 1989). Can these hybrids and resources be matched in a discriminating way?

4.2 The Development of an Endogenous Theory of Heterogeneity

A fundamental premise that distinguishes industrial organization from strategic management is the strategy field's assumption of heterogeneous firms. It seems legitimate to require that the strategy field provide a base for its theoretical foundations. A major advancement in the strategy field is the development of models where firm heterogeneity is an endogenous creation of economic actors.

One approach is to integrate the resource-based view with the organizational economics and dynamic capabilities approach (Teece, Pisano and Shuen, 1990), in which heterogeneity is explained as an outcome of a *disequilibrium process* of Schumpeterian competition (Iwai, 1984), path dependencies (Arthur, 1989), first-mover advantages, irreversible commitments and complementary or co-specialized (Ghemawat, 1991; Grant, 1990; Teece, 1987; Williamson and Winter, 1991).

A second approach utilizes the equilibrium models (Shapiro, 1989) of industrial organization to explain the nature of the heterogeneous firm. Lippman and Rumelt (1982), for example, generate an equilibrium in which firm heterogeneity is an endogenous outcome due to isolating mechanisms and uncertain imitability. Their model provides a persuasive argument that firm heterogeneity may be sustained in equilibrium without invoking *ad hoc* entry barriers. A second type of model stresses 'the heterogeneity (of managerial services), their uniqueness for every individual firm' (Penrose, 1959: 199). Oi (1983) models the heterogeneous firm as the equilibrium outcome of an underlying distribution of entrepreneurial abilities. The resource-based literature is a framework within which an integrated analytical model may be constructed.

An advantage of the disequilibrium approach is that *time* may be viewed as the fourth dimension of resources (along with land, labor, and capital, broadly defined). Time and attention are scarce resources (Becker, 1965; Simon, 1976) and are sources of competitive advantage that are neglected in single-period equilibrium analysis. The approach of organizational economics (Barney and Ouchi, 1986) of real heterogeneous firms, competing in real (calendar) time appears more relevant (and no less rigorous) than orthodox equilibrium models.[14] Nevertheless, contributions to the field may be achieved on both fronts. Amit and Schoemaker (1990), for example, analyze the sustainability of heterogeneous firms both in, and outside of, equilibrium.

4.3 Integration of the Resource-Based View with Strategic Group Analysis

While a morality play of the virtuous resource-based theorists doing battle against the misguided strategic group theorists and industrial organization analysts may provide a crusading faith for the young and naive, a more balanced view, in our estimation, is needed. Intellectual isolating mechanisms which artificially reduce the trading of ideas are not best for the strategy field as a whole.

Albeit at different units of analysis, strategic group research is by no means inconsistent with a resource-based view. In fact, as McGee and Thomas have noted: 'strategic group analysis has interesting parallels with the theory of growth of the firm as first articulated by Downie, Penrose and Marris more than 20 years ago' (1986: 157). Can rare, inimitable resources be a source of sustained strategic group advantages?

4.4 Integration of the Resource-Based View with Industry Analysis

Competitive advantage is a function of industry analysis, organizational governance and firm effects (in the form of resource advantages and strategies). The resource-based model has the potential to coalesce these research streams to provide a rich and rigorous theory of the strategic firm (Conner, 1991; Rumelt, 1984). Indeed, Montgomery and Wernerfelt (1988) give simultaneous attention to the resource-based view, organizational economics and the industrial organization paradigm (see also, Wernerfelt and Montgomery, 1986, 1988). Simultaneous attention to these research streams is precisely the approach that warrants future research.

Notes

1. The importance of assessing a firm's *resource profile* has clearly been a traditional focus within strategic management (e.g. Ackoff, 1970, chap. 4; Hofer and Schendel, 1978: 144–153). Hofer and Schendel (1978: 145) suggest that a resource profile combines the following resources and capabilities: (1) Financial resources (e.g. cash flow, debt capacity, new equity availability); (2) Physical resources (e.g. plant & equipment, inventories); (3) Human resources (e.g. scientists, production supervisors, sales personnel); (4) Organizational resources (e.g. quality control systems, corporate culture, relationships); (5) Technological capabilities (e.g. high quality production, low cost plants). Grant (1991) suggests a sixth type of resource, intangible resources (e.g. reputation, brand recognition, goodwill).

2. Quasi-rent as used by Klein, Crawford and Alchian (K-C-A) (1978) is referred to as a Pareto (Marshallian) rent by Rumelt (1987). Note that in the economics literature a quasi-fixed scarce resource that yields rents is sometimes referred to as a 'quasi-rent' where the meaning is 'quasi-Ricardian rent.' In this paper quasi-rent is used in the K-C-A sense of Pareto (Marshallian) rents.

3. In the agency literature, asymmetric information typically refers to articulable knowledge that has not been revealed by an agent and/or principal. Organizational *capabilities*, however, may involve a closely interrelated mix of routines, tacit knowledge and organizational memory (Nelson and Winter, 1982; Polanyi, 1962; Walsh and Ungson, 1991). Thus, differences in capabilities may go far beyond the issue of nondisclosure of relevant information. A firm may 'know more than it can tell' due to causal ambiguity. The upshot is that differences in firm capabilities do *not* reduce to (articulable) information asymmetries.

4. Penrose's (1959) argument that a firm may achieve competitive advantage by making better use of its resources has been formally modeled in terms of 'dynamic adjustment costs' (Prescott and Visscher, 1980). The firm slowly discovers which tasks suit employees best. The trade-off is between rapid firm growth in which case job assignment errors are large, and slower growth of the firm, in which information about employees' skills have been further processed by managers resulting in improved job assignments.

5. Indeed Chandler thought highly of Penrose (1959); see Chandler (1962: 453, footnote 1).

6. Penrose (1959: 25) makes a crucial distinction between resource and capabilities (services of resources): 'resources consist of a bundle of potential services and can, for the most part, be defined independently of their use, while services cannot be so defined, the very word "service" implying a function, an activity.' In more

modern terms, Penrose (1959) is suggesting that resources are stocks and capabilities (services) are flows. Dynamic capabilities are created over time and may depend on the history of the use of resources in an extremely complex (path dependent) process. Path-dependent capabilities provide the building blocks for the firm's strategic architecture of strategic complexity.

7. While the resource-based view has developed a viable approach for explaining and predicting growth and diversification, a 'resource-based theory of divestment' is clearly lacking.

8. The strategic firm is 'characterized by a bundle of linked and idiosyncratic resources and resource conversion activities' (Rumelt, 1984: 561). In this paper, the firm's potential resource conversion activities are designated firm *capabilities*.

9. The so-called First Fundamental Welfare Theorem of economics articulates a perfectly competitive equilibrium (i.e. zero rents) of price-taking, complete markets, no interdependence of consumer's utilities, no interdependence in production, and perfect information. Organizational economics in general, and the resource-based approach in particular, departs from this stylized world. Economies of scale and asset specificity (sunk costs) violate the price-taking assumption; positive transaction costs result in less than complete markets; externalities violate the assumptions of zero interdependence in consumption and production; and asymmetric information (entrepreneurship and first-mover advantages) violates the assumption of perfect information. To put it economically, one of the assumptions of the 'Theorem' must be violated for a firm to generate (and sustain) positive rents. In fact, one of the assumptions must be violated for the firm to exist. A detailed analysis of the implications of these real-world imperfections for strategy research can be found in Yao (1988).

10. Richardson (1990: 231) notes that: 'we cannot hope to . . . answer our question about the division of labor between firm and market unless the elements of organization, knowledge, experience, and skills are brought back to the foreground of our vision.'

11. A major distinction, however, is that entry (mobility) barriers are a private *collective* asset of an industry's (strategic groups's) incumbents, and investments to augment these assets are subject to free-riding and underprovision. Isolating mechanisms involve firm-level investments in resources and capabilities.

12. Itami's (1987) notion that invisible (intangible) assets are often the only source of competitive edge that can be sustained over time suggests that invisible assets are the most likely candidates for resources that are unique and causally ambiguous.

13. Caves (1982: 4) notes that intangible resources 'are subject to a daunting list of infirmities for being put to efficient use by conventional markets.' Thus, intangible resources are posited as being positively related to the internal development mode of diversification.

14. Penrose (1959) denied the concept of long-run equilibrium analysis in the resource approach. Penrose (1959) suggests that firms are operating in a never-ending state of flux with 'lumpy' resources and excess capacity.

References

Ackoff, R. L. *A Concept of Corporate Planning*, John Wiley, New York, 1970.

Aharoni, Y. and J. P. Sticht. 'In search for the unique: Can firm-specific advantages be evaluated?' Working paper, Leon Recanati Graduate School of Business Administration, Tel Aviv University, 1990.

Alchian, A. A. 'Specificity, specialization, and coalitions', *Journal of Institutional and Theoretical Economics*, **140**, 1984, pp. 34–49.

Alchian, A. A. and H. Demsetz. 'Production, information costs, and economic organization, *American Economic Review*, **62**, 1972, pp. 777–795.

Amit, R. and P. J. Schoemaker. 'Key success factors: Their foundation and application'. Working paper, Northwestern University, 1990.

Andrews, K. *The Concept of Corporate Strategy*, Dow Jones-Irwin, Homewood, IL, 1971.

Ansoff, H. I. *Corporate Strategy: An Analytical Approach to Business Policy for Growth and Expansion*, McGraw-Hill, New York, 1965.

Armour, H. O. and D. J. Teece. 'Organizational structure and economic performance: A test of the multidivisional hypothesis', *Bell Journal of Economics*, **9**, 1978, pp. 106–122.

Arrow, K. *The Limits of Organization*, W. W. Norton & Company, New York, 1974.

Arthur, W. B. 'Self-reinforcing mechanisms in economics'. In P. W. Anderson, K. J. Arrow and D. Pines (eds.), *The Economy as an Evolving Complex System*, Addison-Wesley Publishing, Redwood City, CA, 1988, pp. 9–31.

Arthur, W. B. 'Competing technologies, increasing returns, and lock-in by historical events', *Economic Journal*, **99**, 1989, pp. 116–131.

Bain, J. S. *Industrial Organization*, John Wiley, New York, 1968.

Barney, J. B. 'Organizational culture: Can it be a source of sustained competitive advantage?' *Academy of Management Review*, **11**, 1986a, pp. 656–665.

Barney, J. B. 'Types of competition and the theory of strategy: Toward an integrative framework', *Academy of Management Review*, **11**, 1986b, pp. 791–800.

Barney, J. B. 'Strategic factor markets: Expectations, luck and business strategy', *Management Science*, **32**, 1986c, pp. 1231–1241.

Barney, J. B. 'Returns to bidding firms in mergers and acquisitions: Reconsidering the relatedness hypothesis', *Strategic Management Journal*, **9** (Summer), 1988, pp. 71–78.

Barney, J. B. 'Asset stocks and sustained competitive advantage: A comment', *Management Science*, **35**, 1989, pp. 1511–1513.

Barney, J. B. 'Firm resources and sustained competitive advantage', *Journal of Management*, **17**, 1991, pp. 99–120.

Barney, J. B. and W. Ouchi (eds.) *Organizational Economics: Toward a New Paradigm for Studying and Understanding Organizations*, Jossey-Bass, San Francisco, CA, 1986.

Barzel, Y. *Economic Analysis of Property Rights*, Cambridge University Press, Cambridge, 1989.

Baumol, W. J., J. C. Panzar, and R. D. Willig. *Contestable Markets and the Theory of Industry Structure*, Harcourt Brace Jovanovich, New York, 1982.

Becker, G. S. *Human Capital*, National Bureau of Economic Research, New York, 1964.

Becker, G. S. 'A theory of the allocation of time', *Economic Journal*, **75**, 1965, pp. 493–517.

Bettis, R. A. 'Performance differences in related and unrelated diversified firms', *Strategic Management Journal*, **2**, 1981, pp. 379–393.

Borys, B. and D. B. Jemison. 'Hybrid arrangements as strategic alliances: Theoretical issues in organizational combinations', *Academy of Management Review*, **14**, 1989, pp. 234–249.

Bower, J. L. *Managing the Resource Allocation Process: A Study of Corporate Planning and Investment*, Harvard Business School Press, Boston, MA, 1970.

Bowman, E. H. 'Epistemology, corporate strategy, and academe', *Sloan Management Review*, **15**, 1974, pp. 35–50.

Camerer, C. and A. Vepsalainen. 'The economic efficiency of corporate culture', *Strategic Management Journal*, **9** (Summer), 1988, pp. 115–126.

Castanias, R. P. and C. E. Helfat. 'Managerial resources and rents', *Journal of Management*, **17**, 1991, pp. 155–171.

Caves, R. E. 'Industrial organization, corporate strategy and structure', *Journal of Economic Literature*, **58**, 1980, pp. 64–92.

Caves, R. E. *Multinational Enterprise and Economic Analysis*, Harvard University Press, Cambridge, MA, 1982.

Caves, R. E. 'Economic analysis and the quest for competitive advantage', *American Economic Review*, **74**, 1984, pp. 127–132.

Caves, R. E. and M. E. Porter. 'From entry barriers to mobility barriers: Conjectural decisions and contrived deterrence to new competition', *Quarterly Journal of Economics*, **91**, 1977, pp. 241–261.

Caves, R., M. E. Porter and A. M. Spence. *Competition in the Open Economy*, Harvard University Press, Cambridge, MA, 1980.

Chandler, A. D. *Strategy and Structure: Chapters in the History of the American Industrial Enterprise*, MIT Press, Cambridge, MA, 1962.

Chandler, A. D. *The Visible Hand: The Managerial Revolution in American Business*, Harvard University Press, Cambridge, MA, 1977.

Chandler, A. D. *Scale and Scope: The Dynamics of Industrial Capitalism*, Harvard University Press, Cambridge, MA, 1990.

Chatterjee, S. 'The gains to acquiring firms: The related principle revisited', *Academy of Management Best Papers Proceedings*, 1990a, pp. 12–16.

Chatterjee, S. 'Excess resources, utilization costs, and mode of entry', *Academy of Management*, **33**, 1990b, pp. 780–800.

Chatterjee, S. and B. Wernerfelt. 'Related or unrelated diversification: A resource based approach', *Academy of Management Proceedings*, 1988, pp. 7–16.

Chatterjee, S. and B. Wernerfelt. 'The link between resources and type of diversification: Theory and evidence', *Strategic Management Journal*, **12**, 1991, pp. 33–48.

Coase, R. H. 'The nature of the firm', *Economica*, **4**, 1937, pp. 386–405.

Coase, R. H. 'The problem of social cost', *Journal of Law and Economics*, **3**, 1960, pp. 1–44.

Collis, D. J. 'A resource-based analysis of global competition: The case of the bearings industry', *Strategic Management Journal*, **12** (Summer), 1991, pp. 49–89.

Conner, K. R. 'An historical comparison of resource-based theory and five schools of thought within industrial organization economics: Do we have a new theory of the firm', *Journal of Management*, **17**, 1991, pp. 121–154.

Cooper, A. C., F. J. Gimeno-Gascon and C. Y. Woo. 'A resource-based prediction of new venture survival and growth', *Academy of Management Proceedings*, 1991, pp. 68–72.

Cubbin, J. and P. Geroski. 'The convergence of profits in the long run: Inter-firm and inter-industry comparisons', *Journal of Industrial Economics*, **36**, 1987, pp. 427–442.

Dahlman, C. J. 'The problem of externality', *Journal of Law and Economics*, **22**, 1979, pp. 141–162.

De Gregori, T. R. 'Resources are not; they become: An institutional theory', *Journal of Economic Issues*, **21**, 1987, pp. 1241–1263.

Demsetz, H. 'Industry structure, market rivalry, and public policy', *Journal of Law and Economics*, **16**, 1973, pp. 1–9.

Demsetz, H. 'Two systems of belief about monopoly'. In H. J. Goldschmid, H. Mann, and J. F. Weston (eds), *Industrial Concentration: The New Learning*, Little, Brown, Boston, MA, 1974, pp. 164–184.

Demsetz, H. 'Barriers to entry', *American Economic Review*, **72**, 1982, pp. 47–57.

Dess, G. G. and P. S. Davis. 'Porter's generic strategies as determinants of strategic group membership and organizational performance', *Academy of Management Journal*, **27**, 1984, pp. 467–488.

Dierickx, I. and K. Cool. 'Asset stock accumulation and sustainability of competitive advantage', *Management Science*, **35**, 1989, pp. 1504–1511.

Dosi, G., D. Teece and S. Winter. 'Toward a theory of corporate coherence: Preliminary remarks'. Working paper, University of California, Berkeley, 1990.

Downie, J. *The Competitive Process*, Duckworth, London, 1958.

Duhaime, I. M. and J. L. Stimpert. 'One more time: A look at the factors influencing firm performance'. Working Paper, University of Illinois, 1991.

Edwards, R. S. and H. Townsend. *Business Enterprise: Its Growth and Organization*, Macmillan, London, 1961.

Eisenhardt, K. M. 'Agency theory: An assessment and review', *Acacdemy of Management Review*, **14**, 1989, pp. 57–74.

Farjoun, M. 'Beyond industry boundaries: Human expertise, diversification and resource-related industry groups'. Working paper, University of Illinois, 1991.

Fiol, C. M. 'Managing culture as a competitive resource: An identity-based view of sustainable competitive advantage', *Journal of Management*, **17**, 1991, pp. 191–211.

Friedman, J. W. *Oligopoly Theory*, Cambridge University Press, New York, 1983.

Ghemawat, P. 'Sustainable advantage', *Harvard Business Reivew*, **64**, 1986, pp. 53–58.

Ghemawat, P. *Commitment: The Dynamic of Strategy*, Free Press, New York, 1991.

Ginsberg, A. 'Connecting diversification to performance: A sociocognitive approach', *Academy of Management Review*, **15**, 1990, pp. 514–535.

Gort, M. *Diversification and Integration in American Industry*, Princeton University Press, Princeton, NY, 1962.

Grant, R. M. 'On "dominant logic" and the link between diversity and performance', *Strategic Management Journal*, **9**, 1988, pp. 639–642.

Grant, R. M. 'The competitive process and the basis of competitive advantage', Working paper, Anderson Graduate School of Management, UCLA, 1990.

Grant, R. M. *Contemporary Strategy Analysis: Concepts, Techniques, Application*, Basil Blackwell, Cambridge, MA, 1991.

Grinyer, P. H., P. McKiernan and M. Yasai-Ardekani. 'Market, organizational, and managerial correlates of economic performance in the U.K. electrical engineering industry', *Strategic Management Journal*, **9**, 1988, pp. 297–318.

Grossman, S. and O. Hart, 'Takeover bids, the free-rider problem and the theory of the corporation', *Bell Journal of Economics*, **11**, 1980, pp. 42–64.

Hansen, G. S. and B. Wernerfelt. 'Determinants of firm performance: The relative importance of economic and organizational factors', *Strategic Management Journal*, **10**, 1989, pp. 399–411.

Harrison, J. S., M. A. Hitt, R. E. Hoskisson and R. D. Ireland. 'Synergies and post-acquisition performance: Differences versus similarities in resource allocation', *Journal of Management*, **17**, 1991, pp. 173–190.

Hay, D. A. and D. J. Morris. *Industrial Economics*, Oxford University Press, Oxford, 1979.

Hayek, F. A. *New Studies in Philosophy, Politics, Economics and the History of Ideas*, Routledge & Kegan Paul, London, 1978.

Hayes, R. H. and S. C. Wheelwright. *Restoring our Competitive Edge: Competing Through Manufacturing*, John Wiley, New York, 1984.

Hill, C. W. L. 'Differentiation versus low cost or differentiation and low cost: A contingency framework', *Academy of Management Review*, **13**, 1988, pp. 401–412.

Hill, C. W. L. and G. R. Jones. *Strategic Management: An Integrated Approach*, Houghton Mifflin, Boston, MA, 1989.

Hirshleifer, J. *Investment, Interest and Capital*, Prentice-Hall, Englewood Cliffs, NJ, 1970.

Hitt, M. A. and R. D. Ireland. 'Corporate distinctive competence, strategy, industry and performance', *Strategic Management Journal*, **6**, 1985, pp. 273–293.

Hofer, C. W. and D. Schendel. *Strategy Formulation: Analytical Concepts*, West Publishing, St. Paul, MN, 1978.

Holmstrom, B. 'Moral hazard and observability', *Bell Journal of Economics*, **10**, 1979, pp. 74–91.

Huff, A. S. 'Industry influence on strategy reformulation', *Strategic Management Journal*, **3**, 1982, pp. 119–131.

Itami, H. *Mobilizing Invisible Assets*, Harvard University Press, Cambridge, MA, 1987.

Iwai, K. 'Schumpeterian dynamics: An evolutionary model of innovation and imitation', *Journal of Economic Behavior and Organization*, **5**, 1984, pp. 159–190.

Jacobson, R. 'The persistence of abnormal returns', *Strategic Management Journal*, **9**, 1988, pp. 415–430.

Jensen, M. C. and W. H. Meckling. 'Theory of the firm: Managerial behavior, agency costs and ownership structure', *Journal of Financial Economics*, **3**, 1976, pp. 305–360.

Jones, G. R. 'Transaction costs, property rights, and organizational culture: An exchange perspective', *Administrative Science Quarterly*, **28**, 1983, pp. 454–467.

Karnani, A. 'Generic competitive strategies—An analytical approach', *Strategic Management Journal*, **4**, 1984, pp. 357–380.

Kitch, E. W. (ed.) 'The fire of truth: A remembrance of law and economics at Chicago, 1932–1970', *Journal of Law and Economics*, **26**, 1983, pp. 163–233.

Klein, B., R. G. Crawford and A. A. Alchian. 'Vertical integration, appropriable rents and the competitive contracting process', *Journal of Law and Economics*, **21**, 1978, pp. 297–326.

Klein, B. and K. B. Leffler. 'The role of market forces in assuring contractual performance', *Journal of Political Economy*, **89**, 1981, pp. 615–641.

Koopmans, T. *Three Essays on the State of Economic Science*, McGraw-Hill, New York, 1957.

Kreps, D. M. 'Corporate culture and economic theory'. In J. E. Alt and K. A. Shepsle (eds.), *Perspectives on Positive Political Economy*, Cambridge University Press, Cambridge, 1990, pp. 90–143.

Kreps, D. M. and R. Wilson. 'Reputation and imperfect information', *Journal of Economic Theory*, **27**, 1982, pp. 253–279.

Lamont, B. T. and C. R. Anderson, 'Mode of corporate diversification and economic performance', *Academy of Management Journal*, **28**, 1985, pp. 926–934.

Lemelin, A. 'Relatedness in the patterns of interindustry diversification', *Review of Economics and Statistics*, **64**, 1982, pp. 646–657.

Libecap, G. D. *Contracting for Property Rights*, Cambridge University Press, New York, 1989.

Lieberman, M. B. 'The learning curve, diffusion, and competitive strategy', *Strategic Management Journal*, **8**, 1987, pp. 441–452.

Lieberman, M. B. and D. B. Montgomery. 'First-mover advantages', *Strategic Management Journal*, **9**, 1988, pp. 41–58.

Lippman, S. and R. P. Rumelt. 'Uncertain imitability: An analysis of interfirm differences in efficiency under competition', *Bell Journal of Economics*, **13**, 1982, pp. 418–453.

Lubatkin, M. and R. C. Rogers. 'Diversification, systematic risk and shareholder return: The capital market extension of Rumelt's study', *Academy of Management Journal*, **32**, 1989, pp. 454–465.

MacDonald, J. M. 'R&D and the directions of diversification', *Review of Economics and Statistics*, **67**, 1985, pp. 583–590.

Mahajan, V., S. Sharma and R. A. Bettis. 'The adoption of the M-form organizational structure: A test of imitation hypothesis', *Management Science*, **34**, 1988, pp. 1188–1201.

Mancke, R. 'Causes of interfirm profitability differences: A new interpretation of the evidence', *Quarterly Journal of Economics*, **88**, 1974, pp. 181–193.

Marris, R. L. 'A model of the "managerial" enterprise', *Quarterly Journal of Economics*, **77**, 1963, pp. 185–209.

Marris, R. *The Economic Theory of 'Managerial' Capitalism*, Macmillan, New York, 1964.

Mason, E. S. *Economic Concentration and the Monopoly Problem*, Harvard University Press, Cambridge, MA, 1957.

McCloskey, D. N. *The Rhetoric of Economics*, University of Wisconsin Press, Madison, WI, 1985.

McGee, J. and H. Thomas. 'Strategic groups: Theory of research and taxonomy', *Strategic Management Journal*, 7, 1986, pp. 141–160.

Montgomery, C. A. 'Product-market diversification and market power', *Academy of Management Journal*, 28, 1985, pp. 789–798.

Montgomery, C. A. and S. Hariharan. 'Diversified entry by established firms', *Journal of Economic Behavior and Organization*, 15, 1991, pp. 71–89.

Montgomery, C. A. and B. Wernerfelt. 'Diversfication, Ricardian rents, and Tobin's q', *Rand Journal of Economics*, 19, 1988, pp. 623–632.

Mueller, D. C. 'The persistence of profits above the norm', *Economica*, 44, 1977, pp. 369–380.

Mueller, D. C. 'Persistent profits among large corporations'. In L. G. Thomas (ed.), *The Economics of Strategic Planning*, Lexington Books: Lexington, MA, 1986, pp. 31–61.

Nelson, R. and S. Winter. *An Evolutionary Theory of Economic Change*, Belknap Press, Cambridge, MA, 1982.

Oi, W. Y. 'Heterogeneous firms and the organization of production', *Economic Inquiry*, 21, 1983, pp. 147–171.

Oster, S. M. *Modern Competitive Analysis*, Oxford University Press, New York, 1990.

Ouchi, W. 'Markets, bureaucracies, and clans', *Administrative Science Quarterly*, 25, 1980, pp. 120–142.

Palepu, K. 'Diversification strategy, profit performance and the entropy measure', *Strategic Management Journal*, 6, 1985, pp. 239–255.

Penrose, E. T. 'Limits to the growth and size of firms', *American Economic Review*, 45, 1955, pp. 531–543.

Penrose, E. T. *The Theory of the Growth of the Firm*, John Wiley, New York, 1959.

Penrose, E. T. 'The growth of the firm. A case study: The Hercules Powder Company', *Business History Review*, 34, 1960, pp. 1–23.

Penrose, E. T. *The Theory of the Growth of the Firm: Twenty-five Years Later*, Acta Universitatis Upsaliensis, Uppsala, 1985.

Peteraf, M. A. 'The cornerstones of competitive advantage: A resource-based view'. Discussion Paper No. 90-29, J. L. Kellogg Graduate School of Management, Northwestern University, 1990.

Phillips, A. *Technological Change and Market Structure: A Case Study of the Market for Commercial Aircraft*, D. C. Heath, Boston, MA, 1971.

Phillips, A. 'A critique of empirical studies of relations between market structure and profitability', *Journal of Industrial Economics*, 24, 1976, 241–249.

Phillips, A. and R. E. Stevenson. 'The historical development of industrial organization', *History of Political Economy*, 6, 1974, pp. 324–342.

Polanyi, M. *Personal Knowledge: Towards a Post-critical Philosophy*, University of Chicago Press, Chicago, IL, 1962.

Joseph Mahoney and Rajendran Pandian

Porter, M. E. *Competitive Strategy*, Free Press, New York, 1980.

Porter, M. E. 'The contributions of industrial organization to strategic management', *Academy of Management Review*, **6**, 1981, pp. 609–620.

Porter, M. E. *Competitive Advantage: Creating and Sustaining Superior Performance*, Free Press, New York, 1985.

Prahalad, C. K. and R. Bettis. 'The dominant logic: A new linkage between diversity and performance', *Strategic Management Journal*, **7**, 1986, pp. 485–501.

Prahalad, C. K. and G. Hamel, 'The core competence of the corporation', *Harvard Business Review*, **90**(3), 1990, pp. 79–91.

Prescott, E. and M. Visscher. 'Organizational capital', *Journal of Political Economy*, **88**, 1980, pp. 446–461.

Ramanujam, V. and P. Varadarajan. 'Research on corporate diversification: A synthesis', *Strategic Management Journal*, **10**, 1989, pp. 523–551.

Reed, R. and R. J. DeFillippi. 'Causal ambiguity, barriers to imitation, and sustainable competitive advantage', *Academy of Management Review*, **15**, 1990, pp. 88–102.

Ricardo, D. *Principles of Political Economy and Taxation*, J. Murray, London, 1817.

Richardson, G. B. 'The limits to a firm's rate of growth', *Oxford Economic Papers*, **16**, 1964, pp. 9–23.

Richardson, G. B. 'The organization of industry', *Economic Journal*, **82**, 1972, pp. 883–896.

Richardson, G. B. *Information and Investment* (2nd ed.), Clarendon Press, Oxford, 1990.

Robins, J. G. 'Organizational considerations in the evaluation of capital assets: Toward a resource-based view of strategic investments by firms', *Organization Science*, forthcoming.

Robinson, E. A. G. *The Structure of Competitive Industry*, Harcourt Brace, New York, 1932.

Rubin, P. H. 'The expansion of firms', *Journal of Political Economy*, **81**, 1973, pp. 936–949.

Rumelt, R. P. *Strategy, Structure and Economic Performance*, Harvard University Press, Cambridge, MA, 1974.

Rumelt, R. P. 'Diversification strategy and profitability', *Strategic Management Journal*, **3**, 1982, pp. 359–369.

Rumelt, R. P. 'Toward a strategic theory of the firm'. In R. Lamb (ed.), *Competitive Strategic Management*, Prentice-Hall, Englewood Cliffs, NJ, 1984, pp. 556–570.

Rumelt, R. P. 'Theory, strategy, and entrepreneurship'. In D. J. Teece (ed.), *The Competitive Challenge*, Ballinger Publishing, Cambridge, MA, 1987, pp. 137–158.

Rumelt, R. P. 'How much does industry matter?', *Strategic Management Journal*, **12**, 1991, pp. 167–185.

Scherer, F. M. *Industrial Market Structure and Economic Performance*, Houghton Mifflin Company, Boston, MA, 1980.

Schmalensee, R. 'Entry deterrence in the ready-to-eat breakfast cereal industry', *Bell Journal of Economics*, **9**, 1978, pp. 305–327.

Schmalensee, R. 'Do markets differ much?' *American Economic Review*, **75**, 1985, pp. 341–351.

228

Schoemaker, P. J. H. 'Strategy, complexity and economic rent', *Management Science*, **36**, 1990, pp. 1178–1192.

Schumpeter, J. A. *The Theory of Economic Development*, Harvard University Press, Cambridge, MA, 1934.

Schumpeter, J. A. *Capitalism, Socialism, and Democracy*, Harper & Brothers, New York, 1950.

Scott, J. and G. Pascoe, 'Beyond firm and industry effects on profitability in imperfect markets', *Review of Economics and Statistics*, **68**, 1986, pp. 284–292.

Selznick, P. *Leadership in Administration: A Sociological Perspective*, Harper & Row, New York, 1957.

Shapiro, C. 'The theory of business strategy', *Rand Journal Economics*, **20**, 1989, pp. 125–137.

Sharpe, W. F. *Portfolio Theory and Capital Markets*, McGraw-Hill, New York, 1970.

Shen, T. Y. 'Economics of scale, Penrose-effect, growth of plants and their size distribution', *Journal of Political Economy*, **78**, 1970, pp. 702–716.

Simmonds, P. G. 'The combined diversification breadth and mode dimensions and the performance of large diversified firms,' *Strategic Management Journal*, **11**, 1990, pp. 399–410.

Simon, H. *Administrative Behavior*, (3rd ed.) Free Press, New York, 1976.

Singh, H. and S. J. Chang. 'Corporate reconfiguration: A resource perspective'. Working paper, University of Pennsylvarria. The Wharton School, Management Department, 1991.

Singh, H. and C. Montgomery. 'Corporate acquisition strategies and economic performance', *Strategic Management Journal*, **8**, 1987, pp. 377–386.

Slater, M. 'The managerial limitations to the growth of firms', *Economic Journal*, **90**, 1980a, pp. 520–528.

Slater, M. 'Forword' (2nd ed.) In E. T. Penrose, *The Theory of the Growth of the Firm*, Basil Blackwell, Oxford, 1980b, pp. vii–xxx.

Sodersten, B. *International Economics*, St. Martin's Press, New York, 1980.

Spence, A. M. *Market Signaling, Informational Transfer in Hiring and Related Screening Processes*, Harvard University Press, Cambridge, MA, 1974.

Spence, A. M. 'The learning curve and competition', *Bell Journal of Economics*, **12**, 1981, pp. 49–70.

Spender, J.-C. *Industry Recipes: An Enquiry into the Nature and Sources of Managerial Judgement*, Blackwell, Oxford, 1989.

Starbuck, W. H. 'Organizational growth and development'. In J. March (ed.), *Handbook of Organizations*, Rand McNally, Chicago, IL. 1965, pp. 451–533.

Stewart, J. F., R. S. Harris and W. T. Carleton. 'The role of market structure in merger behavior', *Jounal of Industrial Economics*, **32**, 1984, pp. 293–312.

Stigler, G. *The Organization of Industry*, University of Chicago Press, Chicago, IL., 1968.

Tallman, S. B. 'Strategic management models and resource-based strategies among MNEs in a host market', *Strategic Management Journal*, **12** (Summer), 1992, pp. 68–82.

Teece, D. J. 'Economics of scope and the scope of the enterprise', *Journal of Economic Behavior and Organization*, **1**, 1980, pp. 223–247.

Teece, D. J. 'Towards an economic theory of the multi-product firm', *Journal of Economic Behavior and Organization*, **3**, 1982, pp. 39–63.

Teece, D. J. 'Economic analysis and strategic management', *California Management Review*, **25**, 1984, pp. 87–110.

Teece, D. J. 'Firm boundaries, technological innovation and strategic planning'. In G. L. Thomas. (ed.). *The Economics of Strategic Planning*, D. C. Heath, Lexington, MA, 1986, pp. 187–199.

Teece, D. J. 'Profiting from technological innovation: Implications for integration, collaboration, licensing, and public policy'. In D. J. Teece (ed.), *The Competitive Challenge*, Ballinger, New York, 1987, pp. 185–219.

Teece, D. J. 'Contributions and impediments of economic analysis to the study of strategic management'. In J. Fredrickson (ed.), *Perspectives on Strategic Management*, Harper & Row, New York, 1990, pp. 39–80.

Teece, D. J., G. Pisano and A. Shuen. 'Firm capabilities, resources and the concept of strategy'. Working paper, University of California at Berkeley, 1990.

Teece, D. J. and S. G. Winter. 'The limits of neoclassical theory in management education', *American Economic Review*, **74**, 1984, pp. 116–121.

Tirole, J. *The Theory of Industrial Organization*, MIT Press, Cambridge, MA, 1988.

Tollison, R. D. 'Rent seeking: A survey', *Kyklos*, **35**, 1982, pp. 575–602.

Tomer, J. F. *Organizational Capital: The Path to Higher Productivity and Well-being*, Praeger, New York, 1987.

Ulrich, D. and D. Lake. *Organizational Capability: Competing from the Inside Out*, John Wiley, New York, 1990.

Uzawa, H. 'Time preference and the Penrose effect in a two-class model of economic growth', *Journal of Political Economy*, **77**, 1969, pp. 628–652.

Varadarajan, P. R. and V. Ramanujam. 'Diversification and performance? A reexamination using a new two dimensional conceptualization of diversity in firms', *Academy of Management Journal*, **30**, 1987, pp. 380–393.

Vasconcellos, J. A. and D. C. Hambrick. 'Key success factors: Test of general framework in the mature industrial-product sector', *Strategic Management Journal*, **10**, 1989, pp. 367–382.

Walsh, J. P. and C. R. Ungson. 'Organizational memory', *Academy of Management Review*, **16**, 1991, pp. 57–91.

Wernerfelt, B. 'A resource-based view of the firm', *Strategic Management Journal*, **5**, 1984, pp. 171–180.

Wernerfelt, B. 'From critical resources to corporate strategy', *Journal of General Management*, **14**, 1989, pp. 4–12.

Wernerfelt, B. and C. A. Montgomery. 'What is an attractive industry?' *Management Science*, **32**, 1986, pp. 1223–1229.

Wernerfelt, B. and C. A. Montgomery. 'Tobin's q and the importance of focus in firm performance', *American Economic Review*, **78**, 1988, pp. 246–250.

Williamson, O. E. *Markets and Hierarchies: Analysis and Antitust Implications*, Free Press, New York, 1975.

Williamson, O. E. 'Transaction cost economics: The governance of contractual relations', *Journal of Law and Economics*, **22**, 1979, pp. 233–261.

Williamson, O. E. *The Economic Institutions of Capitalism: Firms, Markets, Relational Contracting*, Free Press, New York, 1985.

Williamson, O. E. 'Comparative economic organization: The analysis of discrete structural alternatives', *Administrative Science Quarterly*, **36**, 1991a, pp. 269–296.

Williamson, O. E. 'Strategizing, economizing, and economic organization', *Strategic Management Journal*, **12** (Winter), 1991b, pp. 75–94.

Williamson, O. E. and S. G. Winter (eds.) *The Nature of the Firm: Origins, Evolution, and Development*, Oxford University Press, New York, 1991.

Winter, S. 'Knowledge and competence as strategic assets'. In D. J. Teece (ed.), *The Competitive Challenge*, Ballinger, Cambridge, MA, 1987, pp. 159–184.

Winter, S. 'On Coase, competence, and the corporation', *Journal of Law, Economics, and Organization*, **4**, 1988, pp. 163–180.

Yao, D. 'Beyond the reach of the invisible hand: Impediments to economic activity, market failures, and profitability', *Strategic Management Journal*, **9**, 1988, pp. 59–70.

Yip, G. S. 'Diversification entry: Internal development versus acquisition', *Strategic Management Journal*, **3**, 1982, pp. 331–345.

IV. THE DYNAMIC CAPABILITIES/CORE COMPETENCIES APPROACH

17 The Core Competence of the Corporation

C. K. Prahalad and Gary Hamel

The most powerful way to prevail in global competition is still invisible to many companies. During the 1980s, top executives were judged on their ability to restructure, declutter and delayer their corporations. In the 1990s, they'll be judged on their ability to identify, cultivate, and exploit the core competencies that make growth possible—indeed, they'll have to rethink the concept of the corporation itself.

Consider the last ten years of GTE and NEC. In the early 1980s, GTE was well positioned to become a major player in the evolving information technology industry. It was active in telecommunications. Its operations spanned a variety of businesses including telephones, switching and transmission systems, digital PABX, semiconductors, packet switching, satellites, defense systems, and lighting products. And GTE's Entertainment Products Group, which produced Sylvania color TVs, had a position in related display technologies. In 1980, GTE's sales were $9.98 billion, and net cash flow was $1.73 billion. NEC, in contrast, was much smaller, at $3.8 billion in sales. It had a comparable technological base and computer businesses, but it had no experience as an operating telecommunications company.

Yet look at the positions of GTE and NEC in 1988. GTE's 1988 sales were $16.46 billion, and NEC's sales were considerably higher at $21.89 billion. GTE has, in effect, become a telephone operating company with a position in defense and lighting products. GTE's other businesses are small in global terms. GTE has divested Sylvania TV and Telenet, put switching, transmission, and digital PABX into joint ventures, and closed down semiconductors. As a result, the international position of GTE has eroded. Non-U.S. revenue as a percent of total revenue dropped from 20% to 15% between 1980 and 1988.

NEC has emerged as the world leader in semiconductors and as a first-tier player in telecommunications products and computers. It has consolidated its position in mainframe computers. It has moved beyond public switching and transmission to include such lifestyle products as mobile telephones, facsimile machines, and laptop computers—bridging the gap between telecommunications and office automation. NEC is the only company in the world to be in the top five in revenue in telecommunications, semiconductors, and mainframes. Why did these two companies, starting with comparable business portfolios, perform so differently? Largely because NEC conceived of itself in terms of 'core competencies,' and GTE did not.

1. Rethinking the Corporation

Once, the diversified corporation could simply point its business units at particular end product markets and admonish them to become world leaders. But with market boundaries changing ever more quickly, targets are elusive and capture is at best temporary. A few companies have proven themselves adept at inventing new markets, quickly entering emerging markets, and dramatically shifting patterns of customer choice in established markets. These are the ones to emulate. The critical task for management is to create an organization capable of infusing products with irresistible functionality or, better yet, creating products that customers need but have not yet even imagined.

This is a deceptively difficult task. Ultimately, it requires radical change in the management of major companies. It means, first of all, that top managements of Western companies must assume responsibility for competitive decline. Everyone knows about high interest rates, Japanese protectionism, outdated antitrust laws, obstreperous unions, and impatient investors. What is harder to see, or harder to acknowledge, is how little added momentum companies actually get from political or macroeconomic 'relief.' Both the theory and practice of Western management have created a drag on our forward motion. It is the principles of management that are in need of reform.

NEC versus GTE, again, is instructive and only one of many such comparative cases we analyzed to understand the changing basis for global leadership. Early in the 1970s, NEC articulated a strategic intent to exploit the convergence of computing and communications, what it called 'C&C.'[1] Success, top management reckoned, would hinge on acquiring *competencies*, particularly in semiconductors. Management adopted an appropriate 'strategic architecture,' summarized by C&C, and then communicated its intent to the whole organization and the outside world during the mid-1970s.

NEC constituted a 'C&C Committee' of top managers to oversee the development of core products and core competencies. NEC put in place coordination groups and committees that cut across the interests of individual businesses. Consistent with its strategic architecture, NEC shifted enormous resources to strengthen its position in components and central processors. By using collaborative arrangements to multiply internal resources, NEC was able to accumulate a broad array of core competencies.

NEC carefully identified three interrelated streams of technological and market evolution. Top management determined that computing would evolve from large mainframes to distributed processing, components from simple ICs to VLSI, and communications from mechanical cross-bar exchange to complex digital systems we now call ISDN. As things evolved further, NEC reasoned, the computing, communications, and components businesses would so overlap that it would be very hard to distinguish among them, and that there would be enormous opportunities for any company that had built the competencies needed to serve all three markets.

NEC top management determined that semiconductors would be the company's most important 'core product.' It entered into myriad strategic alliances—over 100 as of 1987—aimed at building competencies rapidly and at low cost. In mainframe computers, its most noted relationship was with Honeywell and Bull. Almost all the collaborative arrangements in the semiconductor-component field were oriented toward technology access. As they entered collaborative arrangements, NEC's operating managers understood the rationale for these alliances and the goal of internalizing partner skills. NEC's director of research summed up its competence acquisition during the 1970s and 1980s this way: 'From an investment standpoint, it was much quicker and cheaper to use foreign technology. There wasn't a need for us to develop new ideas.'

No such clarity of strategic intent and strategic architecture appeared to exist at GTE. Although senior executives discussed the implications of the evolving information technology industry, no commonly accepted view of which competencies would be required to compete in that industry were communicated widely. While significant staff work was done to identify key technologies, senior line managers continued to act as if they were managing independent business units. Decentralization made it difficult to focus on core competencies. Instead, individual businesses became increasingly dependent on outsiders for critical skills, and collaboration became a route to staged exits. Today, with a new management team in place, GTE has repositioned itself to apply its competencies to emerging markets in telecommunications services.

2. The Roots of Competitive Advantage

The distinction we observed in the way NEC and GTE conceived of themselves—a portfolio of competencies versus a portfolio of businesses—was repeated across many industries. From 1980 to 1988, Canon grew by 264%, Honda by 200%. Compare that with Xerox and Chrysler. And if Western managers were once anxious about the low cost and high quality of Japanese imports, they are now overwhelmed by the pace at which Japanese rivals are inventing new markets, creating new products, and enhancing them. Canon has given us personal copiers; Honda has moved from motorcycles to four-wheel off-road buggies. Sony developed the 8 mm camcorder, Yamaha, the digital piano. Komatsu developed an underwater remote-controlled bulldozer, while Casio's latest gambit is a small-screen color LCD television. Who would have anticipated the evolution of these vanguard markets?

In more established markets, the Japanese challenge has been just as disquieting. Japanese companies are generating a blizzard of features and functional enhancements that bring technological sophistication to everyday products. Japanese car producers have been pioneering four-wheel steering, four-valve-per-cylinder engines, in-car navigation systems, and sophisticated electronic engine-management systems. On the strength of its product features, Canon is now a player in facsimile transmission machines, desktop laser printers, even semiconductor manufacturing equipment.

In the short run, a company's competitiveness derives from the price/performance attributes of current products. But the survivors of the first wave of global competition, Western and Japanese alike, are all converging on similar and formidable standards for product cost and quality—minimum hurdles for continued competition, but less and less important as sources of differential advantage. In the long run, competitiveness derives from an ability to build, at lower cost and more speedily than competitors, the core competencies that spawn unanticipated products. The real sources of advantage are to be found in management's ability to consolidate corporatewide technologies and production skills into competencies that empower individual businesses to adapt quickly to changing opportunities.

Senior executives who claim that they cannot build core competencies either because they feel the autonomy of business units is sacrosanct or because their feet are held to the quarterly budget fire should think again. The problem in many Western companies is not that their senior executives are any less capable than those in Japan nor that Japanese companies possess greater technical capabilities. Instead, it is their adherence to a concept of the corporation that unnecessarily limits the ability of individual businesses to fully exploit the deep

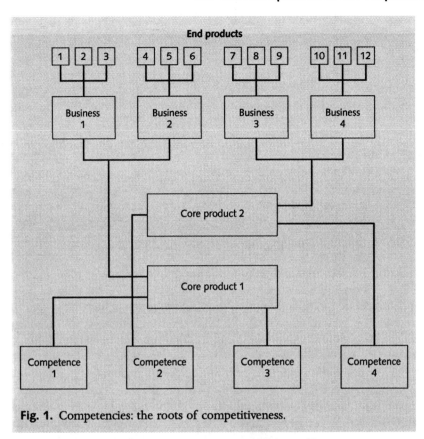

Fig. 1. Competencies: the roots of competitiveness.

reservoir of technological capability that many American and European companies possess.

The diversified corporation is a large tree. The trunk and major limbs are core products, the smaller branches are business units; the leaves, flowers, and fruit are end products. The root system that provides nourishment, sustenance, and stability is the core competence. You can miss the strength of competitors by looking only at their end products, in the same way you miss the strength of a tree if you look only at its leaves. (See Fig. 1, 'Competencies: the roots of competitiveness.')

Core competencies are the collective learning in the organization, especially how to coordinate diverse production skills and integrate multiple streams of technologies. Consider Sony's capacity to miniaturize or Philips's optical-media expertise. The theoretical knowledge to put a radio on a chip does not in itself assure a company the skill to produce a miniature radio no bigger than a business card. To bring off this feat, Casio must harmonize know-how in miniaturization, microprocessor design, material science, and ultrathin precision casing—the same skills it applies in its miniature card calculators, pocket TVs, and digital watches.

If core competence is about harmonizing streams of technology, it is also about the organization of work and the delivery of value. Among Sony's competencies is miniaturization. To bring miniaturization to its products, Sony must ensure that technologists, engineers, and marketers have a shared understanding of customer needs and of technological possibilities. The force of core competence is felt as decisively in services as in manufacturing. Citicorp was ahead of others investing in an operating system that allowed it to participate in world markets 24 hours a day. Its competence in systems has provided the company the means to differentiate itself from many financial service institutions.

Core competence is communication, involvement, and a deep commitment to working across organizational boundaries. It involves many levels of people and all functions. World-class research in, for example, lasers or ceramics can take place in corporate laboratories without having an impact on any of the businesses of the company. The skills that together constitute core competence must coalesce around individuals whose efforts are not so narrowly focused that they cannot recognize the opportunities for blending their functional expertise with those of others in new and interesting ways.

Core competence does not diminish with use. Unlike physical assets, which do deteriorate over time, competencies are enhanced as they are applied and shared. But competencies still need to be nurtured and protected; knowledge fades if it is not used. Competencies are the glue that binds existing businesses. They are also the engine for new business development. Patterns of diversification and market entry may be guided by them, not just by the attractiveness of markets.

Consider 3M's competence with sticky tape. In dreaming up businesses as diverse as 'Post-it' notes, magnetic tape, photographic film, pressure-sensitive tapes, and coated abrasives, the company has brought to bear widely shared competencies in substrates, coatings, and adhesives and devised various ways to combine them. Indeed, 3M has invested consistently in them. What seems to be an extremely diversified portfolio of businesses belies a few shared core competencies.

In contrast, there are major companies that have had the potential to build core competencies but failed to do so because top management was unable to conceive of the company as anything other than a collection of discrete businesses. GE sold much of its consumer electronics business to Thomson of France, arguing that it was becoming increasingly difficult to maintain its competitiveness in this sector. That was undoubtedly so, but it is ironic that it sold several key businesses to competitors who were already competence leaders—Black & Decker in small electrical motors, and Thomson, which was eager to build its competence in microelectronics and had learned from the Japanese that a position in consumer electronics was vital to this challenge.

Management trapped in the strategic business unit (SBU) mind-set almost inevitably finds its individual businesses dependent on external sources for critical components, such as motors or compressors. But these are not just components. They are core products that contribute to the competitiveness of a wide range of end products. They are the physical embodiments of core competencies.

3. How Not to Think of Competence

Since companies are in a race to build the competencies that determine global leadership, successful companies have stopped imagining themselves as bundles of businesses making products. Canon, Honda, Casio, or NEC may seem to preside over portfolios of businesses unrelated in terms of customers, distribution channels, and merchandising strategy. Indeed, they have portfolios that may seem idiosyncratic at times: NEC is the only global company to be among leaders in computing, telecommunications, and semiconductors *and* to have a thriving consumer electronics business.

But looks are deceiving. In NEC, digital technology, especially VLSI and systems integration skills, is fundamental. In the core competencies underlying them, disparate businesses become coherent. It is Honda's core competence in engines and power trains that gives it a distinctive advantage in car, motorcycle, lawn mower, and generator businesses. Canon's core competencies in optics, imaging, and microprocessor controls have enabled it to enter, even dominate, markets as seemingly diverse as copiers, laser printers, cameras, and image scanners. Philips worked for more than 15 years to perfect its optical-media (laser disc) competence, as did JVC in building a leading position in video recording. Other examples of core competencies might include mechantronics (the ability to marry mechanical and electronic engineering), video displays, bioengineering, and microelectronics. In the early stages of its competence building, Philips could not have imagined all the products that would be spawned by its optical-media competence, nor could JVC have anticipated miniature camcorders when it first began exploring videotape technologies.

Unlike the battle for global brand dominance, which is visible in the world's broadcast and print media and is aimed at building global 'share of mind,' the battle to build world-class competencies is invisible to people who aren't deliberately looking for it. Top management often tracks the cost and quality of competitors' products, yet how many managers untangle the web of alliances their Japanese competitors have constructed to acquire competencies at low cost? In how many Western boardrooms is there an explicit, shared understanding of the competencies the company must build for world leadership? Indeed, how many senior executives discuss the crucial distinction between competitive strategy at the level of a business and competitive strategy at the level of an entire company?

Let us be clear. Cultivating core competence does *not* mean outspending rivals on research and development. In 1983, when Canon surpassed Xerox in worldwide unit market share in the copier business, its R&D budget in reprographics was but a small fraction of Xerox's. Over the past 20 years, NEC has spent less on R&D as a percentage of sales than almost all of its American and European competitors.

Nor does core competence mean shared costs, as when two or more SBUs use a common facility—a plant, service facility, or sales force—or share a common component. The gains of sharing may be substantial, but the search for shared costs is typically a post hoc effort to rationalize production across existing businesses, not a premeditated effort to build the competencies out of which the businesses themselves grow.

Building core competencies is more ambitious and different than integrating vertically, moreover. Managers deciding whether to make or buy will start with end products and look upstream to the efficiencies of the supply chain and downstream toward distribution and customers. They do not take inventory of skills and look forward to applying them in nontraditional ways. (Of course, decisions about competencies *do* provide a logic for vertical integration. Canon is not particularly integrated in its copier business, except in those aspects of the vertical chain that support the competencies it regards as critical.)

....

4. Identifying Core Competencies— And Losing Them

At least three tests can be applied to identify core competencies in a company. First, a core competence provides potential access to a wide variety of markets. Competence in display systems, for example, enables a company to participate in such diverse businesses as calculators, miniature TV sets, monitors for laptop computers, and automotive dashboards—which is why Casio's entry into the handheld TV market was predictable. Second, a core competence should make a significant contribution to the perceived customer benefits of the end product. Clearly, Honda's engine expertise fills this bill.

Finally, a core competence should be difficult for competitors to imitate. And it *will* be difficult if it is a complex harmonization of individual technologies and production skills. A rival might acquire some of the technologies that comprise the core competence, but it will find it more difficult to duplicate the more or less comprehensive pattern of internal coordination and learning. JVC's decision in the early 1960s to pursue the development of a videotape competence passed the three tests outlined here. RCA's decision in the late 1970s to develop a stylus-based video turntable system did not.

Few companies are likely to build world leadership in more than five or six fundamental competencies. A company that compiles a list of 20 to 30 capabilities has probably not produced a list of core competencies. Still, it is probably a good discipline to generate a list of this sort and to see aggregate capabilities as building blocks. This tends to prompt the search for licensing deals and alliances through which the company may acquire, at low cost, the missing pieces.

Most Western companies hardly think about competitiveness in these terms at all. It is time to take a tough-minded look at the risks they are running. Companies that judge competitiveness, their own and their competitors', primarily in terms of the price/performance of end products are courting the erosion of core competencies—or making too little effort to enhance them. The embedded skills that give rise to the next generation of competitive products cannot be 'rented in' by outsourcing and OEM-supply relationships. In our view, too many companies have unwittingly surrendered core competencies when they cut internal investment in what they mistakenly thought were just 'cost centers' in favor of outside suppliers.

Consider Chrysler. Unlike Honda, it has tended to view engines and power trains as simply one more component. Chrysler is becoming increasing dependent on Mitsubishi and Hyundai: between 1985 and 1987, the number of outsourced engines went from 252,000 to 382,000. It is difficult to imagine Honda yielding manufacturing responsibility, much less design, of so critical a part of a car's function to an outside company—which is why Honda has made such an enormous commitment to Formula One auto racing. Honda has been able to pool its engine-related technologies; it has parlayed these into a corporatewide competency from which it develops world-beating products, despite R&D budgets smaller than those of GM and Toyota.

Of course, it is perfectly possible for a company to have a competitive product line up but be a laggard in developing core competencies—at least for a while. If a company wanted to enter the copier business today, it would find a dozen Japanese companies more than willing to supply copiers on the basis of an OEM private label. But when fundamental technologies changed or if its supplier decided to enter the market directly and become a competitor, that company's product line, along with all of its investments in marketing and distribution, could be vulnerable. Outsourcing can provide a shortcut to a more competitive product, but it typically contributes little to building the people-embodied skills that are needed to sustain product leadership.

Nor is it possible for a company to have an intelligent alliance or sourcing strategy if it has not made a choice about where it will build competence leadership. Clearly, Japanese companies have benefited from alliances. They've used them to learn from Western partners who were not fully committed to preserving core competencies of their own. As we've argued in these pages before, learning within an alliance takes a positive commitment of resources—travel, a pool of dedicated people, test-bed facilities, time to internalize and test what has been learned.[2] A company may not make this effort if it doesn't have clear goals for competence building.

Another way of losing is forgoing opportunities to establish competencies that are evolving in existing businesses. In the 1970s and 1980s, many American and European companies—like GE, Motorola, GTE, Thorn, and GEC—chose to exit the color television business, which they regarded as mature. If by 'mature' they meant that they had run out of new product ideas at precisely the moment global rivals had targeted the TV business for entry, then yes, the industry was mature. But it certainly wasn't mature in the sense that all opportunities to enhance and apply video-based competencies had been exhausted.

In ridding themselves of their television businesses, these companies failed to distinguish between divesting the business and destroying their video media-based competencies. They not only got out of the TV business but they also closed the door on a whole stream of future opportunities reliant on video-based competencies. The television industry, considered by many U.S. companies in the 1970s to be unattractive, is today the focus of a fierce public policy debate about the inability of U.S. corporations to benefit from the $20-billion-a-year opportunity that HDTV will represent in the mid- to late 1990s. Ironically, the U.S. government is being asked to fund a massive research project—in effect, to compensate U.S. companies for their failure to preserve critical core competencies when they had the chance.

In contrast, one can see a company like Sony reducing its emphasis on VCRs (where it has not been very successful and where Korean companies now threaten), without reducing its commitment to video-related competencies. Sony's Betamax led to a debacle. But it emerged with its videotape recording competencies intact and is currently challenging Matsushita in the 8 mm camcorder market.

There are two clear lessons here. First, the costs of losing a core competence can be only partly calculated in advance. The baby may be thrown out with the bath water in divestment decisions. Second, since core competencies are built through a process of continuous improvement and enhancement that may span a decade or longer, a company that has failed to invest in core competence building will find it very difficult to enter an emerging market, unless, of course, it will be content simply to serve as a distribution channel.

American semiconductor companies like Motorola learned this painful lesson when they elected to forgo direct participation in the 256k generation of DRAM chips. Having skipped this round, Motorola, like most of its American competitors, needed a large infusion of technical help from Japanese partners to rejoin the battle in the 1-megabyte generation. When it comes to core competencies, it is difficult to get off the train, walk to the next station, and then reboard.

5. From Core Competencies to Core Products

The tangible link between identified core competencies and end products is what we call the core products—the physical embodiments of one or more core competencies. Honda's engines, for example, are core products, linchpins between design and development skills that ultimately lead to a proliferation of end products. Core products are the components or subassemblies that actually contribute to the value of the end products. Thinking in terms of core products forces a company to distinguish between the brand share it achieves in end product markets (for example, 40% of the U.S. refrigerator market) and the manufacturing share it achieves in any particular core product (for example, 5% of the world share of compressor output).

Canon is reputed to have an 84% world manufacturing share in desktop laser printer 'engines,' even though its brand share in the laser printer business is minuscule. Similarly, Matsushita has a world manufacturing share of about 45% in key VCR components, far in excess of its brand share (Panasonic, JVC, and others) of 20%. And Matsushita has a commanding core product share in compressors worldwide, estimated at 40%, even though its brand share in both the air-conditioning and refrigerator businesses is quite small.

It is essential to make this distinction between core competencies, core products, and end products because global competition is played out by different rules and for different stakes at each level. To build or defend leadership over the long term, a corporation will probably be a winner at each level. At the level of core competence, the goal is to build world leadership in the design

C. K. Prahalad and Gary Hamel

and development of a particular class of product functionality—be it compact data storage and retrieval, as with Philips's optical-media competence, or compactness and ease of use, as with Sony's micromotors and microprocessor controls.

To sustain leadership in their chosen core competence areas, these companies *seek to maximize their world manufacturing share in core products*. The manufacture of core products for a wide variety of external (and internal) customers yields the revenue and market feedback that, at least partly, determines the pace at which core competencies can be enhanced and extended. This thinking was behind JVC's decision in the mid-1970s to establish VCR supply relationships with leading national consumer electronics companies in Europe and the United States. In supplying Thomson, Thorn, and Telefunken (all independent companies at that time) as well as U.S. partners, JVC was able to gain the cash and the diversity of market experience that ultimately enabled it to outpace Philips and Sony. (Philips developed videotape competencies in parallel with JVC, but it failed to build a worldwide network of OEM relationships that would have allowed it to accelerate the refinement of its videotape competence through the sale of core products.)

	SBU	CORE COMPETENCE
Basis for competition	Competitiveness of today's products	Interfirm competition to build competencies
Corporate structure	Portfolio of businesses related in product-market terms	Portfolio of competencies, core products, and businesses
Status of the business unit	Autonomy is a sacrosanct; the SBU 'owns' all resources other than cash	SBU is a potential reservoir of core competencies
Resource allocation	Discrete businesses are the unit of analysis; capital is allocated business by business	Businesses and competencies are the unit of analysis: top management allocates capital and talent
Value added of top management	Optimizing corporate returns through capital allocation trade-offs among businesses	Enunciating strategic architecture and building competencies to secure the future

Fig. 2. Two concepts of the corporation: SBU or core competence.

JVC's success has not been lost on Korean companies like Goldstar, Sam Sung, Kia, and Daewoo, who are building core product leadership in areas as diverse as displays, semiconductors, and automotive engines through their OEM-supply contracts with Western companies. Their avowed goal is to capture investment initiative away from potential competitors, often U.S. companies. In doing so, they accelerate their competence-building efforts while 'hollowing out' their competitors. By focusing on competence and embedding it in core products, Asian competitors have built up advantages in component markets first and have then leveraged off their superior products to move downstream to build brand share. And they are not likely to remain the low-cost suppliers forever. As their reputation for brand leadership is consolidated, they may well gain price leadership. Honda has proven this with its Acura line, and other Japanese car makers are following suit.

Control over core products is critical for other reasons. A dominant position in core products allows a company to shape the evolution of applications and end markets. Such compact audio disc-related core products as data drives and lasers have enable Sony and Philips to influence the evolution of the computer-peripheral business in optical-media storage. As a company multiplies the number of application arenas for its core products, it can consistently reduce the cost, time, and risk in new product development. In short, well-targeted core products can lead to economies of scale *and* scope.

6. The Tyranny of the SBU

The new terms of competitive engagement cannot be understood using analytical tools devised to manage the diversified corporation of 20 years ago, when competition was primarily domestic (GE versus Westinghouse, General Motors versus Ford) and all the key players were speaking the language of the same business schools and consultancies. Old prescriptions have potentially toxic side effects. The need for new principles is most obvious in companies organized exclusively according to the logic of SBUs. The implications of the two alternate concepts of the corporation are summarized in Fig. 2, 'Two concepts of the corporation: SBU or core competence.'

Obviously, diversified corporations have a portfolio of products and a portfolio of businesses. But we believe in a view of the company as a portfolio of competencies as well. U.S. companies do not lack the technical resources to build competencies, but their top management often lacks the vision to build them and the administrative means for assembling resources spread across mul-

C. K. Prahalad and Gary Hamel

tiple businesses. A shift in commitment will inevitably influence patterns of diversification, skill deployment, resource allocation priorities, and approaches to alliances and out-sourcing.

We have described the three different planes on which battles for global leadership are waged: core competence, core products, and end products. A corporation has to know whether it is winning or losing on each plane. By sheer weight of investment, a company might be able to beat its rivals to blue-sky technologies yet still lose the race to build core competence leadership. If a company is winning the race to build core competencies (as opposed to building leadership in a few technologies), it will almost certainly outpace rivals in new business development. If a company is winning the race to capture world manufacturing share in core products, it will probably outpace rivals in improving product features and the price/performance ratio.

Determining whether one is winning or losing end product battles is more difficult because measures of product market share do not necessarily reflect various companies' underlying competitiveness. Indeed, companies that attempt to build market share by relying on the competitiveness of others, rather than investing in core competencies and world core-product leadership,

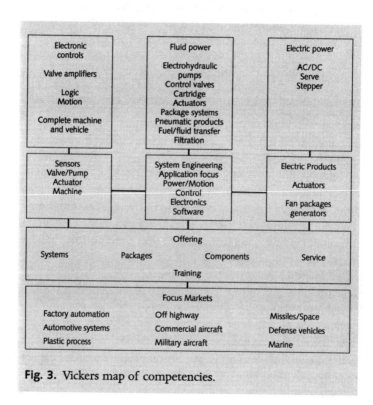

Fig. 3. Vickers map of competencies.

may be treading on quicksand. In the race for global brand dominance, companies like 3M, Black & Decker, Canon, Honda, NEC, and Citicorp have built global brand umbrellas by proliferating products out of their core competencies. This has allowed their individual businesses to build image, customer loyalty, and access to distribution channels.

When you think about this reconceptualization of the corporation, the primacy of the SBU—an organizational dogma for a generation—is now clearly an anachronism. Where the SBU is an article of faith, resistance to the seductions of decentralization can seem heretical. In many companies, the SBU prism means that only one plane of the global competitive battle, the battle to put competitive products on the shelf *today*, is visible to top management. What are the costs of this distortion?

Underinvestment in Developing Core Competencies and Core Products

When the organization is conceived of as a multiplicity of SBUs, no single business may feel responsible for maintaining a viable position in core products nor be able to justify the investment required to build world leadership in some core competence. In the absence of a more comprehensive view imposed by corporate management, SBU managers will tend to underinvest. Recently, companies such as Kodak and Philips have recognized this as a potential problem and have begun searching for new organizational forms that will allow them to develop and manufacture core products for both internal and external customers.

SBU managers have traditionally conceived of competitors in the same way they've seen themselves. On the whole, they've failed to note the emphasis Asian competitors were placing on building leadership in core products or to understand the critical linkage between world manufacturing leadership and the ability to sustain development pace in core competence. They've failed to pursue OEM-supply opportunities or to look across their various product divisions in an attempt to identify opportunities for coordinated initiatives.

Imprisoned Resources

As an SBU evolves, it often develops unique competencies. Typically, the people who embody this competence are seen as the sole property of the business in which they grew up. The manager of another SBU who asks to borrow talented people is likely to get a cold rebuff. SBU managers are not only unwilling to lend their competence carriers but they may actually hide talent to prevent its redeployment in the pursuit of new opportunities. This may be compared to residents of an underdeveloped country hiding most of their cash under their mattresses. The benefits of competencies, like the benefits of the money supply, depend on the velocity of their circulation as well as on the size of the stock the company holds.

Western companies have traditionally had an advantage in the stock of skills they possess. But have they been able to reconfigure them quickly to respond to new opportunities? Canon, NEC, and Honda have had a lesser stock of the people and technologies that compose core competencies but could move them much quicker from one business unit to another. Corporate R&D spending at Canon is not fully indicative of the size of Canon's core competence stock and tells the casual observer nothing about the velocity with which Canon is able to move core competencies to exploit opportunities.

When competencies become imprisoned, the people who carry the competencies do not get assigned to the most exciting opportunities, and their skills begin to atrophy. Only by fully leveraging core competencies can small companies like Canon afford to compete with industry giants like Xerox. How strange that SBU managers, who are perfectly willing to compete for cash in the capital budgeting process, are unwilling to compete for people—the company's most precious asset. We find it ironic that top management devotes so much attention to the capital budgeting process yet typically has no comparable mechanism for allocating the human skills that embody core competencies. Top managers are seldom able to look four or five levels down into the organization, identify the people who embody critical competencies, and move them across organizational boundaries.

Bounded Innovation

If core competencies are not recognized, individual SBUs will pursue only those innovation opportunities that are close at hand—marginal product-line extensions or geographic expansions. Hybrid opportunities like fax machines, laptop computers, hand-held televisions, or portable music keyboards will emerge only when managers take off their SBU blinkers. Remember, Canon appeared to be in the camera business at the time it was preparing to become a world leader in copiers. Conceiving of the corporation in terms of core competencies widens the domain of innovation.

7. Developing Strategic Architecture

The fragmentation of core competencies becomes inevitable when a diversified company's information systems, patterns of communication, career paths, managerial rewards, and processes of strategy development do not transcend SBU lines. We believe that senior management should spend a significant amount of its time developing a corporatewide strategic architecture that establishes objectives for competence building. A strategic architecture is a road map of the future that identifies which core competencies to build and their constituent technologies.

By providing an impetus for learning from alliances and a focus for internal development efforts, a strategic architecture like NEC's C&C can dramatically reduce the investment needed to secure future market leadership. How can a company make partnerships intelligently without a clear understanding of the core competencies it is trying to build and those it is attempting to prevent from being unintentionally transferred?

Of course, all of this begs the question of what a strategic architecture should look like. The answer will be different for every company. But it is helpful to think again of that tree, of the corporation organized around core products and, ultimately, core competencies. To sink sufficiently strong roots, a company must answer some fundamental questions: How long could we preserve our competitiveness in this business if we did not control this particular core competence? How central is this core competence to perceived customer benefits? What future opportunities would be foreclosed if we were to lose this particular competence?

The architecture provides a logic for product and market diversification, moreover. An SBU manager would be asked: Does the new market opportunity add to the overall goal of becoming the best player in the world? Does it exploit or add to the core competence? At Vickers, for example, diversification options have been judged in the context of becoming the best power and motion control company in the world (see 'Vickers Learns the Value of Strategic Architecture', Appendix and Fig. 3).

The strategic architecture should make resource allocation priorities transparent to the entire organization. It provides a template for allocation decisions by top management. It helps lower level managers understand the logic of allocation priorities and disciplines senior management to maintain consistency. In short, it yields a definition of the company and the markets it serves. 3M, Vickers, NEC, Canon, and Honda all qualify on this score. Honda *knew* it was exploiting what it had learned from motorcycles—how to make high-revving, smooth-running, lightweight engines—when it entered the car business. The task of creating a strategic architecture forces the organization to identify and commit to the technical and production linkages across SBUs that will provide a distinct competitive advantage.

It is consistency of resource allocation and the development of an administrative infrastructure appropriate to it that breathes life into a strategic architecture and creates a managerial culture, teamwork, a capacity to change, and a willingness to share resources, to protect proprietary skills, and to think long term. That is also the reason the specific architecture cannot be copied easily or overnight by competitors. Strategic architecture is a tool for communicating with customers and other external constituents. It reveals the broad direction without giving away every step.

8. Redeploying to Exploit Competencies

If the company's core competencies are its critical resource and if top management must ensure that competence carriers are not held hostage by some particular business, then it follows that SBUs should bid for core competencies in the same way they bid for capital. We've made this point glancingly. It is important enough to consider more deeply.

Once top management (with the help of divisional and SBU managers) has identified overarching competencies, it must ask businesses to identify the projects and people closely connected with them. Corporate officers should direct an audit of the location, number, and quality of the people who embody competence.

This sends an important signal to middle managers: core competencies are *corporate* resources and may be reallocated by corporate management. An individual business doesn't own anybody. SBUs are entitled to the services of individual employees so long as SBU management can demonstrate that the opportunity it is pursuing yields the highest possible pay-off on the investment in their skills. This message is further underlined if each year in the strategic planning or budgeting process, unit managers must justify their hold on the people who carry the company's core competencies.

Elements of Canon's core competence in optics are spread across businesses as diverse as cameras, copiers, and semiconductor lithographic equipment and are shown in Fig. 4, 'Core Competencies at Canon.' When Canon identified an opportunity in digital laser printers, it gave SBU managers the right to raid other SBUs to pull together the required pool of talent. When Canon's reprographics products division undertook to develop microprocessor-controlled copiers, it turned to the photo products group, which had developed the world's first microprocessor-controlled camera.

Also reward systems that focus only on product-line results and career paths that seldom cross SBU boundaries engender patterns of behavior among unit managers that are destructively competitive. At NEC, divisional manages come together to identify next-generation competencies. Together they decide how

	PRECISION MECHANICS	FINE OPTICS	MICRO-ELECTRONICS
Basic camera	■	■	
Compact fashion camera	■	■	
Electronic camera	■	■	
EOS autofocus camera	■	■	■
Video still camera	■	■	■
Laser beam printer	■	■	■
Color video printer	■		■
Bubble jet printer	■		■
Basic fax	■		■
Laser fax	■		■
Calculator			■
Plain paper copier	■	■	■
Battery PPC	■	■	■
Color copier	■	■	■
Laser copier	■	■	■
Color laser copier	■	■	■
NAVI	■	■	■
Still video system	■	■	■
Laser imager	■	■	■
Cell analyzer	■	■	■
Mask aligners	■		■
Stepper aligners	■		■
Excimer laser aligners	■	■	■

Fig. 4. Core competence at Canon.

much investment needs to be made to build up each future competency and the contribution in capital and staff support that each division will need to make. There is also a sense of equitable exchange. One division may make a disproportionate contribution or may benefit less from the progress made, but such short-term inequalities will balance out over the long term.

Incidentally, the positive contribution of the SBU manager should be made visible across the company. An SBU manager is unlikely to surrender key people if only the other business (or the general manager of that business who may be a competitor for promotion) is going to benefit from the redeployment. Cooperative SBU managers should be celebrated as team players. Where priorities are clear, transfers are less likely to be seen as idiosyncratic and politically motivated.

Transfers for the sake of building core competence must be recorded and appreciated in the corporate memory. It is reasonable to expect a business that has surrendered core skills on behalf of corporate opportunities in other areas to lose, for a time, some of its competitiveness. If these losses in performance bring immediate censure, SBUs will be unlikely to assent to skills transfers next time.

Finally, there are ways to wean key employees off the idea that they belong in perpetuity to any particular business. Early in their careers, people may be exposed to a variety of businesses through a carefully planned rotation program. At Canon, critical people move regularly between the camera business and the copier business and between the copier business and the professional optical-products business. In midcareer, periodic assignments to cross-divisional project teams may be necessary, both for diffusing core competencies and for loosening the bonds that might tie an individual to one business even when brighter opportunities beckon elsewhere. Those who embody critical core competencies should know that their careers are tracked and guided by corporate human resource professionals. In the early 1980s at Canon, all engineers under 30 were invited to apply for membership on a seven-person committee that was to spend two years plotting Canon's future direction, including its strategic architecture.

Competence carriers should be regularly brought together from across the corporation to trade notes and ideas. The goal is to build a strong feeling of community among these people. To a great extent, their loyalty should be to the integrity of the core competence area they represent and not just to particular businesses. In traveling regularly, talking frequently to customers, and meeting with peers, competence carriers may be encouraged to discover new market opportunities.

Core competencies are the wellspring of new business development. They should constitute the focus for strategy at the corporate level. Managers have to win manufacturing leadership in core products and capture global share through brand-building programs aimed at exploiting economies of scope. Only if the company is conceived of as a hierarchy of core competencies, core products, and market-focused business units will it be fit to fight.

Nor can top management be just another layer of accounting consolidation, which it often is in a regime of radical decentralization. Top management must add value by enunciating the strategic architecture that guides the competence acquisition process. We believe an obsession with competence building will characterize the global winners of the 1990s. With the decade underway, the time for rethinking the concept of the corporation is already overdue.

Appendix: Vickers Learns the Value of Strategic Architecture

The idea that top management should develop a corporate strategy for acquiring and deploying core competencies is relatively new in most U.S. companies. There are a few exceptions. An early convert was Trinova (previously Libbey Owens Ford), a Toledo-based corporation, which enjoys a worldwide position in power and motion controls and engineered plastics. One of its major divisions is Vickers, a premier supplier of hydraulics components like valves, pumps, actuators, and filtration devices to aerospace, marine, defense, automotive, earth-moving, and industrial markets.

Vickers saw the potential for a transformation of its traditional business with the application of electronics disciplines in combination with its traditional technologies. The goal was 'to ensure that change in technology does not displace Vickers from its customers.' This, to be sure, was initially a defensive move: Vickers recognized that unless it acquired new skills, it could not protect existing markets or capitalize on new growth opportunities. Managers at Vickers attempted to conceptualize the likely evolution of (a) technologies relevant to the power and motion control business, (b) functionalities that would satisfy emerging customer needs, and (c) new competencies needed to creatively manage the marriage of technology and customer needs.

Despite pressure for short-term earnings, top management looked to a 10- to 15-year time horizon in developing a map of emerging customer needs, changing technologies and the core competencies that would be necessary to bridge the gap between the two. Its slogan was 'Into the 21st Century.' (A simplified version of the overall architecture developed is shown in Fig. 3.) Vickers is currently in fluid-power components. The architecture identifies two additional competencies, electric-power components and electronic controls. A systems integration capability that would unite hardware, software, and service was also targeted for development.

The strategic architecture, as illustrated by the Vickers example, is not a forecast of specific products or specific technologies but a broad map of the evolving linkages between customer functionality requirements, potential technologies, and core competencies. It assumes that products and systems cannot be defined with certainty for the future but that preempting competitors in the development of new markets requires an early start to building core competencies. The strategic architecture developed by Vickers, while describing the future in competence terms, also provides the basis for making 'here and now' decisions about product priorities, acquisitions, alliances, and recruitment.

Since 1986, Vickers has made more than ten clearly targeted acquisitions, each one focused on a specific component or technology gap identified in the overall architecture. The architecture is also the basis for internal development of new competencies. Vickers has undertaken, in parallel, a reorganization to enable the integration of electronics and electrical capabilities with mechanical-based competencies. We believe that it will take another two to three years before Vickers reaps the total benefits from developing the strategic architecture, communicating it widely to all its employees, customers, and investors, and building administrative systems consistent with the architecture.

C. K. Prahalad and Gary Hamel

Notes

1. For a fuller discussion, see our article, 'Strategic Intent', HBR May–June 1989, p. 63.
2. 'Collaborate with Your Competitors and Win,' HBR January–February 1989, p. 133, with Yves L. Doz.

Why Do Firms Differ, and How Does It Matter?

Richard R. Nelson

1. Firms in Neoclassical Economic Theory

To get at that question from an economist's perspective, one needs to start with a broad understanding of what economic activity is all about, and what constitutes good economic performance or poor. For several reasons, neoclassical theory, which provides the current conventional wisdom on these matters for economists, militates against paying attention to firm differences as an important variable affecting economic performance.

The first reason is the perception of what economic activity is all about. Since the formulation of general equilibrium theory almost a century ago, the focus has largely been on how well an economy allocates resources, given preferences and technologies. This position is far from universal. Empirically oriented economists have been interested in things like technical change, and recently there has been a rash of work on economic institutions and how and why these change over time. Some time ago Schumpeter put forth a strong general theoretical challenge to the effect that innovation ought to be the center of economic analysis. But it is hard to overestimate the degree to which economists continue to see the central economic problem as that of meeting preferences as well as possible, given existing resources, technologies, and institutions. This perspective implies a rather limited view of what firms are about.

The second reason reflects this general orientation, though it is not the only possible formulation of firms' decision processes that is consistent with such a view. Many economists have been wedded to a theory of firm behavior that posits that firms face given and known choice sets (constrained for example by available technologies) and have no difficulty in choosing the action within those sets that is the best for them, given their objectives (generally assumed to be as much profit as possible). Thus the 'economic problem' is basically about getting private incentives right, not about identifying the best things to be doing, which is assumed to be no problem.

The perspective on the economic problem and the theory of firm behavior described above do not invite a careful inquiry into what goes on in firms. However, the tradition in economics of treating firms as 'black boxes' was not inevitable either. The fact that, at least until recently, this has been the norm deserves recognition in its own right.

The overall result is a view that what firms do is determined by the conditions they face, and (possibly) by certain unique attributes (say a choice location, or a proprietary technology) they possess. Firms facing different markets will behave and perform differently, but if the market conditions were reversed, firm behaviors would be too. Where the theory admits product differentiation, different firms will produce different products, but in the theoretical literature any firm can choose any niche. Thus there are firm differences, but there is no essential autonomous quality to them.

The theoretical orientation in economics thus leans sharply away from the proposition that discretionary firm differences matter. Of course economists studying empirical or policy questions have a proclivity to wander away from the tethers of theory when the facts of the matter compel them to do so. Thus in doing industry studies, economists often have been forced to recognize, even highlight, firm differences, and differences that matter. One cannot study the computer industry sensitively without paying attention to the peculiarities of IBM. The recent history of the automobile industry cannot be understood without understanding Toyota and GM. But as the Baumol, Blackman, and Wolff book testifies, the theoretical preconceptions shared by most economists lead them to ignore firm differences, unless they are compelled to attend to them.

Several recent developments in theoretical economics would appear to be changing this somewhat. The same summer that *Made in America* and *Productivity and American Leadership* were published, the long-awaited *Handbook of Industrial Organization* (1989) came out. It included several chapters surveying theoretical work that does recognize firm differences.

There are, first of all, the essays by Ordover and Saloner, and by Gilbert, which are expressly concerned with theoretical work that aims to explain firm differences, or at least some consequences of firm differences. In the models reported, there usually is an incumbent in the industry, or in the production of a particular product, which has certain advantages over firms that might think of joining the action. The presence of these advantages, or threats of action should a newcomer try to encroach, is enough to make the advantages durable. Gilbert deals more generally with models in which firms incur costs if they change their market positions. However, with few exceptions the models surveyed in these chapters do not consider the original sources of firm differences in much depth or detail.

Reinganum's chapter, which surveys modern neoclassical models of technological innovation, is focused on what certainly is an important source of such differences—industrial R&D and the innovation R&D makes possible. In the models she surveys a firm's technology may differ from a rival's because of the luck of an R&D draw, with the advantages made durable by patent protection or subsequent learning curve advantages. Given an initial difference, firms may face different incentives and thus find different courses of action most profitable. However, while these models may rationalize the observation that firms possess different technologies, the explanations offered certainly aren't very deep. And one comes away from them, or at least I do, with very little theoretical insight into why IBM is different, or Toyota, and what their differences mean.

Recently, economists have provided some theoretical work that looks inside firms, at their structure; this work seems to give promise of a theoretical window for a deeper look into why firms differ. The chapters by Holmstrom and Tirole, and by Williamson, report on such contributions. The questions explored in the surveyed work include what determines, through make or buy decisions, the boundaries of a firm, how firms are organized, the relative bargaining power of owners, managers, and workers, and so on. But, again, the ultimate reason for why firms differ is rather superficial. Implicitly they differ because some chance event, or some initial condition, made different choices profitable.

In my view, recent theoretical developments in neoclassical theory have loosened two of the theoretical constraints making it difficult if not impossible to see firm differences as important. Economists are getting away from the theoretical tethers of static general equilibrium theory and are treating technology as a variable, not a given. And they are trying to look inside the black box of the firm. However, for the most part they have failed to get away from the third tether—considering that a firm's choice sets will be obvious to the firm and that the best choice will be similarly clear. And because of that, the reasons for firm differences, in technology or organization, are ultimately driven back to differences in initial conditions, or to the luck of a draw, which may make choice sets different. Given the same conditions, all firms will do the same thing.

As I indicated above, I certainly do not want to play down the role of environment in constraining and molding what firms do. And I do not want to play down the role of chance in causing large and durable subsequent differences among firms. But in my view the models most economists keep playing with do not effectively come to grips with what lies behind the firm differences highlighted in *Made in America,* or the implications of those differences.

The reason, I want to argue, is that while the surveyed work purports to be concerned with 'innovation,' with the introduction of something new to the economy in the form of new technology or a new way of organizing a firm, the models in question completely miss what is involved in innovation. Thus, nowhere in the models Reinganum describes are the fundamental uncertainty, the differences of opinion, the differences in perceptions about feasible paths (which tend to stand out in any detailed study of technical advance) even recognized, much less analyzed in any detail. Williamson's own work on the determinants of firm organization has been much influenced by Chandler, and he dedicates part of his chapter to a transactions cost interpretation of Chandler's account of the rise of the modern corporation. But nowhere does he recognize explicitly the halting, trial-and-error process—often reactive rather than thought through—which led to the new ways of organizing that Chandler describes.

Put compactly, the treatment of technological and organizational 'innovation' described in these chapters simply takes the given 'choice set' and the presumptions of standard neoclassical theory that call for 'maximizing over it' and applies them to 'innovation.' That is, innovation is treated as being basically like any other choice. Investment costs may need to be incurred before the new product or organizational design is ready to be employed, but in neoclassical theory this is true of other capital goods like bridges or machines. There may be high risks involved in doing something new, in a formal sense of that term, but this is treated as statistical uncertainty with the correct probability distribution known to all, as is standard in microeconomic theory. The innovation may yield a new latent or manifest public good, which raises theoretical problems of 'market failure,' but this is no different than investment in, say, public health.

But what if effective treatment of innovation (and perhaps other activities) requires breaking away from the assumptions of clear and obvious choice sets and correct understanding of the consequences of making various choices? Does it really make sense to work with a model that presumes that the transistor, or the M-form of organization, were always possible choices known to all relevant parties, and that they simply were chosen and thus came into existence and use when conditions made profitable the relevant investments? Does the assumption that 'actors maximize' help one to analyze situations where some actors are not even aware of a possibility being considered by others?

If one reflects on these issues, one may be moved to adopt a very different view of the economic problem. Within this view, which I will call evolutionary, firm differences play an essential role.

2. Innovation and Firms in Evolutionary Theory

The models of technological innovation surveyed by Reinganum show economists interested in the theory of the firm struggling to break away from the orientation of general equilibrium theory, which sees the economic problem as allocating resources efficiently, given technologies. So too the new literature on organizational innovation. Here economists seem to be basically interested in how new ways of doing things—technologies, and ways of organizing and governing work—are introduced, winnowed, and where proven useful, spread, as contrasted with how familiar technologies and organizational modes are employed. Many years ago Schumpeter insisted that the focus of general equilibrium theory was on questions that, over the long run, were of minor importance compared with the question of how capitalist economies develop, screen, and selectively adopt new and better ways of doing things. Many of the writers surveyed by Reinganum call themselves 'neo-Schumpeterians.'

However, the dynamic processes Schumpeter described are not captured by the new neoclassical models. As he put it, 'In dealing with Capitalism, you are dealing with an evolutionary process.' He clearly had in mind a context in which people, and organizations, had quite different views about what kinds of innovations would be possible, and desirable, and would lay their bets differently. There are winners and losers in Schumpeter's 'process of creative destruction,' and these are not determined mainly in ex ante calculation, but largely in ex post actual contest.

In his 1911 *Theory of Economic Development*, Schumpeter saw the key innovative actors as 'entrepreneurs.' His 'firms' were the vessels used by entrepreneurs, and by other decision makers forced to adapt to the changes wrought by entrepreneurial innovators or to go under. By the time (1942) he wrote *Capitalism, Socialism, and Democracy*, Schumpeter's view of the sources of innovation had changed, or rather it might be better to say that there had been a transformation of the principal sources of innovation from an earlier era, and Schumpeter's views reflected this transformation. Modern firms, equipped with research and development laboratories, became the central innovative actors in Schumpeter's theory. The chapter by Cohen and Levin in the *Handbook* admirably surveys the wide range of empirical research that has been inspired by Schumpeter, particularly the research concerned with the relationships among innovation, firm size and other firm characteristics, and market structure.

In our book, *An Evolutionary Theory of Economic Change* (1982), Winter and I spent quite a bit of space presenting a 'theory of the firm' which is consistent with, and motivates, a Schumpeterian or evolutionary theoretic view of economic process and economic change. Our formulation drew significantly on Simon (1947), on Cyert and March (1963), and on Penrose (1959), as well as on Schumpeter. With hindsight it is clear that our writing then was handicapped by insufficient study of the writings of Chandler, particularly his *Scale and Scope* (1990b).

Since the time we wrote, there have been a number of theoretical papers on firm capabilities and behavior that draw both on Chandler and on our early formulation, and that add significantly to the picture. Papers by Teece (1980, 1982), Rumelt (1984), Cohen and Levinthal (1989), Dosi, Teece, and Winter (1989), Prahalad and Hamel (1990), Pavitt (1987, 1990), Cantwell (1989, 1990), Kogut (1987), Henderson (1990), Burgelman and Rosenbloom (1989), Langlois (1991), and Lazonick (1990) all present a similar or at least a conformable theoretical view, although with differences in stress. The paper by Teece, Pisano, and Shuen (1990) provides an overview of many of these works, and I believe correctly states that the common element is a focus on firm-specific dynamic capabilities.

This emerging theory of dynamic firm capabilities can be presented in different ways. Here it is convenient to focus on three different, if strongly related, features of a firm that must be recognized if one is to describe it adequately, its strategy, its structure, and its core capabilities. While each has a certain malleability, major changes in at least the latter two involve considerable cost. Thus, they define a relatively stable firm character.

The concept of strategy in this theory of the firm follows the definition of business historians and scholars of management, as contrasted with game theorists. It connotes a set of broad commitments made by a firm that define and rationalize its objectives and how it intends to pursue them. Some of this may be written down; some may not be but is in the management culture of the firm. Many economists would be inclined to propose that the strategy represents a firm's solution to its profit maximization problem, but this seems misconceived to me. In the first place, the commitments contained in a strategy often are as much a matter of faith (coming from top management and company tradition) as they are of calculation. Second, firm strategies seldom determine the details of firm actions, but usually at most the broad contours. Third, and of vital importance, there is no reason to argue a priori that these commitments are in fact optimal or even not self-destructive. If it is proposed that competition and selection force surviving strategies to be relatively profitable, this should be a theorem, not an assumption.

The concept of firm structure in this literature also is in the spirit of Chandler, as is the presumption that strategy tends to define a desired firm structure in a general way, without giving the details. Structure involves how a firm is organized and governed, and how decisions are made and carried out, and thus largely determines what the firm actually does, given the broad strategy. If a firm's strategy calls for it to be a technological leader, and if it lacks a sizeable R&D operation or an R&D director with strong input into firm decision making, it clearly has a structure out of tune with its strategy. However, the high-level strategy may be mute about such matters as links between its R&D lab and universities, whether to have a special biotech group, and so forth.

Change in strategy may require a change in management as well as a change in articulation; indeed, for the latter to be serious may require the former. However, within this theory of the firm, structure is far more difficult to change effectively than is strategy. While changing formal organization, or at least the organization chart, is easy, and sell-offs and buy-ups are possible, significantly changing the way a firm actually goes about making operating-level decisions and carries them out is time-consuming and costly to do. Or rather, while it may not be too difficult to destroy an old structure or its effectiveness, it is a major task to get a new structure in shape and operating smoothly. Thus, to the extent that a major change in strategy calls for a major change in structure, effecting the needed changes may take a long time.

The reason for changing structure, of course, is to change, and possibly to augment, the things a firm is capable of doing well. Which brings the discussion to the concept of core capabilities. Strategy and structure call forth and mold organizational capabilities, but what an organization can do well has something of a life of its own.

Winter and I have proposed that successful firms can be understood in terms of a hierarchy of practiced organizational routines, which define lower-order organizational skills and how these are coordinated, and higher-order decision procedures for choosing what is to be done at lower levels. The notion of a hierarchy of organizational routines is the key building block under our concept of core organizational capabilities. At any time the practiced routines that are built into an organization define a set of things the organization is capable of doing confidently. If the lower-order routines for doing various tasks are absent, or if they exist but there is no practiced higher-order routine for invoking them in the particular combination needed to accomplish a particular job, then the capability to do that job lies outside the organization's extant core capabilities.

The developing theory of dynamic firm capabilities I am discussing here starts from the premise that, in the industries of interest to the authors, firms are in a Schumpeterian or evolutionary context. Simply producing a given set of products with a given set of processes in a competent way will not enable a firm to survive for long. To be successful for any length of time a firm must innovate. The capabilities on which this group of scholars focus are capabilities for innovation and for taking economic advantage of innovation.

In industries where technological innovation is important, a firm needs a set of core capabilities in R&D. These capabilities will be defined and constrained by the skills, experience, and knowledge of the personnel in the R&D department, the nature of the extant teams and procedures for forming new ones, the character of the decision-making processes, the links between R&D and production and marketing, and so forth. This means that at any time there will be certain kinds of R&D projects that a firm can carry out with some confidence and success, and a wide range of other projects that, while other firms might be able to do them, this particular firm cannot with any real confidence.

R&D capabilities may be the lead ones in defining the dynamic capabilities of a firm. However, in a well-tuned firm, the production, procurement, marketing, and legal organizations must have built into them the capabilities to support and complement the new product and process technologies emanating from R&D. In Teece's terms, the firm's capabilities must include control over, or access to, the complementary assets and activities needed to enable it to profit from innovation. And in an environment of Schumpeterian competition, this means the capability to innovate, and to make that innovation profitable, again and again.

The concept of organizational capabilities, and the theory that Winter and I proposed as to what determines and limits them, does not directly imply any coherency to the set of things a firm can do. However, Dosi, Teece, and Winter (1989) argue that, in effective firms, there is a certain coherency. There would appear to be several reasons. The ones stressed by Dosi, Teece, and Winter are associated with localized learning in a dynamic context, and follow on the arguments Winter and I made some time ago that, to be under control, a routine needs to be practiced. Firms need to learn to get good at certain kinds of innovation, and to develop the skills and resources needed to take advantage of these innovations, and this requires concentration or at least coherency, rather than random spreading of efforts. Further, in many technologies one innovation points more or less directly to a set of following ones, and the learning and complementary strengths developed in the former effort provide a base for the next round.

But I think it also is the case that to be effective a firm needs a reasonably coherent strategy, which defines and legitimizes, at least loosely, the way the firm is organized and governed, enables it to see organizational gaps or anomalies given the strategy, and prepares the ground for bargaining over the resource needs for the core capabilities a firm must have to take its next step forward. Absent a reasonably coherent and accepted strategy, decision making about rival claims on resources has no legitimate basis. Decisions from above have no supportive rationale, and there is no way to hold back log-rolling bargaining among claimants other than arbitrary high-level decisions. There is no real guidance regarding the capabilities a firm needs to protect, enhance, or acquire in order to be effective in the next round of innovative competition.

But I think I am simply restating what Chandler, Lazonick, Williamson, and other scholars of the modern corporation have been saying for some time. To be successful in a world that requires firms to innovate and change, a firm must have a coherent strategy that enables it to decide what new ventures to go into and what to stay out of. And it needs a structure, in the sense of a mode of organization and governance, that guides and supports the building and sustaining of the core capabilities needed to carry out that strategy effectively.

If one thinks within the frame of evolutionary theory, it is nonsense to presume that a firm can calculate an actual 'best' strategy. A basic premise of evolutionary theory is that the world is too complicated for a firm to comprehend, in the sense that a firm understands its world in neoclassical theory. There are certain characteristics of a firm's strategy, and of its associated structure, that management can have confidence will enhance the chances that it will develop the capabilities it needs to succeed. There are other characteristics that seem a prescription for failure. However, there is a lot of room in between, where a firm (or its management) simply has to lay its bets knowing that it does not know how they will turn out.

Thus, diversity of firms is just what one would expect under evolutionary theory. It is virtually inevitable that firms will chose somewhat different strategies. These, in turn, will lead firms to develop different structures and different core capabilities, including their R&D capabilities. Inevitably firms will pursue somewhat different paths. Some will prove profitable, given what other firms are doing and the way markets evolve, others not. Firms that systematically lose money will have to change their strategy and structure and develop new core capabilities, or make more effective use of the ones they have, or drop out of the contest.

....

References

Burgelman, R. A., and R. Rosenbloom (1989). 'Technology Strategy: An Evolutionary Process Perspective.' In R. Burgelman and R. Rosenbloom (eds.), *Research on*

Technological Innovation, Management, and Policy Vol. 4. Greenwich, Conn.: JAI Press.

Cantwell, J. (1989). *Technological Innovation and Multinational Corporations*. London: Basil Blackwell.

—— (1990). 'The Technological Competence Theory of International Production and Its Implications.' University of Reading Discussion Paper #149.

Cohen, W., and D. Levinthal (1989). 'Innovation and Learning: The Two Faces of R&D.' *Economic Journal*, September, pp. 11–27.

—— (1990). 'Absorptive Capacity: A New Perspective on Learning and Innovation.' *Administrative Science 35*, pp. 128–152.

Dosi, G., D. J. Teece, and S. Winter (1990). 'Towards a Theory of Corporate Governance: Preliminary Remarks.' Unpublished paper, Center for Research in Management, University of California, Berkeley.

Henderson, R. (1990). 'Underinvestment and Incompetence as Responses to Radical Innovation: Evidence from the Photolithographic Alignment Equipment Industry.' Discussion paper, MIT.

Kogut, B. (1987). 'Country Patterns in International Competition: Appropriability and Oligopolistic Agreement.' In N. Hood and J. Vahlne (eds.), *Strategies in Global Competition*. London: Croom-Helm, pp. 315–340.

Langlois, R. (1991). 'Transaction Cost Economics in Real Time.' *Industrial Corporate Change*, June, pp. 99–127.

Lazonick, W. (1990). *Competitive Advantage on the Shop Floor*. Cambridge, Mass.: Harvard University Press.

Nelson, R., and S. Winter (1982). *An Evolutionary Theory of Economic Change*. Cambridge, Mass.: Harvard University Press.

Pavitt, K. (1987). 'On the Nature of Technology.' Inaugural lecture given at the University of Sussex, June 23.

—— (1990). 'The Stature and Determinants of Innovation: A Major Factor in Firms' (and Countries') Competitiveness.' Paper prepared for the conference on Fundamental Issues in Strategy: A Research Agenda for the 1990s.

Prahalad, C. K., and G. Hamel (1990). 'The Core Competence of the Corporation.' *Harvard Business Review* 68(3), pp. 79–91.

Rumelt, R. P. (1984). 'Towards a Strategic Theory of the Firm.' In R. B. Lamb (ed.), *Competitive Strategic Management*. Englewood Cliffs, N. J.: Prentice-Hall, pp. 556–570.

Schmalensee, R., and R. Willig, eds. (1989). *Handbook of Industrial Organization*. New York: North Holland.

Schumpeter, J. A. (1911/1934). *The Theory of Economic Development*. Cambridge, Mass.: Harvard University Press.

—— (1942). *Capitalism, Socialism, and Democracy*. New York: Harper.

Teece, D. J. (1980). 'Economies of Scope and the Scope of the Enterprise.' *Journal of Economic Behavior and Organization* 1, pp. 223–245.

—— (1982). 'Towards an Economic Theory of the Multiproduct Firm.' *Journal of Economic Behavior and Organization* 3, March, pp. 39–64.

Teece, D. J., G. Pisano, and A. Shuen (1990). 'Dynamic Capabilities and Strategic Management.' Consortium on Competition and Cooperation Working Paper #90-8, Center for Research in Management, University of California, Berkeley.

19 Dynamic Capabilities and Strategic Management

David J. Teece, Gary Pisano, and Amy Shuen

1. Markets and Strategic Capabilities

Different approaches to strategy view sources of wealth creation and the essence of the strategic problem faced by firms differently. The competitive forces framework sees the strategic problem in terms of market entry, entry deterrence, and positioning; game-theoretic models view the strategic problem as one of interaction between rivals with certain expectations about how each other will behave;[1] resource-based perspectives have focused on the exploitation of firm-specific assets. Each approach asks different, often complementary questions. A key step in building a conceptual framework related to dynamic capabilities is to identify the foundations upon which distinctive and difficult to replicate advantages can be built.

A useful way to vector in on the strategic elements of the business enterprise is to first identify what isn't strategic. To be strategic, a capability must be honed to a user need (so that there are customers), unique (so that the products/services produced can be priced without too much regard to competition) and difficult to replicate (so profits won't be competed away). Accordingly, any assets or entity which is homogeneous and can be bought and sold at an established price cannot be all that strategic (Barney, 1986). What is it, then, about firms which undergirds competitive advantage?

To answer this, one must first make some fundamental distinctions between markets and internal organization (firms). The essence of the firm, as Coase (1937) pointed out, is that it displaces market organization. It does so in the main because inside the firms one can organize certain types of economic activity in ways one cannot using markets. This is not only because of transaction costs, as Williamson (1975, 1985) has emphasized, but also because there are many types of arrangements where injecting high powered (market like) incentives might well be quite destructive of the cooperative activity and learning. Indeed, the essence of internal organization is that it is a domain of unleveraged or low-powered incentives. By unleveraged we mean that rewards are determined at the group or organization level, not primarily at the individual level, in an effort to encourage team behavior, not individual behavior, in order to accomplish certain tasks well. Inside an organization, exchange cannot take place in the same manner that it can outside an organization, not just because it might be destructive to provide high powered individual incentives, but because it is difficult if not impossible to tightly calibrate individual contribution to a joint effort. Hence, contrary to Arrow's (1969) view of firms as quasi markets, and the task of management to inject markets into firms, we recognize the inherent limits and possible counterproductive results of attempting to fashion firms into clusters of internal markets. In particular, learning and internal technology transfer may well be jeopardized.

Indeed, what is distinctive about firms is that they are domains for organizing activity in a non market like fashion. Accordingly, as we discuss what is distinctive about firms, we stress competences/capabilities which are ways of organizing and getting things done which cannot be accomplished by using the price system to coordinate activity. The very essence of capabilities/competences is that they cannot be readily assembled through markets (Teece, 1982, 1986a; Kogut and Zander, 1992). If the ability to assemble competences using markets is what is meant by the firm as a nexus of contracts (Fama, 1980), then we unequivocally state that the firm about which we theorize cannot be usefully modeled as a nexus of contracts. By contract we are referring to a transaction undergirded by a legal agreement, or some other arrangement which clearly spells out rights, rewards, and responsibilities. Moreover, the firm as a nexus of contracts suggests a series of bilateral contracts orchestrated by a coordinator, where our view of the firm is that the organization takes place in a more multilateral fashion, with patterns of behavior and learning being orchestrated in a much more decentralized fashion.

The key point, however, is that the properties of internal organization cannot be replicated by a portfolio of business units amalgamated through formal contracts as the distinctive elements of internal organization simply cannot be replicated in the market.[2] That is, entrepreneurial activity cannot lead to the immediate replication of unique organizational skills through simply entering a market and piecing the parts together overnight. Replication takes time, and the replication of best practice may be illusive. Indeed, firm capabilities need to be understood not in terms of balance sheet items, but mainly in terms of the organizational structures and managerial processes which support productive activity. By construction, the firm's balance sheet contains items that can be valued, at least at original market prices (cost). It is necessarily the case, therefore, that the balance sheet is a poor shadow of a firm's distinctive competence.[3] That which is distinctive cannot be bought and sold short of buying the firm itself, or one or more of its subunits.

There are many dimensions to the business firm that must be understood if one is to grasp firm-level distinctive competences/capabilities. In this paper we merely identify several classes of factors that will help determine a firm's dynamic capabilities. We organize these in three categories: processes, positions, and paths.

2 Processes, Positions, and Paths

We advance the argument that the strategic dimensions of the firm are its managerial and organizational processes, its present position, and the paths available to it. By managerial and organizational processes, we refer to the way things are done in the firm, or what might be referred to as its routines, or patterns of current practice and learning. By position we refer to its current endowment of technology and intellectual property, as well as its customer base and upstream relations with suppliers.[4] By paths we refer to the strategic alternatives available to the firm, and the attractiveness of the opportunities which lie ahead. Our focus throughout is on asset structures for which no ready market exits, as these are the only assets of strategic interest. A final section focuses on replication and imitation, as it is these phenomena which determine how readily a competence or capability can be cloned by competitors, and therefore the durability of its advantage.

The firms' processes and positions collectively encompass its capabilities or competences. A hierarchy of competences/capabilities ought be recognized, as some competences may be on the factory floor, some in the R&D labs, some in the executive suites, and some in the way everything is integrated. A difficult to replicate or difficult to imitate competence/capability can be considered a distinctive competence. As indicated, the key feature of distinctive competences and capabilities is that there is not a market for them, except possibly through the market for business units[5] or corporate control. Hence competences and capabilities are intriguing assets as they typically must be built because they cannot be bought. Dynamic capabilities are the subset of the competences/capabilities which allow the firm to create new products and processes, and respond to changing market circumstances.

2.1 *Organizational and Managerial Processes*

Integration

While the price system supposedly coordinates the economy, managers coordinate or integrate activity inside the firm. How efficiently and effectively internal coordination or integration is achieved is very important (Aoki, 1990).[6] Likewise for external coordination.[7] Increasingly, strategic advantage requires the integration of external activities and technologies. The growing literature on strategic alliances, the virtual corporation, and buyer-supplier relations and technology collaboration evidences the importance of external integration and sourcing.

There is some field-based empirical research that provides support for the notion that the way production is organized by management inside the firm is the source of differences in firms' competence in various domains. For example, Garvin's (1988) study of 18 room air conditioning plants reveals that quality performance was not related to either capital investment or the degree of automation of the facilities. Instead, quality performance was driven by special organizational routines. These included routines for gathering and processing information, for linking customer experiences with engineering design choices, and for coordinating factories and component suppliers.[8] The work of Clark and Fujimoto (1991) on project development in the automobile industry also illustrates the role played by coordinative routines. Their study reveals a significant degree of variation in how different firms coordinate the various activities required to bring a new model from concept to market. These differences in coordinative routines and capabilities seem to have a significant impact on such performance variables as development cost, development lead times, and quality. Furthermore, they tended to find significant firm-level differences in coordination routines and these differences seemed to have persisted for a long time. This suggests that routines related to coordination are firm-specific in nature.

Also, the notion that competence/capability is embedded in distinct ways of coordinating and combining helps to explain how and why seemingly minor technological changes can have devastating impacts on incumbent firms' abilities to compete in a market. Henderson and Clark (1990), for example, have shown that incumbents in the photolithographic equipment industry were sequentially devastated by seemingly minor innovations that, nevertheless, had major impacts on how systems had to be configured. They attribute these difficulties to the fact that systems level or 'architectural' innovations often require new routines to integrate and coordinate engineering tasks. These findings and others suggest that productive systems display high interdependency, and that it may not be possible to change one level without changing others. This appears to be true with respect to the 'lean production' model (Womack *et al.*,

1991) which has now transformed the Taylor or Ford model of manufacturing organization in the automobile industry.[9] Lean production requires distinctive shop floor practices and processes as well as distinctive higher order managerial processes. Put differently, organizational processes often display high levels of coherence, and when they do, replication may be difficult because it requires systemic changes throughout the organization and also among interorganizational linkages which might be very hard to effectuate. Put differently, partial imitation or replication of a successful model may yield zero benefits.

The notion that there is a certain rationality or coherence to processes and systems is not quite the same concept as corporate culture, as we understand the latter. Corporate culture refers to the values and beliefs that employees hold; culture can be a *de facto* governance system as it mediates the behavior of individuals and economizes on more formal administrative methods. Rationality or coherence notions are more akin to the Nelson and Winter (1982) notion of organizational routines. However, the routines concept is a little too amorphous to properly capture the congruence amongst processes and between processes and incentives that we have in mind. Consider a professional service organization like an accounting firm. If it is to have relatively high-powered incentives that reward individual performance, then it must build organizational processes that channel individual behavior; if it has weak or low-powered incentives, it must find symbolic ways to recognize the high performers, and it must use alternative methods to build effort and enthusiasm. What one may think of as styles of organization in fact contain necessary, not discretionary, elements to achieve performance. Recognizing the congruences and complementarities among processes, and between processes and incentives, is critical to the understanding of organizational capabilities. In particular, they can help us explain why architectural and radical innovations are so often introduced into an industry by new entrants. The incumbents develop distinctive organizational processes that cannot support the new technology, despite certain overt similarities between the old and the new. The frequent failure of incumbents to introduce new technologies can thus be seen as a consequence of the mismatch that so often exists between the set of organizational processes needed to support the conventional product/service and the requirements of the new. Radical organizational re-engineering will usually be required to support the new product, which may well do better embedded in a separate subsidiary where a new set of coherent organizational processes can be fashioned.[10]

Learning

Perhaps even more important than integration is learning. Learning is a process by which repetition and experimentation enable tasks to be performed better and quicker and new production opportunities to be identified.[11] In the context of the firm, if not more generally, learning has several key characteristics. First, learning involves organizational as well as individual skills.[12] While individual skills are of relevance, their value depends upon their employment, in particular organizational settings. Learning processes are intrinsically social and collective and occur not only through the imitation and emulation of individuals, as with teacher-student or master-apprentice, but also because of joint contributions to the understanding of complex problems. Learning requires common codes of communication and coordinated search procedures. Second, the organizational knowledge generated by such activity resides in new patterns of activity, in 'routines,' or a new logic of organization. As indicated earlier, routines are patterns of interactions that represent successful solutions to particular problems. These patterns of interaction are resident in group behavior, though certain subroutines may be resident in individual behavior. The concept of dynamic capabilities as a coordinative management process opens the door to the potential for inter-organizational learning. Researchers (Doz and Shuen, 1989; Mody, 1990) have pointed out that collaborations and partnerships can be a vehicle for new organizational learning, helping firms to recognize dysfunctional routines, and preventing strategic blindspots.

Reconfiguration and Transformation

In rapidly changing environments, there is obviously value in the ability to sense the need to reconfigure the firm's asset structure, and to accomplish the necessary internal and external transformation (Amit and Schoemaker, 1992; Langlois, 1994). This requires constant surveillance of markets and technologies and the willingness to adopt best practice. In this regard, benchmarking is of considerable value as an organized process for accomplishing such ends (Camp, 1989). In dynamic environments, narcissistic organizations are likely to be impaired. The capacity to reconfigure and transform is itself a learned organizational skill. The more frequently practiced, the easier accomplished.

Change is costly and so firms must develop processes to minimize low payoff change. The ability to calibrate the requirements for change and to effectuate the necessary adjustments would appear to depend on the ability to scan the environment, to evaluate markets and competitors, and to quickly accomplish reconfiguration and transformation ahead of competition. Decentralization and local autonomy assists these processes. Firms that have honed these capabilities are sometimes referred to as 'high flex.'

2.2 Positions

The strategic posture of a firm is determined not only by its learning processes and by the coherence of its internal and external processes and incentives, but also by its location at any point in time with respect to its business assets. By business assets we do not mean its plant and equipment unless they are specialized; rather we mean its difficult-to-trade knowledge assets and assets complementary to them, as well as its reputational and relational assets. These will determine its market share and profitability at any point in time.

Technological Assets

While there is an emerging market for know-how (Teece, 1981), much technology does not enter it. This is either because the firm is unwilling to sell it[13] or because of difficulties in transacting in the market for know-how (Teece 1980). A firm's technological assets may or may not be protected by the standard instruments of intellectual property law. Either way, the ownership protection and utilization of technological assets are clearly key differentiators among firms. Likewise for complementary assets.

Complementary Assets

Technological innovations require the use of certain related assets to produce and deliver new products and services. Prior commercialization activities require and enable firms to build such complementarities (Teece, 1986b). Such capabilities and assets, while necessary for the firm's established activities, may have other uses as well. Such assets typically lie downstream. New products and processes either can enhance or destroy the value of such assets (Tushman et al., 1986). Thus the development of computers enhanced the value of IBM's direct sales force in office products, while disc brakes rendered useless much of the auto industries' investment in drum brakes.

Financial Assets

In the short run, a firm's cash position and degree of leverage may have strategic implications. While there is nothing more fungible than cash, it cannot always be raised from external markets without the dissemination of considerable information to potential investors. Accordingly, what a firm can do in short order is often a function of its balance sheet. In the longer run, that ought not be so, as cash flow ought be more determinative.

Locational Assets

Geography matters too. Uniqueness in certain businesses can stem from locational assets which are non-tradable (e.g., positioning of a refinery in a certain geographic market). While real estate markets are well developed, land use and environmental restrictions often make locational assets non-tradable, and hence may be the source of difficult to replicate advantages which manifest themselves in lower transport costs, superior convenience, and the like.

2.3 Paths

Path Dependencies

Where a firm can go is a function of its current position and the paths ahead. It is of course also shaped by the path behind. In standard economics textbooks, firms have an infinite range of technologies from which they can choose and markets they can occupy. Changes in product or factor prices will be responded to instantaneously, with technologies moving in and out according to value maximization criterion. Only in the short run are irreversibilities recognized. Fixed costs—such as equipment and overhead—cause firms to price below fully amortized costs but never constrain future investment choices. 'Bygones are bygones.' Path dependencies are simply not recognized.

The notion of path dependencies recognizes that 'history matters.' Bygones are rarely bygones, despite the predictions of rational actor theory. Thus a firm's previous investments and its repertoire of routines (its 'history') constrains its future behavior. This follows because learning tends to be local. That is, opportunities for learning will be 'close in' to previous activities and thus will be transaction and production specific (Teece, 1988). This is because learning is often a process of trial, feedback, and evaluation. If too many parameters are changed simultaneously, the ability of firms to conduct meaningful natural quasi experiments is attenuated. If many aspects of a firm's learning environment change simultaneously, the ability to ascertain cause-effect relationships is confounded because cognitive structures will not be formed and rates of learning diminish as a result. One implication is that many investments are much longer term than is commonly thought.

Technological Opportunities

The concept of path dependencies can be given forward meaning through the consideration of an industry's technological opportunities. It is well recognized that how far and how fast a particular area of industrial activity can proceed is in part due to the technological opportunities that lie before it. Such opportunities are usually a lagged function of foment and diversity in basic science, and the rapidity with which new scientific breakthroughs are being made.

However, technological opportunities may not be completely exogenous to industry, not only because some firms have the capacity to engage in or at least support basic research, but also because technological opportunities are often fed by innovative activity itself. Moreover, the recognition of such opportunities are affected by the organizational structures that link the institutions engaging in basic research (primarily the university) to the business enterprise. Hence, the existence of technological opportunities can be quite firm specific.

Important for our purposes is the rate and direction in which relevant scientific frontiers are being rolled back. Firms engaging in R&D may find the path dead ahead closed off, though breakthroughs in related areas may be sufficiently close to be attractive. Likewise, if the path dead ahead is extremely attractive, there may be no incentive for firms to shift the allocation of resources away from traditional pursuits. The depth and width of technological opportunities in the neighborhood of a firm's prior research activities thus are likely to impact a firm's options with respect to both the amount and level of R&D activity that it can justify. In addition, a firm's past experience conditions the alternatives management is able to perceive. Thus, not only do firms in the same industry face 'menus' with different costs associated with particular technological choices, they also are looking at menus containing different choices.[14]

2.4 Assessment

The assessment of a firm's strategic capability at any point in time is presented here as a function of the firm's processes, positions, and paths. What it can do and where it can go is thus heavily constrained by the typography of its processes, positions, and paths. Each component of this capability framework needs to be analyzed in a strategic audit.

We submit that if one can identify each of these components and understand their interrelationships, one can at least predict the performance of the firm under various assumptions about changes in the external environment. One can also evaluate the richness of the menu of new opportunities from which the firm may select, and its likely performance in a changing environment.

The parameters we have identified for determining performance are radically different from those in the standard textbook theory of the firm, and in the competitive forces and strategic conflict approaches to strategy.[15] Moreover, the agency theoretic view of the firm as a nexus of contracts would put no weight on processes, positions, and paths. While agency approaches to the firm may recognize that opportunism and shirking may limit what a firm can do, they do not recognize the opportunities and constraints imposed by processes, positions, and paths. Moreover, the firm in our conceptualization is much more than the sum of its parts—or a team tied together by contracts.[16] Indeed, to some extent individuals can be moved in and out of organizations and, so long as the internal processes and structures remain in place, performance will not necessarily be impaired. A shift in the environment is a far more serious threat to the firm than is the loss of key individuals, as individuals can be replaced more readily than organizations can be transformed. Furthermore, the dynamic capabilities view of the firm would suggest that the behavior and performance of particular firms may be quite hard to replicate, even if its coherence and rationality are observable. This matter and related issues involving replication and imitation are taken up in the section that follows.

....

3. Replicability and Imitatability of Organizational Processes and Positions

Thus far, we have argued that the capabilities of a firm rest on processes, positions, and paths. However, distinctive organizational capabilities can provide competitive advantage and generated rents only if they are based on a collection of routines, skills, and complementary assets that are difficult to imitate.[17] A particular set of routines can lose their value if they support a competence which no longer matters in the marketplace, or if they can be readily replicated or emulated by competitors. Imitation occurs when firms discover and simply copy a firm's organizational routines and procedures. Emulation occurs when firms discover alternative ways of achieving the same functionality. There is ample evidence that a given type of competence (e.g. quality) can be supported by different routines and combinations of skills. For example, the Garvin (1988) and Clark and Fujimoto (1990) studies both indicate that there was no one 'formula' for achieving either high quality or high product development performance.

Replication

Replication involves transferring or redeploying competences from one concrete economic setting to another. Since productive knowledge is embodied, this cannot be accomplished by simply transmitting information. Only in those instances where all relevant knowledge is fully codified and understood can replication be collapsed into a simple problem of information transfer. Too often, the contextual dependence of original performance is poorly appreciated, so unless firms have replicated their systems of productive knowledge on many prior occasions, the act of replication is likely to be difficult (Teece 1976). Indeed, replication and transfer are often impossible absent the transfer of people, though this can be minimized if investments are made to convert tacit knowledge to codified knowledge. Often, however, this is simply not possible.

In short, organizational capabilities, and the routines upon which they rest, are normally rather difficult to replicate[18] Even understanding what all the relevant routines are that support a particular competence may not be transparent. Indeed, Lippman and Rumelt (1992) have argued that some sources of competitive advantage are so complex that the firm itself, let alone its competitors, does not understand them.[19] As Nelson and Winter (1982) and Teece (1982) have explained, many organizational routines are quite tacit in nature. Imitation can also be hindered by the fact few routines are 'stand-alone'; coherence may require that a change in one set of routines in one part of the firm (e.g. production) requires changes in some other part (e.g., R&D).

Some routines and competences seem to be attributable to local or regional forces that shape firms' capabilities at early stages in their lives. Porter (1990), for example, shows that differences in local product markets, local factor markets, and institutions play an important role in shaping competitive capabilities. Differences also exist within populations of firms from the same country. Various studies of the automobile industry, for example, show that not all Japanese automobile companies are top performers in terms of quality, productivity, or product development (see e.g. Clark and Fujimoto 1990). The role of firm-specific history has been highlighted as a critical factor explaining such firm-level (as opposed to regional or national level) differences (Nelson and Winter 1982). Replication in a different context may thus be rather difficult.

At least two types of strategic value flow from replication. One is the ability to support geographic and product line expansion. To the extent that the capabilities in question are relevant to customer needs elsewhere, replication can confer value.[20] Another is that the ability to replicate also indicates that the firm has the foundations in place for learning and improvement. Considerable empirical evidence supports the notion that the understanding of processes, both in production and in management, is the key to process improvement. In short, an organization cannot improve that which it does not understand. Deep process understanding is often required to accomplish codification. Indeed, if knowledge is highly tacit, it indicates that underlying structures are not well understood, which limits learning because scientific and engineering principles cannot be as systematically applied. Instead, learning is confined to proceeding through trial and error, and the leverage that might otherwise come from the application of modern science is denied.

Imitation

Imitation is simply replication performed by a competitor. If self replication is difficult, imitation is likely to be even harder. In competitive markets, it is the ease of imitation that determines the sustainability of competitive advantage. Easy imitation implies the rapid dissipation of rents.

Factors that make replication difficult also make imitation difficult. Thus, the more tacit the firm's productive knowledge, the harder it is to replicate by the firm itself or its competitors. When the tacit component is high, imitation may well be impossible, absent the hiring away of key individuals and the transfer of key organizational processes.

However, another set of barriers impede imitation of certain capabilities in advanced industrial countries. This is the system of intellectual property rights, such as patents, trade secrets, and trademarks, and even trade dress.[21] Intellectual property protection is of increasing importance in the United States, as since 1982 the legal system has adopted a more pro-patent posture. Similar trends are evident outside the United States. Besides the patent system, several other factors cause there to be a difference between replication costs and imitation costs. The observability of the technology or the organization is one such important factor. Whereas vistas into product technology can be obtained through strategies such as reverse engineering, this is not the case for process technology, as a firm need not expose its process technology to the outside in order to benefit from it.[22] Firms with product technology, on the other hand, confront the unfortunate circumstances that they must expose what they have got in order to profit from the technology. Secrets are thus more protectable if there is no need to expose them in contexts where competitors can learn about them.

One should not, however, overestimate the overall importance of intellectual property protection; yet it presents a formidable imitation barrier in certain particular contexts. Intellectual property protection is not uniform across products, processes, and technologies, and is best thought of as islands in a sea of open competition. If one is not able to place the fruits of one's investment, ingenuity, or creativity on one or more of the islands, then one indeed is at sea.

We use the term appropriability regimes to describe the ease of imitation. Appropriability is a function both of the ease of replication and the efficacy of intellectual property rights as a barrier to imitation. Appropriability is strong when a technology is both inherently difficult to replicate and the intellectual property system provides legal barriers to imitation. When it is inherently easy

		Inherent replicability	
		Easy	Hard
Intellectual property rights	Loose	Weak	Moderate
	Tight	Moderate	Strong

Fig. 1. Appropriability regimes.

to replicate and intellectual property protection is either unavailable or ineffectual, then appropriability is weak. Intermediate conditions also exist (see Fig. 1).

4. Strategic Issues from a Dynamic Capabilities Perspective

The dynamic capabilities approach views competition in Schumpeterian terms. This means, at one level, that firms compete on the basis of product design, product quality, process efficiency, and other attributes. However, in a Schumpeterian world, firms are constantly seeking to create 'new combinations,' and rivals are continuously attempting to improve their competences or to imitate the competence of their most qualified competitors. Rivalry to develop new competences or to improve existing ones is critical in a Schumpeterian world. Such processes drive creative destruction. Differences in firms' capabilities to improve their distinctive competences or to develop new distinctive domains of competence play a critical role in shaping long-term competitive outcomes.

The strategic problem facing an innovating firm in a world of Schumpeterian competition is to decide upon and develop difficult to imitate processes and paths most likely to support valuable products and services. Thus, as argued by Dierickx and Cool (1989), choices about how much to spend (invest) on different possible areas are central to the firm's strategy. However, choices about domains of competence are influenced by past choices. At any given point in time, firms must follow a certain trajectory or path of competence development. This path not only defines what choices are open to the firm today, but it also puts bounds around what its repertoire is likely to be in the future. Thus, firms, at various points in time, make *long-term, quasi-irreversible* commitments to certain domains of competence. Deciding, under significant uncertainty about future states of the world, which long-term paths to commit to and when to change paths is the central strategic problem confronting the firm.[23]

Notes

The authors are grateful for helpful comments from two anonymous referees, as well as from Raffi Amit, Susan Athey, Jay Barney, Joseph Bower, Giovanni Dosi, Pankaj Ghemawat, Connie Helfat, Rebecca Henderson, Dan Levinthal, Richard Nelson, Margie Peteraf, Richard Rosenbloom, Richard Rumelt, Carl Shapiro, Oliver Williamson, and Sidney Winter. Useful feedback was obtained from workshops at the Haas School of Business, the Wharton School, the Kellogg School (Northwestern), the Harvard Business School, and the International Institute of Applied Systems Analysis (IIASA) in Vienna.

1. In sequential move games, each player looks ahead and anticipates his rivals' future responses in order to reason back and decide action, i.e., look forward, reason backward.
2. As we note in Teece *et al.* (1994), the conglomerate offers few if any efficiencies because there is little provided by the conglomerate form that shareholders cannot obtain for themselves simply by holding a diversified portfolio of stocks.
3. Owners' equity may reflect, in part, certain historic capabilities. Recently, some scholars have begun to attempt to measure organizational capability using financial statement data. See Baldwin and Clark (1991) and Lev and Sougiannis (1992).
4. We also recognize its strategic alliances with competitors.
5. Such competences may unravel if the subunit is separated from the parent.
6. Indeed, Ronald Coase, author of the pathbreaking 1937 article 'The Nature of the Firm,' which focused on the costs of organizational coordination inside the firm as compared to across the market, half a century later has identified as critical the understanding of 'why the costs of organizing particular activities differs among firms' (Coase 1988: 47). We argue that a firm's distinctive ability needs to be under-

stood as a reflection of distinctive organizational or coordinative capabilities. This form of integration (i.e. inside business units) is different from the integration between business units; they could be viable on a stand-alone basis (external integration). For a useful taxonomy, see Iansiti and Clark (1994)

7. Amy Shuen (1994) examines the gains and hazards of the technology make vs. buy decision and supplier co-development.

8. Garvin (1994) provides a typology of organizational processes.

9. Fujimoto (1994, pp. 18–20) describes key elements as they existed in the Japanese auto industry as follows: 'The typical volume production system of effective Japanese makers of the 1980s (e.g., Toyota) consists of various intertwined elements that might lead to competitive advantages. Just-in-Time (JIT), Jidoka (automatic defect detection and machine stop), Total Quality Control (TQC), and continuous improvement (Kaizen) are often pointed out as its core subsystems. The elements of such a system include inventory reduction mechanisms by Kanban system; levelization of production volume and product mix (heijunka); Reduction of "muda" (non-value adding activities), "mura" (uneven pace of production) and muri (excessive workload); production plans based on dealers' order volume (genyo seisan); reduction of die set-up time and lot size in stamping operation; mixed model assembly; piece-by-piece transfer of parts between machines (ikko-nagashi); flexible task assignment for volume changes and productivity improvement (shojinka); multi-task job assignment along the process flow (takotei-mochi); U-shape machine layout that facilitates flexible and multiple task assignment, on-the-spot inspection by direct workers (tsukurikomi); fool-proof pervention of defects (poka-yoke); real-time feedback of production troubles (andon); assembly line stop cord; emphasis on cleanliness, order, and discipline on the shop floor (5-S); frequent revision of standard operating procedures by supervisors; quality control circles; standardized tools for quality improvement (e.g., 7 tools for QC, QC story); worker involvement in preventive maintenance (Total Productive Maintenance); low cost automation or semi-automation with just-enough functions); reduction of process steps for saving of tools and dies, and so on. The human-resource management factors that back up the above elements include stable employment of core workers (with temporary workers in the periphery); long-term training of multi-skilled (multi-task) workers; wage system based in part on skill accumulation; internal promotion to shop floor supervisors; cooperative relationships with labor unions; inclusion of production supervisors in union members; generally egalitarian policies for corporate welfare, communication and worker motivation. Parts procurement policies are also pointed out often as a source of the competitive advantage; relatively high ratio of parts out-sourcing; multi-layer hierarchy of suppliers; long-term relations with suppliers; relatively small number of technologically capable suppliers at the first tier; subassembly functions of the first-tier parts makers; detail-engineering capability of the first tier makers (design-in, back box parts); competition based on long-term capability of design and improvements rather than bidding; pressures for continuous reduction of parts price; elimination of incoming parts inspection; plant inspection and technical assistance by auto makers, and so on.'

10. See Abernathy and Clark, 1985.

11. For a useful review and contribution, see Levitt and March, 1988.

12. See Mahoney (1994).
13. Managers often evoke the 'crown jewels' metaphor. That is, if the technology is released, the kingdom will be lost.
14. This is a critical element in Nelson and Winter's (1982) view of firms and technical change.
15. In both the firm is still largely a black box. Certainly, little or no attention is given to processes, positions, and paths.
16. See Alchian and Demsetz, 1972.
17. See Dierickx and Cool (1989) for a discussion of the characteristics of assets which make them a source of rents.
18. See Gabriel Szulanski's (1993) discussion of the intra-firm transfer of best practice. He quotes a senior vice president of Xerox as saying 'you can see a high performance factory or office, but it just doesn't spread. I don't know why.' Szulanski also discusses the role of benchmarking in facilitating the transfer of best practice.
19. If so, it is our belief that the firm's advantage is likely to fade, as luck does run out.
20. Needless to say, there are many examples of firms replicating their capabilities inappropriately by applying extant routines to circumstances where they may not be applicable, e.g., Nestles transfer of developed country marketing methods for infant formula to the third world (Hartley, 1989). A key strategic need is for firms to screen capabilities for their applicability to new environments.
21. Trade dress refers to the 'look and feel' of a retail establishment, e.g. the distinctive marketing and presentation style of The Nature Company.
22. An interesting but important exception to this can be found in second sourcing. In the microprocessor business, until the introduction of the 386 chip, Intel and most other merchant semi producers were encouraged by large customers like IBM to provide second sources, i.e., to license and share their proprietary process technology with competitors like AMD and NEC. The microprocessor developers did so to assure customers that they had sufficient manufacturing capability to meet demand at all times.
23. In this regard, the work of Ghemawat (1991) is highly germane to the dynamic capabilities approach to strategy.

References

Abernathy, W. J. and K. Clark. 1985. 'Innovation: Mapping the Winds of Creative Destruction,' *Research Policy*, 14: 3–22.

Alchian, A. A. and H. Demsetz. 1972. 'Production, Information Costs, and Economic Organization,' *American Economic Review*, 62: 777–795.

Amit, R. and P. Schoemaker, 1992. 'Strategic Assets and Organizational Rent,' Working Paper, University of British Columbia, Canada, August 7.

Aoki, M. 1990. 'The Participatory Generation of Information Rents and the Theory of the Firm.' In M. Aoki et al. (eds.), *The Firm as a Nexus of Treaties*. London: Sage.

Arrow, K. 1969. 'The Organization of Economic Activity: Issues Pertinent to the Choice of Market vs. Nonmarket Allocation.' In *The Analysis and Evaluation of Public Expen-*

ditures: The PPB System, 1, U.S. Joint Economic Committee, 91st Session. Washington, DC: U.S. Government Printing Office, 59–73.

Baldwin, C. and K. Clark. 1991. 'Capabilities and Capital Investment: New Perspectives on Capital Budgeting,' Harvard Business School Working Paper #92-004.

Barney, J. B. 1986. 'Strategic Factor Markets: Expectations, Luck, and Business Strategy,' *Management Science*, 32:10 (October 1986), 1231–1241.

Camp, R. 1989. *Benchmarking: The Search for Industry Best Practice That Lead to Superior Performance*. White Plains, NY: Quality Resources.

Clark, K. and T. Fujimoto. 1991. *Product Development Performance: Strategy, Organization and Management in the World Auto Industries*. Cambridge, MA: Harvard Business School Press.

Coase, R. 1937. 'The Nature of the Firm,' *Economica*.

Coase, R. 1988. 'Lecture on the Nature of the Firm, III,' *Journal of Law, Economics and Organization*, 4: 33–47.

Dierickx, I. and K. Cool. 1989. 'Asset Stock Accumulation and Sustainability of Competitive Advantage,' *Management Science*, 35:12 (December), 1504–1511.

Doz, Y. and A. Shuen. 1990. 'From Intent to Outcome: A Process Framework for Partnerships,' INSEAD Working Paper.

Fama, E. F. 1980. 'Agency Problems and the Theory of the Firm,' *Journal of Political Economy*, 88 (April): 288–307.

Fujimoto, T. 1994. 'Reinterpreting the Resource-Capability View of the Firm: A Case of the Development-Production Systems of the Japanese Automakers.' Draft working paper, Faculty of Economics, University of Tokyo (May).

Garvin, D. 1988. *Managing Quality*. New York: Free Press.

Garvin, D. 1994. 'The Processes of Organization and Management,' Harvard Business School Working Paper #94-084.

Ghemawat, P. 1991. *Commitment: The Dynamics of Strategy*. New York: Free Press.

Hartley, R. F. 1989. *Marketing Mistakes*. New York: John Wiley.

Henderson, R. M. and K. B. Clark. 1990. 'Architectural Innovation: The Reconfiguration of Existing Product Technologies and the Failure of Established Firms,' *Administrative Science Quarterly*, 35 (March): 9–30.

Iansiti, M. and K. B. Clark. 1994. 'Integration and Dynamic Capability: Evidence from Product Development in Automobiles and Mainframe Computers,' *Industrial and Corporate Change*, Special Issue, forthcoming.

Kogut, I. and U. Zander. 1992. 'Knowledge of the Firm, Combinative Capabilities, and the Replication of Technology,' *Organizational Science*.

Langlois, R. 1994. 'Cognition and Capabilities: Opportunities Seized and Missed in the History of the Computer Industry,' Working Paper, University of Connecticut. Presented at the conference on Technological Oversights and Foresights, Stern School of Business, New York University, March 11–12, 1994.

Lev, B. and T. Sougiannis. 1992. 'The Capitalization, Amortization and Value-Relevance of R&D.' Unpublished manuscript, University of California, Berkeley, and University of Illinois, Urbana-Champaign (November).

Levitt, B. and J. March. 1988. 'Organizational Learning,' *Annual Review of Sociology*, 14: 319–340.

Lippman, S. A. and R. P. Rumelt. 1992. 'Demand Uncertainty and Investment in Industry-Specific Capital, *Industry and Corporate Change* (forthcoming 1992).

Mahoney, J. 1994. 'The Management of Resources and the Resources of Management,' *Journal of Business Research*.

Mody, A. 1990. 'Learning through Alliances,' Working Paper, The World Bank, Washington, DC, September 6.

Nelson, R., and S. Winter. 1982. *An Evolutionary Theory of Economic Change*. Cambridge, MA: Harvard University Press.

Porter, M. E. 1980. *Competitive Strategy*. New York: Free Press.

Shuen, A. 1994. 'Technology Sourcing and Learning Strategies in the Semiconductor Industry.' Unpublished Ph.D. dissertation, University of California, Berkeley.

Szulanski, G. 1993. 'Intrafirm Transfer of Best Practice, Appropriate Capabilities, Organizational Barriers to Appropriation.' Working Paper, INSEAD (March).

Teece, D. J. 1976. *The Multinational Corporation and the Resource Cost of International Technology Transfer*. Cambridge, MA: Ballinger.

Teece, D. J. 1980. 'Economics of Scope and the Scope of an Enterprise,' *Journal of Economic Behavior and Organization*, 1: 223–247.

Teece, D. J. 1981. 'The Market for Know-how and the Efficient International Transfer of Technology,' *The Annals of the Academy of Political and Social Science*, November 1981, 81–96.

Teece, D. J. 1982. 'Towards an Economic Theory of the Multiproduct Firm,' *Journal of Economic Behavior and Organization*, 3: 39–63.

Teece, D. J. 1986a. 'Transactions Cost Economics and the Multinational Enterprise,' *Journal of Economic Behavior and Organization*, 7: 21–45.

Teece, D. J. 1986b. 'Profiting from Technological Innovation,' *Research Policy*, 15:6 (December).

Teece, D. J. 1988. 'Technological Change and the Nature of the Firm.' In G. Dosi, *et al.* (eds.), *Technical Change and Economic Theory*.

Teece, D. J., R. Rumelt, G. Dosi, and S. Winter. 1994. 'Understanding Corporate Coherence: Theory and Evidence,' *Journal of Economic Behavior and Organization*, 23 (1994), 1–30.

Tushman, M. L., W. H. Newman, and E. Romanelli. 1986. 'Convergence and Upheaval: Managing the Unsteady Pace of Organizational Evolution,' *California Management Review*, 29:1 (Fall), 29–44.

Williamson, O. E. 1975. *Markets and Hierarchies*. New York: Free Press.

Williamson, O. E. 1985. *The Economic Institutions of Capitalism*. New York: Free Press.

Womack, J., D. Jones and D. Roos. 1991. *The Machine That Changed the World*. New York: Harper-Perennial.

20 Transaction-Cost Economics in Real Time

Richard N. Langlois

1. Organization and Capabilities

Although one can find versions of the idea in Smith, Marshall, and elsewhere, the modern discussion of the capabilities of organizations probably begins with Edith Penrose (1959), who suggested viewing the firm as a 'pool of resources.' Among the writers who have used and developed this idea are G. B. Richardson (1972), Richard Nelson and Sidney Winter (1982), and David Teece (1980, 1982). To all these authors, the firm is a pool not of tangible but of intangible resources. Capabilities, in the end, are a matter of knowledge. Because of the nature of specialization and the limits to cognition, organizations as well as individuals are limited in what they know how to do effectively. Put the other way, organizations possess a pool of more-or-less embodied 'how to' knowledge useful for particular classes of activities.

One sort of embodied knowledge is that contained in the firm's physical capital—that is, in machines. By rendering tasks a matter of routine, the division of labor (in the manner of the pinshop) allows for the substitution of skilled machines for skilled labor. But the capabilities embodied in machines are for present purposes the least interesting sorts of capabilities a firm might possess. More important are the sorts of knowledge embodied in the human capital of the firm, especially in those who manage it. Although management is clearly a highly skilled activity, the human capabilities of the firm are nonetheless quite nearly as much a matter of routine as are the skills of machines. 'Routines,' write Nelson and Winter (1982, p. 124), 'are the skills of an organization.' Indeed, as Michael Polanyi (1958) has argued, much of what we think of as skilled human behavior—in sports, the arts, everyday life—is in fact a matter of routine, in the sense that such skill consists in following inarticulate or 'tacit' rules of behavior. Such tacit knowledge is fundamentally empirical: it is gained through imitation and repetition not through conscious analysis or explicit instruction. This certainly does not mean that humans are incapable of innovation; but it does mean that there are limits to what conscious attention can accomplish. It is only because much of life is a matter of tacit knowledge and unconscious rules that conscious attention can produce as much as it does.

In a metaphoric sense, at least, the capabilities of the organization are more than the sum (whatever that means) of the skills of the individuals in the organization. In addition to the 'skill' of the firm's physical capital, there is also the matter of organization. How the firm is organized—how the routines of the humans and machines are linked together—is also part of a firm's capabilities. Indeed, 'skills, organization, and "technology" are intimately intertwined in a functioning routine, and it is difficult to say exactly where one aspect ends and another begins' (Nelson and Winter, 1982, p. 104).

Richardson and Teece have used notions like these to develop a theory of diversification. Just as a technological stage of production may be an 'anti-bottleneck' with excess capacity, so may an organization have excess capacity in its organizational capabilities. In both cases, the result is the taking on of additional work. But in the case of organizational capabilities, the new activity need not be linked technologically to what the firm had previously been doing; rather, the new activity need only require a similar set of capabilities. In Richardson's terminology, the activities needn't be *complementary*; rather, they must be *similar*.

The flip-side of a theory of diversification, of course, is a theory of non-diversification—a theory of specialization. Such a theory would explain, as Coase once put it, 'why General Motors was not a dominant factor in the coal industry, and why A&P did not manufacture airplanes' (Coase, 1971, p. 67). And the basic answer is that capabilities have their limits. There are diminishing returns to spreading one's capabilities over more activities. This is so not merely for the reasons emanating from traditional span-of-control arguments (e.g. Robinson, 1934), but also because each new activity the firm could consider diversifying into will be increasingly dissimilar to—will require capabilities slightly different from—those the firm started out with. Ultimately, a firm will be restricted to activities that are fundamentally similar along one or another dimension.[1]

What gives this observation its salience, however, is that what is similar need not be what is complementary. That is, the various activities in the chain of production may—or may not—each require skills that are quite distinct. The manufacture of silicon wafers, from which integrated circuits begin, requires capabilities quite different from the fabrication of the semiconductors; as a result, the wafers are supplied by chemical companies, like Wacker Chemie, whose other activities are similar. The manufacture of the optical steppers used in the photolithography of the semiconductors is also unlike the fabrication of chips; but it is quite like the making of other precision optical equipment, which is why Nikon and Canon are among the suppliers of these devices (Langlois *et al.*, 1988).

2. Capabilities and Governance Costs

The capabilities view of the firm is in many ways a modern reformulation of the theory of Smith and Marshall: it is a real-time account of production costs in which knowledge and organization have as important a role as technology. Unlike the Smithian theory narrowly understood, however, the capabilities view of the firm does give us some insights into the boundaries of the firm.

One implication of the boundedness of capabilities is that no firm—even the most integrated—has the capabilities necessary for all activities in the chain of production. The result is that firms must link up with other firms. This often takes place through the simplest of market contracts. One can, for example, buy off-the-shelf parts at spot prices and assemble a finished product out of them. But often—and especially when innovation is involved—the links among firms are of a more complex sort, involving everything from informal swaps of information (von Hippel, 1989) to joint ventures and other formal collaborative arrangements (Mowery, 1989). All firms must rely on the capabilities owned by others, especially to the extent those capabilities are dissimilar to those the firm possesses. A firm could—and many do—acquire dissimilar capabilities complementary to the ones they already own. But there is no particular reason to do so unless there are specific transaction costs impeding contractual arrangements. And there are generally costs to owning dissimilar assets, especially when the acquiring firm cannot use or sell their full capacity.

The existence in the market of complementary (but possibly dissimilar) capabilities is, of course, one kind of external economy Marshall thought important. And the level of relevant external capabilities in an economy will be important to the level of vertical integration we observe in that economy. In developing countries, or in developed economies when innovation renders the market's existing capabilities obsolete, a firm may have to integrate into many dissimilar activities in order to generate all the complementary activities it needs (Silver 1984). Consider the case of the American automobile industry

(Langlois and Robertson, 1989). In the early days of the industry, automobile makers were all assemblers, that is, they contracted for almost all the parts that went into the cars, reserving only the assembly stage for themselves. They could do this because the American economy—and the Detroit region in particular—possessed a high level of general purpose machining and metal-working capabilities available in the market. The innovation of the moving assembly line at Ford, however, rendered these capabilities obsolete, in that Ford could mass-produce parts much less expensively than he could buy them on the market.[2] Because Ford could not quickly and cheaply convey to suppliers the (partly tacit) nature of the innovation—which was in any case a slowly unfolding process—he was forced to integrate vertically into parts manufacture. Imitators like General Motors, however, could take advantage of the eventual spread of Ford ideas to the market, and thus needed less integration.

In short, then, the capabilities view of the firm suggests that the boundaries of the firm are determined (at least in part) by the relative strength of internal and external capabilities, that is, capabilities internal to the firm and those available through contract with other firms. Consider Fig. 1.[3] On the X-axis we can array activities or stages of production in order of increasing cost of internal production. Specifically, ΔC graphs the normalized per-unit cost premium the firm must pay for the output of a particular activity if it integrates into that activity, measured relative to the per-unit cost it would incur by obtaining the output on contract from a distinct firm. Whenever this premium is negative, there is a cost advantage to internal organization. And the firm will acquire increasingly dissimilar activities until the premium is zero, in this case at $A^\star$. Activities in the range $OA^\star$ are within the boundaries of the firm; the rest are left to the market.[4]

The cost premium, and therefore the location of $A^\star$, will depend on a number of factors. As transaction-cost economics suggests, it will depend on the bureaucratic costs of internal organization and the transaction costs of market relations. But in this story, the location of the ΔC curve also depends on the internal capabilities of the firm and the external capabilities available in the market. That is to say, the price premium includes both governance-cost and production-cost differences.

If we hold capabilities constant, then we get the familiar account: whatever lowers bureaucratic costs on the margin will increase the extent of integration; whatever lowers transaction costs will reduce the extent of integration. If capabilities were unbounded, then governance costs alone would determine the boundaries of the firm. In such a case, the activities would be ordered according to the normalized per-unit governance-cost premium for internal over market procurement. By contrast, if governance costs were zero, capabilities alone would determine the boundaries of the firm. In this case, the activities would be ordered according to decreasing similarity, measured from the

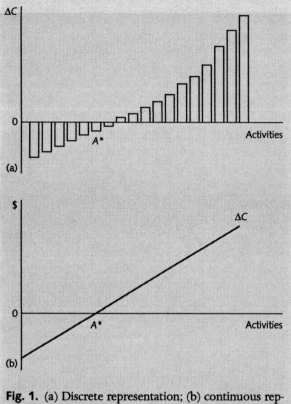

Fig. 1. (a) Discrete representation; (b) continuous representation.

activity in which the firm has the greatest cost advantage over the market. In both polar cases, the firm consists of all the activities in the range OA*; but those are not necessarily the same set of activities in each case (see Fig. 2).

In the long run, I have argued, transaction costs might be expected to approach zero. One might also argue this for governance costs generally. In the long run, activities have become increasingly routine. This reduces the cost of contracting, not in the sense that contracts have become cheaper to write but in the sense that contracts are increasingly unnecessary: everything is done tomorrow the way it was done today. In this sense, then, the long run also arguably reduces the cost of internal management by reducing decision-making costs.[5] Thus, one might argue that, in the long run as I have defined it, the boundaries of the firm are determined entirely by the capabilities of the firm relative to the capabilities of the market.

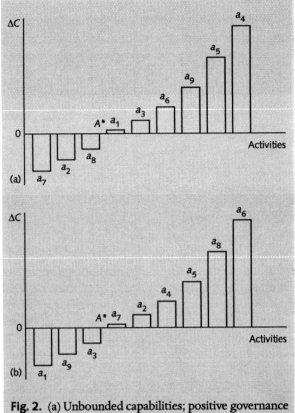

Fig. 2. (a) Unbounded capabilities; positive governance costs. (b) Bounded capabilities; no governance costs.

If, however, we follow Marshall in seeing the long run as the asymptotic end-state of a process of learning, then we also have to consider the ways in which capabilities change over time. And here, it seems to me, there are also two opposing effects. On the one hand, the firm is likely to become more 'capable' over time. As more and more of the firm's activities take on the nature of routines, and as the firm's routines become more finely tuned, both the firm's total managerial capacity and its free managerial capacity will increase. Other things equal, this will shift ΔC down and increase the extent of OA^*. On the other hand, however, the market will also become more 'capable' as time passes. Other firms will also be increasing their capabilities. And techniques pioneered by one firm may diffuse to and be imitated by other firms. All other things equal, this will have the effect of shifting ΔC up and lowering the extent of OA^*.

The classical presumption was that this latter effect predominates: in the longest of runs capability diffuses completely into the market, leading to full specialization and vertical disintegration (see Fig. 3). In general, the relative strengths of these effects will depend on the relative learning abilities of the firm and the market. The firm's learning ability will depend on its internal organization. And the learning ability of the market will depend on technical and institutional factors, as well as on the learning abilities of the firms it comprises, considered both individually and as a system. The remainder of this paper is devoted to considering these two learning systems in slightly more detail. More specifically, it will set out some preliminary generalizations about how the level of capabilities in the firm and the market—and the nature of *change* in those capabilities—effects the boundaries of the firm.

Before turning to that task, however, let me raise a conceptual issue. I have so far tried to portray capabilities as in the nature of production costs, something distinct from transaction costs. But the line is actually far more blurry. Assume no transaction costs of the measurement or hold-up kind. And suppose that a firm chooses to undertake a particular activity internally rather than relying on the market. This must mean that the firm has a cost advantage over the market. But is that advantage in the nature of a production cost or a transaction cost? In a recent critique of the transaction-cost approach to the multinational, Paul Hallwood (1991) argues that much foreign direct investment can be explained simply by production-cost advantages of the foreign firm over indigenous firms. For example, a foreign soft-drink company may choose to set up its own bottling plants in a particular country instead of licensing indigenous bottlers simply because its bottling capabilities are superior to—and thus its costs lower than—those of local plants. Viewed from another perspective,

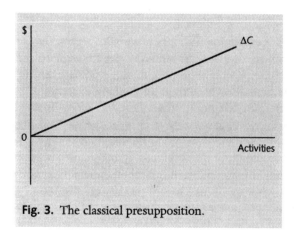

Fig. 3. The classical presupposition.

however, might we not say that the foreign licensor integrates into local production because the transaction costs of using the local market capabilities were prohibitive? This is not merely tautological if we specify that the transaction costs involved are those of somehow transmitting to local market participants the knowledge that would provide them with the necessary capabilities. As Hallwood suggests, this is not necessarily a helpful way to look at the issue, especially when, as we have argued, capabilities involve tacit knowledge that can be gained only by a long process of apprenticeship.

At the same time, of course, 'technology transfer' is in fact an option that presents itself to firms. Instead of producing oneself, one can teach others how to produce and persuade them to do so. In principle, Henry Ford *could* have taught outside parts suppliers the techniques of the moving assembly line and persuaded them to use them for high-volume production. The costs of doing so would have been prohibitive; but they would have been costs, in a straight-forward foregone-opportunity sense. Similarly, a firm that opts to procure an input on the market *might* have chosen to acquire the necessary capabilities to produce internally. The cost of acquiring those capabilities is the diminution in profit from not having taken advantage of the market's capabilities. We might not want to call these transaction costs, but they are certainly information or knowledge costs. And it is these costs that permit the notion of 'capabilities,' unlike the classical or neoclassical notion of production costs, to help explain the boundaries of the firm. Consider the following case. A firm's capabilities grow, allowing it to apply those capabilities to a new activity similar to the ones in which it is already active. If there are truly no transaction costs, and the issue were solely the firm's advantage over other firms in production costs, then there would be no reason for the firm in fact to own the new stage of production. It could costlessly license its knowledge to others and earn a specific contractual return. To say that the firm must extend its boundaries to encompass the new activity implies that it is costly to license its capabilities, which means that there must be transaction costs of *some* kind.[6]

For want of a better term, I propose to call these *dynamic* transaction costs. They are a kind of cost that has been largely neglected in the explanation of the boundaries of the firm. As I will explain more fully below, I will mean by dynamic transaction costs the costs of persuading, negotiating, coordinating and teaching outside suppliers. Another—if perhaps fast and loose—way to look at these transaction costs is as the costs of not having the capabilities you need when you need them. Indeed, if one follows Demsetz (1988) in using the term transaction cost to refer only to costs of using the market and never to costs of internal governance, then one ought to call these dynamic *governance* costs, since, as we'll see, it can also be a cost of internal organization not to have the capabilities one needs at the right time. When the market cannot provide the right capabilities at the right time, vertical integration may result;

and when the firm lacks the right capabilities at the right time, vertical disintegration may occur. Let us examine these two possibilities in order.

3. Capabilities, Learning, and Vertical Integration

3.1 Internal Capabilities

As we have seen, the distinction between capabilities and transaction costs suggests two (non-exclusive) possibilities. On the one hand, a firm may need to internalize a stage of production because the complementary capabilities that stage represents do not exist or are more expensive in the market. This would be a pure capabilities explanation for internalization. Perhaps the case of Henry Ford and the moving assembly line might fit this possibility. His process innovation gave him a cost advantage over outside suppliers, motivating a high degree of vertical integration. On the other hand, a firm may wish to internalize a stage of production even when the market possesses the requisite capabilities to at least the same degree as does the firm itself. If the firm does internalize, it must be because there are other costs to using the markets. An explanation along these lines would be a pure transaction-cost explanation.

What might the sources of these transactions costs be? Asset specificity is a possibility with which the literature is enthralled. In a sense, this fits with the theme I have suggested: when there is a threat of hold-up, one might be afraid of not having the right capabilities available at the right time. For example, Alfred Chandler (1977) sees the backward integration of large manufacturing firms as largely if not entirely a defensive stratagem to avoid supply disruptions and ensure high-volume throughput. As I have already hinted, however, the problem with the hold-up view is that it is neither sufficient nor necessary as an explanation for integration. It is not sufficient because, in the absence of uncertainty and a divergence of expectations about the future, long-term contracts, reputation effects, and other devices can remove the costs of arm's-length arrangements. It is not necessary because, in the presence of uncertainty and a divergence of expectations about the future, arm's-length arrangements can be costly even without highly specific assets.

Consider the case of the diesel locomotive (General Motors Corporation, 1975). In Charles F. Kettering's research laboratories, General Motors developed in the 1920s a generic capability to produce powerful but lightweight diesel engines. Their earliest use was in submarines. But GM chairman Alfred P. Sloan saw the possibility of applying the technology to a diesel-electric railroad locomotive. The existing steam-locomotive firms possessed many necessary capabilities GM lacked, as did General Electric and Westinghouse in all-electric technology. The three sets of capabilities might have combined by some kind of contract or joint venture. But the steam manufacturers—Alco, Baldwin, and Lima—failed to co-operate. This was not, however, because they feared hold-up in the face of highly specific assets. Rather, it was because they actively denied the desirability of the diesel and fought its introduction at every step. General Motors was forced to create its own capabilities in locomotive manufacture, although it did initially buy electrical systems from GE and Westinghouse. As Morris Silver (1984) has argued, the costs that impair market arrangements in such situations are in the nature of persuasion costs—the costs of getting the participants on the same wavelength. The necessity of investing in expensive transaction-specific assets may make such persuasion more difficult, but a divergence of entrepreneurial expectations is enough to do the trick.

Perhaps a more general way to look at these costs of persuasion is as costs of co-ordinating separate stages of production. David Teece encapsulates the argument nicely.

> If there is a high degree of interdependence among successive stages of production, and if occasions for adaptation are unpredictable yet common, coordinated responses may be difficult to secure if the separated stages are operated independently. Interdependence by itself does not cause difficulty if the pattern of interdependence is stable and fixed. Difficulties arise only if program execution rests on contingencies that cannot be predicted perfectly in advance. In this case, coordinated activity is required to secure agreement about the estimates that will be used as a basis for action. Vertical integration facilitates such coordination.
>
> This argument also reduces, at least in some respects, to a contractual-incompleteness argument. Were it feasible to stipulate exhaustively the appropriate conditional responses, coordination could proceed by long-term contract. However, long-term contracts are unsatisfactory when most of the relevant contingencies cannot be delineated. Given these limitations, short-term contracts are likely to be considered instead. . . . Even if short-term contracts are defective neither on account of investment disincentives nor first-mover advantages, the costs of negotiations and the time required to bring the system into adjustment by exclusive reliance on market signals are apt to be greater than the costs of administrative processes under vertical integration. (Teece, 1976, p. 13.)

Another way to say this is that unpredictable change makes it costly to specify contractual provisions, implying the need for expanded residual rights of control.[7]

Teece mentions this possibility as one of a string of possible explanations for vertical integration. My contention is that this is in fact the general explanation, and that all other transaction-cost explanations are either derivative of this argument or apply only on an *ad hoc* basis to special situations. Ultimately, the costs that lead to vertical integration are the (dynamic) transaction costs of persuading, negotiating with, coordinating among, and teaching outside suppliers in the face of economic change or innovation.

When would such costs be likely? That is to say, when would we expect vertical integration? As Teece suggests, the costs of coordinating among stages would be greatest when there is a high degree of interdependence among the relevant stages of production. But more than mere interdependence is necessary: the interdependence must be of a sort such that a change in one stage of production requires a corresponding change in one or more distinct stages.

For simplicity, picture the chain of production as literally that: a linear progression from one stage to the next. We can say that an innovation is *autonomous* if it affects only one stage in the chain. By contrast, an innovation is *systemic* if it requires the coordination of change across more than one stage (Teece, 1986).

It was autonomous innovation that Adam Smith had in mind when he argued that the division of labor enhanced innovation: each operative, by seeking ways to make his or her lot easier, would discover improved methods of performing the particular operation (Smith, 1976, I.i.8, p. 20).[8] The improvements he had in mind were such that they improved the efficiency of a particular stage without any implication for the operation of other stages. Autonomous innovation of this sort may even further the division of labor to the extent that it involves the cutting up of a task into two or more separate operations. Instead of being *differentiating* in this way, however, an innovation may be *integrating*, in the sense that the new way of doing things—a new machine, say—performs in one step what had previously needed two or more steps (Robertson and Alston, 1992). More generally, a systemic innovation may require small modifications of the way work is performed at each of a number of stages, and would thus require coordination among those stages.

This possibility of interconnectedness has been the basis for an argument that vertical disintegration may retard innovation.[9] Innovation may mean replacing assets at more than one stage in the chain of production. If decision-making is decentralized, the costs of coordinating the innovation may be high, and the innovation may never take place. This is particularly significant if some of the existing asset-holders, or the suppliers of factors complementary to the existing assets, have the power to block innovation (through trade unionism, for example) to protect their rent streams. If innovation does occur, it may take place elsewhere in the economy (and perhaps elsewhere in the world) under the direction of a unified asset-holder and decision-maker who can ignore existing task boundaries.

The empirical significance of this argument, especially as applied to the case of Britain at the turn of the twentieth century, is a subject of intense dispute. As a theoretical matter, however, this argument would seem most applicable to particular kinds of innovations, namely those that integrate operations. And what kinds of innovation do this? Surely one class of important systemic innovations comprises major organizational shifts. Examples would include the factory mode of production (Leijonhufvud, 1986), the moving assembly line (Hounshell, 1984), refrigerated meat-packing (Silver, 1984, pp. 28–29), and containerized shipping (Teece, 1986). All of these examples are ultimately *process* innovations. And one might argue that, although process innovation may also proceed in an autonomous way,[10] there are typically advantages to systemic process innovation. For one thing, process innovation is often integrating, requiring the consolidation of several stages of production in a single (usually mechanized) stage. More generally, process innovation is frequently a matter of fine-tuning the production process in the face of steady and predictable growth in demand: learning how to shave time off operations, to eliminate steps, to substitute stamping technology for casting, etc. This class learning- or experience-curve effect arguably proceeds faster in an integrated environment in which systemic change is relatively inexpensive.

How would learning proceed once the integrated organization was established? As change slows, the boundaries between the stages will begin to stabilize, and the costs of coordinating among stages will decrease. One would thus expect a greater decentralization of operations in general,[11] including a spinning off of the activities most dissimilar to the firm's 'core competence.' The extent to which this happens will depend on the relative learning abilities of the market and the firm. If capabilities diffuse easily to the market, we would expect more spinning off and thus less integration with time. If capabilities do not diffuse easily, disintegration will be slowed. Moreover, the firm may be more or less able to learn over time. For example, it may have an R&D lab, or possess a structure and culture conducive to learning.

Cohen and Levinthal (1989, 1990a,b) argue that a firm's ability to learn is governed by its 'absorptive capacity.' This capacity is typically, though not exclusively, a byproduct of R&D. A firm engages in R&D not only to create new knowledge but also, and often more importantly, to increase its ability to perceive and utilize knowledge generated outside the company. That is to say, the ability to learn is itself a capability the firm possesses and in which it can invest. Indeed, since one's ability to assimilate new knowledge is arguably a function of the related knowledge one already possesses, absorptive capacity is cumulative: one's capacity to acquire new capabilities depends on one's existing level of related capabilities. This reinforces the observation that organizations may be good at certain kinds of learning by doing, so long as the economically relevant knowledge the organization needs to learn does not stray far from what it already knows.

3.2 External Capabilities

The possibility that a firm may need to integrate vertically because the market somehow can't deliver has been a theme in the literature at least since Coase. What has received considerably less attention is the way in which failures of internal capabilities can force a firm to disintegrate, that is, to turn to the market for the capabilities it needs. Clearly, the need to coordinate innovation across stages of production can present a decentralized network of firms with transaction costs. But there are also benefits to decentralization. And, in some cases and for some types of innovation, these benefits can greatly outweigh any transaction costs.

In general, vertical disintegration would prove superior to vertical integration when complementary capabilities either don't exist within the firm or are inferior to those available in the market. Marshall talked about external economies as an explanation of economic progress. By analogy, we can talk about *external capabilities* available to the firm through contract. A firm may choose to rely on external capabilities if the (dynamic) governance costs of generating those capabilities internally are high.

Consider the case of the personal computer (Langlois, 1991). In entering the PC market in the early 1980s, IBM understood both (1) that the market possessed a high level of capabilities and (2) that IBM's own capabilities were severely lacking. This latter was the case partly because the company had focused on larger computers and did not possess all the capabilities necessary for smaller machines. But it was also and more importantly because the company's hierarchical structure, internal sourcing procedures, and elaborate system of controls made it too inflexible to respond well to a rapidly changing market. As a result, IBM chose in effect to disintegrate vertically into the production of PCs. They spun off a small group of executives and engineers, exempted them from IBM internal sourcing and other procedures, and treated them as, in effect, a venture-capital investment. The original IBM PC was in fact almost completely assembled from parts available in the market, very few of which were produced in IBM plants. IBM's motives for *disintegration* were in this regard strikingly similar to Henry Ford's motives for *integration*: the need to access quickly capabilities that would not otherwise have been available in time.

With a slower pace of change—and/or the resources to subsidize a short-run cost disadvantage—firms may of course choose to invest in internal capabilities as part of a long-term strategy. But internal capabilities are not always good substitutes for external capabilities. To see why this may be so, we need to turn back to one of the Marshallian themes with which we started: the market as an evolutionary system. Perhaps the central difference between Darwinian and Linnaean biology is that Darwin highlighted not what was common to the organisms in a species but what was *different*: the natural variation among organisms is what made evolutionary selection possible. Marshall saw the economic system in the same way. 'The tendency to variation,' he believed, 'is a chief cause of progress' (Marshall, 1961, V.iv.3, p. 355).[12] Thus, a high degree of variation—a high rate of technological and organizational experiment—is crucial to economic progress (Nelson and Winter, 1977). And the ability of a vertically disintegrated industry to generate, transmit and assimilate new ideas is thus a potentially powerful external capability, external in the same sense that Marshall understood external economies: it is a property of the system as a whole and cannot be reduced to the internal capabilities of firms taken individually. A market form of organization is capable of learning and creating new capabilities, often in a self-reinforcing and synergistic way. Marshall describes just such a system when he talks about the benefits of localized industry.

The mysteries of the trade become no mysteries; but are as it were in the air, and children learn many of them unconsciously. Good work is rightly appreciated, inventions and improvements in machinery, in processes and the general organization of the business have their merits promptly discussed: if one man starts a new idea, it is taken up by others and combined with suggestions of their own; and thus it becomes the source of further new ideas. And presently subsidiary trades grow up in the neigbourhood, supplying it with implements and materials, organizing its traffic, and in many ways conducing to the economy of its materials. (Marshall, 1961, IV.x.3, p. 271.)

In this sense, the ability of a large organization to coordinate the implementation of an innovation, which is clearly an advantage in some situations, may be a *disadvantage* in other ways. Coordination means getting everyone on the same wavelength. But the variation that drives an evolutionary learning system depends on people being on different wavelengths—it depends, in effect, on outbreeding. This is something much more difficult to achieve in a large organization than in a disintegrated system. Indeed, as Cohen and Levinthal (1990a, p. 132) point out, an organization experiencing rapid change ought in effect to emulate a market in its ability to expose to the environment a broad range of knowledge-gathering 'receptors.'

Vertical integration, I argued, might be most conducive to systemic, integrative innovations, especially those involving process improvements when demand is high and predictable. By contrast, vertical integration may be less desirable—and may be undesirable—in the case of differentiating or autonomous innovations. Such innovations require less coordination, and vertical integration in such cases may serve only to cut off alternative approaches. Moreover, disintegration might be most beneficial in situations of high uncertainty: situations in which the product is changing rapidly, the characteristics of demand are still unknown, and production is either unproblematical or production costs play a minor role in competition. In such cases the coordinating benefits of vertical integration are far outweighed by the evolutionary benefits of disintegration.

In part, this is a matter of the so-called product life-cycle (Utterback, 1979). At the early stages of the life-cycle, uncertainty is high and the product is fluid. Here a diversity of approaches can blanket the product space and seek out desirable forms quickly. As the product develops a dominant paradigm, however, change becomes more incremental, and fine-tuning of production for low-cost, high-volume output comes to the fore—and vertical integration gains the advantage. Nevertheless, it may also be the case that disintegration retains its benefits for some time. In some cases product innovation may not slack off very fast. In other cases, low-cost, high-volume production may be already available as an external economy (in a way that it was not available to Henry Ford).[13]

How would learning proceed in a system of decentralized capabilities? As I've already suggested, progress would take place autonomously within the decentralized stages. There would be no need for integration unless a systemic innovation offering superior performance arrives on the scene. Indeed, as we have seen, fixed task boundaries and standardized connections between stages might make innovation difficult within the existing structure, requiring a kind of creative destruction[14] (Schumpeter, 1950). Within the individual (autonomous) stages, however, learning can proceed in systemic fashion. The production process for or internal structure of a modem or stereo amplifier are irrelevant so long as those items can connect in properly with other components. Thus, it may not be surprising to find that vertical integration may be more important in the production of the components of a larger system than in the system itself. To put it another way, one's appraisal of the benefits of vertical integration may depend on how one defines the 'product' under study.

Notes

The author would like to thank Fred Carstensen, Wes Cohen, Joshua Haimson, William Lazonick, Scott Masten, Lanse Minkler, Richard Nelson and Paul Robertson for helpful comments and discussions.

1. I am obviously putting aside the phenomenon of conglomerates. But even here, one could argue that the relevant capability in excess capacity is that of financial management. Such conglomerates function largely as internal capital markets, which, as some have argued, may have advantages over the decentralized stock markets during periods in which inflation injects noise into the price system. (For the characterization of the conglomerate as an internal capital market, see Williamson (1985, p. 288). For an argument about the role of inflation, see Boudreaux and Shughart (1989).) Conglomerates now seem out of fashion,

however, and many business analysts are arguing that firms are returning—or ought to return—to their 'core competences' (Prahalad and Hamel, 1990). For an interesting discussion of diversification strategies from the point of view of organizational capabilities, see Robertson (1990).

2. Contrary to popular notions, the moving assembly line was significant not primarily as a way to assemble cars but as a way to manufacture parts for cars.

3. This figure is inspired by, but modified from, Silver (1984, p. 44).

4. Such a diagram captures what Coase meant when he wrote that 'a firm will tend to expand until the costs of organizing an extra transaction within the firm become equal to the costs of carrying out the same transactions by means of an exchange in the open market or the costs of organizing in another firm' (Coase, 1937, p. 395).

5. This is not to say, of course, that the long run favors internal organization. Since, as we will see, the benefits of internal management lie largely in the superior flexibility (of a specific kind) such management offers, we might well expect the *benefits* of internal management to decline faster than the costs in the long run, since flexibility becomes less important in a world of routine.

6. For a discussion of the cost of licensing that is somewhat in the spirit of the present essay, see Caves *et al.* (1983)

7. For an argument that this was ultimately Frank Knight's theory of the firm, see Langlois and Cosgel (1990). One could also make an argument that this was in the end Coase's theory as well. Consider the following passage.

It may be desired to make a long-term contract for the supply of some article or service. . . . Now, owing to the difficulty of forecasting, the longer the period of the contract is for the supply of the commodity or service, the less possible, and indeed, the less desirable it is for the person purchasing to specify what the other contracting party is expected to do. It may well be a matter of indifference to the person supplying the service or commodity which of several courses of action is taken, but not to the purchaser of that commodity or service. But the purchaser will not know which of these several courses he will want the supplier to take. Therefore, the service which is being provided is expressed in general terms, the exact details being left until a later date. . . . The details of what the supplier is expected to do is not stated in the contract but is decided later by the purchaser. When the direction of resources (within the limits of the contract) becomes dependent on the buyer in this way, that relationship which I term a 'firm' may be obtained. (Coase, 1937, pp. 391–392.)

8. In fact, however, Smith also saw the division of labor as leading to systemic innovations: 'All the improvements in machinery, however, have by no means been the inventions of those who had occasion to use the machines. Many improvements have been made by the ingenuity of the makers of the machines, when to make them became the business of a peculiar trade; and some by that of those who are called philosophers or men of speculation, whose trade it is, not to do any thing, but to observe every thing; and who, upon that account, are often capable of combining together the powers of the most distant and dissimilar objects.' (I.i.9, p. 21) More on this below.

Richard Langlois

9. An early version of the argument is by Marvin Frankel (1955). (See also Gordon, 1956, and Frankel, 1956.) The idea has more recently found a champion in William Lazonick (1981; Elbaum and Lazonick 1986). Such notables as Sir Arthur Lewis (1957, pp. 583–584) and Charles Kindleberger (1969, pp. 146–147) have also pointed to vertical fragmentation as a cause of British industrial decline.

10. There are in fact many examples of this in industry. An example at the forefront of modern technology is semiconductor fabrication. A large group of (mostly American) firms is pushing for a modular equipment architecture standard (MESA) that will allow a fabricator of semiconductors to mix and match process equipment from many different manufacturers (Winkler, 1990). Each unit will be able to 'bolt on' to the system so long as it obeys the standard. This will allow a greater degree of autonomous innovation in process technology. The main reasons for this development seem to be the highly decentralized nature of American capabilities in semiconductor fabrication equipment and the inadequate capabilities of even the largest producers to create all the elements necessary for the increasingly integrated process technology of modern semiconductors.

11. This was in fact true in the case of the moving assembly line. Once the innovation had taken its basic form, Ford found it desirable, in the face of a growing extent of the market, increasingly to set up geographically dispersed plants specializing in the fabrication of particular parts (Langlois and Robertson, 1989, p. 368). In this way, he replicated something like the network of decentralized producers existing before the innovation—except that the new network used the moving assembly line and was all owned by Ford.

12. On this see also Loasby (1990).

13. More interestingly, perhaps, the product may develop into a modular system (Langlois and Robertson, 1990). In such a system, the connections among the parts making up the product become standardized, rendering innovation much more autonomous than in cases in which the connections among parts are fluid.

14. Tushman and Anderson (1986) talk of technological change that is competence enhancing or, as in this case, competence destroying.

References

Boudreaux, D. J. and W. F. Shugart, II (1989), 'The Effects of Monetary Instability on the Extent of Vertical Integration,' *Atlantic Economic Journal*, 17, 1–10.

Caves, R., H. Crookell and P. J. Killing (1983), 'The Imperfect Market for Technology Licenses,' *Oxford Bulletin of Economic Statistics*, 45, 249–267.

Chandler, A. D. (1977), *The Visible Hand: The Managerial Revolution in American Business*. Cambridge: The Belknap Press.

Coase, R. H. (1937), 'The Nature of the Firm,' *Economica (N.S.)* 4, 386–405.

Coase, R. H. (1972), 'Industrial Organzation: A Proposal for Research,' in V. R. Fuchs (ed.), *Policy Issues and Research Opportunities in Industrial Organization*. New York: NBER.

Cohen, W. M. and D. A. Levinthal (1989), 'Innovation and Learning: the Two Faces of R&D,' *The Economic Journal*, 99, 569–596.

Cohen, W. M. and D. A. Levinthal (1990a),' Absorptive Capacity: A New Perspective on Learning and Innovation,' *Administrative Science Quarterly*, 35, 128–152.

Cohen, W. M. and D. A. Levinthal (1990b), 'Fortune Favors the Prepared Firm,' Mimeo, Carnegie Mellon University.

Demsetz, H. (1988), 'The Theory of the Firm Revisited,' *Journal of Law, Economics, and Organization*, 4, 141–161.

Elbaum, B. and W. Lazonick (1986), 'An Institutional Perspective on British Decline,' in B. Elbaum and W. Lazonick, (eds), *The Decline of the British Economy*. Oxford: Clarendon Press, pp. 1–17.

Frankel, M. (1955), 'Obsolescence and Technological Change in a Maturing Economy,' *American Economic Review*, 45, 296–319.

Frankel, M. (1956), 'Reply,' *American Economic Review*, 46, 652–656.

General Motors Corporation (1975), 'The Locomotive Industry and General Motors,' in Y. Brozen (ed.), *The Competitive Economy*. Morristown, NJ: General Learning Press.

Gordon, D. F. (1956), 'Obsolescence and Technological Change: Comment,' *American Economic Review*, 46, 646–652.

Hallwood, C. P. (1991), 'Production Costs, Measurement Costs, and the Theory of the Multinational Corporation,' Working Paper 91–1001, Department of Economics, University of Connecticut.

Hounshell, D. A. (1984) *From the American System to Mass Production, 1800–1932*. Baltimore: Johns Hopkins University Press.

Kindleberger, C. (1969), *Economic Growth in France and Britain, 1851–1950*. New York: Simon and Schuster.

Langlois, R. N. (1988), 'Economic Change and the Boundaries of the Firm,' *Journal of Institutional and Theoretical Economics*, 144, 635–657, reprinted in Bo Carlsson (ed.), *Industrial Dynamics: Technological, Organizational, and Sutructural Changes in Industries and Firms*. Dordrecht: Kluwer Academic Publishers, 1989, pp. 85–107.

Langlois, R. N. (1991), 'External Economies and Economic Progress: The Case of the Microcomputer Industry,' Working Paper 91–1502, Department of Economics, University of Connecticut.

Langlois, R. N. and M. M. Cosgel (1990), 'Knight on Risk, Uncertainty, and the Firm: A New Interpretation,' manuscript, University of Connecticut.

Langlois, R. N. and P. L. Robertson (1989), 'Explaining Vertical Integration: Lessons from the American Automobile Industry,' *Journal of Economic History*, 49, 361–375.

Langlois, R. N. and P. L. Robertson (1990), 'Networks and Innovation in a Modular System: Lessons from the Microcomputer and Stereo Component Industries,' Discussion Paper, Department of Economics and Management, University College, University of New South Wales (forthcoming in *Research Policy*).

Lazonick, W. (1981), 'Competition, Specialization, and Industrial Decline,' *Journal of Economic History*, 41, 31–38.

Leijonhufvud, A. (1986), 'Capitalism and the Factory System', in R. N. Langlois (ed.), *Economics as a Process: Essays in the New Institutional Economics*. New York: Cambridge University Press, pp. 203–223.

Lewis, W. (1957), 'International Competition in Manufacturers,' *American Economic Review*, 47, 583–584 (supplement).

Loasby, B. J. (1990), 'Firms, Markets, and the Principle of Continuity,' in J. K. Whitaker (ed.), *Centenary Essays on Alfred Marshall*. Cambridge: Cambridge University Press.

Marshall, A. (1961), *Principles of Economics*. London: Macmillan, 9th (variorum) edition, volume I.

Mowery, D. (1989), 'Collaborative Ventures Between U.S. and Foreign Manufacturing Firms,' *Research Policy*, 18, 19–32.

Nelson, R. R. and S. G. Winter (1977), 'In Search of More Useful Theory of Innovation,' *Research Policy*, 5, 36–76.

Nelson, R. R. and S. G. Winter (1982), *An Evolutionary Theory of Economic Change*. Cambridge: Harvard University Press.

Penrose, E. T. (1959), *The Theory of the Growth of the Firm*. Oxford: Basil Blackwell.

Polanyi, M. (1958), *Personal Knowledge*. Chicago: University of Chicago Press.

Prahalad, C. K. and G. Hamel (1990), 'The Core Competence of the Corporation,' *Harvard Business Review*, pp. 79–91 (May–June).

Richardson, G. B. (1972), 'The Organisation of Industry', *Economic Journal*, 82, 883–896.

Robertson, P. L. (1990), 'Economies of Scope, Organizational Culture, and the Choice of Diversification Strategies,' Economics and Management Working Paper #2, University College, University of New South Wales.

Robertson, P. L. and L. J. Alston (1992), 'Technological Choice and the Organization of Work in Capitalist Firms,' *Economic History Review*, 45.

Robinson, E. A. G. (1934), 'The Problem of Management and the Size of Firms,' *Economic Journal*, 44, 242–257.

Schumpeter, J. A. (1950), *Capitalism, Socialism, and Democracy*. New York: Harper and Brothers, 2nd edition.

Silver, M. (1984), *Enterprise and the Scope of the Firm*. London: Martin Robertson.

Smith, A. (1976), *An Inquiry into the Nature and Causes of the Wealth of Nations*. Glasgow edition. Oxford: Clarendon Press. (First published in 1776.)

Teece, D. J. (1976), *Vertical Integration and Vertical Divestiture in the US Oil Industry: Analysis and Policy Implications*. Stanford: Stanford University Institute for Energy Studies.

Teece, D. J. (1980), 'Economies of Scope and the Scope of the Enterprise,' *Journal of Economic Behavior and Organization*, 1, 223–247.

Teece, D. J. (1982), 'Towards an Economic Theory of the Multiproduct Firm,' *Journal of Economic Behavior and Organization*, 3, 39–63.

Teece, D. J. (1986), 'Profiting from Technological Innovation: Implications for Integration, Collaboration, Licensing, and Public Policy,' *Research Policy*, 15, 285–305.

Tushman, M. and P. Anderson (1986), 'Technological Discontinuities and Organizational Environments,' *Administrative Science Quarterly*, 31, 439–465.

Utterback, J. M. (1979), 'The Dynamics of Product and Process Innovation,' in C. T. Hill and J. M. Utterback (eds), *Technological Innovation for a Dynamic Economy*. New York: Pergamon Press, pp. 40–65.

von Hippel, E. (1989), 'Cooperation Between Rivals: Informal Know-how Trading,' in B. Carlsson (ed.), *Industrial Dynamics: Technological, Organizational, and Structural Changes in Industries and Firms*. Dordrecht: Kluwer Academic Publishers.

Williamson, O. E. (1985), *The Economic Institutions of Capitalism*. New York: The Free Press.

Winkler, E. (1990), 'MESA, Applied Fued Stirring Over Pact,' *Electronic News*, April 16, p. 26.

21 Knowledge of the Firm, Combinative Capabilities, and the Replication of Technology

Bruce Kogut and Udo Zander

A fundamental puzzle, as first stated by Michael Polanyi (1966), is that individuals appear to know more than they can explain. That knowledge can be tacit has broad implications for understanding the difficulty of imitating and diffusing individual skills, a problem lying at the heart of artificial intelligence to the competitive analysis of firms. Though the idea of tacit knowledge has been widely evoked but rarely defined—as if the lack of definition is itself evidence of the concept, it represents a dramatically different vantage point by which to analyze the capabilities and boundaries of firms.

This article seeks to lay out an organizational foundation to a theory of the firm. To rephrase Polanyi's puzzle of tacit knowledge, organizations know more than what their contracts can say. The analysis of what organizations are should be grounded in the understanding of what they know how to do.

It is curious that the considerable attention given to how organizations learn has obscured the implication that organizations 'know' something. In fact, the knowledge of the firm, as opposed to learning, is relatively observable; operating rules, manufacturing technologies, and customer data banks are tangible representations of this knowledge. But the danger of this simple characterization is that everything that describes a firm becomes an aspect of its knowledge. While this is definitionally true, the theoretical challenge is to understand the knowledge base of a firm as leading to a set of capabilities that enhance the chances for growth and survival.

In our view, the central competitive dimension of what firms know how to do is to create and transfer knowledge efficiently within an organizational context. The following article seeks to describe these capabilities by analyzing the contention put forth by Winter (1987) that technology transfer and imitation are blades of the same scissor. The commonality is that technology is often costly to replicate, whether the replication is desired by the firm or occurs by imitation and unwanted diffusion. Though the terminology may differ, the underlying phenomena impacting the costs of technology transfer and imitation share similarities, regardless whether the replication occurs within the firm, by contract, or among competitors.

That similar factors may determine both the costs of imitation and technology transfer presents an interesting dilemma to the firm. In the efforts to speed the replication of current and new knowledge, there arises a fundamental paradox that the codification and simplification of knowledge also induces the likelihood of imitation. Technology transfer is a desired strategy in the replication and growth of the firm (whether in size or profits); imitation is a principal constraint.

Our view differs radically from that of the firm as a bundle of contracts that serves to allocate efficiently property rights. In contrast to the contract approach to understanding organizations, the assumption of the selfish motives of individuals resulting in shirking or dishonesty is not a necessary premise in our argument. Rather, we suggest that organizations are social communities in which individual and social expertise is transformed into economically useful products and services by the application of a set of higher-order organizing principles. Firms exist because they provide a social community of voluntaristic action structured by organizing principles that are not reducible to individuals.

We categorize organizational knowledge into information and know-how based, a distinction that corresponds closely to that used in artificial intelligence of declarative and procedural knowledge. To move beyond a simple classification, these types of knowledge are argued to carry competitive implications through their facility to be easily replicated within an organization but difficult to imitate by other firms. Following the suggestions of Rogers (1983) and Winter (1987), the characteristics of both types of knowledge are analyzed along the dimensions of codifiability and complexity. By examining first personal expertise and then social knowledge, the capabilities of the firm in general are argued to rest in the organizing principles by which relationships among individuals, within and between groups, and among organizations are structured.

But organizations serve as more than mechanisms by which social knowledge is transferred, but also by which new knowledge, or learning, is created. The theoretical problem is that if the knowledge of the firm is argued to be competitively consequential, learning cannot be characterized as independent of the current capabilities. To explore this dynamic aspect, we introduce the concept of a **combinative capability** to synthesize and apply current and acquired knowledge. This concept is, then, explored in the context of a competitive environment. By this discussion, we ground such concepts as localized learning to path dependence by developing a micro-behavioral foundation of social knowledge, while also stipulating the effects of the degree of environmental selection on the evolution of this knowledge.

To ground the abstraction of the argument in an example, we reexamine the empirical findings on the make-buy decision of firms. The importance of the ability to generate new knowledge suggests a different view on the 'boundaries' of the firm, that is, what a firm makes and what it buys. Firms invest in those assets that correspond to a combination of current capabilities and expectations regarding future opportunities. Or, in other words, the knowledge of a firm can be considered as owning a portfolio of options, or platforms, on future developments.[1]

Figure 1 provides a roadmap to our argument. We begin by analyzing the knowledge of the firm by distinguishing between information regarding prices and the know-how, say, to divisionalize. This static portrait is the basis by which we explore how knowledge may be recombined through internal and external learning. An important limitation to the capability of developing new skills is the opportunity (or potential) in the organizing principles and technologies

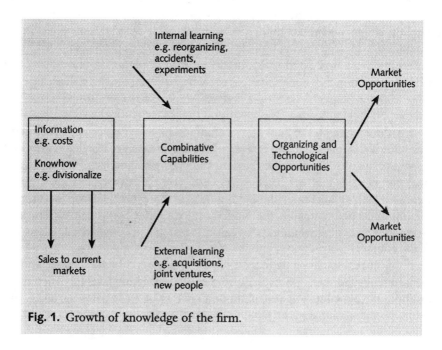

Fig. 1. Growth of knowledge of the firm.

for further exploitation. Eventually, there are decreasing returns to a given technology or method of organizing, and there, consequently, results in an incentive to build new, but related skills. These investments in new ways of doing things, we suggest, serve as platforms on future and uncertain market opportunities.

It is important to underline the presumption that the knowledge of the firm must be understood as socially constructed, or, more simply stated, as resting in the organizing of human resources. The issue of the organizing principles underlying the creation, replication, and imitation of technology opens a window on understanding the capabilities of the firm as a set of 'inert' resources that are difficult to imitate and redeploy.[2] It is the persistence in the organizing of social relationships in which knowledge is embedded that is the focus of inquiry developed in this article.

1. Information and Know-How

There have been many suggestions as to how the knowledge of the firm might be categorized. Nelson (1982), for example, separates techno from logy, the former belonging to a firm, the latter to the public arena. A more common distinction is between research and development, or that between process and product.

For our purposes, we distinguish between two categories of knowledge as information and know-how.[3] By information, we mean knowledge which can be transmitted without loss of integrity once the syntactical rules required for deciphering it are known. Information includes facts, axiomatic propositions, and symbols. Nelson's idea of logy is, in fact, a recognition that within scientific communities, there exists a social agreement regarding the factual evidence by which to communicate the reliability of scientific findings. Similarly, public firms are required to report data to shareholders in a common format so as to facilitate analysis and appraisal. For the objective of public dissemination, information is standardized and released in order to be understood at minimal cost to those with the requisite training.

Of course, information is often proprietary. Firms maintain, as a rule, two sets of accounting data, one for external use, the other to aid managerial decisions and evaluation. Data can also be of competitive value. An obvious example is the value of information to traders of financial securities, but a more prosaic example is the data acquired by grocery stores on consumer expenditures.

Know-how is a frequently used, but rarely defined term. Von Hippel offers the definition that 'know-how is the accumulated practical skill or expertise that allows one to do something smoothly and efficiently' (von Hippel 1988). The pivotal word in this definition is 'accumulated,' which implies that know-how must be learned and acquired.

Knowledge as information implies knowing *what* something means. Know-how is, as the compound words state, a description of knowing *how* to do something. In economics, this distinction is, implicitly, preserved in the often made distinction between exchange and production economies, where the former consists of only traders responding to prices, and the latter to how inputs are transformed into outputs. To use a current example, the problems of the adoption economy in Eastern Europe consist not only of just finding the right prices, but also learning how to organize a market and a firm efficiently.

Though this distinction between information and know-how appears to be a fundamental element in the analysis of organizational knowledge, most efforts in this direction have tended, following March and Simon (1958) and Cyert and March (1963), to investigate the notion of routines in the context of organizational learning. Yet, this vantage point for the investigation of firm knowledge is ill-chosen. Learning has little significance in the absence of a theory of organizational knowledge.

A routine is in itself an insightful but incomplete characterization of knowledge. Because of the broad coverage of the term routine, an appeal is often made to the analogy of a blueprint, an analogy favored by a number of authors.[4] But a blueprint favors much more a description of information than know-how. Knowing how to do something is much like a recipe; there is no substantive content in any of the steps, except for their capacity to produce a desired end.[5] The information is contained in the original listing of ingredients, but the know-how is only imperfectly represented in the description.

It is revealing that this distinction between information and know-how as blueprints and recipes is similar to that made between declarative and procedural knowledge used in computer science. Declarative knowledge consists of a statement that provides a state description, such as the information that inventory is equal to a 100 books. Procedural knowledge consists of statements that describe a process, such as a method by which inventory is minimized. This distinction is robust to other phenomena than software, even to a furniture set where the inventory of parts is first described and then the recipe of assembly laid out.

Know-how, like procedural knowledge, is a description of what defines current practice inside a firm. These practices may consist of how to organize factories, set transfer prices, or establish divisional and functional lines of authority and accountability. The knowledge displayed in an organizational chart, as in any blueprint, is limited to providing information on personnel and formal authority. The know-how is the understanding of how to organize a firm along these formal (and informal) lines. It is in the regularity of the structuring of work and of the interactions of employees conforming to explicit or implicit recipes that one finds the content of the firm's know-how.

2. The Inertness of Knowledge

Firms differ in their information and know-how and these differences, when they are economically interesting, have persisting effects on relative performance. Thus, a central characteristic to be explained is the persisting difference in capabilities, that is, the difficulty in their transfer and imitation. The persistence of differentials in firm performance lies in the joint problem of the difficulty of transferring and imitating knowledge.

There is a need, therefore, to go beyond the classification of information and know-how and consider why knowledge is not easily transmitted and replicated. The transferability and imitability of a firm's knowledge, whether it is in the form of information or know-how, are influenced by several characteristics (Kogut and Zander 1990). Rogers (1983) and Winter (1987) have proposed that knowledge can be analyzed along a number of dimensions.

Consider the two dimensions of codifiability and complexity. Codifiability refers to the ability of the firm to structure knowledge into a set of identifiable rules and relationships that can be easily communicated. Coded knowledge is alienable from the individual who wrote the code. Not all kinds of knowledge are amenable to codification. Drafting a recipe for the manufacturing of a musical instrument is unlikely to capture the requisite skills of a craftsperson.

Nor is this limitation only applicable to know-how. It is not always possible to identify the relevant information which operates as the data to an actor or set of actions. There may be no 'theory' (in the sense used above) by which to identify the relevant information, such as drawing the blueprint. This argument bears similarities to the artificial intelligence debate on the obstacles to formalizing noncodified 'background knowledge' to scientific theories (Dreyfus and Dreyfus 1988). Codifiability is a question of the degree that there exists in implied theory by which to identify and symbolically represent knowledge. A theory may be as lacking for information as for know-how.[6]

Though codifiability is a central characteristic, it does not capture other aspects of knowledge. Knowledge can vary in complexity. There are many ways to define complexity. From a computer science perspective, it can be defined as the number of operations (or CPU time) required to solve a task. Indeed,

Simon's notion of nearly decomposable systems is closely related. An ordered system reduces the cost and necessity of complex communication patterns. Drawing upon information theory, Pringle (1951) draws the distinction between order and complexity, defining the latter as the number of parameters to define a system. Within any given ordering (or what we call a code), complexity can be accommodated, but at a cost.

These dimensions are not independent. Codifiability and complexity are related, though not identical. To return to Pringle's definition, it is obvious that the number of parameters required to define, say, a production system is dependent upon the choice of mathematical approaches or programming languages. For a particular code, the costs of transferring a technology will vary with its complexity. A change of code changes the degree of complexity.

3. Transformation of Personal to Social Knowledge

The final element in our characterization of the static properties of organizational knowledge is the distinction between the knowledge of an individual and that of the organization. Any discussion of firm knowledge confronts, ultimately, the problem of unit of analysis. We leave to the side the important task of specifying a more explicit integration of individual and organizational knowledge (such as via a shared culture, mechanisms of socialization, or an assumption of affiliative needs), but turn rather to laying out a description of the problem by distinguishing between personal, group, organizational, and network knowledge. The following discussion is summarized in Fig. 2.[7]

Nelson and Winter (1982) have provided an important contribution by separating skills from routines. Individuals can be skilled in certain activities, such as driving a car or playing tennis. These skills may indeed be difficult to pass on. Variations in human intelligence alone may render difficult the transfer of technology, especially if intelligence is decomposed into aptitudes for solving differentiated tasks.

It is, in fact, the problem of communicating personal skills that underlies Polanyi's (1966) well-known idea of tacit knowledge, an idea similar to the dimensions of noncodifiable and complex knowledge. As noted earlier, to Polanyi, the central puzzle is the following: why do individuals know more than they can express. An interpretation of his argument is that tacit knowledge con-

	INDIVIDUAL	GROUP	ORGANIZATION	NETWORK
INFORMATION	Facts	Who knows what	Profits Accounting data Formal & informal structure	Prices Whom to Contact who has what
KNOW-HOW	Skill of how to communicate Problem solving	Recipes of organizing such as Taylorist methods or craft production	Higher-order organizing principles of how to coordinate groups and transfer knowledge	How to cooperate How to sell and buy

Fig. 2. The relationship of the knowledge of the individual, group, organization, and network.

sists of search rules, or heuristics, that identify the problem and the elements consisting of the solution (Polanyi 1966, pp. 23–24). The act of solving a problem rests on a sense of how the phenomena function; the formal expression of the solution is unlikely to capture fully this procedural knowledge, or even the data and information (or clues, as Polanyi describes it) leading to the solution. Thus, even in the arena of problem identification and solving, the know-how of heuristic search precedes the formal knowledge of the solution.[8]

The teaching of know-how and information requires frequently interaction within small groups, often through the development of a unique language or code. Part of the knowledge of a group is simply knowing the information who knows what. But it also consists of how activities are to be organized, e.g., by Taylorist principles.

It is the sharing of a common stock of knowledge, both technical and organizational, that facilitates the transfer of knowledge within groups. This view is widely held across a disparate literature. Arrow (1974) views one of the advantages of the organization as its ability to economize in communication through a common code. Piore (1985, p. xxv) likens the theory of internal labor markets to a 'conception of production knowledge as being like a language' common to a particular group of workers. By shared coding schemes, personal knowledge can be transmitted effectively within close-knit groups (Katz and Kahn 1966). Personal knowledge can be transmitted because a set of values are learned, permitting a shared language by which to communicate (Berger and Luckman 1967). It is this language which provides a normative sanction of how activities are to be organized or what information is to be collected and evaluated.

But whereas the accumulation of small group interactions facilitate the creation of shared coding schemes within functions, a fundamental problem arises in the shifting of technologies from research groups to manufacturing and marketing (Dougherty forthcoming). At this point, the identification with a professional orientation conflicts with the need to integrate within the organization. The problems of different professional languages are attenuated when technology transfer is horizontal, that is, within the same function, as when a second plant identical to the first is built. To facilitate this communication, certain individuals play pivotal roles as boundary spanners, both within the firm as well as between firms (Allen and Cohen 1969; Tushman 1977).

The vertical transfer of technology, as when a product is moved from development to production, poses additional problems insofar that the shared codes of functional groups differ. Leonard-Barton's (1988) finding that technology transfer success is dependent upon the mutual adaptation between the two parties highlights the critical transformation of personal and group knowledge in the process of codification. To facilitate this transfer, a set of higher-order organizing principles act as mechanisms by which to codify technologies into a language accessible to a wider circle of individuals. These principles establish how the innovation is transferred to other groups, the responsibility of engineers to respond to complaints, and the allocation of incentives to establish authority over decisions. These organizing principles, which we call higher-order as they facilitate the integration of the entire organization, are also supported by data regarding profitability, costs, or task responsibility (as represented in an organizational chart).

In this sense, a firm's functional knowledge is nested within a higher-order set of recipes that act as organizing principles. Complex organizations exist as communities within which varieties of functional expertise can be communicated and combined by a common language and organizing principles. To the extent that close integration within a supplier or buyer network is required, long-term relationships embed future transactions within a learned and shared code. In fact, the trading of know-how among firms often requires the establishment of long-term relationships (von Hippel 1988). In this wider perspective, a firm's knowledge consists also of the information of other actors in the network, as well as the procedures by which resources are gained and transactions and cooperation are conducted.

4. The Paradox of Replication

There is an important implication for the growth of the firm in the transformation of technical knowledge into a code understood by a wide set of users. An individual is a resource severely restrained by physical and mental limitations. Unless able to train large numbers of individuals **or** to transform skills into organizing principles, the craft shop is forever simply a shop. The speed of replication of knowledge determines the rate of growth; control over its diffusion deters competitive erosion of the market position.

For a firm to grow, it must develop organizing principles and a widely-held and shared code by which to orchestrate large numbers of people and, potentially, varied functions. Whereas the advantages of reducing the costs of intra- or inter-firm technology transfer encourage codification of knowledge, such codification runs the risk of encouraging imitation. It is in this paradox that the firm faces a fundamental dilemma.

The problems of the growth of the firm are directly related to the issues of technology transfer and imitation. Once organizing principles replace individual skills of the entrepreneur, they serve as organizational instructions for future growth. Technology transfer is, from this perspective, the replication of existing activities. The goal of the firm is to reduce the costs of this transfer while preserving the quality and value of the technology.

Because personal and small group knowledge is expensive to re-create, firms may desire to codify and simplify such knowledge as to be accessible to the wider organization, as well as to external users. It is an interesting point, with far-reaching implications, that such a translation rarely occurs without a transformation in the nature of the knowledge. Computer software packages not only reduce the complexity of the knowledge required to use a computer's hardware; knowing how to use software is, in fact, substantively different from knowing how the computer works.

The reason why software has been successful is that it is codified so as to demand a lower fixed cost on the part of the general user. The user is required to understand the function of the program without knowledge of the substantive technology. (A function is an attribute to the product; substantive technology is the knowledge by which the product is created or produced.) The cost of this transformation is that the user's choices are restricted to the expressed functions. The specificity of a software language cannot expand the capabilities of the hardware; rather, it can only reduce the costs of its accessibility. It is, in fact, the possibility to separate the expertise to generate the technology and the ability to use it that permits the nesting of a firm's knowledge, as described above. But it is also this separation, as discussed below, that facilitates the ease of imitation. Being taught the functional skills of how to do something is different than being taught how to create it. We turn to these static and dynamic considerations below.

5. Combinative Capabilities

The issue of being able to use and being able to create software reflects a distinction commonly made in the literature on technology transfer regarding know-how and know-why.[9] It is, in fact, this distinction between exploiting and developing capabilities that lies at the foundation of Rosenberg's (1976) observation that 'reliance on borrowed technology (by developing countries) perpetuates a posture of dependency and passivity.' For example, activities involved in a manufacturing production process can be codified and imitated without requiring the knowledge of how the machinery functions. A Japanese factory shop might, conceivably, be organized by rules for inventory management and these rules might be transferred to American operations. Yet, the knowledge that leads to the development of such practices is unlikely to be transferred as easily. Being taught the functional skills of how to do something is different than being taught how to create it.

To return to the development of software as a problem in codifying knowledge, Papert (1979, p. 77) notes the paradox that some languages are simple to learn but become complex in application. He writes:

But what do we mean by 'simpler' and what do we mean by 'learn the language'? Indeed, the (user) . . . would learn its vocabulary very quickly, but they would spend the rest of their time struggling with its constraints. They would have to search for devious ways to encode even mildly complex ideas into this small vocabulary. Thus it is well-known that the programming language BASIC . . . is quickly learned, but its programs quickly become labyrinths.

Papert's objection raises two important points. Some codes may be qualitatively better than others. They might facilitate certain technologies or practices better; the language of chemical pharmaceuticals may be inadequate for the development and transfer of biotechnologies. Even for the same technology, some firms may have evolved codes that differ in their efficacy.

The observation that some languages are more 'easily learned' suggests, superficially, a contradiction in the argument. Basic is 'simpler' but becomes quickly complex. But in what sense is it simpler other than through its familiarity to what the user already knows and through its design to address specific applications familiar to the user? Then why does it become a 'labyrinth'? The implicit suggestion is that Basic does not provide an efficient capability to address a change in the required application.

Let us migrate the argument from the individual to the organizational level by sorting out the two issues of familiarity to the user and, as discussed later, of the capability to create new applications to address changes in the environment, such as changes in market demand. Creating new knowledge does not occur in abstraction from current abilities. Rather, new learning, such as innovations, are products of a firm's **combinative capabilities** to generate new applications from existing knowledge. By combinative capabilities, we mean the intersection of the capability of the firm to exploit its knowledge and the unexplored potential of the technology, or what Scherer (1965) originally called the degree of 'technological opportunity.'

In the technological literature, the determinants of 'opportunity' are often regarded as physical in character; the speed of electrons is inferior to that of light. But since physical laws are eternally given, the critical question would then seem to be the social laws of their discovery and innovative application. Schumpeter (1934) argued that, in general, innovations are new combinations of existing knowledge and incremental learning.[10] He writes:

> To produce other things, or the same things by a different method, means to combine these materials and forces differently . . . Development in our sense is then defined by the carrying out of new combinations (Schumpeter 1934, pp. 65–66).

As widely recognized, firms learn in areas closely related to their existing practice. As the firm moves away from its knowledge base, its probability of success converges to that for a start-up operation (as implicit in Lippman and Rumelt 1982). The abstract explanation for this claim is that the growth of knowledge is experiential, that is, it is the product of localized search as guided by a stable set of heuristics, or, in our terminology, know-how and information (Cyert and March 1963, Nelson and Winter 1982). It is this local search that generates a condition commonly called 'path dependence,' that is, the tendency for what a firm is currently doing to persist in the future.

It should be clear that individual limitations in learning new skills are not a sufficient explanation. For even if mature individuals do not relearn—as psychological evidence suggests, an organization may reconstitute its knowledge by recruiting new workers with the requisite skills. The problem of the 'inertness' of what an organization knows is not reducible to individuals, except for the degenerate case of restrictions on the recruitment and retirement of human resources.

What makes the innovative search localized is that 'proximate' technologies do not require a change in an organization's recipes of organizing research. If current knowledge is inadequate, it may well be that a firm does not know what changes are required in the existing principles and structure of relationships.

Even if identified, they may not be feasible, because the relational structure in the organization would be disturbed. Knowledge advances by recombinations because a firm's capabilities cannot be separated from how it is currently organized.

6. Selection Environment

Up to now, we have been concerned with explaining the role of organizing principles to facilitate the transfer of technology and ideas within the organization of the firm. The distinction between the ability to produce a product and the capability to generate it is fundamental to broadening our perspective to the competitive conditions of imitation. The ability to build on current technology is instrumental in the deterrence of the imitation of a firm's knowledge by competitors.

Imitation differs from technology transfer in a fundamental sense. Whereas technology transfer is concerned with adapting the technology to the least capable user, the threat of imitation is posed by the most capable competitors. In abstraction from a particular technology, it is, *a priori*, impossible to state in general what aspects of the transformation of ideas into marketable products will deter imitation. No matter which factor, however, is the most important, imitation is impeded by the possession of at least one bottleneck capability, as long as this capability is rewarded in the market.[11] This bottleneck can possibly arise through the benefits of reputation among consumers, patent protection, or the exercise of monopoly restrictions.

When these entry-deterring benefits are absent, competition switches from traditional elements of market structure to the comparative capabilities of firms to replicate and generate new knowledge. The nature of this competition is frequently characterized as a race between an innovator and the ability of the imitating firm either to reverse engineer and to decode the substantive technology. The growth of the firm is determined by a combination of the speed of technology transfer and of the imitative efforts of rivals.

Reverse engineering is often not a required response by competitors to new innovations. Incumbent competitors may simply respond to new product innovations by relying on other capabilities, such as brand labeling or distribution channels. Of more interest to our concerns, some competitors can imitate the function of the technology without necessitating reverse engineering of the substantive code. (As an example, many distinctive kinds of software can provide a spreadsheet function; the function is imitated, but not the underlying technology.) Many new products are only re-designs (i.e., recombinations) of existing components (Henderson and Clark 1990). In this kind of competition, the need to decipher the elements of the innovator's knowledge that generated the product can be simply bypassed.

In this on-going competition, there is a short-term consideration, i.e., at what speed and cost can a firm replicate its current technology and imitate others. In innovative industries, competition is frequently a question of the speed and efficiency by which diverse groups within a corporation cooperate, a problem exacerbated when multi-functional coordination is required in order to increase transfer times to the market (Dougherty forthcoming). Over time and across multiple products, small differences in efficiencies can generate significant variations in profitability and (as well established in evolutionary biology) survival.

Short-term competitive pressures can, however, draw from the investments required to build new capabilities. The direct effect of selection is on the acceptance and rejection of new products, but indirectly it is operating to reward or to penalize the economic merits of the underlying stock of knowledge.[12] Knowledge, no matter how resistant to imitation, is of little value if it results in products that do not correspond competitively to consumers' wants. Selection on product types acts to develop and retard the capabilities of firms.

The ability to indulge in a forward-looking development of knowledge is strongly contingent on the selection environment. Long-term survival involves a complex tradeoff between current profitability and investing in future capability. Future capabilities are of little value if the firm does not survive. In this sense, we have returned to Papert's concerns. Basic may be a poor language by which to address new applications or changes in the market. But for the student facing a deadline, programming in Basic may have clear survival value.

An important question, then, is the critical balancing between short-term survival and the long-term development of capabilities. A too strong reliance on current profitability can deflect from the wider development of capabilities (Stiglitz 1987). By their ability to buffer internal ventures from an immediate market test, organizations have the possibility to create new capabilities by a process of trial-and-error learning.

Thus luxury is often too exorbitant for companies or, for that matter, developing countries facing strong survival pressures. Yet, because investments in new ways of doing things are expensive, it is possible for a firm to continue to develop capabilities in ways of doing things which it knows, in the long run, are inferior (Arthur 1989). A too rigid competitive environment, especially in the early years of a firm's development, may impede subsequent performance by retarding a firm's ability to invest in new learning.

7. The Make Decision and Firm Capabilities

The merits of the above argument can be better evaluated by considering an example. An interesting application is the make-buy question, that is, whether a firm should source a component from the outside or make it internally. The examination of this problem throws into relief how an approach based on the knowledge of the firm differs from a contracting perspective.

It has become standard to argue that markets for the exchange of technology fail because of an appeal to a poker-hand metaphor; once the cards are revealed, imitation rapidly ensues since draws from the deck are costless. Because of the work of Teece (1977), Mansfield, Schwartz, and Wagner (1981), and Levin et al. (1987), it is widely recognized this argument is a shibboleth. Yet, the consequences of this recognition are scarcely to be seen in the literature on technology transfer.

In fact, the costliness of its transfer has often been reconstrued as market failure (Teece 1980). Because a buyer cannot ascertain its value by observation, technology cannot be priced out. Thus, markets fail for the selling of technology since it is costly to transact.

The problem of this market failure argument is not only that markets for technology do exist, but also that it is over-determined. The public good argument turns on the opportunism of the buyer; the costs of transfer do not necessitate a similar behavioral assumption, though one can always throw it in for good measure. Opportunism is not a necessary condition to explain why technology is transferred within a firm instead of the market. Rather, the issue becomes why and when are the costs of transfer of technology lower inside the firm than alternatives in the market, independent of contractual hazards. The relevant market comparison, in this sense, are the efficiencies of other firms.

This issue extends to the more commonly studied case of contractual hazards affecting the make or buy decision, that is, whether to source from outside the firm. In the seminal empirical study of Walker and Weber (1984), evidence was found for the claim that the transaction costs of relying on outside suppliers lead to decisions to source internally. Yet, the most important variable is the indicator of differential firm capabilities, that is, whether the firm or the supplier has the lower production costs. Transaction cost considerations matter but are subsidiary to whether a firm or other suppliers are more efficient in the production of the component.

In the Monteverde and Teece (1982) paper that also supported the transaction cost argument, the most significant variable is the dummy for the firm. In other words, despite controls, the heterogeneous and unobserved firm effects were the dominant influence on the make-buy decision. Yet, both firms faced the same environment and transactional hazards.

While the boundaries of the firm are, unquestionably, influenced by transactional dilemmas, the question of capabilities points the analysis to understanding why organizations differ in their performance. The decision which capabilities to maintain and develop is influenced by the current knowledge of the firm and the expectation of the economic gain from exploring the opportunities in new technologies and organizing principles as platforms into future market developments. (See Fig. 1.) We propose that firms maintain those capabilities in-house that are expected to lead to recombinations of economic value.

The evaluation of this economic gain rests critically upon a firm's ability to create and transfer technology more quickly than it is imitated in the market. Many investment decisions inside a firm do not include a make-buy calculation, for the presumption is that the new assets are extensions, or combinations, of the existing knowledge base.[13] Nor should it be surprising that there is a sense of ownership over the right to make and control the investment, for the physical assets are embedded within the replication of the existing social relationships and political structure of the firm. Because these relationships exist, an ongoing firm should have a greater capability to expand in current businesses than new entrants.

Path dependence is a rephrasing of the simple statement that firms persist in making what they have made in the past; for existing firms, knowledge advances on the basis of its current information and ways of doing things. To return to the Monteverde and Teece study, the finding that firms tended to produce internally those parts with high engineering content is a confirmation that auto companies specialize in engineering design and production. They make those parts that reflect their knowledge. (In fact, we should expect that they imitate those technologies which correspond closely to their knowledge.)

There are, of course, investment opportunities which are uncertain in terms of the applicability of a firm's current knowledge. Internal development, and imitation, are deterred because the organizing principles and information cannot be easily identified. Thus, investments in new knowledge often have a characteristic of trial-and-error learning, much like buying options on future opportunities.

Joint ventures frequently serve as options on new markets distantly related to current knowledge by providing a vehicle by which firms transfer and combine their organizationally-embedded learning. A common purpose of joint ventures is to experiment with new ways by which relationships are structured. That they frequently end by acquisition is a statement of their value as an ongoing entity of enduring social relationships which serve as platforms into new markets (Kogut 1991).

The decision to make or buy is, thus, dependent upon three elements: how good a firm is currently at *doing* something, how good it is at *learning* specific capabilities, and the value of these capabilities as *platforms* into new markets. To formalize the implications of these elements in terms of propositions, we would expect the following to hold:

1. Firms make those components that require a production knowledge similar to their current organizing principles and information.
2. The purchasing of technologies is carried out by the market when suppliers have superior knowledge which is complex and difficult to codify; by licensing when the transferred knowledge is close to current practice.
3. Firms develop internally projects that build related capabilities leading to platforms into new markets or rely on joint ventures (or acquisitions) when the capabilities are distantly related.
4. Immediate survival pressures encourage firms towards a policy of buying.

Similar propositions could be made in reference to other applications, such as acquisitions, the composition of a technology portfolio, and the sequence by which a firm invests in a foreign market.

8. Conclusions

The study of the knowledge of a firm raises issues, such as relatedness, technical core, or corporate culture, that are familiar to organizational theorists, but that have been hard to pin down. To a large extent, the theory of firm knowledge, as we have sketched it above, neglects the problem of individual motivation by focusing on organizing principles as the primary unit of analysis for understanding the variation in firm performance and growth. Because these principles are expressions of how a firm organizes its activities, they represent the procedures by which social relations are recreated and coordinated in an organizational context.

In contrast to a perspective based on the failure to align incentives in a market as an explanation for the firm, we began with the view that firms are a repository of capabilities, as determined by the social knowledge embedded in enduring individual relationships structured by organizing principles. Switching to new capabilities is difficult, as neither the knowledge embedded in the current relationships and principles is well understood, nor the social fabric required to support the new learning known. It is the stability of these relationships that generates the characteristics of inertia in a firm's capabilities.

Without question, there are issues, such as the creation of compatible incentives to induce behavior from individuals in accordance with the welfare of the organization, that can be fruitfully examined from a contracting perspective. But the transaction as the unit of analysis is an insufficient vehicle by which to examine organizational capabilities, because these capabilities are a composite of individual and social knowledge. After nearly two decades of research in organizational and market failure, it is time to investigate what organizations do.

Notes

We would like to thank Ned Bowman, Farok Contractor, Deborah Dougherty, Lars Hakanson, Gunnar Hedlund, Arie Lewin, and the anonymous referees for their comments. Partial funding for the research has been provided by AT & T under the auspices of the Reginald H. Jones Center of The Wharton School.

1. This notion of a platform is investigated in Kogut (1991) and Kogut and Kim (1991).
2. See Lippman and Rumelt (1982), Wernerfelt (1984), Rumelt (1984), Barney (1986), and Kogut (1987), as well as the publications that appeared while this article was under review by Dierickx and Cool (1989) and Prahalad and Hamel (1990).
3. Steve Kimbrough has pointed out in conversation that the terms are similar to Bertrand Russell's distinction between know-that and know-how.
4. See Nelson and Winter (1982); Hannan and Freeman (1977); March and Simon (1958).
5. In light of the wide appeal genetics has for organizational analogies, it is of interest to refer to Dawkins' (1987) discussion of genes as recipes (and the phenotype as a blueprint). See also Simon (1962).
6. Contrary to Dreyfus' and Dreyfus' doubts, the organization behaviorists, Argyris and Schoen (1978, p. 11), believe it possible to derive the 'theory-in-use' from 'directly observable data of behavior . . . to ground . . . construction of the models of action theories which guide interpersonal behavior.'
7. As a way of summarizing our argument, this figure was suggested to us by Gunnar Hedlund. See also Hedlund and Nonaka (1991).
8. In the philosophy of the science, this distinction corresponds to the difference between the logic of discovery and the logic of demonstration. See also Dreyfus and Dreyfus (1988) for a discussion in relation to artificial intelligence.
9. In the interest of avoiding a proliferation of terms, we would add the caveat that since formal science is characterized by recipes through which causal relationships are identified, this distinction may be simply a restatement of the question, identified in footnote 8, whether the methods of scientific discovery can be codified.
10. The view that knowledge can be created only as combinations of what is already known has a long lineage, from Plato's *Meno* to Polanyi's (1966) idea of tacitness.

11. This point is captured in empirical work using the survey results, whereby appropriability is defined as the item that indicates the maximum deterrence to imitation (Levin et al. 1987).
12. This point, of course, lies at the heart of the genes versus phenotype controversy in biology. See, for example, Dawkins (1976).
13. We would like to thank Gordon Walker for emphasizing that many new investment decisions entail only whether to and not to make internally; there is often no external evaluation.

References

Allen, Thomas and Stephen Cohen (1969), 'Information Flow in Research and Development Laboratories,' *Administrative Science Quarterly*, 14, 12–20.

Argyris, Chris and Donald Schoen (1978), *Organizational Learning: A Theory of Action Perspective*, Reading, MA: Addison-Wesley.

Arrow, Kenneth (1974), *The Limits of Organization*, New York: Norton.

Arthur, Brian (1989), 'Competing Technologies, Increasing Returns, and Lock-in by Historical Events,' *Economic Journal*, 99, 116–131.

Barney, Jay (1986), 'Strategic Factor Markets: Expectations, Luck, and Business Strategy,' *Management Science*, 32, 1231–1241.

Cyert, Richard M. and James G. March (1963), *A Behavioral Theory of the Firm*, Englewood Cliffs, NJ: Prentice-Hall.

Dawkins, Richard (1976), *The Selfish Gene*, Oxford: Oxford University Press.

Dawkins, Richard (1987), *The Blind Watchmaker*, New York: Basic Books.

Dierickx, Ingemar and Karel Cool (1989), 'Asset Stock Accumulation and Sustainability of Competitive Advantage,' *Management Science*, 33, 1504–1513.

Dougherty, Deborah (1992), 'Interpretative Barriers to Successful Product Innovation in Large Firms,' *Organization Science*, 3, 2, 179–202.

Dreyfus, Hubert and Stuart Dreyfus (1988), 'Making a Mind versus Modeling the Brain: Artificial Intelligence Back at a Branchpoint,' in *The Artificial Debate*, Stephen Graubard (Ed.), Cambridge: MIT Press.

Hannan, Michael and John Freeman (1977), 'The Population Ecology of Organizations,' *American Journal of Sociology*, 82, 929–964.

Hedlund, Gunnar and Ikujiro Nonaka (1991), 'Models of Knowledge Management in the West and Japan,' mimeo, Stockholm School of Economics.

Henderson, Rebecca and Kim Clark (1990), 'Architectural Innovation: The Reconfiguration of Existing Product Technologies and the Failure of Established Firms,' *Administrative Science Quarterly*, 35, 9–31.

Kogut, Bruce (1987), 'Country Patterns in International Competition: Appropriability and Oligopolistic Agreement,' *Strategies in Global Competition*, N. Hood and J.-E. Vahlne (Ed.), London: Croom Helm.

Kogut, Bruce (1991), 'Joint Ventures and the Option to Expand and Acquire,' *Management Science*, 37, 19–33.

Kogut, Bruce and Dong Jae Kim (1991), 'Technological Platforms and the Sequence of Entry,' Working Paper, Reginald H. Jones Center, Wharton School.

Kogut, Bruce and Udo Zander (1990), 'The Imitation and Transfer of New Technologies,' mimeo.

Leonard-Barton, Dorothy (1988), 'Implementations as Mutual Adaptation of Technology and Organization,' *Research Policy*, 17, 251–267.

Levin, Richard, Alvin Klevorick, Richard Nelson and Sidney Winter (1987), 'Appropriating the Returns from Industrial Research and Development,' *Brookings Papers on Economic Activity*, 3, 783–831.

Lippman, Stephen and Richard Rumelt (1982), 'Uncertain Imitability: An Analysis of Interfirm Differences in Efficiency Under Competition,' *Bell Journal of Economics*, 13, 418–438.

March, James and Herbert Simon (1958), *Organizations*, New York: John Wiley.

Monteverde, Kirk and David Teece (1982), 'Supplier Switching Costs and Vertical Integration in the Automobile Industry,' *Bell Journal of Economics*, 13, 206–213.

Nelson, Richard (1982), 'The Role of Knowledge in R & D Efficiency,' *Quarterly Journal of Economics*, 96, 453–470.

Nelson, Richard and Sidney Winter (1982), *An Evolutionary Theory of Economic Change*, Cambridge: Belknap Press.

Papert, Seymour (1979), 'Computers and Learning,' in M. Dertouzos and J. Moses (Eds.), *The Computer Age: A Twenty-Year View*. Cambridge, MA: MIT Press.

Piore, Michael (1985), 'Introduction,' in P. Doeringer and M. Piore, *Internal Labor Markets and Manpower Analysis*, New York: M. E. Sharpe Inc.

Polanyi, Michael (1966), *The Tacit Dimension*, New York: Anchor Day Books.

Prahalad, C. K. and Gary Hamel (1990), 'The Core Competence of the Corporation,' *Harvard Business Review*, (May–June), 79–91.

Pringle, J. W. S. (1951), 'On the Parallel Between Learning and Evolution,' *Behavior*, 3, 175–215.

Rogers, Everett (1983), *The Diffusion of Innovations* (Third Ed.) (First Ed., 1962), New York: Free Press.

Rosenberg, Nathan (1976), *Perspectives on Technology*, Cambridge, UK: Cambridge University Press.

Rumelt, R. P. (1984), 'Towards a Strategic Theory of the Firm,' In *Competitive Strategic Management*, Robert Boyden Lamb (Ed.), Englewood Cliffs, NJ: Prentice-Hall, Inc.

Schumpeter, Joseph (1934), *The Theory of Economic Development*, Cambridge, MA: Harvard University Press (first published in 1911; republished 1968).

Simon, Herbert (1962), 'The Architecture of Complexity,' *Proceedings of the American Philosophical Society*, 106, 467–482.

Teece, David (1977), 'Technology Transfer by Multinational Corporations: The Resource Cost of Transferring Technological Know-how,' *Economical Journal*, 87, 242–261.

Bruce Kogut and Udo Zander

Teece, David (1980), 'Economies of Scope and the Scope of an Enterprise,' *Journal of Economic Behavior and Organization*, 1, 223–247.

Tushman, Michael (1977), 'Special Boundary Roles in the Innovation Process,' *Administrative Science Quarterly*, 22, 587–605.

von Hippel, Eric (1988), *The Sources of Innovation*, Cambridge: MIT Press.

Walker, Gordon and David Weber (1984), 'A Transaction Cost Approach to Make or Buy Decisions,' *Aministrative Science Quarterly*, 29, 373–391.

Wernerfelt, Birger (1984), 'A Resource-Based View of the Firm,' *Strategic Management Journal*, 5, 171–180.

Winter, Sidney (1987), 'Knowledge and Competence as Strategic Assets,' in *The Competitive Challenge—Strategies for Industrial Innovation and Renewal*, D. Teece (Ed.), Cambridge, MA: Ballinger.

22 Related Diversification, Core Competences and Corporate Performance

Constantinos C. Markides and Peter J. Williamson

A fundamental part of any firm's corporate strategy is its choice of what portfolio of businesses to compete in. According to the academic literature, this decision should reflect the 'superiority' of related diversification over unrelated diversification (e.g., Ansoff, 1965; Bettis, 1981; Lecraw, 1984; Palepu, 1985; Rumelt, 1974; Singh and Montgomery, 1987). This is because related diversification presumably allows the corporate center to exploit the interrelationships that exist among its different businesses (SBUs) and so achieve cost and/or differentiation competitive advantages over its rivals. But despite 30 years of research on the benefits of related diversification, there is still considerable disagreement about precisely how and when diversification can be used to build long-run competitive advantage (e.g., Hoskisson and Hitt, 1990; Ramanujam and Varadarajan, 1989; Reed and Luffman, 1986). In this paper we argue this disagreement exists for two main reasons:

1. Traditional measures of relatedness provide an incomplete and potentially exaggerated picture of the scope for a corporation to exploit interrelationships between its SBUs. This is because traditional measures look at relatedness only at the industry or market level. But as we explain below, the relatedness that really matters is that between 'strategic assets' (i.e., those that cannot be accessed quickly and cheaply by nondiversified competitors.)[1] Therefore, to accurately measure whether two businesses are related, we need to go beyond broad definitions of relatedness that focus on market similarity; we need to look at the similarities between the underlying strategic assets of the various businesses that a company is operating in (see also Hill, 1994).

2. The way researchers have traditionally thought of relatedness is limited. This is because it has tended to equate the benefits of relatedness with the static exploitation of economies of scope. While we would not deny that economies of scope are an important short-term benefit of related diversification, we believe the real leverage comes from exploiting relatedness to create and accumulate *new* strategic assets more quickly and cheaply than competitors (rather than simply amortizing existing assets—i.e., reaping economies of scope). To predict how much a strategy of related diversification will contribute to superior, *long-run* returns it is necessary to distinguish between four types of potential advantages of related diversification.

   a. the potential to reap economies of scope across SBUs that can share the same strategic asset (such as a common distribution system);

   b. the potential to use a core competence amassed in the course of building or maintaining an existing strategic asset in one SBU to help improve the quality of an existing strategic asset in another of the corporation's SBUs (for example, what Honda learns as it gains more experience managing its existing dealer network for small cars may help it improve the management of its largely separate network for motorbikes);

   c. the potential to utilize a core competence developed through the experience of building strategic assets in existing businesses, to create a *new* strategic asset in a *new* business faster, or at lower cost (such as using the experience of building motorbike distribution to build a new, parallel distribution system for lawn mowers—which are generally sold through a different type of outlet);

   d. the potential for the process of related diversification to expand a corporation's existing pool of core competences because, as it builds strategic assets in a new business, it will learn new skills. These, in turn, will allow it to improve the quality of its stocks of strategic assets in its existing businesses (in the course of building a new distribution system for lawn mowers, Honda may learn new skills that allow it to improve its existing distribution system for motorbikes).

We term these four potential advantages of related diversification 'asset amortization,' 'asset improvement,' 'asset creation' and 'asset fission' respectively.

We will argue that the long-run value of a related diversification lies *not so much* in the exploitation of economies of scope (asset amortization)—where the benefit is primarily short-term—but in allowing corporations to more cost efficiently expand their stocks of strategic assets. Relatedness, which opens the way for asset improvement, asset creation and asset fission, holds the key to the long-run competitive advantages of diversification.

This means that in most cases, similarities in the *processes* by which strategic assets are expanded and new strategic assets are created are more important than static similarities between the strategic assets that are the *outcome* of those processes. Firms that are diversified across a set of 'related markets' where the strategic assets are either few, or the processes required to improve and create them are context-specific cannot be expected to out-perform unrelated diversifiers.

1. The Measure of Relatedness

The strategy of related diversification is considered superior to unrelated diversification because it allows the firm to exploit interrelationships among its different business units. Specifically, the corporate center in related diversifiers is expected to *identify* important assets residing in any one of its SBUs and then *transfer* these assets and *utilize* them in another SBU. Canon's deployment of technology from its camera SBU in developing its photocopier business is a good example.[2]

Even though the advantages of the strategy of related diversification are usually cast in terms of the cost of differentiation benefits that arise from the cross-utilization of the firm's *underlying assets*, the actual measurement of relatedness between two businesses often does not even consider the underlying assets residing in these businesses. Relatedness has been traditionally measured in two basic ways (e.g., Montgomery, 1982; Pitts and Hopkins, 1982): (i) using an objective index like the entropy index of SIC count (e.g., Caves *et al.*, 1980; Jacquemin and Berry, 1979; Palepu, 1985) which assumes that if two businesses share the same SIC they must have common input requirements and similar production/technology functions; and/or (ii) using a more subjective measure such as Rumelt's (1974) diversification categories which consider businesses as related '. . . when a common skill, resource, market, or purpose applies to each.' (Rumelt, 1974: 29).

We do not doubt that the traditional measures could be acceptable proxies for what they are trying to measure. In fact, if these measures did not suffer from any *systematic* bias, one would consider them as a 'good enough' way to substitute for a costly and time consuming ideal measure. However, they do suffer from one systematic bias. Consider a firm using the strategy of related diversification so as to exploit the relatedness of its SBU-level assets. Suppose, however, that the SBU-level assets that the corporate center is trying to exploit are not 'strategically important' (as defined below). For example, suppose that the asset services that Firm X provides to an SBU by cross-utilizing the assets of a sister subsidiary are such that any other firm can easily purchase on the open market at close to marginal cost. In that case, even if Firm X achieves short-term competitive advantage through exploitation of economies of scope, it will not really achieve any sustainable competitive advantage *over time*; other firms will quickly achieve similar positions by purchasing similar asset services. The opportunity for a diversified firm to amortize the costs of running a trucking fleet by sharing it across two SBUs is often a case in point. If nondiversified firms could buy similar trucking services from a common carrier (which itself achieves the economies of scope across customers) at close to marginal cost, then there would be no competitive advantage to diversification even though the two markets were closely 'related' according to traditional measures like SIC similarity.

This implies that any measure of relatedness should take into consideration not only whether the underlying SBU-level assets of a firm are related, but also consider whether these assets are a potential source of competitive advantage. Even if the traditional measures of relatedness do a good job in capturing the relatedness of the underlying assets, they *consistently* ignore the evaluation of whether these assets are 'strategic' assets; and they do so because in measuring relatedness, they do not *explicitly* consider the underlying assets.

1.1 Strategic Assets

To win competitive advantage in any market, a firm needs to be able to deliver a given set of customer benefits at lower costs than competitors, or provide customers with a bundle of benefits its rivals cannot match (Porter, 1980). It can do so by harnessing the drivers of cost and differentiation in its specific industry. For example, if scale is an important driver of cost leadership then those firms that operate large-scale plants will outperform their subscale competitors. However, to effectively exploit these cost and differentiation drivers, the firm needs to access and utilize a complex set of tangible and intangible assets. For example, to reap the benefits of scale economies in production, it may require the services of tangible assets like a large-scale plant and intangible assets like the skills to manage this scale facility effectively and distributor loyalty to support a constant high volume of sales.[3]

Given that a particular set of asset stocks is necessary to allow a firm to exploit cost and differentiation advantages, the crucial question for a firm is: 'How can I access these assets?' A firm can secure these required asset services in a number of ways. It may obtain them with the *endowment* which establishes the business. A company established to exploit a proprietary technology, for example, often receives a valuable patent asset from its founder. It may *acquire* the assets on the open market, or contract directly for the services of an asset (as in the case of an equipment lease). It might access the required asset services by *sharing* the asset with a sister SBU or an alliance partner. Finally, it may *accumulate* the required asset through a process of combining tradeable inputs with existing asset stocks and learning by doing (Dierickx and Cool, 1989).

Firms that possess assets which underpin competitive advantage will earn rents (Rumelt, 1987). To the extent that competitors can identify these rent producing assets, they can decide between two alternative ways in replicating this competitive advantage: they may seek to imitate the assets through one of the four mechanisms above, or they may try to substitute them with other assets which can earn similar rents by producing equivalent or superior customer benefits. *The assets on which long-term competitive advantage critically depends (strategic assets) are, therefore, those that are imperfectly imitable and imperfectly substitutable* (Barney, 1986; Dierickx and Cool, 1989).

1.2 The Importance of Asset Accumulation Processes

The conditions above imply that assets which are readily tradeable cannot act as sources of long-term competitive advantage (Williamson, 1975). Similarly, assets which can be quickly and/or cheaply accessed through endowment, acquisition or sharing can only provide competitive advantage which is short-lived. In the long run, internal accumulation is likely to be the most significant source of imperfectly imitable and imperfectly substitutable assets. This is because most assets will be subject to erosion over time (see e.g., Eaton and Lipsey, 1980). Customer assets like brands, for example, will decay as new customers enter the market or former customers forget past experience or exit the market. The value of a stock of technical know-how will tend to erode in the face of innovation by competitors. Patents will expire. Thus, assets accessed through initial endowment or an initial asset base shared with another SBU will tend to lose their potency as sources of competitive advantage over time unless they are replenished by internal accumulation processes.

Moreover, even when an asset can be accessed through acquisition, alliance, or sharing, it is quite likely that the existing assets available will not perfectly fit the requirements of the market they will be used to serve. Existing assets generally need some adaptation to a specific market context and integration with existing asset bundles. Internal asset accumulation processes therefore play a role in molding assets which an SBU accesses externally into a competitive, market-specific bundle.

Regardless of whether the initial stock of strategic assets within an SBU is obtained by endowment or acquisition, or accessed through sharing, therefore, the long-term competitive advantage of a firm will largely depend on its ability to continuously adapt and improve its strategic assets to meet market-specific demands and to create new strategic assets that it can exploit in existing or new markets.

If these asset accumulation processes were frictionless and firms could speed them up at little cost, then it would be difficult for a firm that gained an initial advantage in respect of a set of assets (e.g., through endowment, sharing or first mover experience in a new, growing segment of the market) to maintain this lead. In practice, however, there are many impediments which prevent laggards from replicating or surpassing the asset positions of the leaders. Dierickx and Cool (1989) identify four separate categories of these impediments to asset accumulation: time compression diseconomies, asset mass efficiencies, asset interconnectedness and causal ambiguity.[4] These impediments also lie behind the concept of barriers to mobility (Caves and Porter, 1977) and Rumelt's 'isolating mechanisms' which include property rights on scarce resources, lags, information asymmetries and other sources of friction in processes of asset imitation (Rumelt, 1987).

When the process necessary to accumulate an asset suffers from one or more of these impediments, all firms will face higher costs and time delays in building it. This will restrict their ability to satisfy their market by offering the differentiation or cost advantages that the elusive asset would underpin. Impediments like time compression diseconomies, asset mass efficiencies and asset interconnectedness, however, will impose higher costs on later entrants to a business, making it more difficult for them to catch up with first movers and established firms who have had longer to accumulate non-tradeable assets. Diversifiers entering a market for the first time against established firms would therefore suffer a handicap from late arrival, other things being equal.

It may be, however, that by deploying its existing core competences a diversifier can overcome some of these frictions. By drawing on its existing competence pool, such a corporation may be able to imitate valuable, non-tradeable assets, or accumulate new, substitute ones, or create entirely new strategic assets more cheaply and quickly than competitors who lacked access to similar core competences: to grow new trees more rapidly and more cheaply by drawing on a common, existing root stock. Likewise, by properly deploying core competences between business units, a diversified corporation may also be able to maintain or extend its competitive advantage in its existing businesses through its ability to augment its nontradeable, market-specific assets more quickly and cheaply than its competitors. This is especially important in market environments that are undergoing significant change. Even firms with massive asset bases will lose their competitive advantage if they are unable to develop the new, strategic assets necessary to serve a changing market.

1.3 Core Competences as Catalysts in the 'Production Function' of Strategic Assets

If strategic assets are the imperfectly imitable, imperfectly substitutable and imperfectly tradeable assets necessary to underpin an SBU's cost or differentiation advantage in a particular market, then core competences can be viewed as the pool of experience, knowledge and systems, etc. that exist elsewhere in the same corporation which can be deployed to reduce the cost or time required either to create a new, strategic asset or expand the stock of an existing one. Competences are potential *catalysts* to the process of accumulating strategic assets. If the firm knows from past experience how to efficiently build the type of distribution network which will improve the competitiveness of its product (i.e., the 'competence' in building a suitable type of distribution network exists), then it will be able to put the necessary asset in place more quickly and cheaply than a firm which lacks this competence. Competences may also act as catalysts to the processes of adapting and integrating assets that an SBU has accessed through acquisition, alliances or sharing. Prahalad and Hamel (1990), for example, cite the case of NEC's competency in managing collaborative arrangements as an important factor in their ability to access and then internalize technological assets and skills from their alliance partners.

This catalytic role of competences in the 'production function' for building assets which are nontradeable, nonsubstitutable and difficult to accumulate is illustrated in Fig. 1. Inputs include time, readily tradeable assets, existing nontradeable assets and the catalyst to the construction process: competences.

The obvious next question is: where can a firm get hold of the competences that would allow it to speed up its rates of asset accumulation, adaptation and integration? The first place to look is the open market. But competences themselves often have characteristics which render markets inefficient as a mechanism for exchange. Characteristics such as information impactedness and scope for opportunism make competences, like other intangible assets, difficult to sell at arms-length (Williamson, 1973; Caves, 1982, Ch. 1). This leads to excess capacity in competences which cannot be easily utilized by seeking buyers in the open market. Unique competences developed by an SBU through learning by doing therefore risk becoming 'imprisoned' in that unit, even though they could be potentially valuable catalysts to the process of asset accumulation in other businesses (Prahalad and Hamel, 1990).

Compared with the problems associated with trading competences in the open market, it is often more efficient to transfer competences between businesses using conduits *internal* to a single organization (Williamson, 1975). Such internal mechanisms include posting staff from one business unit to another,

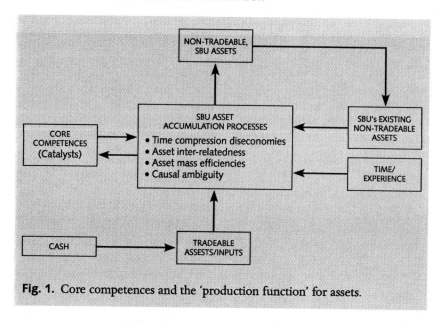

Fig. 1. Core competences and the 'production function' for assets.

bringing together a corporate task force with individuals from a number of businesses to help solve a problem for one of them, and passing market intelligence or other information between SBUs which could act as catalysts to asset accumulation.

Not all of the competences of a corporation which can act as catalysts in expanding the asset base of a new or existing SBU, however, will make an equal contribution to improving the competitive advantage of an SBU. Honda's competence in building networks of dealers for consumer durables may speed up the rate and improve the cost at which it can build an effective, specialized distribution network for its new lawn mower product. But if a competitor could effectively substitute this by a distribution agreement with one or two national retail chains, the Honda Corporation's competence may afford its lawn-mower SBU little or no competitive edge. Likewise, if a rival could acquire a suitable network at a competitive price, or obtain access to one through a strategic alliance, access to Honda Corporation's competence might provide its related SBU with little or no competitive advantage. In both of these cases, while the competence is both available and transferable, it does not lead to the creation of a strategic asset that is both hard to substitute and difficult to imitate.

By contrast, Honda's competence in small petrol engines may enable its lawn mower SBU to quickly and cost effectively bring a superior product to market, backed by a superior production process. If competitors had no way of matching the resulting buyer benefits, except by spending a great deal of money over a long period of time, Honda's engine design organization and the combination of its manufacturing hardware and software would represent extremely potent strategic assets for the lawn mower SBU once they were in place. So access to Honda's engine competence would be a very significant source of competitive advantage for its lawn mower SBU.

We therefore have two conditions which must be satisfied for internal transfer of competences between SBUs to create advantage for the corporation:

1. it must be more efficient to transfer the competence internally between businesses in the same group than via an external market;
2. the competence must be capable of acting as a catalyst to the creation of market-specific assets which are nontradeable, nonsubstitutable and slow or costly to accumulate, thereby acting as a source of competitive advantage for the recipient SBU.

The larger the efficiency advantage of internal transfer, and the more costly the resulting asset is to accumulate, the greater the advantage to be gained from shifting a competence from one business unit to another existing or new SBU.[5]

2. A Dynamic View of Relatedness

So far we have established that an SBU's competitive advantage depends importantly on its access to strategic assets. We have also discussed how core competences can be used as catalysts in the processes of expanding an SBU's stock of strategic assets. The real, long-run benefits of relatedness should therefore lie in opening up opportunities to quickly and cheaply create and accumulate these strategic assets. It is then possible to distinguish five different types of relatedness.[6] These distinctions help pinpoint exactly when and how related diversification will lead to competitive advantage for a corporation (and when it will not).

The first category, we term 'exaggerated relatedness.' This is where the markets served by two SBUs share many similarities, but there is little potential to exploit these similarities for competitive advantage. The relatedness is 'exaggerated' in the sense that looking at the overall similarity (which traditional measures of market-relatedness tend to do, as we explain below), overstates the likelihood that a corporation will achieve superior performance by diversifying across both markets. This exaggeration may arise under any of a number of different conditions. It may be that while the diversified firm can quickly and cheaply build the asset stocks necessary to supply the market, so can any other firm, because most of these assets are easily imitable. Even if other, nondiversified firms cannot replicate the assets built by the diversifier, they may be able to substitute some other, readily available asset at no disadvantage to their competitiveness. In short, the assets that that relatedness helps a diversifier build may be *non-strategic*. A manufacturer of fashion knitwear in Europe or North America, for example, may have the competence to bring a local production facility for knitting standard, men's socks onstream quickly and efficiently. But such a facility may prove a nonstrategic asset against competitors who rely on off-shore sourcing for this type of nontime sensitive, nonfashion product. This type of relatedness, therefore, would not create an opportunity for profitable diversification.

Similarly, exaggerated relatedness may arise when the market-specificity of the strategic assets and the competences that can help build them, are underestimated by the indicators a diversifier chooses to consider. Diversification by Levis from jeans into men's suits, for example, was recognized as a failure. The two businesses may appear highly related on many dimensions from production through to marketing and distribution, but the strategic assets and competences required to build competitive advantage turned out to be very different.

The second type of relatedness arises where the strategic assets in one SBU can be shared with another to achieve economies of scope (e.g., Porter, 1987; Teece, 1982). This type of relatedness underpins what we term 'amortization advantage,' by allowing related diversifiers to amortize the cost of an existing asset by using it to serve multiple markets. This type of relatedness can offer important, short-term advantages in the form of reduced costs and improved differentiation. But, for most corporations, diversification is a long-term step that could be costly to reverse. And simply exploiting its *existing* stock of assets (even if they are the 'right' assets) cannot be enough to create *long-term* competitive advantages (e.g., Prahalad and Hamel, 1990). The truly successful firms over the long term will be the ones that continuously *create new* strategic assets.

The third category of relatedness is where the strategic asset itself cannot be shared or transferred between two SBUs (because it is market-specific), but the competence gained in the process of building or maintaining an existing strategic asset in one SBU can be used as a catalyst to help improve the quality of an existing strategic asset in another SBU. This role of competences in asset accumulation is illustrated with the example of Canon's camera, photocopier and laser printer divisions in Fig. 2.

Consider the position at Canon at the point where the company has successfully established itself in both the camera and photocopier businesses. Many of the strategic assets which underpin these respective SBUs cannot be

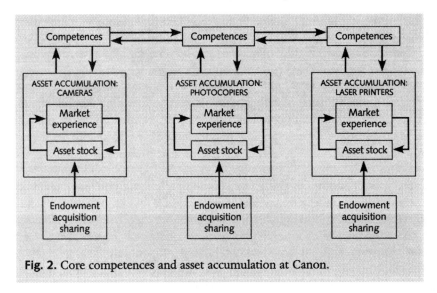

Fig. 2. Core competences and asset accumulation at Canon.

shared directly. The dealer networks and component manufacturing plans are largely specific to each SBU. But in the course of its operations producing and marketing cameras, the camera division has extended this initial asset stock by a mix of learning-by-doing and further purchases of assets in the market. As a by-product of this asset accumulation process, the camera business also developed a series of competences like knowledge of how to increase the effectiveness of a dealer network, how to develop new products combining optics and electronics and how to squeeze better productivity out of high-volume assembly lines.

Because Canon is in two businesses, cameras and photocopiers, where the processes of improving dealer effectiveness, speeding up product development or improving assembly-line productivity are similar, it can improve the quality of the strategic assets in its photocopier business, by transferring competences learned in its camera business and vice versa. This type of relatedness, similarities in the *processes* required to improve the effectiveness and efficiency of separate, market-specific stocks of strategic assets in two businesses, opens up opportunities for what we call 'asset improvement' advantages for related diversifiers.

The fourth type of relatedness emerges where there is potential to utilize a core competence developed through the experience of building strategic assets in existing businesses, to create a *new* strategic asset in a *new* business faster, or at lower cost. For example, in the course of operating in the photocopier market, and building the asset base required to out-compete rivals, this SBU also accumulated its own, additional competences that the camera SBU had not developed. These may have included how to build a marketing organization targeted to business, rather than personal buyers, and how to develop and manufacture a reliable electrostatic printing engine.

When Canon diversified into laser printers, this new SBU started out with an endowment of assets, additional assets acquired in the market and arrangement to share facilities and core components. But even more important for its long-term competitiveness, the new laser printer SBU was able to draw on the competences built up by its sister businesses in cameras and photocopiers to create new, market-specific strategic assets faster and more efficiently than its competitors (illustrated by the arrows pointing to the right in Fig. 2). This kind of relatedness, where the competences amassed by existing SBUs can be deployed to speed up and reduce the cost of creating new market-specific strategic assets for the use of a new SBU, we term the 'asset creation' advantage of related diversifiers. Again, only where the processes required to build the particular strategic assets needed by the new SBU are 'related' in the sense that they can benefit from existing core competences, will this type of diversification advantage be available.

The fifth, and final, type of relatedness is where in the process of creating the new strategic assets required to support diversification into a new business (like laser printers), the corporation learns new competences that can then be used to enhance its existing SBUs. For example, in creating the assets required to support the design, manufacture and service of the more sophisticated electronics demanded by the laser printer business, Canon may have developed new competences that could be used to improve its photocopier business. Alternatively, by combining the competences developed in its photocopier and laser printer businesses, may have helped it to quickly and cheaply build the strategic assets required to succeed in a fourth market: that for plain paper facsimiles. This kind of advantage over single-business firms or unrelated diversifiers, we term 'asset fission' advantage.

It is these last three types of relatedness that are likely to offer the greatest advantages from related diversification over the long-run. As the label suggests, exaggerated relatedness offers little or no scope for a strategy of related diversification to deliver superior performance, despite what may be a high degree of similarity between two markets. Related diversification designed to reap economies of scope, helping to amortize existing assets, is likely to provide only ephemeral advantage. Only relatedness that allows a corporation to access asset improvement, asset creation and asset fission promises long-run competitive advantage to related diversifiers. The problem is that traditional measures of relatedness have not been designed to distinguish between these profitable and unprofitable types of diversification.

Notes

We would like to thank Harbir Singh, Julia Liebeskind, Robert Hoskisson, two anonymous reviewers and especially Gary Hamel for many helpful suggestions on earlier drafts.

1. It is important here to clarify the difference between 'strategic assets' and 'core competences.' Strategic assets are assets that underpin a firm's cost or differentiation advantage in a particular market and that are imperfectly imitable, imperfectly substitutable and imperfectly tradeable. These assets also tend to be market-specific. An example would be Honda's dealer network distributing and servicing its motorbikes. On the other hand, core competences are the pool of experience, knowledge and systems, etc. that exist elsewhere in the same corporation and can be deployed to reduce the cost or time required either to create a new, strategic asset or expand the stock of an existing one. Thus Honda's experience in building competitive dealer networks for a particular class of consumer durables would be an example of a core competence. Each of these networks (one for motorbikes and another for lawn mowers, for example) would be a separate strategic asset: 'different trees, sharing the same (core competence) root stock.'
2. An extension of this argument has been proposed by Hill (1988): the corporation will be in a better position to exploit the interrelationships among its businesses if it is *structured* appropriately. Hill finds that related diversifiers are better served by the CM-form organizational structure than the M-form structure.
3. See Verdin and Williamson (1994) for a fuller discussion of the link between Porter's cost and differentiation drivers and the assets on which exploitation of these drivers depend.
4. *Time compression diseconomies* are the extra cost associated with accumulating the required assets under time pressure (the cost of compressing an activity in time). For example, it may take more than twice the amount of marketing to achieve in 1 year the same level of brand awareness as an established competitor may have been able to develop over a period of 2 years (other things equal). *Asset mass efficiencies* refer to the fact that some types of assets are more costly to accumulate when the firm's existing stock of that asset is small. It is more difficult, for example, to build the customer base of a credit card when it has few existing users. *Asset interconnectedness* refers to the fact that a lack of complementary assets can often impede a firm from accumulating an asset which it needs to successfully serve its market. *Causal ambiguity* refers to the impediment associated with the uncertainty of pinpointing which specific factors or processes are required to accumulate a required asset (the precise chain of causality is ambiguous).
5. The role of organizational structure in allowing a firm to exploit the benefits of related diversification is explored in more detail in Markides and Williamson (1993).
6. We would like to thank Gary Hamel for his contribution in the formulation of these ideas.

References

Ansoff, H. I. (1965). *Corporate Strategy*. McGraw-Hill, New York.

Bailey, E. L. (1975). *Marketing Cost Ratios of U.S. Manufacturers*. Conference Board Report No. 662. Conference Board, New York.

Barney, J. B. (October 1986). 'Strategic factor markets: Expectations, luck and business strategy', *Management Science*, 32, pp. 1231–1241.

Bettis, R. A. (1981). 'Performance differences in related and unrelated diversified firms', *Strategic Management Journal*, 2(4), pp. 379–393.

Caves, R. E. (1982). *Multinational Enterprise and Economic Analysis*. Cambridge University Press, Cambridge, MA.

Caves, R. E. and M. E. Porter (1977). 'From entry barriers to mobility barriers: Conjectural variations and contrived deterrence to new competition'. *Quarterly Journal of Economics*, 91, pp. 241–262.

Caves, R. E., M. E. Porter, M. A. Spence and J. T. Scott (1980). *Competition in the Open Economy: A Model Applied to Canada*. Harvard University Press, Cambridge, MA.

Cowling, K. (1976). 'On the theoretical specification of industrial structure-performance relationships', *European Economic Review*, 8(1), pp. 1–14.

Dierickx, I. and K. Cool (December 1989). 'Asset stock accumulation and sustainability of competitive advantage', *Management Science*, 35, pp. 1504–1514.

Eaton, B. and R. Lipsey (1980). 'Exit barriers are entry barriers: The durability of capital as a barrier to entry', *Bell Journal of Economics*, 11, pp. 721–729.

Hill, C. W. L. (1988). 'Internal capital market controls and financial performance in multidivisional firms', *Journal of Industrial Economics*, 37(1), pp. 67–83.

Hill, C. W. L. (1994). 'Diversification and economic performance: Bring structure and corporate management back into the picture'. In R. Rumelt, D. Schendel and D. Teece (eds.), *Fundamental Issues in Strategy*. Harvard Business School Press, Boston, MA, pp. 297–321.

Hoskisson, R. E. and M. A. Hitt (1990). 'Antecedents and performance outcomes of diversification: Review and critique of theoretical perspectives', *Journal of Management*, 16, pp. 461–509.

Jacquemin, A. P. and C. H. Berry (1979). 'Entropy measure of diversification and corporate growth', *Journal of Industrial Economics*, 27(4), pp. 359–369.

Lecraw, D. J. (1984). 'Diversification strategy and performance', *Journal of Industrial Economics*, 33(2), pp. 179–198.

Markides, C. C. and P. J. Williamson (1993). 'Corporate diversification and organizational structure: A resource-based view', Working paper, London Business School.

Montgomery, C. A. (1982). 'The measurement of firm diversification: Some new empirical evidence', *Academy of Management Journal*, 25(2), pp. 299–307.

National Science Foundation (1978). *Research and Development in Industry*, Technical Notes and Detailed Statistical Tables, Washington, DC.

Palepu, K. (1985). 'Diversification strategy, profit performance, and the entropy measure', *Strategic Management Journal*, 6(3), pp. 239–255.

Pitts, R. A. and H. D. Hopkins (1982). 'Firm diversity: Conceptualization and measurement', *Academy of Management Review*, 7(4), pp. 620–629.

Porter, M. E. (1976). *Interbrand Choice, Strategy and Bilateral Market Power*, Harvard University Press, Cambridge, MA.

Porter, M. E. (1980). *Competitive Strategy: Techniques for Analyzing Industries and Competitors*, Free Press, New York.

Porter, M. E. (May–June 1987). 'From competitive advantage to corporate strategy', *Harvard Business Review*, pp. 43–59.

Prahalad, C. K. and G. Hamel (May–June 1990). 'The core competence of the corporation', *Harvard Business Review*, pp. 71–91.

Ramanujam, V. and P. Varadarajan (1989). 'Research on corporate diversification: A synthesis', *Strategic Management Journal*, **10**(6), pp. 523–551.

Ravenscraft, D. J. and F. M. Scherer (1987). *Mergers, Sell-offs and Economic Efficiency*. The Brookings Institution, Washington, DC.

Reed, R. and G. A. Luffman (1986). 'Diversification: The growing confusion', *Strategic Management Journal*, 7(1), pp. 29–35.

Rumelt, R. (1974). *Strategy, Structure and Economic Performance*. Division of Research, Harvard Business School, Cambridge, MA.

Rumelt, R. P. (1987). 'Theory, strategy and entrepreneurship'. In D. Teece (ed.), *The Competitive Challenge*. Cambridge, Ballinger, MA, pp. 137–158.

Singh, H. and C. A. Montgomery (1987). 'Corporate acquisition strategies and economic performance', *Strategic Management Journal*, 8(4), pp. 377–386.

Teece, D. J. (1982). 'Towards an economic theory on the multiproduct firm', *Journal of Economic Behavior and Organization*, **3**, pp. 39–63.

U. S. Bureau of Census (1980). 'Job classification statistics', *Census of Population*, U.S. Government Printing Office, Washington, DC.

Verdin, P. J. and P. J. Williamson (1994). 'Core competences, market analysis and competitive advantage: Forging the links'. In G. Hamel and A. Heene (eds.), *Sustainable Competitive Advantage through Core Competence*. Wiley, New York.

Williamson, O. E. (May 1973). 'Markets and hierarchies: Some elementary considerations', *American Economic Review*, **63**, pp. 316–325.

Williamson, O. E. (1975). *Markets and Hierarchies*. Free Press, New York.

V. RETROSPECT AND PROSPECT

23 Resources and Strategy: Problems, Open Issues, and Ways Ahead

Nicolai J. Foss

1. Evaluating the Resource-Based Perspective

In the introductory chapter to this Reader, I claimed—following Montgomery (1995)—that the emergence of the resource-based perspective (RBP) warrants optimism on behalf of the strategy field in both the practical as well as the academic dimension. This claim may be supported by pointing to a number of circumstances.

For example, one may argue that because it relies more on economics than most other approaches to strategy (the Porter industry analysis approach exempted), the RBP represents an increase in rigor and precision relative to most previous strategy research. Among other benefits, this allows for a more cumulative type of research in strategy. On the other hand, the perspective still maintains the contact to practical reality that should always exist in strategy research. Thus, on the practical side, the successes of the RBP in terms of acceptance by managers are registered by the increasing amount of corporations that now establish inter-divisional competence-centers, competence-facilitators, emphasize the importance of strategic intent, and in other ways conform to ideas and prescriptions from resource-based thought.[1]

One may also point to more specific circumstances, such as the fact that the resource-based theory of diversification, as represented and developed in several of the contributions to this Reader, now seems to be the dominant perspective on diversification in both strategy research and in economics (Montgomery, 1994). Finally, one may point to the RBP's integrative potential, as Mahoney and Pandian do in 'The Resource-Based View Within the Conversation of Strategic Management'.[2] The potentials for intellectual joint-ventures are apparent, not only with respect to organizational economics or other approaches to strategy, but also with respect to organization theory, simply because resource-based theorists are very much interested in the competitive implications of the phenomena that capture the minds of organization theorists. Moreover, the more dynamic developments in the RBP—what has been called 'the core competence/dynamic capabilities approach' in this Reader—rather naturally link up with ideas on organizational learning (Mahoney, 1995).

All in all, it is therefore not surprising that the RBP has in fact met with such relative success and has been greeted with considerable enthusiasm by academics and practitioners alike. However, there may be reason to hold your breath and curb your enthusiasm somewhat; for taken as a whole, the selections in this Reader demonstrate rather clearly that the RBP is an *emerging* perspective. There is agreement on important basic assumptions and insights, to be sure; and there has also been a certain cumulative theory development; for example, there has been a gradual refinement in the understanding of the conditions that resources must meet in order to yield rent.

However, there are also many unsolved problems and issues in need of clarification. Most conspicuously, perhaps, there is a considerable amount of terminological soup, with various resource-based theorists using concepts such as 'resources', 'competences', 'capabilities', 'assets', etc. for what is often essentially the same thing(s). Such problems may be overcome as certain terminological standards gradually become dominant in the community of resource-based theorists. But there are also deeper issues in need of clarification and potentially conflicting insights—issues of which terminological confusion is merely a reflection.

Perhaps most fundamentally, there is little clarity and agreement as to how one actually goes on developing resource-based theories. How should it be done? On which disciplines should we primarily draw? Should economics still be a dominant source of inspiration or are there dangers associated with relying too much on economics? What are the relevant standards of excellence for resource-based research? What are the relevant benchmarks for theoretical development? And so on.

Assuredly, any theoretical perspective carries with it an open horizon, as it were. A perspective or, more ambitiously, a paradigm, is first and foremost a box of tools that is used to attack problems of both a theoretical and practical nature. And we cannot—as a purely logical matter—exactly know in advance how our perspective will fare with respect to future problem-solving. In this sense, therefore, a theoretical perspective will always imply uncertainty because it frames unsolved problems (Loasby, 1976).

That being said, however, the hallmark of a well-developed perspective is that the tool-box is internally consistent—the theoretical concepts, tools and models should not be in conflict—and that there is 'a cookery book', that is to say, a set of agreed upon rules as to how one actually solves problems within the perspective.[3] The problems that a well-developed perspective confronts are therefore more in the nature of problems of application and problems of how the perspective should be extended and modified under the impact of empirical reality than they are matters of problems of internal consistency and terminology.

Even more basic is the fact that those who employ the tools and models should be aware of, and in agreement about, their strengths and weaknesses, where it is legitimate to apply them and where it is not. Although some may claim that this is really an ideal state, modern economics is not that very far from conforming to it. Indeed, it is precisely because of the relative agreement on concepts and heuristics and because of the presence of well-developed models of wide applicability in economics that drawing on this discipline has been so attractive to strategy theorists—and not the least resource-based strategy theorists.

It is the aim of this concluding chapter to debate the consistency of the resource-based tool-box, to diagnose problems and to speculate on how they may be overcome. The next section constructs a catalogue of problems and issues in need of solution and clarification. These have to do with such issues as the role of statics and dynamics in the RBP, the role of equilibrium assumptions, how the environment should be factored in the RBP, what is the unit of analysis, the problem of measuring resources, etc. In the following, I discuss these problems more or less *seriatim*, and then speculate on the future development of the RBP.

2. A Catalogue of Problems and Open Issues

The overall objective that informs the RBP, it has been argued, is to account for the creation, maintenance and renewal of competitive advantage in terms of the characteristics and dynamics of the internal resources of firms. That is an ambitious and demanding task. However, if one thinks of the selections in this Reader as constituting one integrated perspective on strategic management, one may argue that the RBP does meet the overall objective reasonably well.

However, the problem is that the RBP is not yet 'one integrated perspective'. It is a set of contributions published over approximately the last fifteen years (plus some important precursors to these contributions) that share a number of basic themes, such as the importance of emphasizing and understanding the resource-side of firms when accounting for the sources of competitive advantage. But, apart from that, the contributions that may be seen as constituting the RBP are undeniably quite heterogeneous in terms of, for example, style (written for managers or written for academics, formalization, rigor, etc.) and in terms of the disciplines on which they draw (economics, sociology, psychology, decision theory). For example, it is hard to see what are the shared ideas in Prahalad and Hamel's 'The Core Competence of the Corporation' and Lippman and Rumelt's highly formal 1982 paper on 'Uncertain Imitability: An Analysis of Interfirm Differences Under Competition'. However, they are usually both seen as important contributions to the RBP. Many other instances of the same phenomenon can be found.[4]

In the ensuing pages, it will be argued that existing differences among resource-based contributions can to a large extent be rationalized in terms of whether the underlying approach is a static or a dynamic approach. A basically static and equilibrium oriented approach—that is, an approach drawn from standard economics—admittedly implies a premium in terms of clarity and rigor. However, it easily neglects the more dynamic issues—such as the creation and renewal of competitive advantage. In order to put these problems into perspective, it will prove instructive to begin with dynamics, as it were, and take a look at firm development.

2.1 The 'Unfolding Process' of Firm Development

Edith Penrose (1959: 1) referred to the development of firms as an 'unfolding' process—a process that is based on the endogenous change of the firm's resources and the services these resources yield. Hers is certainly an evolutionary theory in a broad sense of the word. Since the specifics of resource-accumulation processes are different across firms, firms will end up holding different bundles of resources and services and will therefore articulate different strategies based on these resources and services. This, we note in passing, is a quite revolutionary insight, because economists have normally assumed that firms differ either because they come equipped from their 'birth' with different endowments of resources (e.g. different endowments of entrepreneurial talent, cf. Lucas, 1978) or because they are placed in different industries. Endogenous change through managerial discretion has not normally played a role in economic analysis, because economists have traditionally worked with an extremely stylized view of the firm and because equilibrium methodology and the comparative static method of analysis have both hindered the development of theories of endogenous change in general.

Now, what precisely is meant by saying that the development of firms describes 'an unfolding process'? An old idea is to argue that firms go through a life-cycle much like the life-cycle that biological organisms go through—an idea that was strongly criticized by Penrose (1952). However, it may not be entirely unreasonable to assume that there is a sort of overall development that takes place in identifiable stages to the history of most firms. Indeed, in a rough way, such an argument lies behind such claims that diversification naturally follows growth, that efficiency considerations normally dictate that diversified companies have M-form structures, that decentralized M-form corporations in turn face a significant risk of losing innovation ability, etc. I here discuss a modern stage theory of firm development, one that allows some of the strengths and weakness of the RBP to be put into perspective.

Hogarth et al. (1991) develop a four stage framework for analyzing firm activities, specifically in order to gain insight into how different types of activities influenced long-term viability. Thus, their aim is to combine the analysis of firm growth and change with the analysis of sustained competitive advantage,[5] to combine, in other words, process issues with content issues. Hogarth et al. argue that the activities of firms could be described in terms of the stages of:

1. *Privileged access.* Activities in this stage result from some privileged access to primary resources and/or markets.
2. *Transformation.* Firms transform resources into products, for example, by superior processes inherited from the past. However, firms at this stage lack ability to change processes. In the longer run, these processes will become imitable. Thus, long-run above-normal returns cannot be obtained from stage 2 processes.
3. *Leverage.* At this stage, firms are capable of renewing their processes of transformation (their productive capabilities), and thereby hinder competitive imitation and substitution (for at least some time). This means that they can obtain above-normal returns for long periods of time. However, stage 3 activities become stage 2 activities as imitators catch up.
4. *Regeneration.* At this final stage firms are not only capable of changing their methods of transformation, but also their ways of searching for new methods of transformation (their dynamic capabilities). In other words, stage 4 activities operate on stage 3 activities, as it were.

There is no presumption in this stage theory that all firms must by some inevitable logic pass through all stages or must pass through the stages one at a time. Many firms do not reach stage 4 or even stage 3, and most firms contain activities that are at more than one stage. In fact, the stage framework is more of a normative nature than of a descriptive nature: it is a theoretical attempt to examine the conditions for sustained competitive advantage in terms of development possibilities. Thus, the bottomline of Hogarth et al.'s paper is essentially that in order to secure sustained competitive advantage, firms have to control certain resources, notably a core-group of managers and dynamic capabilities or core competences. This basically comes to the same thing as the argument that ultimately learning is the only sustainable source of competitive advantage (Williams, 1992).

In the context of understanding the strengths and weaknesses of the RBP, the Hogarth et al. framework has the clear advantage that its sequential mode of analysis allows an identification of precisely where—that is, with respect to which kinds of firm activities—the RBP suffers from weaknesses and where it possesses strengths. Moreover, the framework points to the need of more fully integrating process issues—such as organizational learning—with content issues, such as the analysis of sustained competitive advantage (Mahoney, 1995).

Thus, we can rather safely say that the resource-based approach is strong on aspects of the analysis of stage 1 activities ('Privileged access'). In resource-based terminology, privileged access means to control valuable and rare resources. More specifically, Jay Barney's factor market analysis (see 'Strategic Factor Markets') clearly belongs here with its point that a necessary condition for a resource to yield rent to its owner is that the resource in question is acquired at a price that is below the expected value of the resource. Another example is Foss and Eriksen's (1995) concept of 'industry capabilities'. These are resources that are shared by incumbents but are not available to outsiders, such as trust relations, specific ways of diffusing and sharing technological knowledge, etc. Foss and Eriksen argue that such shared resources may yield rents to incumbents, for example, firms in industrial districts. This clearly also links up with Michael Porter's (1990) recent analysis of national 'diamonds' and how these are defined by, among other things, the resource endowments of the nation.

Now, privileged access says nothing about how the resources to which one has a privileged access are actually employed in production. Stage 2 activities ('Transformation') refer to processes of production that may be unique in the short run, and thus give rise to a competitive advantage. However, stage 2 firms have not yet learned how to change and adapt processes—they only possess what may be called 'static capabilities'. As a result, competitive advantage can only be temporary. Clearly, the resource-based analysis of the competitive dynamics of imitation and substitution (as summed up in Peteraf's 'The Cornerstones of Competitive Advantage' by what she calls 'ex post limits to competition') relates to the understanding of the implications of stage 2 activities for competitive advantage. In general, basic microeconomics helps in understanding much of the content and dynamics of stage 2 activities.

Stage 3 ('Leverage') activities involve *changes* in established processes of production (including routines and capabilities/competences), where these changes may help the firm pursue generic strategies, such as cost or quality leadership, or change its information systems, organization design, etc. In other words, stage 3 activities are a matter of innovations in products, processes or organization. The shift from a U-form to an M-form in large American diversified corporations described by Alfred Chandler ('**Strategy and Structure**') is an example of a stage 3 activity. Nelson and Winter in '**An Evolutionary Theory of Economic Change**' capture the distinction between stage 2 and stage 3 activities by introducing a hierarchy of routines, where higher-order (stage 3) R&D routines are characterized by operating on lower-order routines (stage 2).

What characterizes stage 4 ('Regeneration') firms is their ability to achieve sustained competitive advantage by means of an ability to generate a continuous stream of stage 3 activities. Whereas stage 3 activities involve the ability to invent and exploit new products, processes, organizational forms, etc., stage 4 activities involve the ability to invent and/or absorb new ways of accomplishing this. Thus, stage 4 firms would seem to be 'hypercompetitive' in the sense of Aveni (1994) and their characteristic capabilities correspond to what Teece, Pisano, and Shuen call 'dynamic capabilities' ('**Dynamic Capabilities and Strategic Management**').

More generally, one may conjecture that activities at the four different stages of development are supported by different types of resources. Thus, resources that support the relatively trivial (in terms of the analysis of competitive advantage) stage 2 activities may be rather different from the type of resources that support stage 3 or 4 activities. Whereas important stage 2 resources may be physical resources, it is plausible to presume that important stage 3 or 4 resources are organizational resources, such as learning capabilities. Moreover, there is a presumption that the latter type of resources may better satisfy the basic resource-based criteria for being rare, valuable, costly to imitate, etc. This is so because they are—almost by definition—more likely to be strongly firm-specific, (therefore) hard to trade, socially complex, characterized by causal ambiguity, etc.—all following from their being internally accumulated through history-bound, path-dependent processes of change. Thus, in this way the analysis of firm development, the analysis of resource categories, and the analysis of sustainability of competitive advantage join hands.

2.2 Firm Development and the Resource-Based Perspective

As already stated, the Hogarth *et al.* framework is useful in our context because it points to some weak points in the RBP—such as the lack of integration of the analysis of firm growth and change with the analysis of sustained competitive advantage—and more generally because it allows us to isolate where the RBP is strong and where it is not. Moreover, it also provides a way of identifying and illustrating some of the differences among the various approaches and contributions that together constitute the RBP.

With respect to the strengths/weaknesses issue, it has already been noted that the RBP is strong with respect to the analysis of the stage 1 activities of privileged access and that it has interesting things to say about the stage 2 activities of transformation and their competitive implications. The resource-based analysis of stage 3 activities ('Leverage') is represented, for example, by Dierickx and Cool's analysis in '**Asset Stock Accumulation and the Sustainability of Competitive Advantage**', which is one of the first and still most important attempts to take the RBP in a more dynamic direction. Dierickx and Cool's concepts of, for example, asset–mass efficiencies, asset stock interconnectedness, etc.—as well as their overall stock–flow approach—brought the RBP much further with respect to placing the analysis of sustained competitive advantage in a dynamic framework. But much work clearly remains to be done here.

It is clearly with respect to the analysis of stage 4 activities ('Regeneration')— the most 'dynamic' stage of the Hogarth *et al.* framework—that the RBP is weakest. Assuredly, regeneration activities have been a dominant issue in the many contributions that have been inspired by Prahalad and Hamel's 1990 paper on '**The Core Competence of the Corporation**' (roughly, the contributions in Part IV of this Reader). Indeed, their understanding of core competences as the 'collective learning in the organization, especially how to coordinate diverse production skills and integrate multiple streams of technology', and involving the ability to 'spawn new unanticipated products' seems to be one way of approaching the nature of the competences/capabilities that underlie stage 4 activities. Teece, Pisano, and Shuen's analysis in '**Dynamic Capabilities and Strategic Management**' points to much the same, but is more explicitly built on (evolutionary) economics. However, these contributions are recent, few in number and often highly informal. Here, too, much more work needs to be done.

To sum up, viewing the RBP through the lens provided by the Hogarth *et al.* stage framework reveals a general difficulty of handling the more dynamic issues of resource creation. More formal contributions to the RBP largely neglect these issues, while less formal contributions (such as Prahalad and Hamel's contributions) are admittedly concerned with these, but reason in such broad, and sometimes diffuse, terms that their real contribution to the advancement of the RBP is questionable.

The underlying problem in this context is *that there is no clear conceptual model of the endogenous creation of new resources to be found in the RBP*. This lack accounts for the inability of the RBP really to come to grips with what was in the Hogarth *et al.* framework called stage 3 and 4 activities. And it explains the co-existence in resource-based strategy theorizing of two widely different styles of discourse, one stark, rigorous and static; the other one loose, informal and oriented toward dynamics.

One may argue that it is in the nature of the RBP that there is no model of endogenous creation of resources, for it would imply (1) generalizing about the unique (namely resources), and (2) that there is a 'rule for riches' (which there is not). But this argument would be wrong, for in a limited sense the RBP itself generalizes about the unique (e.g. resources have to be rare, valuable, non-imitable, etc. in order to yield rents), and a theory abut the creation of resources does not necessarily imply a rule for riches. In fact, a few of the contributions in this Reader are clearly reaching for a model of endogenous resource-creation, notably Dierickx and Cool's paper on '**Asset Stock Accumulation and Sustained Competitive Advantage**' and Wernerfelt's '**A Resource-Based View of the Firm**' (see also Wernerfelt, 1995). But again, these are first beginnings, albeit important ones.

Before speculating on how this important weakness may be remedied, let us consider the deeper reasons *why* the RBP suffers from such a weakness. The above observations point to more fundamental discussions that are well-known to economists and also to strategy theorists influenced by economics; namely the issue of the role of equilibrium in work in strategy research (e.g. whether equilibrium models inherently introduce a static bias). Numerous economists have pointed out that equilibrium assumptions and the restrictive behavioral assumptions that normally accompany equilibrium models (such as admitting only maximizing rationality) will seriously impede the development of models of endogenous change (e.g. Nelson and Winter, 1982).

Relatedly, one may also argue that one reason why there is not one clear-cut resource-based approach, bur rather a somewhat heterogeneous literature with a few shared organizing themes, is that economics (and equilibrium models) is relied upon to varying extent by different contributors to the approach. For example, Prahalad and Hamel at most rely on economics in a background way, while contributors such as Wernerfelt, Montgomery, Barney and others quite explicitly rely on economics. Arguably, this influences not only the *form* of the contributions (i.e. whether economic concepts are actually used, the degree of abstraction and rigor, whether mathematical models are used, etc.), but also the *content*. Those who are skeptical with respect to the economic turn in strategy thinking are usually so because they hold the position that relying too much on economics (particularly neoclassical economics) cuts off some phenomena. Thus, they would argue economics introduces a static bias to strategy thinking, this means that it becomes different to approach and understand dynamic phenomena such as innovation and learning. They may have a point. Let us take a closer look at the issues.

2.3 Equilibrium, Statics and Dynamics

The concept of equilibrium is, of course, a cornerstone in most economic thinking. However, the concept is not entirely unambiguous. There are several different and not necessarily compatible meanings of equilibrium. In its simplest version, equilibrium simply means equality between supply and demand at a given point of time. In this version, the concept is rather uncontroversial: most economists and strategy scholars would accept that product and factor markets are often in equilibrium in this sense, and that a tendency towards such an equilibrium can be relied upon (cf. Kirzner, 1973). Controversy may begin when equilibrium is given an intertemporal dimension—for example, equilibrium as consistency of plans—and an informational interpretation, for example, equilibrium as obtaining when prices reflect all public and private information. These constructs are much more restrictive than simply supply–demand equilibrium.

It is clearly the case that equilibrium assumptions play a key role in many contributions to the RBP. This is the case for Margaret Peteraf's '**The Cornerstones of Competitive Advantage**', in which the concept of Ricardian rent is developed using efficiency differences across firms under competitive equilibrium as a benchmark. And it is also the case for Jay Barney's '**Strategic Factor Markets**', in which the finance concepts of strong and weak efficiency are (implicitly) used to elucidate the reasoning behind the concepts of perfect factor markets and factor market imperfections. Indeed, the very concept of sustained competitive advantage is often defined in equilibrium terms: it is that advantage which lasts after all attempts at imitation have ceased. This has the implication, unfortunately, that sustained competitive advantage has no meaning outside equilibrium, and that the concept is hard to operationalize.

Now, equilibrium theories may take different forms. It is one thing to say that all phenomena should be represented as if in equilibrium—what may be called 'hard' neoclassical equilibrium economics. And it is quite another thing to admit equilibrium as a legitimate tool of analysis, for example, as a state that real-world markets are constantly tending toward (but perhaps not reaching)—what may be called a 'weaker' or more 'Austrian' type of equilibrium economics (Kirzner, 1973).

The RBP is not by necessity committed to the first kind of equilibrium theory; it is perfectly possible to cast the key resource-based ideas in terms of the 'weaker' type of equilibrium economics. Moreover, a tight connection between the understanding of competitive advantage and 'hard' equilibrium economics surely hinders an understanding of a number of real world phenomena. As a general matter, we are cut off from approaching the disequilibrium aspect of competitive advantage; for example, maintaining competitive advantage through engaging in a stream of what was called 'stage 3' and 'stage

4' activities above. Learning and innovation activities involve by definition novelties in the sense of the acquisition or creation of novel knowledge—and such novelties are hard to force into an equilibrium straitjacket.

Equilibrium models may be useful in connection with tracing the effects of the creation of new knowledge—for example, the effects on factor prices of the creation and diffusion of new technical knowledge—but they tell us next to nothing about the process of creation of new knowledge.[6] Thus, one important reason why the RBP lacks a clear model of the endogenous creation of resources may simply be that (hard) equilibrium economics has been such an important force in the development of the RBP. Notice that this is not a call for abandoning the reliance on economics; it is rather a call for being open to other types of economics than standard neoclassical equilibrium economics, such as evolutionary economics (Nelson and Winter, 1982) (more about this later).

2.4 What Is The Unit of Analysis?

The role of economics may also be relevant in another issue of at least potential disagreement within the RBP, namely what should be the relevant unit of analysis. The problem of finding the appropriate unit of analysis in the study of firms is a general one. For example, phenomena relating to firms may be approached using, in ascending order of aggregation, decisions and decision premises, transactions, contracts, activities, processes, routines, capabilities, strategic business units, core competences, even the firm itself as the relevant unit of analysis. Clearly, what one chooses to use depends on what one wishes to examine and illuminate. For example, if the objective is to examine a firm's relations to suppliers, contracts are likely to be the appropriate unit of analysis. However, if one aims at understanding the creation of a corporate technology base, the level of core competences may be the appropriate unit of analysis.

However, most contributions within the RBP take the individual resource as the relevant unit of analysis. For example. Peteraf's analysis in 'The Cornerstones of Competitive Advantage' clearly applies to the individual resource: it is isolated and evaluated in terms of heterogeneity, whether it was acquired at a price below cost, etc. Arguably, this approach may owe something to the influence of economics on the RBP, because economics is often seen to promote a tendency to analytical atomism. On the substantial level, there may be dangers of taking the individual resource as the unit of analysis. Admittedly, this procedure may in some cases be completely legitimate because the relevant resource is sufficiently well-defined and free-standing. An example may be a pharmaceutical firm that wishes to evaluate the rent-yielding potential of a new patent. But it may also lead analysis astray and result in wrong advice.

This is particularly so, when there are strong relations of complementarity and co-specialization among individual resources, so that it is not really the individual resources, but rather the way resources are clustered and how they interplay, that is important to competitive advantage. Arguably, it is this clustering and interplay that those contributors to the RBP who prefer to talk about 'capabilities' or 'competences' rather than 'resources' wish to emphasize. In terms of Dierickx and Cool's framework in '**Asset Stock Accumulation and the Sustainability of Competitive Advantage**', internally accumulated asset stocks often represent clustered resources (i.e. 'asset stock interconnectedness' effects) and individual resources are primarily important because they help maintain or build stocks of such clustered resources.

The upshot of all this is that one should exercise much care when analyzing resources on an individual and free-standing basis, for example, asking whether the relevant resource is 'unique', 'rare', etc. It may often not be the uniqueness or rareness of the resource that matters, but rather its ability to fit into a system. This question of embeddedness leads into a broader embeddedness issue, namely the firm's embeddedness in its environment.

2.5 The Environment

It has been a commonplace criticism in the debate in strategy on the RBP that it 'neglects the environment'. This is not entirely accurate, but it is not entirely wrong either. For example, Dierickx and Cool argue in '**Asset Stock Accumulation and Sustainability of Competitive Advantage**' that 'product market positioning and unique resources work together to determine competitive advantage' (1980: 1510). And in '**A Resource-Based View of the Firm**', Wernerfelt argues much the same, pointing out that product market perspectives and the RBP 'should ultimately yield the same perspectives'. Thus, the environment is at least not completely neglected. Moreover, environmental analysis—the analysis of how to achieve the best position in a product-market—and the RBP may be seen as at least complementary. Specifically, the Porter industry analysis approach would not seem to be opposed to the RBP.

In one form of this argument, the approaches are complementary for the simple reason that they have different domains of application: in the context of the SWOT framework, the domain of application of the RBP is the analysis of the strengths and weaknesses of firms, while the analysis of environmental threats and opportunities is the domain of, for example, the Porter industry analysis approach. Such an argument has been made quite explicitly by, for example, Barney (1991).

The argument provokes some comments, however. First, it is correct that the environment has not been treated in detail in the RBP. Second, it is probably to give in too much to say that the domain of application of the RBP is restricted to the firm and not to the environment. A resource-based approach may in fact be helpful when analyzing environmental phenomena. For example, Schoemaker and Amit (1994) coined and analyzed the concept of 'strategic industry factors', which are industry-specific sets of resources that affect industry profitability. Dierickx and Cool (in 'Asset Accumulation and Sustained Competitive Advantage') noted that firms do not necessarily have to own resources in order to reap rents from exploiting them. For example, firms may benefit from positive externalities, as when a firm that sells skiing equipment benefits from being placed close to a popular ski-resort.

More generally, resource-based insights may further an understanding of industry-level competitive dynamics. For example, the RBP may be helpful for understanding the nature of mobility and entry-barriers, since it directs attention to the resources that underlie these barriers. For example, it is not sufficient to know what is the minimum efficient scale in terms of produced units in an industry; an entrant may also wish to have information about the resources that are necessary for efficiently producing at this scale of production. In addition the RBP may be helpful for understanding competitor expectations, since these expectations are partly formed on the basis of knowledge about competitors' resources. For example, the path-dependency that a firm's resources introduce constrains that firm's possible competitive moves. Thus, applying the RBP aids a better understanding of the nature of competitive threats. In sum, the RBP may in fact add some more fine-grained analysis to current industry analysis based on industrial organization economics. There is at least a basis for fertile dialogue here.

2.6 Testing and Measuring the RBP

In a perceptive critique of the RBP, Michael Porter (1994) argued that

[a]t its worst, the resource-based view is circular. Successful firms are successful because they have unique resources. They should nurture these resources to be successful. But what is a unique resource? What makes it valuable? Why was a firm able to create or acquire it? Why does the original owner or current holder of the resource not bid the value away? What allows a resource to retain its value in the future? There is once again a chain of causality that this literature is just beginning to unravel.

Because Porter's objection that the RBP may suffer from circular reasoning is purely logical, it will not do to dismiss this criticism with the argument that he attacks the RBP from a competing perspective. It has to be taken seriously. Elaine Mosakowski and Bill McKelvey (1995: 1–2) elaborated on Porter's charge of tautological reasoning:

The current state of the strategic management work on the resource-based view represents tautological reasoning of the sort that 1) rents are often used to define a firm's critical resources in that these resources are identified by comparing successful versus unsuccessful firms; and then 2) the question is asked whether critical resources generate rents, to which a resounding YES is heard.

Obviously, this methodology is unacceptable; for example, it makes the RBP completely unfalsifiable. But in principle there is also a way out, and this is to *operationalize* the key criteria that resources have to meet in order to yield long-lived rents. Thus, one has to construct proxy variables to, for example, the analytical categories that Peteraf lists in 'The Cornerstones of Competitive Advantage' or perhaps Barney's (1991) simpler argument that sustained competitive advantage hinges on whether resources are *valuable, rare,* and *very costly to imitate and substitute*. In principle, this can be done: for example, expert panels can be used for obtaining information about the cost of imitation, estimates of rareness may be obtained from simple counting of the resources possessed by competing firms, etc. These proxy variables can then be used as independent variables to examine how much they explain of returns, for example, of the dispersal of returns within a population of firms or of changes in returns as explained by changes in the characteristics of resources.

3. Ways Ahead

Well-defined problems often suggest their own solutions, and the more so, the more well-defined and understood they are. And the above problems, to the extent that they are well-defined, may point to various remedies. So, let us take stock and recapitulate some of the main problems to which no ready answer was given in the above:

- The RBP has difficulties coming to grips with processes of creation of new resources.
- The RBP may be too much wedded to equilibrium methodology.
- There is a tendency to evaluate resources as individual and free-standing entities.

Admittedly these problems do not characterize all contributions to the RBP. For example, the more informal literature on core competences discusses processes for creation of resources, innovation, learning, etc., and it does not evaluate resources as individual and free-standing entities. However, this literature suffers from a certain looseness and imprecision, which is not only a matter of its more explicitly managerial orientation, but also a product of its attempt to grapple with complex and dynamic issues.

What the RBP needs, therefore, is more agreement that the dynamic issues that are featured in such contributions as Prahalad and Hamel's 'The Core Competence of the Corporation' are crucial, but should be approached in a more precise and analytical way. If this does not happen, there is a real danger that the RBP may split even more visibly into, first, a formal, stark, abstract branch strongly inspired by economics and gradually losing contact with the managerial reality, and, second, an increasingly loose and free-wheeling branch where almost anything goes on the analytical level. Whether this will happen or not may crucially depend on successfully approaching and solving some of the problems that were identified above. In the following, I shall briefly discuss some possible remedies to these problems.

3.1 Equilibrium, Process, and the RBP

There is no reason for resource-based theorists to completely abandon equilibrium ideas. As previously stated, equilibrium concepts are useful, both in an ex ante sense where they give us some understanding of the direction of the market process, and in an ex post sense where they help us in organizing historical experience. Moreover, they may be helpful as benchmarks; for example, perfectly efficient markets rule out competitive advantages. But equilibrium concepts may also introduce a static bias and they may, if used in too heavy-handed a way, hinder understanding of process (disequilibrium) phenomena.[7] Intuitively, strategy is very much about exploiting and perhaps even initiating (à la Schumpeter) periods of disequilibrium, and we wish to theorize this aspect of strategy, too. In general, there is a need for bringing process issues more directly into the focus of resource-based theorists.

It is understandable that economics and particularly equilibrium economics has had such an influence on the RBP: it is not only that it becomes possible to understand more phenomena better—it is also a matter of making *heuristic* progress (e.g. clearer concepts, mathematical RBP models (such as Wernerfelt, 1995)). Some resource-based theorists may fear that interest in process issues may sacrifice this heuristic progress, because process issues are notoriously more fuzzy and difficult to understand than equilibrium.

This does not necessarily have to happen. Specifically, theorizing disequilibrium phenomena does not mean that formalization is ruled out. In fact, there are now many formal models in *evolutionary economics* (beginning with Nelson and Winter's **An Evolutionary Theory of Economic Change**). These models are not only about the market process, that is, the process of interaction of firms. They also address internal organization issues. For example, Luigi

Marengo (1992) develops a formal simulation model of a firm in which agents do not have any prior knowledge of the environment they are facing, but are able to learn and coordinate their actions through a common knowledge basis. Marengo is particularly interested in the coordination of individual learning processes inside the firm, and how a stock of organizational knowledge emerges from the interaction of these learning processes. In his simulation model, agents do not have any prior knowledge of the environment they are facing and they do not possess a shared partition of the states of the world (that is, there is no common knowledge).

However, such a shared partition is necessary for coordination to take place, for example, understanding the demands of the exogenous market and coordinating this with the different shops inside the firm. And as demonstrated by Marengo's simulations, coordination in fact emerges gradually and spontaneously, as agents interact under given organizational structures and under the impact of given environments. Thus, it is possible to model mathematically what resource-based theorists would refer to as 'organizational capabilities'. And it is possible to mathematically model the process of creation of new resources.

More generally, evolutionary economics and the RBP are both characterized by emphasizing fundamental heterogeneity of firms as a *necessary* starting point for theorizing. There are many other important similarities between the two approaches (see Foss *et al.*, 1995; Foss, 1996), and the RBP in particular may benefit from being infused with a dose of evolutionary economics. For example, evolutionary economists have cultivated an advanced understanding of the mechanisms of technological change—insights that may both help develop a more refined resource-based analysis of the environment and help understanding the process of creation of new resources through innovation. Thus, one attractive way ahead for the RBP is to strike a closer intellectual strategic alliance with evolutionary theorists, most importantly because evolutionary economics adds a dynamic dimension and does so in a rather precise and formal way. However, there are also other types of recent work in economics and strategy research that may be helpful in the context of making the RBP more dynamic. These are considered in the following section.

3.2 Creating New Resources

The argument here has been that an important shortcoming of the RBP is that there is no well-developed model of endogenous resource creation. Mostly, theorists analyze the end-states of previous processes of resource-creation (including processes of organizational learning). However, in order to account for the emergence and maintenance of the systematic heterogeneity among firms that is a basic premise of the RBP, it would seem to be necessary to develop some model(s) of endogenous change. At the present state of analysis, heterogeneity is simply asserted. However, there are different types of work in strategy thinking and economics that may help overcome this deficiency. For example, there is important contemporary work on:

- *Real options* (Sanchez, 1993).
- *Path-dependency* (Arthur, 1989).
- *Organizational learning* (Huber, 1991; Marengo, 1992).
- *Complementarities* (Milgrom and Roberts, 1995).

In the context of furthering the RBP, work on *real options* may be the most immediately useful contribution. In the theory of real options, one conceptualizes firms not as bundles of resources *per se*, but rather as portfolios of real options. In analogy with the finance notion of an option, firms are seen as having at any point of time a number of strategic options which they may exercise in their input (e.g. spot markets, alliances, long contracts, vertical integration, etc.) and output markets (e.g. different products, different designs, different marketing channels, etc.). The aim of strategy in this perspective becomes the acquisition of an optimal bundle of options where optimality is a matter of striking a balance between the costs of acquisition of options and the benefits these options may bring in terms of added flexibility.

A clear advantage of this work in relation to the furtherance of the RBP is that it is a step in the direction of a better understanding of the endogenous creation of resources. Thus, the creation of new resources may often be understood in option terms as a matter of creating new product options. In other words, firms' processes of resource creation may be seen as a matter of creating product options and then finding ways to defer and make contingent their acquisition of the resources they need to produce those products in the future (Sanchez, 1993: 269). Thus, the accumulation and/or acquisition of resources become contingent on managerial expectations and aspirations, and the real options perspective therefore goes some way towards furthering our understanding of the mechanisms underlying endogenous change in firms' stocks of resources.

On the other hand, the RBP may complement the options perspective by pointing out that new options are often—and generally should be—acquired in areas of competence that are 'close in' to the firm's existing area of competence. This is simply one consequence of the general resource-based emphasis on relatedness in investment projects such as diversification and the acquisition of options—a view that is fundamentally, if implicitly, rooted in the connected notions of *path-dependency, organizational learning,* and *complementarity.*

Firms generally seem to learn more and better in learning domains that are not far away from existing learning domains. Among the reasons why this is so is that much of the relevant learning is essentially organizational in nature. One interpretation of 'organizational' here is that the learning in question is synergistic because of *complementarities* among individual learning processes.[8] That is, these learning processes feed on each other, and it is this characteristic that makes the relevant learning genuinely organizational rather than individual. Moreover, learning implies sunk costs. As a result firms are strongly constrained in their abilities to change paths of development. On the theoretical level, such path-dependency effects help in understanding persistent heterogeneity across firms, serve as predictors of the future process of accumulation of resources, and adds conceptual meat to the concept of 'relatedness'—a concept that is important to the resource-based analysis of diversification. Most importantly, however, all the four concepts above help us add a dynamic dimension to the RBP and they allow us to do this in a relatively rigorous way.

4. Conclusion

The RBP is not a complete approach to strategy. It does not feature a distinct approach to analyzing the environment; it is concerned with the content rather than the process side of strategy; it has difficulties accounting for the process of creation of new resources, etc. Admittedly, these are all shortcomings, some more serious than others, some more easily remedied than others.

Perhaps, and in spite of the optimism I have flagged in this chapter and in the introductory chapter, we should not expect over much of an approach that in its modern manifestation has only been in existence for little more than a decade. Some modesty may be appropriate. Tensions and unsolved problems will stay with the RBP for a long time to come. What we can do, however, is to evaluate the RBP on what has so far been accomplished and what it promises to deliver in the future.

On balance, the impression that is conveyed by perusing the selections in this Reader is one of considerable achievement: the RBP has rediscovered, revitalized and refined crucial, but somewhat neglected, ideas associated with older writers. It has brought increasing rigor and precision to the strategy field, without losing contact with practical reality. Perhaps most importantly, it has asked and with considerable success answered some of the basic questions of strategy in novel and stimulating ways.

But we should also ask basic questions of the RBP, as in the present chapter. The RBP is not in such a developed state that we are entitled to set the basic questions completely aside. We need these in order to challenge and in this way advance the RBP. And, yes, we should also recognize the possibility that the RBP is not necessarily the last word in strategy.

....

Notes

1. Of course, we should be wary of attributing all these changed practices solely to the breakthrough of the RBP: as is usually the case, there has been a rich process of interchange among managers, consultants, and strategy theorists in the development of the RBP. Thus, it would be wrong to claim that changing practices have been entirely theory-driven.
2. As in the introduction to this Reader, whenever a paper or a book that is included among the selections is mentioned it is set in **bold**.
3. Philosophers of science call this 'a positive heuristic' (Lakatos, 1970).
4. The 'two resource-based approaches' argument is presented and elaborated in different ways in Schulze (1994) and Foss (1996). Against this argument may be said that what primarily differs is the *style* in which the two resource-based approaches present their arguments. Richard Nelson and Sidney Winter (1982: 46) noted the simultaneous existence in economics of two different styles of theorizing, what they called 'formal' and 'appreciative' theory. As they explain: 'When economists are doing or teaching economic theory *per se* . . . the theoretical work is stark, logical, formalized. In contrast, when economists are undertaking applied work . . . or are explaining to an audience interested in the question *per se*, why certain economic events happened, theoretical ideas tend to be used less formally and more as a means of organizing analysis. These two different styles of theorizing, we shall call *formal* and *appreciative*' (ibid.; emphasis in original). However, formal and appreciative theorizing may diverge—and this is what may be happening to the RBP.
5. For an argument that these two issues have normally lived separate lives and that they are particularly hard to harmonize, see Knudsen (1996).
6. This is also true for recent work in economics on 'patent-races' (Reinganum, 1989): everything except who is going to commercialize the innovation is known in advance.
7. In **The Theory of the Growth of the Firm**, Edith Penrose explicitly rejected equilibrium theories of the firm, pointing out that 'The attainment of such a "state of rest" [i.e. equilibrium] is precluded by three significant obstacles: those arising from the familiar difficulties posed by the indivisibility of resources; those arising from the fact that the same resources can be used differently under different circumstances, and, in particular, in a specialized manner; and those arising because in the ordinary processes of operation and expansion new productive services are continually being created' (1959: 68).
8. The economic concept of complementarity is that the returns from investing in an asset stock varies positively with the height of other asset stocks. For example, the return from further investments in R&D may be an increasing function of how much marketing knowledge is accumulated.

References

Arthur, W. Brian (1989), 'Competing Technologies, Increasing Returns, and Lock-In by Historical Events,' *Economic Journal*, 99, 116–31.

Aveni, R. (1994), *Hypercompetition: Managing the Dynamics of Strategic Maneuvering*, New York: Free Press.

Barney, Jay B. (1991), 'Firm Resources and Sustained Competitive Advantage', *Journal of Management*, 17, 99–120.

Barney, Jay B. (1995), 'The Resource Based View: Evolution, Current Status, and Future', handout for a presentation, Third International Workshop on Competence-Based Competition, Ghent, Belgium, November, 1995.

Foss, Nicolai J. (1996), 'Whither the Competence Perspective?', in Nicolai J. Foss and Christian Knudsen, eds. (1996), *Towards a Competence Theory of the Firm*, Routledge, London.

Foss, Nicolai J. and Bo Eriksen (1995), 'Industry Capabilities and Competitive Advantage', in Cynthia A. Montgomery, ed. (1995), *Resource-Based and Evolutionary Theories of the Firm*, Kluwer Academic Publishers, Boston, MA.

Foss, Nicolai J., Christian Knudsen, and Cynthia A. Montgomery (1995), 'An Exploration of Common Ground: Integrating Evolutionary and Strategic Theories of the Firm', in Cynthia A. Montgomery, ed. (1995), *Resource-Based and Evolutionary Theories of the Firm*, Kluwer, Boston, MA.

Hogarth, Robin M., Claude Michaud, Yves Doz and Ludo Van der Heyden (1991), 'Longevity of Business Firms: A Four-Stage Framework For Analysis', unpublished manuscript.

Huber, George P. (1991), 'Organizational Learning: The Contributing Processes and The Literatures,' *Organization Science*, 2, 88–115.

Kirzner, Israel M. (1973), *Competition and Entrepreneurship*, Chicago: University of Chicago Press.

Knudsen, Christian (1996), 'The Competence Perspective: A Historical View', in Nicolai J. Foss and Christian Knudsen, eds. (1996), *Towards a Competence Theory of the Firm*, Routledge, London.

Lakatos, Imre (1970), 'Falsification and the Methodology of Scientific Research Programmes', in Imre Lakatos (1978), *The Methodology of Scientific Research Programmes*, Cambridge University Press, Cambridge.

Lippman, Stephen A. and Richard P. Rumelt (1982), 'Uncertain Imitability: An Analysis of Interfirm Differences Under Competition', *Bell Journal of Economics*, 13, 418–38.

Loasby, Brian J. (1976), *Choice, Complexity, and Ignorance*, Cambridge University Press, Cambridge.

Lucas, Robert E. (1978), 'On the Size Distribution of Business Firms', *Bell Journal of Economics*, 9, 508–23.

Mahoney, Joseph T. (1995), 'The Management of Resources and the Resource of Management', *Journal of Business Research*, 33, 91–101.

Marengo, Luigi (1992), 'Structure, Competence, and Learning in an Adaptive Model of the Firm,' *Papers edited by the European Study Group for Evolutionary Economics, #9203,* Freiburg.

Milgrom, Paul and John Roberts (1995), 'The Economics of Modern Manufacturing: Technology, Strategy and Organization', *American Economic Review*, 80, 511–28.

Montgomery, Cynthia A. (1994), 'Corporate Diversification', *Journal of Economic Perspectives*, 8, 163–78.

Montgomery, Cynthia A. (1995), 'Of Diamonds and Rust: A New Look at Resources', in Cynthia A. Montgomery ed. (1995), *Resource-Based and Evolutionary Theories of the Firm*, Kluwer Academic Publishers, Boston, MA.

Mosakowski, Elaine and Bill McKelvey (1995), 'Bringing the Environment Into the Resource-Based View of Strategy', forthcoming in Aimé Heene and Ron Sanchez, eds. (1997), *Competence-Based Strategic Management*, Elsevier, Oxford.

Penrose, Edith T. (1952), 'Biological Analogies in the Theory of the Firm', *American Economic Review*, 42, 804–19.

Penrose, Edith T. (1959), *The Theory of the Growth of the Firm*, OUP, Oxford.

Porter, Michael E. (1990), *The Competitive Advantage of Nations*, New York: Free Press.

Porter, Michael E. (1994), 'Toward a Dynamic Theory of Strategy', in Richard P. Rumelt, Dan E. Schendel, and David J. Teece, eds., *Fundamental Issues in Strategy*, Harvard Business School Press, Boston, MA.

Reinganum, Jennifer (1989), 'The Timing of Innovations', in Richard D. Schmalensee and Robert D. Willig, eds., *Handbook of Industrial Organization, vol. 1*, North-Holland, Amsterdam.

Sanchez, Ron (1993), 'Strategic Flexibility, Firm Organization, and Managerial Work in Dynamic Markets: A Strategic Options Perspective', *Advances in Strategic Management*, 9, 251–91.

Schoemaker, Paul and Raphael Amit (1994), 'Investment in Strategic Assets: Industry and Firm-Level Perspectives', *Advances in Strategic Management*, 10, 3–33.

Schulze, William (1994), 'The Two Schools of Thought in Resource-Based Theory', *Advances in Strategic Management*, 10, 127–52.

Wernerfelt, Birger (1995), 'Resource-Based Strategy in a Stochastic Model', in Cynthia A. Montgomery, ed. (1995), *Resource-Based and Evolutionary Theories of the Firm*, Kluwer Academic Publishers, Boston, MA.

Williams, Jeffrey A. (1992), 'How Sustainable is Your Competitive Advantage?', *California Management Review*, 34(3), 29–51.

Index

Index

Index

Index

jackpot model of R&D assets 167
Jacobson, R. 210
Jacquemin, A. P. 329
Japan: stepping stones strategy 128
Jemison, D. B. 218
Jensen, M. C. 183, 211
joint ventures 321
Jones, G. R. 211, 212
JVC 241, 243, 245, 246, 247

Kahn 314
Karnani, A. 214
Katz 314
Kay, J. 7
Kia 247
Kimberly, J. 151
King, B. F. 180
Kirzner, I. 106–7, 354
Kitch, E. W. 217
Klein, B. 111, 147, 194
  and strategic management conversion 206, 213
knowhow
  contracting 108–9
  and economies of scope 106–10
  as firm-specific asset 163
  hazards of contracting 108
  and information, compared 309–11
  marginal costs of 106
  as public good 106
knowledge of firm 8, 306–23
  and combinative capabilities 316–18
  inertness of 311–12
  information and knowhow 309–11
  make-buy decision 320–2
  personal to social 312–14
  and replication 315–16
  selection environment of 318–19
Kodak 249
Kogut, B. 8, 12, 262, 269
  on knowledge of the firm 306–23
Komatsu 238
Koopmans, T. 211
Kreps, D. M. 174

Lake, D. 209
Lamont, B. T. 218
Langois, R. 8, 12, 262, 273
  on transaction-cost economics 286–305
Lazonick 262, 265
leadership 21–6
  creative role of 25
  efficiency in 21
  and goals 21–2
  and integrity of organizations 23
  security under 25–6

self-knowledge in 24
lean production 272
learning 361
  and internal competences 297
  in strategic management 272–3
  and vertical integration 294–300
Lecraw, D. J. 178, 180, 327
Leijonhufvud, A. 297
Lemelin, A. 209
Lenz, R. T. 156
Leonard-Barton, D. 314
leverage in development of firms 349, 350–1, 352
Levin 261
Levin, R. 320
Levinthal, D. A. 262, 297, 299
Libecap, G. D. 212
Lieberman, M. B. 211
life-cycle of development of firms 349
Lindenberg, E. B. 178, 179
Lippman, S. A. 14, 135, 168, 174, 277, 317
  and competitive advantage 187, 192, 199
  and strategic factor markets 151, 155
  and strategic management conversion 212, 213, 217, 218
Lipsey, R. 167, 330
Livingston, M. 180
Loasby, B. J. 346
locational assets in strategic management 274
loyalty as firm-specific asset 163, 164
Lucas, R. E. 348
Luckman 314
Luffman, G. A. 327

MacDonald, J. M. 209
machine capacity in resource-based theory of firm 120–1
Mahoney, J. T. 12, 15, 17, 188
  on strategic management conversion 204–31, 345, 346, 350
make-buy decision of firms 320–2
management team in theory of firm 32–4
managerial constraints on diversification 208
managerial services in theory of firm 34
Mancke, R. 217
Mandelkar, G. 146
Mansfield 320
Mansfield, E. 166
March, J. 86, 262, 310, 317
Marengo, L. 359–60, 361
market failure
  and economies of scope 110–12
  and excess capacity of productive factors 173
  and resource-based theory of firm 213
market transactions and inter-firm co-operation 64, 67

372

Index

Index

Index

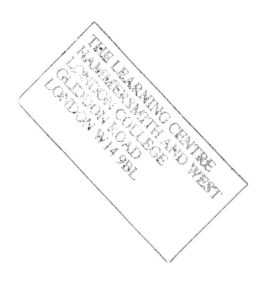